Antique

FURNITURE

PRICE GUIDE • 2ND EDITION

Edited by Kyle Husfloen
Mark Moran, Contributing Editor

©2004 by Krause Publications

Published by

krause publications
An F+W Publications Company

700 East State Street • Iola, WI 54990-0001
715-445-2214 • 888-457-2873
www.krause.com

Our toll-free number to place an order or obtain
a free catalog is (800) 258-0929.

Library of Congress Catalog Number: 2004101590
ISBN: 0-87349-777-5

Edited by Kyle Husfloen
Designed by Kay Sanders

Printed in the United States of America

TABLE OF CONTENTS

INTRODUCTION

Antique Trader Books published its first *Furniture Price Guide* in 1997, updating it in 2001. We are proud to introduce here an all-new and expanded Second Edition of this comprehensive guide. Our focus continues to be on antique furniture from the 18th through the early 20th centuries. However, as the market has continued to evolve, you'll find that we are offering a broader selection of collectible furniture up through the mid-20th century. American-made furniture comprises a majority of the listings here, but in order to reflect the full spectrum of the furniture marketplace we also include pieces from England, France, Germany and other European countries as well as the Orient.

We always strive to provide the most accurate and detailed descriptions for each item listed as well as abundant photographs. A special highlight for this new edition is printing all of these pictures in FULL COLOR! This provides a rare opportunity to see hundreds of pieces of furniture in the finest detail possible.

This book can also serve as a good general reference to furniture, not just a pricing guide. We include several special features including a section of sketches to help you identify the various components of most furniture pieces, a timeline to major furniture styles, a select bibliography of furniture books and two helpful appendices, one listing major auction houses that deal in furniture and then a carefully illustrated chart with "Stylistic Guidelines" to American and English furniture.

My contributing editor, Mark Moran, provided a large selection of the illustrations and descriptions included here, as well as preparing an overview of the furniture marketplace in a special feature, "Antique Furniture in the New Millennium." Special thanks to Mark for his valuable assistance.

We also must acknowledge our debt to a large number of dealers, auction houses and photographers who generously shared information and photographs of pieces sold in recent years. We list them below in alphabetical order and also include the letter code for each that we have included in the caption of each color photograph.

Albrect Auction Service, Vassar , Mich. . . . . . AL
Jay Anderson Antiques, Wabasha, Minn. . . . .J.A.
Brunk Auction Service, Asheville, N.C. . . . . . BR

Charlton Hall Galleries, Columbia, S.C. . . . C.H.
Copake Country Auctions, Copake, N.Y. . . . . CP
Craftsman Auctions, Pittsfield, Mass. . . . . . . CR
DeFina Auctions, Austenburg, Ohio. . . . . . . DE
William Doyle Galleries, New York, N.Y. . . . . D
DuMouchelle's, Detroit, Mich. . . . . DU
Susan Eberman, Bedford, Ind. . . . . .S.E.
Fontaine's Gallery, Pittsfield, Mass. . . . . FO
Garth's Auctions, Delaware, Ohio . . . . G
Green Valley Auctions, Mt. Crawford, Va. . . G.V.
Gene Harris Antique Auction Center, Marshall-
    town, Iowa. . . . . G.H.
Michael Ivankovich, Doylestown, Pa. . . . . . M.I.
Jackson's International Auctioneers,
Cedar Falls, Iowa . . . . .JK
Greg Kowles, Winona, Minn. . . . . G.K.
Mark Moran, Rochester, Minn. . . . . M.M.
New Orleans Auction Galleries, New
Orleans, La. . . . . N.O.
Northeast Auctions, Portsmouth, N.H. . . . . . . NE
Rago Arts & Crafts, Lambertville, N.J. . . . . . .R
Skinner, Inc., Bolton, Mass. . . . . SK
Slawinski Auction Company, Felton, Calif. . . .SL
Treadway Gallery, Cincinnati, Ohio . . . . TR
York Town Auctions, York, Pa. . . . . YK

It is my hope that our efforts will provide you with the most comprehensive, detailed, accurate and well-illustrated pricing guide to the wide world of antique furniture. It will serve all our readers well, whether they are collectors, dealers, appraisers or simply students of American material culture. We always welcome letters from our readers and will do our best to reply if you have questions about this volume.

– Kyle Husfloen, Editor

Please note: Though listings have been double-checked and every effort has been made to insure accuracy, neither the compilers, editors nor publisher can assume responsibility for any losses that might be incurred as a result of consulting this guide, or of errors, typographical or otherwise.

ON THE COVER: An early 20th century S-roll rolltop desk.

Antique Furniture in the New Millennium

By Mark Moran

The antiques marketplace has changed dramatically since this price guide was last updated eight years ago, and depending on who you talk to, the Internet and the cell phone have either been the trade's savior or its curse. Consider this:

Only a decade ago, the average dealer in Fond du Lac or Flagstaff, Bakersfield or Bangor had to rely on word of mouth, an ad in the regional trade paper, or the luck of a drop-in customer to sell merchandise that was unusual, eclectic or just plain odd. And good furniture—no matter how creatively presented or reasonably priced—is still the hardest sell of all.

And the retail customer—not the seasoned collector, but the average buyer seeking an accent piece or the right accessory—was limited by regional tastes and local bias: Refinished oak or old paint? Classic influences or country primitive? Victorian formal or folk-art funky?

The Internet has given buyers and sellers a global reach, but not all have embraced its influence. Some antique malls and shops have actually put up signs trumpeting "We don't sell on eBay!" They think this is something to be proud of, but when the market changes in such a profound way, those who ignore opportunities presented by technology are left to wonder why other dealers are thriving and the tech-fearing are not.

And the cell phone has reached to even the most remote and bucolic auction site, meaning the out-of-the-way farm sale with a rare painted kas, or the minor-league estate sale with the overlooked gem of a landscape are less likely to be the province of a select few, and more likely the target of the sharp-eyed (and sharp-eared) collector or dealer with unlimited roaming capabilities.

The book you are holding represents a meeting of minds on the question of antique sales in a high-tech world.

On the one hand, it offers hundreds of detailed photos and descriptions of furniture from virtually every stylistic era from the 17th to the 20th centuries, and the prices range from less than $200 to more than $30,000. So it's an excellent traditional guide for the beginning collector trying to get a handle on what's out there, and what fits best in their lives.

On the other hand, its scope represents an opportunity for a new generation of buyer to establish a collecting legacy in a marketplace where regional price differences are breaking down but still linger. This means that with the click of a mouse or the chirp of a cell phone (and this guide close at hand), even the most stay-at-home shopper can come up with just the right table, chair, chest or bed at a price that is hundreds or even thousands of dollars less than the prevailing rate in certain areas of the country.

The best advice for antique collectors remains unchanged by technology: Learn all you can from a variety of sources, take a chance now and then if your checkbook permits, and buy the best available pieces within your budget. And while you're out there shopping, whether it's on the road or on the 'net, remember that no one can have all the answers on price, style and rarity, but by tapping into the resources in print, online and from personal contacts, anyone can build a collection to be proud of.

This book would not have been possible without access to the resources of Jay Anderson Antiques in Wabasha, Minnesota.

I am especially indebted to my good friend Greg Kowles of Country Comfort Antiques in Winona, Minnesota, who generously gave of his time, knowledge and coffee.

Dedication: For Catherine

Mark Moran

FURNITURE DATING CHART

AMERICAN FURNITURE
Pilgrim Century – 1620-1700
William & Mary – 1685-1720
Queen Anne – 1720-50
Chippendale – 1750-85
Federal – 1785-1820
Hepplewhite – 1785-1800
Sheraton – 1800-20
Classical (American Empire) – 1815-40
Victorian – 1840-1900
Early Victorian – 1840-50
Gothic Revival – 1840-90
Rococo (Louis XV) – 1845-70
Renaissance Revival – 1860-85
Louis XVI – 1865-75
Eastlake – 1870-95
Jacobean & Turkish Revival – 1870-90
Aesthetic Movement – 1880-1900
Art Nouveau – 1895-1918
Turn-of-the Century
    (Early 20th Century) – 1895-1910
Mission-style
    (Arts & Crafts movement) – 1900-15
Colonial Revival – 1890-1930
Art Deco – 1925-40
Modernist or Mid-Century – 1945-70

ENGLISH FURNITURE
Jacobean – Mid-17th Century
William & Mary – 1689-1702
Queen Anne – 1702-14
George I – 1714-27
George II – 1727-60

George III – 1760-1820
Regency – 1811-20
George IV – 1820-30
William IV – 1830-37
Victorian – 1837-1901
Edwardian – 1901-10

FRENCH FURNITURE
Louis XV – 1715-74
Louis XVI – 1774-93
Empire – 1804-15
Louis Philippe – 1830-48
Napoleon III
    (Second Empire) – 1848-70
Art Nouveau – 1895-1910
Art Deco – 1925-35

Germanic Furniture
Since the country of Germany did not exist before 1870, furniture from the various Germanic states and the Austro-Hungarian Empire is generally termed simply "Germanic." From the 17th century onward furniture from these regions tended to follow the stylistic trends established in France and England. General terms are used for such early furniture usually classifying it as "Baroque," "Rococo" or a similar broad stylistic term. Germanic furniture dating from the first half of the 19th century is today usually referred to as Biedermeier, a style closely related to French Empire and English Regency.

AMERICAN FURNITURE TERMS

CHAIRS

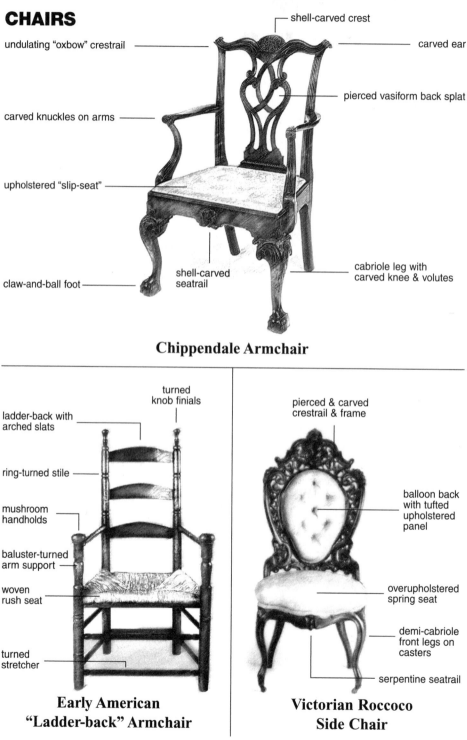

shell-carved crest

undulating "oxbow" crestrail

carved ear

pierced vasiform back splat

carved knuckles on arms

upholstered "slip-seat"

cabriole leg with
carved knee & volutes

claw-and-ball foot

shell-carved
seatrail

Chippendale Armchair

turned
knob finials

ladder-back with
arched slats

pierced & carved
crestrail & frame

ring-turned stile

balloon back
with tufted
upholstered
panel

mushroom
handholds

baluster-turned
arm support

woven
rush seat

overupholstered
spring seat

demi-cabriole
front legs on
casters

turned
stretcher

serpentine seatrail

**Early American
"Ladder-back" Armchair**

**Victorian Roccoco
Side Chair**

CHESTS & TABLES

shaped
molded edge

pierced
brass pull

pierced brass
keyhole
escutcheon

graduated
drawers

beaded drawer
dividers & stiles

straight
bracket feet

serpentine front

Chippendale Chest of Drawers

leather-covered
top with tack trim

corbel

mortise & tenon
through-construction

medial shelf

Mission Oak Library Table

FURNITURE PEDIMENTS & SKIRTS

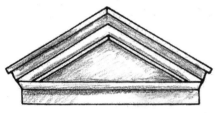

Classic Pediment

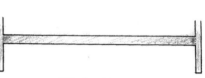

Plain Skirt

Broken Arch Pediment

Arched Skirt

**Bonnet Top with
Urn & Flame Finial**

Valanced Skirt

**Bonnet Top with Rosettes &
Three Urn & Flame Finials**

Scalloped Skirt

FURNITURE FEET

Trestle Foot

Pad Foot

Block Foot

Slipper Foot

Spade Foot

Snake Foot

Tapered or Plain Foot

Spanish Foot

FURNITURE FEET

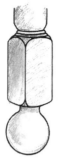

Ball Foot

Trifid Foot

Bun Foot

Hoof Foot

Turnip Foot

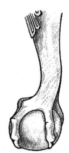

Claw-and-Ball Foot

Arrow or Peg Foot

Paw Foot

BEDROOM SUITES

English Arts & Crafts Bedroom Suite - G.K.

Arts & Crafts style: double bed, tall chest of drawers, wardrobe, nightstand, dressing table & bench & free-standing mirror; oak, each piece w/the main panels decorated w/a rectangular reserve enclosed by an arch & leaftip design, cabinet pieces w/vertical panels, doors w/long flat wrought-iron strap hinges & ring pulls in the shape of inverted hearts, original finish, ca. 1915, England, wardrobe 16 x 48", 78" h. (ILLUS. of part) **$2,000**

light inlay all bordered by brass bands w/gilt-brass mounts on the top rails & on the legs, serpentine siderails, the armoire w/an arched crest w/gilt-brass scroll mount above a pair of tall cupboard doors w/tall beveled mirrors, delicate marquetry band above the doors & on the drawer across the bottom, demountable, original finish, France, ca. 1890, armoire 20 x 50", 96" h., the set (ILLUS. of bed) . **15,000**

Louis XV-Style Marquetry Bed - G.K.

Louis XV-Style: double bed & two-door armoire; mahogany marquetry, each of undulating outline, the bed w/the head- and footboard ornately decorated w/leafy scrolls, urns & other classical designs in

Renaissance-Style Armoire - N.O.

Victorian Aesthetic Movement Bedroom Suite - M.M.

Renaissance-Style: bed, chest-of-drawers, cheval mirror, two-door armoire, pair of nightstands; burled elm & walnut, the large armoire w/a widely flaring stepped cornice w/blocked ends over a dentil-carved band above a frieze band w/lion mask carved blocks at the sides & a scroll-carved center panel flanked by narrow burl panels, all above the tall burl-paneled doors flanked by side pilasters carved w/angel heads, fruit clusters & scallops, blocked & stepped base on carved grotesque mask front feet, the other pieces w/matching details, Italy, ca. 1900, bed 74 x 87", 71" h., armoire 31 x 80", 91" h., the set (ILLUS. of armoire previous page) **4,830**

Victorian Aesthetic Movement substyle: double tester bed, wardrobe & washstand; walnut & burl walnut, the high-backed headboard supporting a half-tester w/a ornate stepped crown-form crestrail w/a pierced lattice band & quarter-round cut corner ears, the headboard w/a matching crestrail over an arched rectangular burl panel over lower burl panels, the low footboard w/a flat crestrail over a row of sunbursts; the wardrobe w/a matching crestrail above a pair of tall burl panel doors over a pair of base drawers; the washstand w/a matching crestrail above a square mirror swiveling between tall uprights above a white marble backsplash & rectangular top over a case w/a single long drawer over two small draw-

ers beside a small paneled door, refinished, ca. 1880, bed overall 10' 5" h., the set (ILLUS. above) **7,500**

Top-quality Aesthetic Design Pieces - M. M.

Top-quality Aesthetic Design Pieces - M. M.

Aesthetic Movement Bed from Suite - M. M.

Victorian Aesthetic Movement substyle: half-tester double bed, chest of drawers, washstand & knockdown wardrobe; walnut & burl walnut, the high-back bed w/a large half-tester w/a gently arched crestrail centered by a narrow rectangular panel of leaf carving over a long frieze of leaf carving, the headboard w/a matching carved crestrail above large burl veneer panels & twist-carved colonette, low footboard w/flat crestrail over matching carved panels, the other pieces w/matching crestrails, the chest of drawers & washstand w/carved uprights flanking large square beveled swiveling mirrors over rectangular pink marble tops, the chest case w/a row of three drawers over two long drawers, the washstand w/two long drawers over a pair of paneled doors, the wardrobe w/tall doors w/bev

eled mirrors, original hardware & finish, ca. 880, bed 64 x 85", 10' h., the set (ILLUS. of bed, chest & washstand previous page, & top left) **35,000**

Victorian Aesthetic Movement substyle: high-backed double bed, chest of drawers & washstand; oak, each piece w/a flat-topped crestrail w/dentil carving over a band of leafy scrolls centered by a small shield & flanked by rounded scroll-carved corner ears, the headboard w/a further bands of dentil carving over a narrow rectangular leaf-carved panel flanked by square panels w/carved rosettes, a matching low footboard, the chest of drawers & washstand w/swiveling mirrors, original hardware, refinished, ca. 1890, bed 58 x 78", 6' 6" h., the set (ILLUS. of bed above) **2,800**

Aesthetic Movement Suite with Grapevine Carving - M. M.

Aesthetic Suite with Fancy Crests - M. M.

Victorian Aesthetic Movement substyle: high-backed double bed, chest of drawers & washstand; quarter-sawn oak, the bed & chest w/a flat flaring crestrail over a thin beaded band over a grapevine-carved band flanked by knob finials, the bed w/carved side pilasters flanking a large rectangular raised panel, the low footboard w/round fan-carved corners over a rectangular panel over a band of grapevine carving; the chest crestrail raised on narrow uprights w/pilasters flanking the large rectangular beveled mirror above the rectangular top over a case w/two small & one long raised panel drawers over a single long drawer over a shorter drawer beside a small square cupboard door all flanked by pilasters; the washstand w/a rectangular grey marble top above a case w/a single long drawer over two drawers & a square door, original hardware, original finish, ca. 1890, bed 60 x 78", 7' h., the set (ILLUS. bottom, previous page) **4,000**

Victorian Eastlake Bedroom Suite - M. M.

Victorian Aesthetic Movement substyle:
high-backed double bed, chest of drawers & washstand; walnut & burl walnut
veneer, the bed & chest w/high ornate
crestrails w/a pierced sunburst center
crest above a wide panel centered by a
pierced lattice panel centered by a
carved florette flanked by triangular
raised burl & leaf-carved panels, the bed
w/long rectangular burl veneer panels,
the chest w/flat uprights w/can-
dleshelves flanking the large square
swiveling mirror above the rectangular
white marble top on the case w/a row of
three burl veneer drawers over two long
burl veneer drawers, flat apron, washstand w/white marble tall splashback on
a case w/a long narrow burl panel drawer over two burled drawers & small door,
flat apron, original fancy brass hardware, refinished, ca. 1880, chest overall
7' 8" h., the set
(ILLUS. top, previous page) **3,500**

Victorian Eastlake substyle: double bed,
chest of drawers & washstand; walnut &
burl walnut, the bed & chest w/high
backs topped w/a wide molded crestrail
w/a carved central roundel & pointed
carved corner ears above a scallop-cut
frieze band, the bed headboard
w/stepped narrow panels of burl & a
matching low footboard, the chest w/a
large swiveling square mirror flanked by
small quarter-round shelves at the base
of the side supports above the rectangular top over a case w/a row of three
drawers over two long drawers; the
washstand w/a marble splashback over
a case w/a long narrow drawer over two
small drawers beside a small raised-
panel door, original narrow rectangular
brass pulls, ca. 1880, chest 21 x 42", 6'
8" h., the set (ILLUS., bottom previous
page) **6,500**

Eastlake Washstand from Set - N.O.

Victorian Eastlake substyle: half-tester
double bed, two-door armoire, chest-of-
drawers & washstand; walnut & burl walnut, each w/a high stepped crestrail
carved w/scrolls & flanked by tapering
block corner finials above a narrow dentil
& block band, the washstand w/a large
rectangular mirror swiveling between uprights above the rectangular red marble
top w/a high splashback over a case
w/two long narrow burl-paneled drawers
slightly stepped-out above a pair of burl-
paneled cupboard doors, molded base
on casters, bed 62 x 74", 92 1/2" h.,
washstand 18 x 32 1/4", 78 1/2" h., the
set (ILLUS. of washstand)........................ **4,370**

Four-piece Golden Oak Suite - M. M.

Golden Oak Bed & Chest with Simple Details - M. M.

Victorian Golden Oak style: double bed, chest of drawers, chiffonier & washstand; oak & oak veneer, the high-backed bed w/a double-arch crestrail centered by a carved shell over large C-scrolls & smaller leafy scrolls, a plain low footboard; the chest w/a serpentine crestrail w/small shell & scroll carving curves down to form an oblong tall frame around a large beveled mirror swiveling between S-scroll uprights w/scroll-carved trim over the rectangular top w/serpentine edges over a conforming serpentine case w/a pair of drawers over two long drawers over a serpentine apron & short legs w/paw feet; the tall chiffonier w/a matching rectangular serpentine frame around a long rectangular beveled mirror of S-scroll uprights above a serpentine top over a case w/a pair of drawers over a stack of four long drawers, serpentine apron & paw feet; the washstand w/a towel bar supported by S-scroll scroll-carved uprights over the serpentine top & case w/a long drawer over two small drawers beside a small door, on paw feet, refinished, ca. 1900, bed 6' h., the set (ILLUS., bottom, previous page) **4,000**

Victorian Golden Oak style: high-backed double bed & chest of drawers; oak, the headboard w/a central shell-and-scroll-carved low crest on a slightly serpentine crestrail above a scroll-carved cluster on the wide plain backboard, the low footboard w/a rod crestrail over a scroll-carved cluster; the chest of drawers w/a large rectangular beveled mirror in a molded frame w/matching crestrail, swiveling between S-scroll supports w/scroll-carved trim above the rectangular top w/a double-serpentine front over the conforming case w/a pair of drawers over two long lower drawers, serpentine apron & simple curved legs, original brass hardware, original dark finish, ca. 1900, bed 58 x 78", 6' h., 2 pcs. (ILLUS., above) **1,400**

Heavy Golden Oak Bedroom Suite - M. M

Simple Golden Oak Bedroom Suite - M. M.

Victorian Golden Oak style: high-backed double bed, chest of drawers & washstand; each piece w/a serpentine crestrail centered by a shell carved over leafy scrolls on a wide half-round rail; the bed headboard w/half-round columns flanking a rectangular molding panel w/a scroll-and-cartouche crest, the low footboard w/a matching raised panel; the chest w/columnar uprights flanking an arched rectangular beveled swiveling mirror over a rectangular top over a case w/a pair of projecting drawers over two long graduated bow-front drawers flanked by half-round columns over heavy paw feet; the washstand also w/columnar uprights flanking a narrow rectangular oblong beveled mirror over a towel bar, the rectangular top over a pair of projecting drawers over a single long bow-front drawer over a pair of bow-front doors all on heavy paw feet, original dark finish, ca. 1895, bed 58 x 78", 7' 7" h., the set (ILLUS., bottom, previous page) ... **8,500**

Victorian Golden Oak style: high-backed double bed, chest of drawers & washstand; oak, the headboard w/a slightly serpentine crestrail over delicate leafy scroll carving above plain panels, the chest w/a matching crestrail over flat uprights flanking a large rectangular swiveling mirror above the rectangular top over a case w/three long drawers, flat apron; the washstand w/a towel bar on uprights above the rectangular top & case w/a long drawer over two small drawers & a small door, refinished, ca. 1910, chest of drawer overall 6' 6" h., the set (ILLUS., above) **1,600**

Golden Oak Pieces with Delicate Carving - M. M.

Victorian Golden Oak style: high-backed
double bed & chests of drawers; quarter-
sawn oak, each piece w/a flat molded
crestrail centered by an arched scroll-
carved crest, the headboard w/a large flat
panel decorated w/delicate leafy scroll
carving w/matching carving on the low
footboard, the chest of drawers crest
above a large oblong beveled mirror
swiveling between S-scroll scroll-carved
supports over a rectangular top w/ser-
pentine edges over a double-serpentine
case w/a pair of drawers over two long
drawers over simple curved feet,
refinished, ca. 1900, bed 58 x 78", 6'
6" h., 2 pcs. (ILLUS., bottom previous
page) **2,750**

between narrow stiles w/raised burl panels & candle shelves above a drop-well
top w/three sections w/faux black marble
painted tops, pairs of small paneled drawers w/large drop pulls flank the center well
all above a long concave-front drawer
w/matching pulls over a concave deep
molded base, similar set attributed to Thomas Brooks, Brooklyn, New York, ca.
1875, washstand marble top replaced,
bed 65 x 84", 95 1/2" h., chest-of-drawers
24 x 57 1/2", 95" h., the set (ILLUS. of
chest of drawers photo below).................. **8,050**

Renaissance Revival Tall Bed - N.O.

Victorian Renaissance Revival substyle:
bed & chest of drawers; walnut & burl
walnut, the bed w/a tall headboard w/a
palmette & leafy scroll crest flanked by
scrolled ears above an arched molding
w/roundel above a tall rectangular burl
panel flanked by half-round ring-turned
columns & bars flanked by lower arched
burl panels & short blocked & baluster-
turned side stiles, the low footboard w/a
raised & arched center crest over long
burl panels & ring-turned rails, the chest
of drawers w/similar carving & a tall
arched mirror above a drop-well case
w/white marble tops, ca. 1875, bed
68 x 85", 106" h., the pair (ILLUS. of bed) **12,650**
Victorian Renaissance Revival substyle:
bed, chest of drawers & washstand; walnut & burl walnut, the bed & chest w/a tall
back topped by an ornately carved
arched pediment centered by a carved
winged angel head over raised burl panels above large scrolls at the top corners,
the chest w/a very tall rectangular mirror

Renaissance Revival Tall Chest - N.O.

Victorian Renaissance Revival substyle:
double bed, chest of drawers & washstand; walnut, the high-backed bed &
chest w/tall broken-scroll arched crests
centered by carved fruit finials above
shaped raised burl panels, the bed w/a
low arched footboard w/raised fruit &
scroll carving, the chest w/an arched
molding below the crest over a tall arched
mirror flanked by shaped sides w/small
candle shelves & raised burl panels
above the drop-well white marble top
w/stacks of four small drawers flanking
two longer center drawers; the washstand w/an arched white marble splashback over a long narrow single drawer
over a pair of arched-panel doors, original black pear-shaped drawer pulls, ca.
1875, refinished, chest overall 8' h., the
set (ILLUS., top next page) **3,500**

Simple Renaissance Revival Bedroom Suite - M. M.

Renaissance Bed & Chest of Drawers - M. M.

Victorian Renaissance Revival substyle:
high-backed double bed & chest of drawers; walnut & burl walnut, each piece w/a high crestrail centered by a large pointed palmette-and-scroll-carved crest flanked by pierced leafy scrolls over an angled pediment w/burl panels, the headboard w/further shaped burl panels flanking a large roundel flanked by urn-form finials all above three tall narrow molded panels, the lower footboard w/a peaked top over matching burl panels & angled paneled legs, the chest w/scroll-cut sides flanking the tall rectangular mirror above the drop-well white marble top over a case w/pairs of small drawers over two long drawers all w/raised burl panels, original black pear-shaped drops, 1870s, bed 58 x 78", 8' h., 2 pcs. (ILLUS.) **5,800**

Fine Renaissance Revival Bed - M. M.

Victorian Renaissance Revival substyle:
high-backed double bed & chest of drawers; walnut & burl walnut, each w/a matching crestrail w/peaked leafy scroll center bracket crest w/burl panel above an arched molding over further burl & molded panels flanked by brackets, the headboard w/block-and-roundel corner finials above block-molded sides flanking long narrow panels, the low arched footboard w/a central diamond-shaped

burl panel flanked by shaped panels over long rectangular panels & heavy square blocked legs; the crest on the chest above a tall arched rectangular mirror flanked by paneled sides w/small candle shelves & scroll-carved lower sides above the drop-well top w/white marble tops, two small drawers at each side above two long lower drawers w/raised burl panels & original pulls, refinished, ca. 1875, bed 58 x 78", overall 7' 10" h., 2 pcs. (ILLUS. of bed previous page).. **6,500**

Fancy Renaissance Chest from Set - M.M.

Victorian Renaissance Revival substyle: high-backed double bed & chest of drawers, walnut & burl walnut, each w/a tall ornately carved broken-scroll crestrail centered by a large palmette & fruit-carved finial over further carved scrolls & a blocked crestrail, the headboard w/half-round columns below the blocked rail flanking a very tall raised burl panel flanked by shorter side panels below urn-form finials palmette-carved drops, the low footboard w/a flat crestrail over an arrangement of raised burl panels, the chest of drawers w/a similar design of columns & scroll-carved sides flanking a tall beveled mirror w/a paneled top above the white marble drop-well top, the side sections w/outset beveled corners above a conforming section w/two small burl paneled drawers above two long burl paneled drawers flanked by slender side columns, original T-form pulls, refinished, ca. 1875, bed 58 x 78", 8' 6" h., pr. (ILLUS. of chest of drawers) **7,500**

Elaborate Renaissance Suite - M.M.

Victorian Renaissance Revival substyle: high-backed double bed & chest of drawers; walnut & burl walnut; each piece w/an extremely ornate crest w/a large urn finial above a broken-arch raised center pediment flanked by turned T-form spindles above a heavy molded arch flanked by large angled side pediments w/fanned ears, the headboard w/a large arched burl center panel flanked by smaller rectangular panels each separated by short heavy turned columns on blocked brackets separating further burl panels, the lower arched footboard w/panels, a roundel & columns matching the headboard, the ornate chest crest above columns & blocks flanking the long rectangular mirror flanked by two side compartments w/square inset marble tops supporting a block & column w/a round disk shelf, each compartment w/a shaped & carved molding over three small drawers, refinished, ca. 1870, bed 68 x 80", 9' h., 2 pcs. (ILLUS. of bed) **25,000**

Victorian Renaissance Revival substyle: high-backed double bed & chest of drawers; walnut & burl walnut, the bed w/a tall palmette-and-scroll-carved center crest flanked by scrolls above the molded broken-arch pediment above triangular raised burl panels over a wide section w/scroll-carved sides flanking a large center oval burl panel surrounded by small triangular raised burl panels all flanked by urn-form finials on the block-carved sides flanking three tall vertical rectangular panels, the low footboard w/matching carving & panels; the chest of drawers w/a matching crest above wide tapering scroll-carved sides w/candle shelves flanking a tall rectangular mirror over the drop-well white marble top, the case w/pairs of small burl drawers over a single long drawer w/raised burl panels flanking a center roundel, ca. 1875, original finish, bed 60 x 80", 8' 4" h., 2 pcs. (ILLUS. of bed below) **6,500**

Ornate Renaissance Revival Bed - M.M.

Ornately Carved Renaissance Chest - M.M.

Victorian Renaissance Revival substyle: high-backed double bed & chest of drawers; walnut & burl walnut, the headboard w/a very high arched crest topped by a full-figure carved cupid w/quiver flanked by small dolphins above carved scrolls all above a large arched burl panel flanked by detailed urn corner finials

above three molded arched panels, the low footboard w/an arched crestrail over three arched burl panels flanked by rounded corners w/burl panels, the chest of drawers w/a matching finial & crestrail over a tall arched mirror flanked by scroll-carved sides w/burl panels & candle shelves over the drop-well top w/white marble, the rectangular raised side section w/chamfered corners above a conforming case w/a stack of three burl-paneled drawers at each side flanking the low center section w/a concave front over a conforming long burl-paneled drawer, original pulls, refinished, ca. 1870, bed 58 x 78", 9' h., 2 pcs. (ILLUS. of chest below left) **25,000**

Victorian Rococo substyle: high-backed double bed & chest of drawers; carved mahogany, the chest of drawers w/a very high superstructure topped by a Prince-of-Wales plumes carved finial over a broken-arched pediment w/scroll-pierced panels above wide pierced scroll-carved sections supporting two half-round shelves on each side & flanking a tall arched swiveling mirror, the rectangular white marble top w/a serpentine front & outset chamfered corners above a conforming case w/four long bow-front drawers w/ornate scroll-carved panels & pulls, molded bow-front apron; the bed headboard w/a pierced & scroll-carved finial on the wide arched & molded crestrail above a wide arched flame veneer panel flanked by heavy side posts w/large urn-form finials, low footboard w/raised scroll-carved corners & arched center crest above a cartouche-carved roundel, deep side rails, by Mitchell & Rammelsburg Co., Cincinnati, Ohio, ca. 1850-60, bed 62 x 80", overall 9' h., pr. (ILLUS. of chest, photo below)................................ **10,000**

Fine Mitchell & Rammelsberg Chest - M.M.

Ornate Rosewood Chest - M.M.

Ornate Rosewood Bed- M.M.

Victorian Rococo substyle: high-backed double bed & chest of drawers; carved rosewood, the bed headboard w/a high pierced arched crest elaborately carved w/scrolling leafy vines w/an exotic bird perched at each side over the arched & stepped crestrail above the three-panel backboard w/further scroll carving flanked by block-and-column-carved stiles w/urn-form finials, the lower arched footboard w/ornate scroll carving centered by a large oval knob above two arched panels, curved low corner boards; the chest w/a tall superstructure w/ornately pierced-carved twining branches w/an exotic bird on each side & resting on tall square plinths w/round candle shelves all enclosing a tall oblong swiveling mirror, the rectangular white marble top w/a serpentine front above a conforming case w/ three long drawers w/scroll-carved pulls flanked by canted front corners w/further carved scrolls, low serpentine apron, Mitchell & Rammelsberg Co., Cincinnati, Ohio, ca. 1855, original finish, bed 64 x 82", 8' 6" h., pr. (ILLUS. photo of each at left) **20,000**

Victorian Rococo substyle: high-backed double bed & chest of drawers; feather-grained walnut; the high bed headboard w/an arched crest w/ornately carved scrolls on an open C-scroll above the arched crestrail w/further scrolls above a large oval grained panel flanked by narrow arched rectangular panels between the serpentine stiles w/further scroll carving, the low footboard w/a raised, arched center w/fruit-and-flower carving & curved low corner posts; the chest w/a tall superstructure w/a high pierced scroll-carved crest & upturned corners over a tall rectangular mirror w/serpentine top swiveling between ornate shaped & scroll-carved uprights above the rectangular white marble top over a case w/two long, deep drawers decorated w/raised banded panels w/scroll carving, serpentine apron w/scroll carving between bun feet, labeled "O. P. Merriman, Baltimore," original finish, ca. 1860, bed 64 x 82", 6' 6" h., pr. (ILLUS. of bed, photo below) **8,500**

Feather-grained Rococo Bed - M.M.

Extraordinary Rococo Bedroom Suite - M.M. -

Victorian Rococo substyle: high-backed double bed, chest of drawers & washstand; carved rosewood, the bed headboard w/a large arched & peaked pierce-carved crest composed of ornate scrolls centered by a Prince of Wales plumes finial above the arched & molded crestrail above raised burl panels over three small pierced-carved panels above three tall arch-topped veneer panels all flanked by block-and-scroll-carved stiles, the low arched footboard w/three arched veneer panels centered w/a scroll-carved cluster, curved & paneled corner boards; the chest w/a tall superstructure w/a pierced crest matching the bed above pierced & scroll carved uprights w/small half-round shelves flanking a tall, swiveling arched-topped rectangular mirror, the rectangular white marbled top w/projecting canted corners above columns flanking a conforming case w/three long drawers decorated w/raised oval banding & fruit-carved pulls, the washstand w/a rectangular white marble top over a case of three long drawers, Mitchell & Rammelsberg Co., Cincinnati, Ohio, ca. 1860, original finish, bed 64 x 84", overall 9' 6" h., the set (ILLUS.)............................. **35,000**

BEDS

Art Nouveau-influenced Bed - M.M.

Art Nouveau style bed, quarter-swan oak, the high oval headboard w/molded edges topped by a cartouche-carved crest, a flat-topped matching lower footboard w/scroll-carved trim & short outswept legs w/paw feet, refinished, ca. 1900, 58 x 78", 6' 2" h. (ILLUS.) **$800**

Early Classical Low-post Bed - M.M.

Classical low-poster bed, mahogany, matching head- and footboards w/curved tops w/scrolled ends above pairs of rectangular burl veneer panels, ropetwist posts w/large knob finials above blocked sections on heavy tapering ovoid legs, brass bolt covers, refinished, ca. 1830s, 58 x 76", 45" h. (ILLUS.) 1,200

Classical low-poster bed, mahogany, the flat-topped headboard w/a knob-ended bar over delicate applied bronze cupids flanking swags, acanthus leaf & ribbed knob carved side posts w/small bronze pineapple finials & heavy acanthus-carved turned legs, matching foot posts joined by a rail, original finish, ca. 1840, 60 x 80", 5' h. (ILLUS. top next column).... 2,400

Classical low-poster bed, mahogany, the gently arched headboard w/scroll-cut end flanked by ornate baluster-turned & leaf-carved sections topped by acorn finials, matching foot posts joined by a wide rail, bulbous tapering ovoid legs, brass bolt covers, probably original finish, ca. 1840, 40 x 74", 42" h. (ILLUS., bottom of column) 800

Classical Bed with Bronze Trim - M.M.

Classical Bed with Ornate Posts - M.M.

Classical "sleigh" bed, mahogany, double-size, the even upright S-scroll head- and footboards joined by shaped side rails on flat rounded feet, American, ca. 1830-40, 57 1/2 x 75", 41 1/2" h. (ILLUS. top of next page) 1,160

American Classical Double Sleigh Bed - N.O.

Classical Bed with Ornate Tall Posts - M.M.

Classical tall-poster bed, mahogany, the arched & scroll-carved headboard over two large rectangular flame veneer panels flanked by tall knob-, ring- and acanthus leaf-carved tall posts w/knob finials, matching foot posts, short baluster-turned legs, original brass bolt covers, original dark finish, ca. 1835, 58 x 80", 7' h. (ILLUS.) **5,500**

Classical tall-poster tester bed, mahogany, a wide cove-molded rectangular tester frame raised on columnar posts, an arched headboard w/a cartouche-and-scroll-carved finial, wide side & foot rails, short ring-turned feet, original finish, ca. 1840, 60 x 78", 9' h. (ILLUS. next column).. **2,500**

Classical Full-tester Bed - M.M.

Classical Revival tall-poster bed, mahogany, each post w/ring-turned segments alternating w/reeded segments & carved pineapple designs, the narrow cut-out headboard w/a carved crest bar w/rosette ends, on pineapple- and paw-carved legs, late 19th c., 52 x 79", 96" h. (ILLUS. top next page)............................ **3,680**

Classical Revival tall-poster bed, mahogany, high flame veneer headboard w/flat crestrail w/knob ends above cutout scrolls flanked by leaf-carved spiraling posts w/ring-turned & pineapple finials, matching foot posts joined by a turned leaf-carved upper rail & a flat lower rail, short heavy tapering turned legs w/bun feet, original finish, ca. 1890-1910, 56 x 76", 6' h. (ILLUS. bottom next page)................ **1,500**

Classical Revival Mahogany Bed - N.O.

Classical Revival Four-Post Bed - M.M.

Classical Revival Tall-poster Bed - M.M.

Classical Revival tall-poster bed, mahogany, the high flat-topped headboard w/scroll trim over a leaf-carved band w/roundel above a rectangular panel w/beaded molding, flanked by posts w/baluster- and ring-turned leaf-carved sections below tall tapering reeded sections w/carved knob finials, matching shorter footrails joined by a wide rail, tapering reeded short legs, late 19th c., 60 x 78", 6' h. (ILLUS. below top right)...... **1,500**

Classical Revival Mahogany Bed - M.M.

Classical Revival tall-poster bed, mahogany, the wide arched headboard centered by a pair of large delicate cutout scrolls, heavy paneled tapering side posts w/flattened knob finials, matching foot posts joined by a paneled narrow upper rail & gently arched lower rail, heavy C-scroll feet, original finish, ca. 1890-1910, 60 x 80", 5' 6" h. (ILLUS. above)..... **1,000**

Classical Revival tall-poster bed, mahogany, the wide headboard w/a broken-scroll crestrail centered by a pointed knob finial & flanked by rope-twist-turned posts w/knob-turned finials, the slightly shorter foot posts joined by a ropetwist-, knob- and ring-turned rail above a wide scroll-ended lower rail, short knob-turned feet, refinished, early 20th c., 58 x 78", 5' h. (ILLUS. next page) **850**

Classical Revival Fancy Bed - M.M.

Classical Transitional Bed - M.M.

Classical-Rococo transitional tall-poster bed, mahogany, the high arched head-board w/ornate carved scrolls flanked by tall posts formed by a cluster of four columns topped w/a ball finial, shorter matching foot posts, serpentine scroll-trimmed side- and foot rails, possibly original finish, ca. 1845, 66 x 84", 6' h. (ILLUS. below left) **4,500**

Colonial Revival Tall-poster Bed - M.M.

Colonial Revival tall-poster bed, mahogany, the high broken-scroll headboard w/turned center finial flanked by slender leaf-carved baluster- and ring-turned posts w/carved pineapple finials, matching foot posts joined by a turned & leaf-carved upper rail & flat lower rail, short legs w/claw-and-ball feet, original finish, full-sized, early 20th c., 58 x 78", 6' h. (ILLUS. above) **2,400**

French Empire-Style Bed - N.O.

Empire-Style bed, ormolu-mounted mahogany, the high flat-topped headboard w/a rounded crestrail fitted w/a small figural ormolu boss over an arched panel w/corner bosses flanked by free-standing side columns w/ormolu capitals, the matching lower footboard trimmed w/ormolu bar mounts & a large wreath, on short, square tapering legs, France, ca. 1900, 59 1/2 x 81", 4' 4" h. (ILLUS. bottom, previous page) **1,265**

ropetwist columns w/carved pineapple finials, matching foot posts joined by a rail, ropetwist legs on original brass feet, original bolt covers, original finish, ca. 1820s, 60 x 80", 7' 8" h. (ILLUS. left) **7,500**

Rare Early New Orleans Bed

Federal tall-poster bed, mahogany, the high shaped headboard topped by a baluster- and ringed-turned bar w/acorn terminals, slender baluster- and ring-turned posts w/baluster-turned finials, matching foot posts joined by a lower rail, bulbous turned & tapering legs, original finish, made in New Orleans, ca. 1825-35, 60 x 80", 7' 6" h. (ILLUS. above) **10,500**

Fine Federal Tall-Poster Bed - M.M.

Federal tall-poster bed, mahogany, the headboard w/an arched crestrail over two rectangular panels flanked by tall slender

Simple Federal Revival Twin Beds - M.M.

Federal Revival tall-poster twin-sized beds, mahogany, the wide flat headboard w/a narrow flat crestrail w/scrolled ends flanked by slender tapering reeded posts topped by stylized plume finials, matching foot posts joined by a knob-turned reeded upper rail & a flat bottom rail, early 20th c., 42 x 74", 5' 6" h., pr. (ILLUS. previous page) **1,800**

French Louis Philippe Bed - N.O.

Louis Philippe bed, mahogany, the even head- and footboards w/arched scroll-carved crests above plain panels flanked by paneled stiles w/turned button finials, deep shaped siderails, heavy tapering ring- and knob-turned legs, France, mid-19th c., 40 1/2 x 74", 39" h. (ILLUS.)............ **805**

Ornate Chinese Rosewood Bed - N.O.

Oriental canopy bed, rosewood, the rectangular canopy top pierce-carved w/rectangular panels & raised on six slender tapering posts above the platform base enclosed by a three-quarters gallery pierce-carved w/squares & quatrefoils, raised on high incurved blocked legs, the top w/overall subtle low-relief carved foliage sprays, China, late 19th c., 59 x 87", 94" h. (ILLUS. bottom left)........................ **3,450**

Fine Victorian Spool-turned Bed - M.M.

Victorian cottage-style tall-poster bed, walnut, a flat-topped headboard w/scroll-carved sides over a row of short spool-turned spindles above a spool-turned rail, flanked by tall spool-turned posts, matching foot posts joined by a spool-turned upper rail & flat lower rail, tall spool-turned legs, original finish, mid-19th c., 58 x 76", 6' h. (ILLUS.) **1,200**

Victorian country-style double bed, carved butternut, high matching head- and footboards w/stepped crestrails over three wide panels flanked by flattened posts carved at the top w/a cornucopia above raised leaf-carved panels centered by a roundel, wide side rails w/scroll-carved top brackets & long raised panels carved w/leafy vines & centered by a carved roundel, heavy block feet, original finish, ca. 1870s, 56 x 76", 4' h. (ILLUS., top next page) **750**

Interesting Country-style Carved Bed - M.M.

Tall Golden Oak Double Bed - G.K.

Victorian Golden Oak bed, the high squared headboard w/a heavy rounded crestrail centered by a pointed & scroll-carved crest over a wide section w/a delicate large panel of applied leafy scrolls flanked by squared stiles w/simple scroll carving, the low footboard w/a heavy rounded crestrail over delicate scrolling, original dark finish, ca. 1900, 58 x 78", 80" h. (ILLUS.) **1,400**

Golden Oak Child's Bed - M.M.

Victorian Golden Oak child's bed, demountable, the high headboard w/a serpentine top w/carved scroll trim above a raised oval scroll band, side stiles w/scroll-carved ears, matching lower footboard, deep slatted side rails, original finish, ca. 1900 24 x 48", 40" h. (ILLUS.) **500**

Compact Victorian "Murphy" Bed - M.M.

Victorian Golden Oak "Murphy" bed, a high scalloped & scroll-carved crestrail above the rectangular top of the conforming case, the wide flat paneled & scroll-carved front folds out to expose the bed springs & mattress, original finish, ca. 1900, closed 20 x 50", overall 5' 4" h. (ILLUS.) **650**

Early Wardrobe-style "Murphy" Bed - M.M.

Victorian Golden Oak "Murphy" bed, wardrobe-style, the tall case w/a serpentine crestrail, delicate leafy scroll carving on the door-like panel enclosing an arched beveled mirror, the tall side panels w/rod cornices above tall slightly serpentine panels over flat panels, paneled & shaped side panels, full front folds down to expose the bed mattress & springs, patent-dated 1886, refinished, 22 x 60", 7' h. (ILLUS. below left)............. **1,250**

Rare Gothic Revival Half-tester Bed - M.M.

Victorian Gothic Revival half-tester bed, mahogany, the rectangular bow-fronted tester frame cut w/repeating low Gothic arches & cutout trefoils, raised on tall baluster-turned & paneled posts w/Gothic arch brackets, the tall headboard w/a gently arched scroll-carved crestrail over three tall Gothic arch flame veneer panels, the low footboard w/a serpentine crestrail over three arched panels between heavy paneled legs w/urn-form finials & raised on knob feet, refinished, ca. 1840, 60 x 80", 9' 9" h. (ILLUS.)........................ **5,500**

Victorian Renaissance Revival bed, walnut & burl walnut veneer, the tall arched headboard w/a fan- and scroll-carved crest centered by a raised burl shield above narrow curved burl panels over small burl panels flanking a roundel over two large arched burl panels, flat side stiles w/carved drop decoration, the low arched footboard w/a central flattened block finial over further raised burl panels, heavy square legs w/matching finials & carved drops, heavy square block feet, refinished, ca. 1875, 60 x 80", 8' 6" h.
 .... **3,500**

Child's Simple Tall-poster Bed - M.M.

Victorian Renaissance Revival tall-poster child's bed, walnut, the arched & scallop-cut headboard over a row of short turned spindles between rod-and-baluster-turned tall posts w/ball finials, matching foot posts joined by a low gently arched footboard, heavy baluster-and ring-turned legs, brass bolt covers, old refinish, ca. 1870s, 42 x 76", 5' 4" h. (ILLUS.).. **600**

Victorian Rococo bed, carved rosewood, the arched headboard w/a high arched crestrail pierced & carved w/heavy scrolls centered by an oval button, heavy rounded columnar legs w/flattened urn-form finials, the side- and foot rails w/scroll-carved corner brackets & cartouche-carved aprons, shorter columnar footboard legs w/matching finials, refinished, ca. 1860, 68 x 80", 5' h. (ILLUS. below).. **6,500**

Rosewood Bed with Bold Carving - M.M.

Rococo Carved Rosewood Bed - M.M.

Victorian Rococo bed, carved rosewood, the high headboard w/a tall broken-arch crest composed of ornate carved scrolls & pierced scroll panels centered by a turned urn finial, the arched crestrail above a simple paneled board flanked by matching turned urn corner finials, the lower arched footboard w/matching turned finials, wide sideboards, probably New York City, ca. 1855, original finish, 60 x 80", 6' h. (ILLUS. above) **2,800**

Victorian Rococo bed, carved rosewood, the very tall headboard w/an extremely or-

nate crest, a wide arched & pierced & scroll-carved crest centered by a full-figure seated putti above an arched molding over further elaborate leafy scroll & flower carving above three tall rectangular panels w/arched & serpentine tops flanked by heavy paneled side posts w/disk-turned finials, the low arched footboard w/further ornate scroll carving flanked by heavy panel legs w/disk finials, heavy disk-turned feet, ca. 1850s, 64 x 82", 8' 10" h. (ILLUS. of complete bed below left).......... **10,000**

Elaborately Carved Rococo Bed - M.M.

Simple Victorian Rococo Bed - M.M.

Victorian Rococo bed, chestnut & walnut, the high headboard w/an arched, stepped crestrail topped by a scroll-carved cartouche finial above a central scroll-carved cartouche over an oval raised band, blocked top corners w/knob-turned finials, the matching low footboard w/curved leg panels, refinished, ca. 1860, 58 x 78", 5' h. (ILLUS. previous page) **950**

Victorian Country-style Rococo Bed - M.M.

Victorian Rococo country-style bed, cherry & mahogany, the high arched headboard w/an ornate scroll-carved crestrail over the tall panels flanked by rod-turned posts w/ring-turned finials, low foot posts joined by narrow rails, original finish, ca. 1850s, 56 x 76", 6' h. (ILLUS.).. **1,000**

Fine Full-Tester Rococo Bed - M.M.

Victorian Rococo full-tester bed, mahogany, the deep cove-molded tester frame raised on slender paneled tapering posts above heavy tapering columnar posts above large columnar lower legs, the high headboard w/a pierced & scroll-carved crestrail over a wide veneer panel, the wide side- and foot rails w/scroll-carved corner brackets & serpentine aprons, refinished, ca. 1845, 68 x 84", overall 10' 6" h. (ILLUS. below left) **15,000**

Wonderful Rococo Half-tester Bed - M.M.

Victorian Rococo half-tester bed, carved rosewood, the rectangular half-tester w/a deep frame w/a coved cornice over a band of delicate scroll carving w/rounded projecting corners w/further detailed carving, supported by ornate scroll brackets above heavy columnar posts flanking the high arched headboard w/a scroll-carved central cartouche & scroll trim over a raised burl panel, the low footboard w/a serpentine top & a lower vine-carved panel flanked by short heavy paneled legs w/knob finials, refinished, Philadelphia, ca. 1855, 66 x 84", overall 10' h. (ILLUS.) **18,000**

Victorian Rococo half-tester bed, mahogany, the top half-tester frame w/serpentine sides w/a button- and scroll-carved front crest & reeded urn-turned corner finials, the tall arched headboard w/a shell- and roundel-carved crest & scroll-carved stepped crestrails above a rectangular burled panel flanked by heavy tapering tall posts, shaped & scroll-carved side rails & footboard flanked by heavy short columns w/arched raised panels & ring- and knob-turned pointed finials, attributed to Charles Lee, Manchester, Massachusetts, ca. 1860, 74 1/2 x 88 1/2", headboard 113" h. (ILLUS., next page) **19,550**

Very Rare Victorian Rococo Half-Tester Bed - N.O.

BENCHES

Early Ohio Bucket Bench - G

Bucket (or water) bench, country-style, painted pine, a narrow rectangular top shelf atop wide board upright ends w/bootjack feet & chamfered at the top over two open dovetailed medial shelves, original deep red paint, attributed to Ohio, mid-19th c., good patina, minor age splits & wear, 13 x 43", 41 1/2" h. (ILLUS.)................................. **$2,760**

Bucket (or water) bench, country-style, painted poplar, the narrow rectangular top above a narrow stepped-back enclosed shelf & chamfered one-board ends w/bootjack feet flanking two lower open shelves, old red wash, 19th c., wear to back corners of lower shelves, 12 x 43 1/4", 47" h. (ILLUS. top right) **1,093**

Painted Poplar Bucket Bench - G

Charles II bench, oak, long narrow rectangular seat cushion on a conforming frame raised on six block- and knob-turned legs joined by barley-twist turned rails, last quarter 17th c. or later, England, 22 x 60", 18 1/2" h. (ILLUS., below)......... **2,070**

Louis XV-Style bench, carved fruitwood, the long, narrow, rectangular upholstered seat cushion decorated w/gros & petit point designs of birds & animals in Aubusson-style cartouche, the apron w/carved frieze of shell & acanthus leaf decoration, cabriole legs w/shell-carved knees & scrolled feet, base missing original stretcher, France, late 19th c., 15 x 39", 22" h. (ILLUS. top next page) ... **1,045**

Early Charles II English Bench - N.O.

Upholstered Window Seat Bench - BR

George Nelson Modern-style Bench - C.H.

Modern-style bench, a rectangular long seat composed of solid maple slats raised on three ebonized wood trapezoidal open legs, designed by George Nelson, produced by Herman Miller, ca. 1956, 72" l., 14" h. (ILLUS. above).. **1,500-1,600**

Oriental hall bench, carved mahogany w/ebonized finish, the very ornately carved tall back top w/a wide undulating pierce-carved dragon & clouds above the two-panel back carved w/facing scenes of birds & flowers & borders w/carved scrolls, large carved dragon, open arms on scroll-carved supports above the rectangular lift-seat, the deep apron carved overall w/leafy scrolls & flowers, foo lion-head legs w/paw feet, China, ca. 1900-10, 24 x 60", 60" h. (ILLUS. right) **2,500**

Very Ornate Carved Chinese Bench - G.K.

Wicker Photographer's Bench - FO

Photographer's bench, wicker, the ornate stepped back w/an arched band of tight scrolls above panels of tight woven wicker & bobbins beside a lower section of slender strands & bobbins, a high rolled arm at one end composed of rows of bobbins, oblong wooden seat, ring- and scroll-trimmed front apron, slender wrapped legs, natural finish, ca. 1880 (ILLUS.).. **825-850**

Regency curule bench, carved, rosewood-grained & parcel-gilt wood, flaring U-form outswept upper rails raised on inverted U-form legs ending in giltwood paw feet, seat upholstered in green velvet w/brass tack trim, England, first quarter 19th c., 28 1/4" w., 29" h. (ILLUS.top right)............ **4,370**

Regency-Style benches, mahogany, long rectangular upholstered seat above a line-incised flat apron raised on turned tapering reeded legs on brass casters, England,   19th   c.,   25 1/2 x 47 1/2", 21 1/2" h., pr. (ILLUS., below).................. **2,300**

Fine Regency Curule Bench - N.O.

Victorian Baroque-style bench, carved fruitwood, the high arched back ornately carved w/a figural lion head at the top center over scrolls above wide border band w/concave sides centering bold carving of military trophies & cornucopias & flanked by figural seated putti playing horns, the wide serpentine-sided seat above an ornately carved front panel centering a panel w/a carved grotesque face & the sides w/carved profile grotesque crouching figures above scroll-carved feet, original finish, ca. 1870s, Europe, 20 x 36", 42" h. (ILLUS., top next page).. **1,000**

Nice Regency-Style Benches - N.O.

Carved Bench with Figures - M.M.

Very Ornate Victorian Bench - M.M.

Baroque-style Paneled Hall Bench - M.M.

Victorian Baroque-style bench, carved fruitwood, the high stepped back composed of three panels, the largest center rectangular panel topped by a high crest carved w/facing griffins & the panel carved w/a pair of scrolling griffins flanking a center round reserve w/a Cupid, the small side panels w/scrolled griffin crests & each carved w/scrolling designs, heavy end arms each carved w/a reclining lion flanking the long lift-top seat above a three-panel front further carved w/ornate scrolls & scrolling beasts, raised on two central short legs carved w/winged masks & large figural griffin corner legs, original finish, Europe, last quarter 19th c., 26 x 70", 44" h. (ILLUS. bottom previous page)........ **5,000**

Victorian Baroque-style bench, carved walnut, the high rectangular back w/a large panel carved overall w/ornate leafy scrolls centering a fruit-filled urn, heavy scroll end arms on block supports flank the rectangular leather-covered hinged seat above the front w/two scroll-carved panels, deep paneled apron w/front kick board missing, original finish, Europe, ca. 1870s, 18 x 50", 40" h. (ILLUS. top of page) **1,000**

Victorian Zebra-covered Ottoman - N.O.

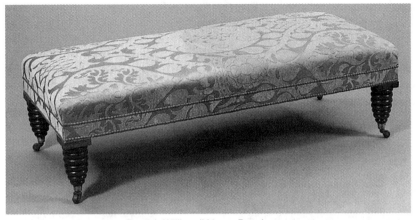

English William IV Long Bench - *N.O.*

Victorian ottoman, upholstered mahogany, deep rectangular form, the hinged top opening to storage, narrow wood base molding on bun feet, covered in zebra skin, third quarter 19th c., 18 1/2 x 49", 19" h. (ILLUS., bottom, previous page)..... **3,910**

William IV bench, mahogany, rectangular padded & upholstered top raised on heavily reeded short legs raised on brass caps & casters, England, mid-19th c., 24 x 54", 15" h. (ILLUS.) **1,380**

BOOKCASES

Arts & Crafts Leaded Glass Bookcase - M.M.

Arts & Crafts bookcase, mahogany & mahogany veneer, rectangular top w/narrow cornice above a pair of tall finely leaded glass doors, flat molded base, divided interior w/adjustable shelves, original dark finish & brass hardware, ca. 1900, 16 x 44", 5' h. (ILLUS.) **$1,400**

Rare Roycroft Oak Bookcase - C.A.

Arts & Crafts bookcase, oak, the rectangular top above tall paneled sides w/corner corbels & a tall wide door w/ornate geometric glazing, flat base, Roycroft mark, early 20th c. (ILLUS.) **11,600**

Fine American Classical Bookcase - N.O.

Classical bookcase, mahogany, the peaked pediment w/a thin edge ribbon molding above a tall case w/a pair of tall arched glazed doors opening to six adjustable wooden shelves, a slightly projecting base w/a pair of drawers raised on simple bracket feet, old finish, probably Boston, ca. 1840-50, 14 x 47 1/4", 7' 3" h. (ILLUS.) **3,910**

Fancy Classical Revival Bookcase - M.M.

Classical Revival bookcase, mahogany & mahogany veneer, an arched & ornately pierced scroll-carved crest board flanked by small urn finials above the rectangular back above a pair of tall glazed doors opening to adjustable wooden shelves w/a mirror behind the top shelves, all flanked by acanthus leaf-carved baluster-turned side columns, flat base on heavy paw feet, original finish, ca. 1890, 18 x 40", 5' 8" h. (ILLUS. previous page) .. **1,800**

Simple Classical Revival Bookcase - M.M.

Classical Revival bookcase, mahogany & mahogany veneer, the rectangular top above a pair of tall bow-front glazed doors flanked by long serpentine pilasters above a rounded bowed apron, rolled front feet, refinished, ca. 1910, 18 x 48", 5' 4" h. (ILLUS.) **1,400**

Classical Revival bookcase, mahogany & mahogany veneer, the rectangular top w/blocked front corners over a conforming case w/two tall glazed doors opening to three wooden shelves flanked by acanthus leaf & pineapple-carved side columns above a pair of bow-front base drawers, raised on front paw feet, original finial, ca. 1900, 18 x 42", 5' 4" h. (ILLUS. top right column) **1,500**

Colonial Revival bookcase, mahogany & mahogany veneer, the rectangular arched top centered by a shell-carved crest above a pair of tall arched glazed doors w/applied geometric grillwork, glass side panels, serpentine apron raised on cabriole legs ending in claw-and-ball feet, original casters, refinished, ca. 1920s, 18 x 48", 6' h. (ILLUS. bottom right column) **1,800**

Early Classical Revival Bookcase - M.M.

Nice Colonial Revival Bookcase - M.M.

Fine Colonial Revival Bookcase - M.M.

Colonial Revival bookcase, mahogany, the long rectangular top w/a high backboard w/a flat crestrail centered by ribbon carving & flanked by turned finials above a narrow shelf raised on short carved balusters in front of a long narrow raised panel all flanked by incurved end brackets, the top w/a coved molding over a thin beaded band over a long leaf-carved central band all above a case of four tall glass doors w/beveled glass opening to adjustable wooden shelves in the maple interior, raised on eight tapering blocked & carved legs joined by simple stretchers, original finish, late 19th c., 20 x 84", 6' h. (ILLUS. above) **4,000**

Early 20th century bookcase, oak, four-section stacking lawyer's-type, the rectangular top w/rounded crestrail above four lift-front geometrically-leaded doors, narrow base drawer, Macy Stacking Bookcase Co., ca. 1900, 12 x 34", 4' 8" h. (ILLUS. below left) **1,800**

Leaded Glass Stacking Bookcase - M.M.

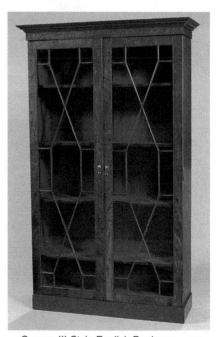

George III-Style English Bookcase - N.O.

George III-Style bookcase, mahogany, the rectangular top w/a narrow flaring & stepped cornice above a pair of tall geometrically-glazed doors opening to four adjustable wooden shelves, flat plinth base, England, late 19th - early 20th c., 18 x 51", 6' 10" h. (ILLUS. previous page) **2,990**

Rare Harvey Ellis-designed Bookcase - R/CR

Mission-style (Arts & Crafts movement) bookcase, oak, the rectangular top w/a low back rail above a pair of tall two-pane glazed doors opening to three adjustable shelves, side stiles continue down to form tapering front legs flanking the slightly arched apron, round copper pulls, medium brown finish, branded mark of Charles Limbert Co., Grand Rapids, Michigan, early 20th c., 14 x 40 1/2", 4' 9" h. **2,760**

Quality Globe-Wernicke Bookcase - M.M.

Late Victorian bookcase, mahogany & mahogany veneer, four-section stacking lawyer's-type, the rectangular top w/carved projecting front corners flanking a dentil-carved band above a stack of four long lift-front beveled glass doors each flanked by reeded half-columns, the projecting base w/a long drawer w/brass bail pulls flanked by leaf-carved brackets, the Ideal Model by Globe-Wernicke, original dark finish, ca. 1890, 16 x 38", 5' h. (ILLUS.) **2,000**

Mission-style (Arts & Crafts movement) bookcase, oak, a thin rectangular top overhanging a tall case w/a single door w/a row of three small four-pane glazed panels over three long glass panes, arched front & side aprons, designed by Harvey Ellis for Gustav Stickley, early 20th c. (ILLUS. top, next column) **19,550**

Early Oak Revolving Bookcase - M.M.

Mission-style (Arts & Crafts movement) bookcase, quarter-sawn oak, revolving-type, a square top above two sides composed of narrow slats flanking three shelves, a wide adjustable book shelf at the side, rotating on a cross-form base on casters, refinished, ca. 1910, 22" w., 44" h. (ILLUS.) **750**

Large Neoclassical Bookcases - M.M.

Regency Marble-topped Bookcase - N.O.

Neoclassical Revival bookcases, mahogany, a rectangular top w/one end angled out above a tall corner alcove w/a tall raised panel over a paneled lower door carved w/a classical urn & swags, the main case w/a pair of tall & wide glass doors opening to three adjustable wooden shelves, deep molded base, original finish, ca. 1900, 18 x 70", 5' h., pr. (ILLUS. top of page).............. **2,800**

Regency breakfront-style bookcase, rosewood, the long rectangular white marble top w/a stepped-out center section w/two doors set w/diamond lattice metal grills flanked by large scroll blocks at the top, the set-back end sections w/matching doors, conforming plinth base, England, first quarter 19th c., 17 x 72 1/2", 37" h. (ILLUS., above).......... **5,750**

Victorian Aesthetic Movement bookcase, walnut, the high superstructure w/a tall square central panel w/flat crestrail & finials above a recessed panel boldly carved w/leaves, half-round carved crests & corner blocks w/finials topping the side sections each w/a narrow shelf raised on short knob-turned spindles, the rectangular top w/a flaring cornice above a pair of tall beveled glass doors opening to fixed shelves all flanked by slender reeded side columns, the projecting base w/a pair of

drawers each centered by a raised half-round panel, original cast-brass bail pulls, deep molded base, refinished, ca. 1885, 18 x 38", 6' 4" h. (ILLUS., below) **2,400**

Aesthetic Movement Bookcase - M.M.

Extraordinary Aesthetic Movement Bookcase - N.O.

Victorian Aesthetic Movement break-front-style bookcase, walnut, amboyna & ebonized wood, the long rectangular top w/a stepped-out center section over a pair of tall arched glazed doors opening to wooden shelves, the top glass pane in stained amber green glass in a leaded frame, all above a wide mid-molding over a pair of four-panel cupboard doors, the set-back side sections w/pairs of similar doors above matching pairs of doors in the base, on eight small knob feet, ebonized trim, attributed to Gillow, probably designed by Bruce Talbot, England, third quarter 19th c., 20 1/4 x 120", 7' 4" h. (ILLUS.)............... **13,800**

Victorian Aesthetic Movement break-front-style bookcase, walnut, the superstructure w/a high projecting central section w/an arched crest carved w/leaves & acorns above a scalloped apron raised on reeded baluster-turned supports backed by a rectangular mirror, the backboard sides w/a flat crest over a band of blocks over dentil carving & a rectangular panel also carved w/acorns & leaves all flanked by blocked ends w/acorn finials, the rectangular top w/projecting center section above the conforming case, the projecting center section w/a narrow leaf & acorn-carved panel over the tall glazed door opening to adjustable wooden shelves, the setback side sections w/a tall glazed door opening to four adjustable wooden shelves, each section w/drawers w/brass butterfly pulls on the molded base band, original hardware & finish, ca. 1885, 20 x 72", 7' h. (ILLUS., next column)........................ **4,500**

Fine Victorian Aesthetic Bookcase - M.M.

Victorian Baroque Revival bookcase, beech, demountable, the rectangular top w/four blocked sections above a conforming case w/a wide frieze band cased in the projecting blocks carved w/turbaned heads flanking bands of large carved shells all above the tall glazed arched doors each separated by tall ornately carved panels featuring caryatids, grotesque masks & leafy scrolls, the base w/three deep scroll-carved drawers separated by blocks carved w/grotesque masks, on flattened bun feet, Europe, late 19th c., sold refinished, 22 x 84", 7' h. (ILLUS. top, next page) **5,000**

Ornate Baroque Revival Bookcase - *M.M.*

Ornately Carved Horner Bookcase - *M.M.*

Victorian Baroque Revival bookcase, mahogany, a long rectangular top w/a deep curved & ornately carved cornice raised on two inner turned columns & two figural seated winged lion end supports all backed by a long beveled mirror over a rectangular top w/a convex center section above a conforming base, a wide bowed glass central door opening to shelves & flanked by scroll-and-button carved columns flanked by tall flat glazed doors also flanked by matching side columns, the molded base on compressed paw feet, original finish, made by Horner of New York City, ca. 1880s, 18 x 84", 6' h. (ILLUS. above) **8,000**

Boldly Carved Baroque Bookcase - M.M.

Victorian Country-style Bookcase - M.M.

Victorian Baroque Revival bookcase, oak, the long rectangular top w/projecting block ends, a wide flaring leaf-carved cornice over a frieze band carved w/scrolling leafy vines flanked by florette side blocks over a pair of tall arched glazed doors opening to wooden shelves, side columns boldly carved w/fruits & leaves above the coved carved apron matching the top cornice, refinished, ca. 1880s, 21 x 54", 6' 8" h. (ILLUS.) **3,500**

Victorian country-style bookcase, walnut, the arched crestrail centered by a high peaked scroll-and-leaf-carved crest, the case w/a single tall & wide glazed door opening to two shelves flanked by chamfered front corners carved w/thin reeded quarter-columns, a long deep base drawer w/brass bin pulls, flat base, original finish, may have had a base at one time, ca. 1880, 18 x 36", 6' 8" h. (ILLUS.).................. **700**

Finely Detailed Eastlake Bookcase - M.M.

Victorian Eastlake bookcase, walnut, a low stick-and-ball gallery rail w/carved palmettes above a case w/two tall side cabinets flanking a shorter center cabinet, the center section w/a narrow band of carved spearpoints above a glazed door topped by a narrow band of carved crosses, the tall side sections w/tall glazed doors also carved w/a band of crosses, each section w/adjustable wooden shelves, the slightly stepped-out base w/a carved band of spearpoints above three burl-paneled drawers w/original brass ring pulls, refinished, ca. 1880, 22 x 60", 6' h. (ILLUS. bottom, previous page) **5,000**

High-crested Golden Oak Bookcase - M.M.

Oak Bookcase with Pierced Gallery - M.M.

Victorian Golden Oak bookcase, oak, a high arched & delicate scroll-pierced top back rail & low cutout sides on the rectangular top w/a deep flaring molding over a pair of tall glazed cupboard doors w/pierced scroll-cut bands at the top of each & narrow scroll-cut panels at the base, on a narrow scroll-incised apron w/scroll feet on casters, refinished, ca. 1900, 16 x 40", 5' 8" h. (ILLUS.) **2,000**

Victorian Golden Oak bookcase, oak, a high, deeply scalloped & scroll-carved back crest on the rectangular top, a pair of tall glazed doors w/serpentine scroll-carved top borders, a wide serpentine base on block feet, adjustable shelves, original finish, ca. 1900, 16 x 42", 5' 8" h. (ILLUS. top, next column) **1,750**

Golden Oak Bookcase with Gallery - M.M.

Victorian Golden Oak bookcase, oak, the superstructure w/a low top gallery w/a knob rail over a narrow shelf raised on baluster-turned front supports & a back panel divided into three beveled mirrors, the top over a case w/a pair of tall glazed doors w/downswept tops highlighted by tapering panels of carved scrolls, the bottom of each door w/matching carved panels, simple block feet on casters, adjustable wooden shelves, original finish, ca. 1900, 16 x 42", 6' h. (ILLUS.) **1,500**

Open Oak Bookcase with Spindles - M.M.

Victorian Golden Oak bookcase, oak, the high three-quarters gallery top w/a back rail topped w/a low raised crestrail over tiny spindles over a carved thin block band flanked by scrolled corner brackets & knob-turned finials above curved solid ends over a rectangular top shelf above a three-part serpentine apron supported by two turned tall spindles flanked by low spindle rails all flanked by large round end cutouts, three open lower shelves over a scroll-cut short apron, original finish, ca. 1895, 15 x 42", 5' 4" h. (ILLUS.) **950**

Victorian Renaissance Revival bookcase, oak, three-section, the rectangular top w/a wide cornice centered by a broken-scroll pediment w/a large urn finial above the carved face of a classical woman flanked by wide leafy scrolls, all above a tall recessed center section backed by a tall beveled mirror & w/pierced scroll upper corner brackets flanked by slender colonettes, tall glazed doors at the sides flanked by larger reeded & knob-turned freestanding side columns above the stepped-out lower cabinet, the lower section w/a rectangular top w/a bowed center section over a stack of three paneled drawers w/pierced brass pulls flanked by narrow leaf-carved pilasters & large paneled side cupboard doors & wide leaf-

carved pilasters topped by lion heads at the sides, refinished, ca. 1890, 24 x 72", 8' 4" h. (ILLUS., below) **5,500**

Fine Oak Renaissance Bookcase - M.M.

One-door Renaissance Bookcase - M.M.

Victorian Renaissance Revival bookcase, walnut, an arched & stepped cornice w/carved leaves, blocks & center roundel above a deep flaring blocked cornice over a single tall glazed door flanked by plain raised pilasters & raised side panels, the stepped-out base w/two small drawers over the deep flat molded base, adjustable wooden shelves, refinished, original pulls, ca. 1875, 18 x 32", 7' h. (ILLUS.) **1,800**

Large Breakfront Walnut Bookcase - M.M.

Handsome Renaissance Bookcase - M.M.

Victorian Renaissance Revival bookcase, walnut & burl walnut, the top section w/a high broken-scroll pediment centered on a platform w/an urn-form finial over triangular raised burl panels, a deep coved cornice above a pair of tall glazed doors w/rounded top corners flanked by slender quarter-round corner columns, the stepped-out lower section w/a pair of cupboard doors w/raised burl panels, deep molded base w/rounded corners, refinished, ca. 1875, 24 x 48", 8' 6" h. (ILLUS.) **3,000**

Victorian Renaissance Revival breakfront-style bookcase, figured circassian walnut, the high stepped-out center section w/an arched crestrail centered by a carved cartouche above a frieze band of roundels over blocked corners above the tall rectangular glazed arched door above a narrow base drawer, the shorter side cabinets w/crestrails carved w/upright pierced leaf bands over a flaring cornice, each side w/a band of roundels above shorter matching glazed doors above a narrow base shelf, adjustable wooden shelves, deep molded base, ebonized wood pulls, refinished, ca. 1875, 20 x 88", 6' 6" h. (ILLUS., above) **5,500**

Very Large Renaissance Bookcase - M.M.

Victorian Renaissance Revival break-front-style bookcase, walnut & burl walnut, the tall stepped-out central section w/a high arched pierced scroll-carved crest over a flaring blocked crest rail over a tall arched glazed door w/raised burl panels at the top & flanked by blocked & leaf-carved designs, the lower side cabinets w/a carved scroll above the flaring cornice over matching narrower glazed doors; the stepped-out lower case w/a pair of raised-panel arched center doors w/wide matching doors at each side, deep molded base, original finish, ca. 1875, 24 x 84", 10' 3" h. (ILLUS. previous page) **10,000**

Simple Victorian Rococo Bookcase - M.M.

Extraordinary Rococo Bookcase - N.O.

Victorian Rococo bookcase, carved rosewood, the top front w/a high pointed pierced leafy-scroll-carved crest over a wide arched molding above a fan carving above a tall glazed door opening to four shelves, the angled top side moldings topped by four pointed finials over angled tall side panels each flanked by slender spiral-twist colonnettes & framing a tall slender arched mirror below a scroll-carved top panel, deep stepped conforming base, possibly by J. & J. Meeks, New York, New York, ca. 1850s, 20 x 57", 8' 9 1/2" h. (ILLUS.) **20,125**

Victorian Rococo bookcase, walnut, the rectangular top w/a low arched & ornately scroll-carved crestrail above a flared cornice over a pair of tall glazed arched doors separated by three tall slender incised oval bands, opening to adjustable wooden shelves, the stepped-out lower section w/a molded edge above a group of four drawers w/carved wooden fruit pulls, deep molded base, ca. 1865, refinished, 18 x 54", 7' 10" h. (ILLUS. top right) **2,500**

English William IV Bookcase - N.O.

William IV bookcase, mahogany, two-part construction: the upper section w/a rectangular top w/a deep, flaring round-cornered cornice above a conforming case w/a pair of tall glazed doors opening to four wooden shelves; the stepped-out lower section w/a pair of drawers above a pair of arched-panel cupboard doors, on a plinth base, England, mid-19th c., 18 1/2 x 53 1/2", 7' 5" h. (ILLUS.)............. **2,530**

BUREAUX PLAT

Louis XV-Style Bureau Plat - N.O.

Louis XV-Style bureau plat, mahogany, kingwood & parquetry, the shaped rectangular top w/an inset leather writing surface & ormolu banding above an apron w/three drawers each inset w/diamond pattern parquetry panels & fitted w/scrolling ormolu mounts, on cabriole legs headed by ormolu mounts & ending w/ormolu foot mounts, France, third quarter 19th c., 31 1/4 x 57 1/2", 32 3/4" h. (ILLUS., above) .. **$575**

Louis XV-Style bureau plat, ormolu-mounted hardwood, the rectangular top w/serpentine sides decorated w/elaborate inlay surrounding the writing surface, the serpentine floral-inlaid apron fitted w/three hand-dovetailed drawers, the cabriole legs w/elaborate female head ormolu mounts, traces of original gilding, France, early 20th c., separations & chips to veneer, 31 x 63", 32" h. (ILLUS., below) **1,980**

Louis XV-Style Bureau Plat - BR

Simple Louis XVI-Style Bureau Plat - N.O.

Louis XVI-Style Bureau Plat - N.O.

Louis XVI-Style bureau plat, mahogany, the rectangular top w/a floral-carved edge above an apron fitted w/a central foliate-carved drawer flanked by plain drawers w/bail pulls, simple square fluted tapering legs, France, ca. 1900, 32 x 68", 30" h. (ILLUS. bottom, previous page)...... **2,185**

Louis XVI-Style bureau plat, ormolu-mounted mahogany, the rectangular top w/a brass-bound border enclosing a yellow leather writing surface, one apron fitted w/pairs of small drawers w/ormolu mounts flanking a single center drawer over the kneehole opening, the corner blocks fitted w/ormolu swag drops, on tapering reeded legs w/ormolu mounts & ending in brass foot caps, France, early 20th c., 30 x 60 1/2", 30" h. (ILLUS. above).......... **920**

Napoleon III bureau plat, brass-inlaid ebonized wood, the serpentine rectangular top centered by elaborate brass inlay & brass edge banding above an apron fitted w/one end drawer & brass banding on the serpentine edges, on cabriole legs headed by large ormolu shields & scrolls & ending in feet w/ormolu mounts, France, third-quarter 19th c., 31 1/2 x 51 1/2", 30" h. (ILLUS. below) **2,530**

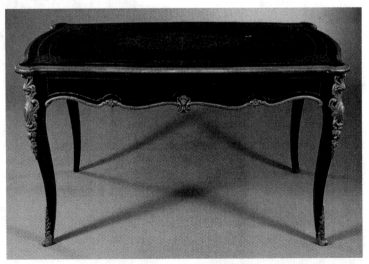

Brass-inlaid Napoleon III Bureau Plat - N.O.

CABINETS

Old Oriental Apothecary Cabinet - G

Apothecary cabinet, painted & decorated wood, a nearly square top w/molded edges above a tall case w/three rows of nine small square drawers, decorated overall in old reddish brown paint w/dark mustard yellow drawer panels w/Oriental characters on each, drawers w/small ring pulls, probably China, 19th c., later background, 23 1/2 x 26", 5' 6 1/2" h. (ILLUS.) .. **$805**

Delicate Art Nouveau Cabinet - M.M.

China cabinet, Art Nouveau-influenced, mahogany & mahogany veneer, the narrow rectangular top w/an upright short superstructure w/narrow shelf flanked by pierced scroll-carved ears & raised on a slender center leg backed by a narrow beveled mirror, the top above a central tall curved glass door opening to a mirrored compartment above a lower open compartment w/delicate curved legs, the center cabinet flanked by two open shelves backed w/narrow vertical mirrors & supported by delicate incurved corner supports, the base supported on slender cabriole legs, original dark finish, ca. 1890s, 17 x 34", 5' h. (ILLUS. bottom left)............. **1,500**

Small Mirrored Art Nouveau Cabinet - M.M.

China cabinet, Art Nouveau-influenced, mahogany, the superstructure w/an arched crestrail w/scroll-carved crest over an arch-topped beveled mirror flanked by small shelf on slender serpentine supports backed by pierced scroll-brackets over a half-round top above a pair of curved glass doors opening to mirror-backed compartment raised on an S-scroll support over a lower half-round open shelf backed by a mirror, flat outswept base, refinished, ca. 1900, 16 x 22", 4' 10" h. (ILLUS.)........................... **800**

Early Classical Rosewood Cabinet - M.M.

China cabinet, Classical style, rosewood, two-part construction: the upper section w/a rectangular top w/a deep flaring coved cornice w/a beaded band above a pair of wide glazed doors flanked by free-standing columns & opening to wooded shelves; the stepped-out lower section w/a pair of deep drawers projecting over a pair of cupboard doors flanked by bold S-scrolls ending in paw feet on platforms, original hardware, refinished, ca. 1850s, 24 x 42", 6' 10" h. (ILLUS.) **1,500**

Simple Colonial Revival Cabinet - M.M.

China cabinet, Colonial Revival, mahogany, a flat plain wide crest board above the half-round D-form top over a conforming case w/two curved glass panels, one forming a hinged door opening to a mirror-backed interior w/two glass shelves, molded half-round apron on three simple curved legs

w/scroll-carved corner brackets & ending in paw feet, ca. 1910, refinished, 16 x 24", 5' 6" h. (ILLUS. bottom left) **1,200**

Nice Colonial Revival China Cabinet - M.M.

China cabinet, Colonial Revival, mahogany & mahogany veneer, rectangular top above a veneered frieze band over a pair of wide glazed doors overlaid w/decorative scroll-cut fretwork, a medial band over the lower section w/a very long single drawer w/decorative veneer & butterfly brass pulls, serpentine scroll-carved apron raised on cabriole legs w/scrolled returns & claw-and-ball feet, original finish, ca. 1920s, 21 x 42", 6' h. (ILLUS.) **750**

Ebonized Colonial Revival Cabinet - M.M.

China cabinet, Colonial Revival, mahogany w/ebonized finish, two-part construction: the upper section w/a rectangular top & pierced broken-scroll pediment over a frieze band carved w/lunettes over a pair of glazed doors w/applied geometric grill-work; the stepped-out lower section w/a rectangular top over two long serpentine-fronted florette-carved drawers all raised on slender square tapering legs joined by a curved cross-stretcher, original hardware, late 19th c., 20 x 38", 7' 4" h. (ILLUS. previous page).. **1,600**

Unusual Oriental China Cabinet - M.M.

French Provincial China Cabinet - M.M.

China cabinet, French Provincial, mahogany & hardwood, the rectangular top above a narrow rectangular light wood inlaid band above the tall glass door w/an asymmetrical pane of glass over an asymmetrical light wood panel above two narrow base drawers w/shell-carved pulls flanked by light wood panels, serpentine apron on short scroll front legs, paneled sides, adjustable interior shelves, France, mid-19th c., original finish, 18 x 26", 6' h. (ILLUS.) **1,200**

China cabinet, Oriental-style, inlaid mahogany, an ornate superstructure composed on one side w/a large upper cupboard w/a stepped pagoda-style top over a mother-of-pearl inlaid band above a glass cupboard door raised on slender spindles, the other side w/a smaller open compartment w/a pierced scroll crest & front spindles over a narrow inlaid drawer; the rectangular lower section top w/one end curled up & the other curled down, above an ornate arrangement of mother-of-pearl inlaid doors beside a stack of small carved drawers over a stepped small shelf & long bottom shelf all trimmed w/pierced scrolls, the narrow serpentine apron carved w/Oriental scrolls above short paw-footed legs, probably China, ca. 1880, original finish, 20 x 36", 6' h. (ILLUS. top right) **2,000**

Large Renaissance-Style Cabinet - N.O.

China cabinet, Renaissance-Style, fumed oak, the large rectangular top w/a widely flaring dentil-carved cornice over a wide blocked frieze band centered by a long panel carved w/an urn issuing leafy vines above a pair of tall 12-pane glazed doors flanked by boldly carved caryatids atop carved pilasters, the deep base w/a carved band over a plain band all raised on scroll-carved feet, Flanders, ca. 1900, 24 x 59 1/2", 6' 1" h. (ILLUS.).................... **1,380**

Fine French Rococo China Cabinet - M.M.

China cabinet, Rococo Revival style, bleached figured walnut veneer, the arched serpentine top w/a bold scroll-carved center crest over a conforming frieze band above a very wide serpentine-topped glazed door w/applied ornate scrollwork flanked by wide rounded corners, a lower gadrooned band over a wide bombe base band w/a wide drawer, ornate scroll-carved serpentine apron raised on scrolled cabriole legs, original finish, France, early 20th c., 20 x 36", 6' h. (ILLUS.) **3,600**

Large French Rococo China Cabinet - M.M.

China cabinet, Rococo Revival style, mahogany, arched serpentine center crestrail w/a carved cartouche flanked by ornate carved scroll bands above a pair of arched glazed doors open to a mirrored back & fixed shelves above three long serpentine-front drawers, each side w/a shorter cabinet w/serpentine short cornice over a narrow conforming glass door & ends backed by a mirror above paneled front & sides; serpentine scroll-carved apron raised on four front cabriole legs w/scroll feet, original finish, France, early 20th c., 22 x 72", 7' h. (ILLUS. bottom left) **1,800**

Ornately Carved Baroque Cabinet - M.M.

China cabinet, Victorian Baroque Revival, carved oak, two-part construction: the upper section w/a rectangular top w/a high arched scroll-carved crest centered by a large cartouche over the flaring cornice above a frieze band of carved fruit & scrolls above the tall glazed door opening to shelves & flanked by fruit-carved side drops; the stepped-out lower section w/a long fruit-carved drawer over a wide rectangular door boldly carved w/figures of dead game & flanked by fruit-carved side bands, flaring carved base on compressed bun feet, original dark finish, probably Europe, late quarter 19th c., 20 x 36", 8' 8" h. (ILLUS.) **2,800**

China cabinet, Victorian Baroque Revival, mahogany, a rectangular top w/a narrow cornice over a pair of tall paneled doors flanked by rounded & carved front corners raised on heavy incurved carved supports on blocks backed by a valanced backboard over a rectangular top above a pair of wide paneled cupboard doors, heavy front bun feet, original hardware, probably Europe, refinished, ca. 1900, 20 x 34", 5' h. (ILLUS. next page) **900**

Smaller Baroque Revival Cabinet - M.M.

Large Colonial Revival Cabinet - M.M.

China cabinet, Victorian Colonial Revival, mahogany, the half-round top w/a projecting center section w/an arched palmette & scroll-carved crest over a band w/scrolls above the wide arched glass door flanked by slender turned & reeded columns, curved glass sides, flaring molded base on short cabriole legs w/paw feet, original dark finish, ca. 1890, 19 x 56", 6' 3" h. (ILLUS.)......................... **3,000**

Fancy Classical Revival Cabinet - M.M.

China cabinet, Victorian Classical Revival style, quarter-sawn oak, the large half-round top w/blocked projecting front corners over carved lion heads, scrolls & cartouche above tall columns flanking a tall curved glass door topped by an ornately scroll-carved band, curved glass sides, mirrored interior back, molded base w/blocks over large paw feet, original dark finish, ca. 1895, 20 x 48" h., 6' h. (ILLUS.).. **4,800**

Ornate Eastlake China Cabinet - M.M.

China cabinet, Victorian Eastlake substyle, walnut & burl walnut, the tall crestrail w/a flat dentil-carved center section above a narrow rectangular scroll-carved panel flanked by angled sides over a long narrow rectangular shelf over an arrangement of two stepped open shelves backed by a tall rectangular & a narrow rectangular beveled mirror, one side w/a tall door w/a row of three small square beveled glass panes over a tall beveled glass pane opening to adjustable shelves, the other side w/a shorter door w/a beveled glass pane, trimmed w/turned spindles & narrow burl panels, stepped & molded base on tiny bun feet, refinished, ca. 1880, 18 x 40", 6' h. (ILLUS. previous page)........ **4,800**

High-crested Oak China Cabinet - M.M.

Oak Cabinet with Fancy Top Shelf - M.M.

China cabinet, Victorian Golden Oak style, a high superstructure w/a low arched gadrooned crest on a top shelf raised on flat S-scroll supports in front of a wide backboard w/scroll & leaf carving & rounded reeded ends, the half-round top over a tall flat glazed door above a long bow-fronted base drawer flanked by curved glass sides over plain lower panels, four wooden shelves, original hardware, carved paw feet on casters, refinished, ca. 1900, 19 x 58", 6' 4" h. (ILLUS.) **3,000**

China cabinet, Victorian Golden Oak style, quarter-sawn oak, a high top back crest w/an arched broken scroll centering a large feather finial over delicate leafy scrolls, the D-form top w/projecting blocks over carved lion heads & scrolls atop columns flanking the wide curved glass door, curved glass sides, three wooden shelves, molded base on two short cabriole legs w/paw feet & plain square back legs, refinished, ca. 1900, 18 x 48", 6' h. (ILLUS. top right) **2,800**

Large China Cabinet with Lions - M.M.

China cabinet, Victorian Golden Oak style, quarter-sawn own, the half-round case w/a deep flaring cornice w/a central serpentine projection above a tall curved glass door flanked by columns topped by lion heads above paw feet, curved glass sides, four wooden shelves, conforming shaped molded apron on heavy paw feet, refinished, ca. 1900, 20 x 48", 6' h. (ILLUS.) **3,500**

Oak Cabinet with Tambour Base - M.M.

China cabinet, Victorian Golden Oak style, the D-form top w/a deep carved band of stylized leaves over wide central curved glass door flanked by curved glass sides above a conforming lower case w/a tambour-style base w/a curved cabinet door centered by a large round carved medallion, beaded base band on heavy turned & tapering feet, refinished, ca. 1900, 18 x 30", 6' 6" h. (ILLUS.)........................... **1,600**

Mirrored Crest on Oak Cabinet - M.M.

China cabinet, Victorian Golden Oak style, the high arched back crestrail w/a shell finial over a shaped oblong beveled mirror flanked by tiny shelves on the half-round top w/flattened center section over the flat

tall glass door trimmed w/ornate scrolls, curved glass sides, four wood shelves w/mirrored back in upper half, on simple squared cabriole legs, refinished, ca. 1900, 18 x 48", 6' 3" h. (ILLUS. bottom left) . **2,000**

Heavily Carved Oak Cabinet - M.M.

China cabinet, Victorian Golden Oak style, the wide half-round top w/a wide flattened center section w/a large arched & scroll-carved crest above a conforming frieze band ornately carved w/scrolls, the curved glass center door flanked by dividers, boldly carved blocks & bands of leaf carving resting on heavy blocks over large paw feet, curved glass sides, mirrored interior w/four wooden shelves, refinished, ca. 1890s, 22 x 48", 6' h. (ILLUS.).................... **3,500**

European Rococo China Cabinet - M.M.

China cabinet, Victorian Rococo substyle, carved beechwood, two-part construction: the upper section w/a high arched & scroll-carved pediment centered by a large carved cartouche above a flaring cornice over a wide scroll-carved frieze band above a pair of tall glazed doors w/arched serpentine tops flanked by carved corner bands; the stepped-out lower section w/a rectangular molded edge overhanging a pair of leafy band-carved drawers over a pair of paneled cupboard doors boldly carved w/large clusters of fruits & vegetables, carved corner bands, paneled projecting front feet & molded flat base, original dark finish, Europe, ca. 1870, 22 x 45", 8' 6" h. (ILLUS. previous page) **3,200**

Mahogany Rococo China Cabinet - M.M.

China cabinet, Victorian Rococo substyle, mahogany & mahogany veneer, two-part construction: the upper section w/an arched pierced scroll-carved crestrail over a deep ogee cornice above a pair of glazed doors w/pierced scroll-carved grillwork at the top, flanked by chamfered front corners w/carved top & bottom drops; the stepped-out lower section w/four long graduated crotch grain-veneered drawers w/ornate scroll-carved center pulls, chamfered front corners w/carved drops, deep scroll-carved apron, polished original finish, ca. 1855-60, 20 x 42", 7' 8" h. (ILLUS.) **3,000**

Nice Rosewood Rococo Cabinet - M.M.

China cabinet, Victorian Rococo substyle, carved rosewood, two-part construction: the upper section w/an arched broken-scroll pediment centered by an ornate pierced scroll crest above an arched beaded frieze band over a pair of tall glazed doors w/ornate scrolling grillwork opening to shelves; the projecting lower section w/a narrow white marble shelf over a pair of narrow long drawers w/leaf-carved pulls over a pair of paneled cupboard doors w/carved leaf sprigs in each corner & a central carved cartouche, deep scalloped & scroll-carved apron on short cabriole legs w/scroll feet on casters, New York City, ca. 1855, refinished, 22 x 42", 7' 6" h. (ILLUS.) **4,800**

Rococo China Cabinet with Mirror - M.M.

China cabinet, Victorian Rococo substyle, mahogany, two-part construction: the upper section w/a very tall pointed pierced scroll-carved crest & urn-form finials above the arched cornice over a wide single door centered by a large round mirror & flanked by chamfered corners w/scroll-carved drops; the stepped-out lower section w/a rectangular top w/serpentine edges overhanging a case w/a long drawer over a pair of cupboard doors w/large oval veneered panels, chamfered front corners w/scroll-carved drops, projecting rounded base corners on squatty bulbous front feet, 18 x 40", 7' 10" h. (ILLUS. previous page) **3,000**

Pair of Colonial Revival Cabinets - M.M.

China cabinets, Colonial Revival style, mahogany & mahogany veneer, each w/a rectangular top above a cornice w/dentil carving & carved spearpoints over a single tall glass door w/geometric applied grillwork opening to adjustable wooden shelves, a medial band over the bowfronted base top & conforming case w/a single bowed door w/a panel of raised banding, molded base over a serpentine apron ending in French feet, original finish, ca. 1920s, 18 x 22", 6' 6" h., pr. (ILLUS.) **1,000**

China corner cabinet, Chippendale, mahogany, the top w/a pierced broken-scroll pediment over a carved cornice above a pair of tall geometrically glazed cupboard doors opening to shelves & surrounded by blind fretwork carving & scroll-carved side panels, a medial rail above a pair of short geometrically glazed doors also surrounded by carving, molded base on bracket feet, George III period, Ireland, last quarter 18th c., 21 x 43", 8 1/2" h. (ILLUS., top next column) **11,500**

Fine Irish Chippendale Cabinet - N.O.

Two-piece Corner Cupboard - BR

China corner cabinet, Rococo-style, mahogany, two-piece dovetailed construction: the top section w/molded cornice & five garniture platforms above two domed doors, each w/18 panes of glass w/through muntins & pull-out platform & two shelves w/shaped fronts; the base section w/two domed doors, each w/12 panes of glass w/through muntins, partially replaced bracket feet, possibly Dutch, late 18th or early 19th c., 20 x 40", 82" h. (ILLUS.) **4,840**

Unusual Rococo Corner Cabinet - *M.M.*

China corner cabinet, Victorian Rococo substyle, rosewood, the superstructure composed of two wide quarter-round open shelves topped by a delicate pierced scroll-carved crest, each backed by low pierced-carved back rails & supported on pierced S-scroll front brackets & slender ring-turned spindles, the quarter-round top w/molded edge above a case w/small center drawer flanked by recessed panels over a pair of curved glass doors bordered w/ornate scroll carving & slender side colonettes, molded curved apron, lower interior in maple, original finish, ca. 1855, 20 x 36", 6' h. (ILLUS.) **3,000**

Simple Oak Corner China Cupboard - *M.M.*

China corner cupboard, Victorian Golden Oak style, a low scalloped crest on the flat top above a wide flat glass door opening to a mirrored interior w/three glass shelves, slightly shaped apron on simple cabriole front legs, refinished, ca. 1900, 18 x 28", 5' h. (ILLUS. bottom left) **900**

Ornate Oak Corner China Cupboard - *M.M.*

China corner cupboard, Victorian Golden Oak style, quarter-sawn oak, the high superstructure w/a pointed center scroll-carved crest flanked by low flat side crests over a narrow curved shelf supported by slender spindles, a central square mirror flanked by shaped beveled side mirrors & S-shaped scroll corners, the oblong top over a tall central flat door w/an upper panel enclosing an oval center surrounded by angled corners all in beveled glass above a plain tall glass panel, curved glass side panels, original finish, ca. 1900, 24 x 44", 6' h. (ILLUS.).... **3,400**

Nice Victorian Dental Cabinet - *M.M.*

Dental cabinet, Victorian Eastlake substyle, mahogany, a low slightly arched & paneled top crest board on the rectangular top w/molded edges over a stack of three drawers beside a small square beveled glass door above a pair of tall beveled glass lower doors opening to two shelves, deep scalloped apron encloses base drawer, on blocked curved legs, paneled sides, original brass hardware, refinished, 14 x 22", 40" h. (ILLUS. previous page) **1,400**

Unusual Tall Oak Dentil Cabinet - S.E.

Dentil cabinet, Victorian Golden Oak style, the top w/a narrow rectangular shelf & three-quarters arched gallery w/scroll-carved trim above a top section w/a stack of seven small drawers at the left, two small cupboard doors in the center & a rectangular beveled-mirror door on the right, all above a mid-section w/a stack of five long graduated drawers beside a tall flat cupboard door, the bottom section w/a pair of paneled cupboard doors, raised on ogee bracket feet on casters, ca. 1900 (ILLUS.) **3,600**

Display cabinet, Baroque-Style, walnut, the rectangular top w/a narrow coved cornice above a frieze band w/black & white inset marble panels flanking a long panel carved w/an eagle & swags, all above four tall reeded & carved Corinthian columns fronting the case, the upper section w/a stepped-out central square-paneled cupboard door carved w/leafy scrolls & flanked by small black & white marble inset panels, set-back raised panels at each side, the center section w/a long front drawer carved w/a reclining nude & raised on four tapering

trumpet-form supports, the deep base w/a flaring coved apron raised on four heavy bun front feet, Europe, late 19th c., 19 x 51 1/2", 5' 1 1/2" h. (ILLUS. below) ... **2,300**

Fine Baroque-Style Display Cabinet - G

Finely Carved Chinese Cabinet - N.O.

Display cabinet, Oriental-style, rosewood, the tall case w/a stepped Chinese pagoda-style top w/an ornately pierce-carved top crest above a stepped roof w/out-swept pierce-carved corners, a glazed door at the front & glass sides all trimmed along the top w/pierced fretwork, the lower front w/a single two-panel door w/bold tree carving in each panel, an ornately carved serpentine apron raised on claw feet, China, late 19th c., 33 1/2 x 46", 8' 4 1/2" h. (ILLUS.) **7,188**

English Aesthetic Display Cabinet - N.O.

Display cabinet, Victorian Aesthetic Movement style, ebonized wood, the superstructure w/a central shaped crest over a spindled gallery centered by a plaque featuring an avian scene, w/a beveled mirror below, flanked at each side by a spindled gallery & open shelf, the lower section canted & fitted w/a central drawer over a tri-paneled cupboard door featuring an avian scene, flanked at each side by open shelves, joined to a lower open shelf, raised on turned bulbous feet, incised overall w/gilt-decorated designs on the black ground, England, late 19th c., 16 x 59 1/2", 6' 6 1/2" h. (ILLUS.).................. **920**

Victorian Bamboo Display Cabinet - N.O.

Display cabinet, Victorian bamboo-style, the superstructure w/a bamboo framework w/short spindles & frames enclosing two rectangular lacquered panels above the rectangular cabinet w/a pair of tall glazed cupboard doors, bamboo front stiles continuing to outswept front legs, Anglo-Indian, late 19th c., 11 x 23 1/2", 5' h. (ILLUS. bottom left) **805**

Dyer's cabinet, painted & decorated wood, rectangular top above a case fitted w/four rows of four drawers each over a bottom row of three drawers, each drawer w/block letter stenciled dye color names, flat molded base, Pennsylvania, late 19th c., 16 1/2 x 44 1/2", 40 1/2" h. **6,463**

Very Large Oak Filing Cabinet - M.M.

File cabinet, oak, a tall case w/a rectangular top above a top section composed of 15 narrow & small drawers over a section of 24 card file drawers over two sections each w/seven vertical wide file drawers above a pair of long base drawers, original brass hardware, molded base, refinished, ca. 1900, 15 x 48", 6' h. (ILLUS.) **1,600**

Music cabinet, Louis XV-Style "Vernis Martin" type, a rectangular top w/serpentine sides above the bombé cabinet w/a single wide door w/gilt-brass border band & center reserve enclosing a colorful romantic landscape scene, gilt-brass scroll front corner mounts above slender outswept legs, dark gold painted background, open to shelves, ca. 1910, 18 x 22", 34" h. (ILLUS. top, next page) **750**

Fancy Louis XV-Style Music Cabinet - M.M.

Rococo Revival Music Cabinet - M.M.

Music cabinet, Rococo Revival style, mahogany-finished wood, a serpentine low three-quarters gallery on the rectangular top above a pair of tall flat doors decorated w/gilt-metal borders & centered by a two-part h.p. romantic courting scene, base corner brackets above the simple tapering & slightly shaped legs, original finish, ca. 1900, 14 x 22', 38" h. (ILLUS. left) **450**

Fine Eastlake Music Cabinet - M.M.

Music cabinet, Victorian Eastlake substyle, mahogany, a superstructure w/a low three-quarters gallery w/knob finials on the rectangular shelf supported by slender spiral-twist spindles & cutout sides above a rectangular beveled mirror over a rectangular top w/knob front finials over a single door w/line-incised bands & centered by a large round bronze plaque showing children playing musical instruments, ornate brass hinges, flat apron, small turned front legs, original finish, ca. 1880, 16 x 20", 4' h. (ILLUS. previous page).......... **650**

Nice Golden Oak Music Cabinet - M.M.

Music cabinet, Victorian Golden Oak style, rectangular top w/narrow carved cornice above a pair of tall paneled doors centered by wreath-and-ribbon-carved decoration, side panels w/matching carving, wide curved apron raised on simple squared cabriole legs, interior w/shelves for records & cylinders, original finish, ca. 1900, 16 x 26", 36" h. (ILLUS.) **600**

Renaissance Revival Music Cabinet - N.O.

Music cabinet, Victorian Renaissance Revival substyle, walnut & burl walnut, the rectangular top above a single door w/a

raised molding panel w/roundels & carved musical instruments on the burl ground over a narrow long drawer, ring- and rod-turned quarter-round columns at each side, raised on tapering turned & blocked legs joined by a shaped medial shelf, on pointed knob feet on casters, American, ca. 1870s, 19 3/4 x 31", 43" h. (ILLUS.) **633**

Country-style Pantry Cabinet - M.M.

Pantry cabinet, country-style, pine, a rectangular top above a square paneled door beside an arrangement of five drawers over a wide cylindrical-roll bin cover w/iron bin handle, narrow long drawer at the bottom w/small wood pulls, scalloped apron, refinished, second half 19th c., 18 x 24", 4' 6" h. (ILLUS.)........................ **1,000**

Golden Oak Sewing Cabinet - M.M.

Sewing cabinet, Victorian Golden Oak style, a low spindled three-quarters gallery w/shaped crest on the rectangular top w/molded edges above a case w/a pair of scroll-carved drawers over a pair of scroll-carved doors flanked by ropetwist side columns, refinished, ca. 1900, 16 x 30", 35" h. (ILLUS.) **550**

Louis XV-Style Inlaid Side Cabinet - M.M.

Side cabinet, Louis XV-Style, inlaid mahogany, the rectangular red marble top w/tapering serpentine sides above a bombé case w/two long drawers inlaid w/a continuous design of leafy flower-ing vines, serpentine apron w/a gilt-brass scroll mount, gilt-brass corner mounts above the simple cabriole legs w/gilt-brass foot mounts, scrolled gilt-brass pulls, probably France, ca. 1920, original finish, 18 x 30", 30" h. (ILLUS. left).. **1,600**

Side cabinet, Neoclassical, mahogany, rectangular Susini marble top w/elaborate multi-colored composition inlay, black & pale salmon rocaille border, central rectangular panel w/two classical figures, signed below "Clemente Susini F. en Firenze 1797," flanked by two side panels w/neoclassical scroll & foliate decoration w/putti; the ormolu-mounted cabinet w/ebonized surface & cast gilt bronze mounts, two doors each w/oval panel w/figures similar to those in marble top & scrolled spandrels, ormolu rocaille frieze, molded base w/bracket feet, back w/paper label reading "Preaubert...S M. Madgar Re (??)," possibly a marriage, extensive losses to veneer & molding, one spandrel missing from one door, cabinet in poor condition, Italy, 18th c., 21 x 43 1/2", 39 1/2" h. (ILLUS. below & top next page)... **8,800**

Italian Neoclassical Side Cabinet - BR

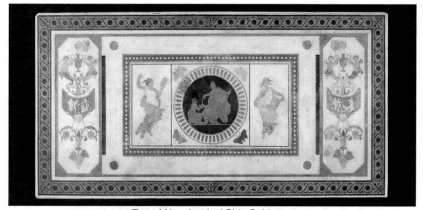

Top of Neoclassical Side Cabinet- BR

Provincial French Empire Cabinet - N.O.

Side cabinet, provincial Empire-Style, fruit-wood, the long rectangular top w/molded edges above a concealed long drawer over two paneled cupboard doors flanked by engaged columns w/ormolu mounts, on short turret feet, France, mid-19th c., 21 x 51", 35" h. (ILLUS.)............... **1,955**

Side cabinet, Victorian Renaissance Revival substyle, inlaid walnut & burl walnut, a rectangular top inset w/white marble above a raised section w/a single long drawer w/raised burl panels centered by a flower-inlaid center oval & flanked by raised corner blocks, all raised on four tapering turned & leaf-carved columns above the lower rectangular top over a long rectangular door w/a raised burl panel centered by a flower-inlaid cartouche panel & flanked by raised veneer side panels, flaring molded base on compressed ring-turned feet, original hardware, possibly by Herter, ca. 1875, 16 x 20", 30" h. (ILLUS. right) **2,000**

Fancy Marble-top Inlaid Cabinet - M.M.

Elaborate Renaissance Side Cabinet - M.M.

Side cabinet, Victorian Renaissance Revival substyle, mahogany & marquetry inlay, the top w/a raised, stepped center rectangular platform on the top w/wide incurved sides above a conforming case, the flat front section w/a leaf-inlaid frieze above a large paneled door centered by an elaborate marquetry panel centered by a bow supporting a leafy swag w/trophies all framed by a wide band w/scrolls, the door flanked by carved & gilt-trimmed blocked pilasters, the concave side panels w/similar marquetry panels, the apron band w/incised geometric gilt bands, original finish, ca. 1875, 24 x 60", 4' h. (ILLUS.) **3,500**

figural plaque among gilt incising & foliate carving, flanked by niches w/arched mirrors & supported by fluted columns, the mirror fronted by a display shelf, the base edged in Greek key marquetry, the back of the cabinet marked in heavy ink "Elbio 4565," attributed to Pottier & Stymus, New York City, ca. 1875, 20 x 61", 5' 1" h. (ILLUS. left).................................... **16,100**

Rosewood Renaissance Side Cabinet - M.M.

Side cabinet, Victorian Renaissance Revival substyle, rosewood, nearly square top inset w/marble, ovolu front corners over ring-and-rod-turned reeded corner posts flanking a single drawer w/leaf-carved cartouche & wood pulls over a single raised-panel door w/scroll-carved keyhole escutcheon, carved front apron flanked by projecting round corners, refinished, ca. 1870, 17 x 18", 28" h. (ILLUS.) **1,800**

Extraordinary Renaissance Cabinet - N.O..

Side cabinet, Victorian Renaissance Revival substyle, marquetry-inlaid & bronze-mounted rosewood, the large case w/a central shell-carved crest over a marquetry-inlaid panel, the projecting central cupboard door w/a panel framed by marquetry banding & centered by a bronze

Ornate Renaissance Side Cabinet - M.M.

Side cabinet, Victorian Renaissance Revival substyle, walnut & burl walnut, the high back crest w/a horizontal spindle between blocks w/pointed finials above carved side scrolls flanking a small rectangular veneer panel over a raised rectangular platform on the rectangular top w/rounded sides, the conforming case w/a narrow drawer slightly projecting above a single door w/an arched molding over an arched burl panel & flanked by half-round tapering columns, incurved side panels on a conforming base molding on low block feet, refinished, ca. 1875, 21 x 44", overall 5' h. (ILLUS.) **2,500**

Ornately Carved Burmese Cabinet - N.O.

Side cabinet, Victorian Rococo substyle, carved hardwood, the very high serpentine backsplash pierce-carved overall w/birds among intertwined leaves & vines, the rectangular top w/a bowed center section above a case w/a pair of tall doors centered by narrow rectangular pierce-carved panels flanking a bowed central door w/a similar panel, the doors separated by boldly fruit-carved pilasters, deep scalloped & pierce-carved aprons & carved front feet, Burma, mid- to late 19th c., 15 x 48 1/2", overall 4' 3 1/2" h. (ILLUS. below left) **1,610**

Unique Folk Art Spice Cabinet - M.M.

Spice cabinet, Victorian folk art-style, walnut & maple, the tall arched three-quarters gallery composed of ornately pierce-carved scrolls centered at the top by an oval maple plaque marked inside w/pyrography initials, the rectangular top over a case w/a central scroll-pierced band over a tall pierce-carved rectangular door centered by a round maple plaque w/a pyrography scene of a young maiden & flowers above a narrow pierce-fronted drawer, each side w/a stack of four tin-lined drawers w/scroll-pierced fronts, each inset w/a narrow maple rectangular plaque incised w/the name of a different spice, scalloped cutout bands down the front sides, all above a wide arched & ornately pierce-carved apron, original finish, ca. 1890, 5 x 21", 27" h. (ILLUS.) ... **1,200**

Spool cabinet, oak, a rectangular top above a case of six long narrow drawers each w/an inset glass panel in gold & black, blocked stiles & flat molded base, wording on panels reads "Clark's - George A. Clark - Sole Agent - O.N.T. - White. - Fast Black" (ILLUS. bottom w/Chadwick's spool cabinet top of next page) **1,100**

Chadwick's & Clark's Spool Cabinets - S.B.

Spool cabinet, oak, a rectangular top above a stack of four narrow drawers w/small black wood knobs & each w/an inset glass panel w/silver lettering, panels read "Six Cord - Spool - Chadwick's Cotton," scroll-cut corners & flat molded base, slight paint damage, late 19th c. (ILLUS. top w/Clark's spool cabinet above) **650**

Storage cabinet, inlaid & decorated lacquer, a rectangular top above a pair of tall flush doors w/ornate scroll-cut brass hardware, the stiles & door borders in black w/red & green Oriental designs & the recessed door centers w/red ground inlaid & applied w/a continuous scene of vases w/flowers & writing accessories in soapstone, a deep lower drawer w/similar decoration, the recessed side panels w/further soapstone decoration of large vases & tall flowers, scalloped aprons & short block feet, shelved interior, Oriental, probably China, ca. 1920-40, 20 x 26", 4' h. (ILLUS. right) **400**

Oriental Decorated Lacquer Cabinet - G.K.

Mission Oak Vice Cabinet - CR

Vice cabinet, Mission-style (Arts & Crafts movement), oak, a rectangular top overhanging a case w/a thin pullout bar shelf inset w/hammered glass above a long narrow drawer over a pair of flat cupboard doors, square brass pulls, cleaned finish & hardware, branded mark of the Limbert Furniture Co., early 20th c., 19 x 31", 36" h. (ILLUS.) **2,300**

Inlaid Vitrine with Lower Shelf - M.M.

Vitrine cabinet, Louis XV-Style, inlaid mahogany, the rectangular top w/serpentine edges above a conforming case w/floral-inlaid frieze bands, the wide curved glass door w/gilt-brass edging flanked by glass sides, curved apron w/floral inlay flanked by gilt-brass scroll mounts above the simple tall cabriole front legs joined by an open lower shelf to the square tapering rear legs, brass mounts on front feet, original finish, France, ca. 1900, 18 x 26", 5' 4" h. (ILLUS. below left) **1,800**

Louis XV-Style Vitrine Cabinet - M.M.

Vitrine cabinet, Louis XV-Style, mahogany, the half-round top w/a low gilt-brass gallery over a gilt-brass scroll band above a tall curved glass door w/gilt-brass edge trim, curved glass sides w/gilt-brass trim, serpentine front apron, simple cabriole legs w/gilt-brass mounts, two adjustable shelves, original shelves, France, ca. 1910, 18 x 24", 5' h. (ILLUS.)...................... **950**

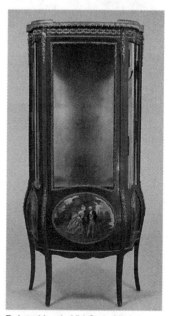

Painted Louis XV-Style Vitrine - N.O.

Vitrine cabinet, Louis XV-Style, the half-round top w/a low three-quarters pierced brass gallery above a tall door w/a long glazed panel above a bowed lower section centered by an oval reserve painted in the Vernis Martin style, matching sides w/painted panels, raised on slender square splayed legs ending in brass caps, accented overall w/ormolu mounts & millwork, France, late 19th c., 29 1/2" w., 5' 7" h. (ILLUS. previous page) **1,840**

Early American Hanging Cabinet - M.M.

Large Vernis Martin Vitrine - N.O.

Vitrine cabinet, Louis XV-Style, the high arched & molded crestrail centered by a pierced scroll crest above the swelled frieze band & conforming bombé case decorated in the Vernis Martin style, the top frieze painted w/a large floral bouquet above a pair of tall curved glass panels over serpentine lower panels painted w/figures of lovers in a landscape, glass side panels above further bowed landscape panels, on cabriole legs w/ormolu mounts, France, late 19th c., 14 1/2 x 39", 6' 2" h. (ILLUS.) **2,070**

Wall cabinet, early American country-style, walnut & tiger stripe maple, a high arched & scroll-cut crest board pierced w/a hanging hole above a rectangular top over a roll-up tambour front w/two small brass knobs opening to a shelved interior above a single cockbeaded drawer w/small ring pulls & brass keyhole escutcheon, ca. 1820, 9 x 14", 22" h. (ILLUS. above right) .. **1,200**

Unusual Golden Oak Wall Cabinet - M.M.

Wall cabinet, Victorian Golden Oak style, a rectangular top w/dentil- carved cornice & scalloped apron overhanging an open shelf w/a scroll-carved back panel above a pair of short rectangular glass doors opening to a mirror-backed compartment, a narrow recessed base shelf backed by a narrow scroll-carved panel above a serpentine, scroll-carved apron, deep shaped sides, refinished, ca. 1900, 12 x 30", 36" h. (ILLUS.) **1,000**

CHAIRS

French Art Deco Club Chairs - N.O.

Art Deco club chairs, leather & mahogany, the rectangular russet leather back above deep squared arms & a deep cushion seat, on short wooden block feet, France, ca. 1930, 30" h., pr. (ILLUS.) **$1,955**

Art Nouveau side chair, giltwood, the asymmetrical back composed of ornate scrolls enclosing a long fan-shaped caned panel above the wide caned seat, slender cabriole front legs w/scroll-carved knees & seatrail, Europe, late 19th c., 35" h. (ILLUS., next column) **575**

Baroque Revival armchairs, oak, the square upholstered back w/arched crest above open S-scroll molded arms raised on baluster-and-block-turned supports flanking the wide upholstered seat, block-and-baluster-turned front legs w/disk feet joined by a high knob-turned stretcher, turned H-stretchers joining all the legs, original finish, Europe, ca. 1900, 38" h., pr. (ILLUS. below) **2,000**

Unusual Art Nouveau Side Chair - N.O.

Fine Baroque Revival Armchairs - M.M.

Ornately Carved Baroque Rocker - CP

Baroque Revival rocking chair w/arms, oak, the tall back w/arched crest over ornately scrolling pierce-carved back flanked by square stiles w/knob finials, open arms resting on boldly carved winged sphinx arm supports on ornate scrolling legs on knob-carved rockers, Europe, late 19th c. (ILLUS.)..................... **4,500**

Italian Baroque-Style Armchair - N.O.

Baroque-Style armchair, oak, the wide arched & scroll-carved crestrail flanked by scroll-carved ears above the rectangular leather-upholstered back panel raised above the leather seat & flanked by open shaped arms, square legs w/a wide arched & ornate scroll-carved front stretcher & small carved side stretchers, Italy, possibly Tuscan, late 19th c., 47" h. (ILLUS.).. **518**

Italian Baroque Revival Side Chair - M.M.

Baroque Revival side chairs, carved fruit wood, a rectangular upholstered back below scroll-carved finials, rectangular upholstered seat above a deep front seat rail carved w/ornate scrolls around a center cartouche, plain square legs, remnants of original upholstery, Italy, late 19th c., 36" h., pr. (ILLUS. of one) **400**

Stone-inlaid Chinese Side Chair - M.M.

Chinese side chair, carved hardwood, the low rounded crestrail carved w/scrolls above a wide pierced scroll-carved lower rail centered by a round red soapstone insert above the rectangular seat inset w/soapstone, narrow pierce-carved apron between plain square legs joined by box stretchers, China, late 19th c., original finish, 36" h. (ILLUS.) **650**

*Chippendale Country-style
Side Chair - BR*

Chippendale country-style side chair,
mahogany, openwork splat, scrolled crestrail & ears, drop-in seat w/later upholstery, original glue blocks & hand-
wrought nails, America, probably Virginia, late 18th c., damage & repair to top of
crestrail, 37" h. (ILLUS.) **1,760**

Decorated Chippendale Side Chair - G

Chippendale country-style side chair,
painted mahogany, the serpentine crestrail, outswept stiles & pierced vasiform
splat all painted w/a finely alligatored design of green & yellow vining w/red flowers on a black ground, paper rush seat,
square legs w/molded edges, America,
late 18th c. w/later paint, 36" h. (ILLUS.) **518**

Chippendale Cherry Side Chair - G

Chippendale country-style side chairs,
cherry, pierced scroll, diamond & heart
back splat w/serpentine crest & shaped
ears, square legs w/beaded edges &
cross stretchers, molded seat frame
w/two-tone brown or tan upholstery,
America, attributed to Massachusetts,
one slip seat damaged, a few later pegs
& glued splits, seats 17 1/2" h., overall
38 1/2" h., set of 4 (ILLUS. of one w/two-
tone brown upholstery) **4,600**

Nicely Carved Corner Chair - M.M.

Chippendale Revival corner chair, mahogany, the low U-form crestrail continuing to flat arms over ornately pierce-
carved sea serpent supports flanking a
curved center upholstered back panel,
upholstered seat on carved seatrail
raised on three cabriole legs w/leaf-
carved knees & bold paw feet, refinished,
new upholstery, late 19th c., 34" h.
(ILLUS.).. **850**

Chippendale Revival Corner Chair - M.M.

Chippendale Revival corner chair, mahogany, the low U-form crestrail curving to rounded hand grips, three columnar spindles alternating w/loop-pierced back splats, spring-upholstered seat, cabriole front leg ending in paw foot, square back legs joined by two ring-turned & two plain stretchers, late 19th c., old needlepoint upholstery, refinished, 34" h. (ILLUS. left)........................... **850**

Chippendale Revival dining chairs, mahogany, a serpentine crestrail centered by a shell carving over a rounded hand grip over the vasiform splat centered by a large carved rayed diamond & a small pierced lower diamond, wide overupholstered spring seat on a serpentine gadroon-carved seatrail centered by a carved shell, cabriole legs w/carved knees & claw-and-ball feet, original finish, late upholstery, late 19th c., 42" h., set of 6 (ILLUS. below) **3,500**

Finely Carved Chippendale Revival Dining Chairs - M.M.

Chippendale Revival Dining Chairs with Pierced Splats - M.M.

Simple Chippendale Revival Dining Chairs - M.M.

Chippendale Revival dining chairs, mahogany, an ox-yoke crestrail w/ears above slightly canted stiles flanking a pierced scroll-carved vasiform splat, wide upholstered seat, cabriole front legs w/leaf-carved knees & ending in ball-and-claw feet, original finish, new upholstery, ca. 1900, 38" h., set of 6 (ILLUS. bottom, previous page) **15,000**

Chippendale Revival dining chairs, walnut, simple ox-yoke crest above solid vasiform splat over a woven rush seat, cabriole front legs ending in claw-and-ball feet, legs joined by turned H-stretcher, two chairs w/shaped open arms, original finish, five side chairs & two armchairs, 42" h., set of 7 (ILLUS. above) **1,750**

Chippendale Revival Side Chair - M.M.

Chippendale Revival side chair, mahogany, the ox-yoke crest centered by a carved shell above the pierced vasiform splat, wide upholstered seat over a seatrail w/a small center drop, cabriole front legs ending in claw-and-ball feet, turned H-stretcher, ca. 1900, 38" h. (ILLUS. below left) **300**

Pair of Chippendale Revival Chairs - M.M.

Chippendale Revival side chairs, walnut, an ox-yoke crestrail centered by a carved shell above a solid scroll-cut back splat, wide upholstered seat on a seatrail w/a carved shell, cabriole front legs ending in claw-and-ball feet, refinished, ca. 1900, 40" h., pr. (ILLUS.) **600**

Chippendale Revival wing-back armchair, mahogany, the high upholstered back w/a serpentine crest flanked by serpentine upholstered wings over rolled upholstered arms, cushion seat over upholstered seatrail, cabriole front legs w/leaf-carved knees & claw-and-ball feet, probably original finish & upholstery, ca. 1930s, 4' h. (ILLUS. next page) **400**

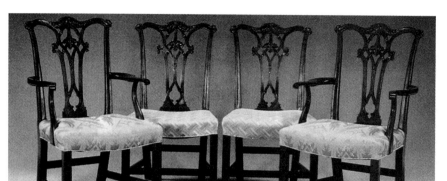

Set of Chippendale-Style Chairs - BR

Chippendale Revival Wing Chair - M.M.

Chippendale-Style Lolling Chair - G

Chippendale-Style chairs: two armchairs & two side chairs; mahogany, openwork splats & carved crestrails, square front legs w/chamfered interior corners & stretcher bases, upholstered shaped seats, late 19th or early 20th c., wear, scratches & minor chips, 40" h., set of 4 (ILLUS. top of page) .. **1,430**

Chippendale-Style "lolling" armchair, mahogany, the tall upholstered rectangular back flanked by shaped open arms w/incurved arm supports above the wide upholstered seat, square reeded legs joined by H-stretchers, early 20th c., 42" h. (ILLUS. right column) **316**

Chippendale-Style side chairs, mahogany, the back composed of four pierced ribbon rails between the canted reeded styles over the upholstered slip seat, square legs joined by an H-stretcher, old brown finish, America, late 19th - early 20th c., 39" h., set of six (ILLUS. of one bottom right) **1,208**

Chippendale-Style Ribbon-back Chair - G

Elaborate Chippendale-Style Chair - N.O.

Chippendale-Style side chairs, mahogany, the double-arch crestrail w/fancy notch carving & scroll-carved ears above an elaborate pierce-carved splat composed of ribbons & scrolls & flanked by scroll-carved S-form stiles, the wide upholstered seat on a scalloped scroll-carved seatrail & boldly carved front cabriole legs ending in scroll feet, England, late 19th c., 35" h., set of 12 (ILLUS. of one) **5,750**

One of a Pair of Classical Armchairs - M.M.

Classical armchairs, mahogany, a flat slightly curved crestrail raised on fanning leaf-carved brackets continuing to form a lower rail over long scrolled open arms, original horsehair-upholstered seat, on saber legs, old refinish, ca. 1830, 30" h., pr. (ILLUS. of one) **1,000**

Curly Maple Country Side Chair - G

Classical country style side chairs, curly maple, two arched back slats, scrolled finials, seat frames graduating into rear stiles, saber legs, one back leg w/pegged restoration, seats 17 1/2" h., overall 32 3/4" h., pr. (ILLUS. of one) **460**

Classical country-style rocking chair w/arms, painted pine & maple, the tall back w/a wide flat crestrail w/rounded corners & traces of original stenciled decoration above a thin rail & wider rail over a rail of arrow slats, S-scroll arms over two arrow slats & canted turned arm support, wide rounded plank seat, canted turned front legs joined by a simple stretcher, carpet-cutter rockers, overall traces of original painted & stenciled decoration, ca. 1840s, 46" h. (ILLUS. right with side chair, next page) **300**

Nicely Decorated Classical Chair - M.M.

Classical Country Side Chair & Rocker - M.M.

Classical country-style side chair, painted & stenciled, the long curved crestrail w/rounded ends decorated w/original stenciled fruit basket & scrolls above the wide shaped splat decorated w/gold stenciled leaf scrolls, caned seat, saber front legs joined by a flattened arrow-style front stretcher, original caned seat, ca. 1830s, 34" h. (ILLUS. previous page) **350**

Classical country-style side chair, tiger stripe maple, the wide curved & rolled crestrail above a vasiform splat over a caned seat, front sabre legs joined by a flat curved stretcher, ca. 1840, 32" h. (ILLUS. left w/rocking chair, above) **200**

Classical dining chairs, mahogany & mahogany veneer, a low rolled crest on the wide rounded crestrail continuing down to form shaped stiles flanking the vasiform splat, upholstered slip seat, sabre front legs, refinished, reupholstered, ca. 1840, 32" h., set of 8 (ILLUS. of one below left)... **1,600**

Rare Classical Highchair - M.M.

Classical highchair, mahogany & mahogany veneer, a serpentine crestrail w/rounded corners above a vasiform splat flanked by open scrolled arms joined by a protection bar, upholstered slip seat, raised on tall front sabre legs joined by a rounded footrest, refinished, new upholstery, ca. 1840, 40" h. (ILLUS.) **800**

Classical Dining Chair from a Set - M.M.

American Classical Side Chair - BR

Classical side chair, mahogany, the flat shaped acanthus-carved crestrail above a boss & leaf-carved lower rail, backswept molded stiles flanking the upholstered slip seat, front saber legs w/finely carved hairy ankle & paw feet, America, probably New York, old refinishing, repair to one rear post & one front foot, 34 1/2" h. (ILLUS.) **1,650**

Classical Mahogany Side Chair - *M.M.*

Classical side chairs, mahogany, two double-arched back rails centered by fan-carving above slip seats (not shown), front saber legs between serpentine front seatrail, original finish, ca. 1840s, 34" h., pr. (ILLUS. of one).. **500**

Classical Revival armchair, hardwood, wide squared back w/upholstered panel flanked by serpentine open arms on stylized carved dolphin arm supports, upholstered seat, square slightly curved front sabre legs, probably Europe, ca. 1910, 35" h. **259**

Classical-Victorian transitional side chairs, mahogany, an open balloon back w/triple-arch crestrail over incurved sides joined by a pierced double-scroll splat, overupholstered seat on a serpentine seatrail on simple sabre front legs w/scroll feet, refinished, ca. 1845, 37" h., pr. (ILLUS. of one, top next column) **500**

Classical-Victorian transitional side chairs, mahogany, open balloon-back w/a pierced scroll-carved crestrail & scroll-carved lower rail above the wide overupholstered seat, serpentine seatrail over baluster-and-ring-turned front legs on small paw feet, refinished, later upholstery, ca. 1840s, 32" h., pr. (ILLUS. of one right) **600**

Mahogany Transitional Side Chair - *M.M.*

One of a Pair of Transitional Chairs - *M.M.*

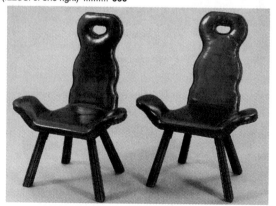

Unusual English Cock-fighting Chairs - *N.O.*

Cock-fighting chairs, mahogany, tall, narrow, oblong & serpentine leather-upholstered back w/pierced hand hole above the leather-upholstered seat w/outswept low sides, raised on canted square molded legs, England, early 20th c., 32" h., pr. (ILLUS., bottom previous page) **3,450**

Colonial Revival Chair from a Set - M.M.

Colonial Revival dining chairs, oak, a wide serpentine crestrail carved w/leafy floral scrolls centered by a cartouche & w/carved lion head corner ears, zipper-carved stiles flanking the square upholstered back panel w/a scroll-carved lower rail, the wide upholstered spring seat on heavy cabriole front legs w/leafy scroll-carved knees & returns & ending in paw feet, simple H-stretcher, labeled by the Phoenix Furniture Co., Grand Rapids, Michigan, original finish, ca. 1890s, 42" h., set of 12 (ILLUS. of one) **12,000**

Child's Country Rocking Chair - BR

Early American child's country-style rocking chair, ash & hickory, turned elements w/later hickory bark seat by Hunter Maney, North Carolina, two splats, backs w/drawknife marks, old red paint w/minor chips & losses, 21" h. (ILLUS. below left) **99**

Early American Shaker Highchair - G

Early American country-style highchair, birch, the tall turned canted back legs forming the back stiles w/small knob finials & flanking three arched slats above simple rod arms joining the canted front legs, woven splint seat, traces of red stain, from the Alfred, Maine, Shaker colony, 19th c., 37" h. (ILLUS.) **1,725**

Early American Maple Highchair - M.M.

Early American country-style highchair, maple, the back w/three graduated flat slats between square stiles, simple rod arms on baluster-turned arm supports continuing into the front legs, original woven rush seat, simple double stretchers on three sides, original finish, early 19th c., 40" h. (ILLUS.) **300**

Decorated Country-style Rocker - M.M.

Early American country-style rocking chair w/arms, painted & decorated, the wide flat crestrail w/rounded corners decorated w/fruit & floral stencil decor on black, five slender slightly curved spindles between straight tapering stiles, flattened S-scroll arms over an arrow slat & canted baluster-turned arm supports, wide plank seat on ring-turned front legs joined by a stretcher, on rockers, original dark finish & decoration, ca. 1840s, 42" h. (ILLUS.) **350**

Early Country-style Rocker - M.M.

Early American country-style rocking chair w/arms, pine & maple, a stepped oblong crestrail above four tall simple spindles flanked by twisted serpentine stiles, simple rod arms on baluster-and-ring-turned arm supports over the S-roll seat, canted baluster-turned legs joined by stretchers, carpet-cutter rockers, old refinish, ca. 1840, 44" h. (ILLUS.) **300**

American Country Side Chair - BR

Early American country-style side chair, hardwood, two splats w/canted corners between unusual shaped back stiles shaped to a point, damaged original oak split seat, ring-turned legs w/flared feet, probably black paint w/traces of gold highlights, 19th c., scuffs, paint chips, surface wear, seat in poor condition, 30" h. (ILLUS.) **99**

Walnut Ladder-back Side Chairs - BR

Early American "ladder-back" side chairs, walnut, the back w/three splats between ring- and rod-turned stiles w/pointed knob finials, woven fiber seat, ring- and rod-turned front legs w/double stretchers, old varnish surface, one leg w/wooden peg construction, replaced seats, 35" h., pr. (ILLUS.) **330**

Fine French Empire-Style Armchairs - N.O.

Mace-made Ladder-back Chair - BR

Early Ohio Decorated Side Chair - G

Early American-Style "ladder-back" chair, walnut & hickory, five arched splats, ice cream cone finials, corn-shuck seat, double stretchers, peg feet, Shadrick Mace, North Carolina, 1930s-1950s, scattered chips & flakes, 46" h. (ILLUS.) **358**

Empire-Style armchairs, mahogany, a square upholstered back w/a back-scrolled frame w/ormolu mounts above padded open arms ending in ormolu eagle head handrests above incurved arm supports, the wide overupholstered seat on a narrow seatrail, shaped tapering squared front legs ending in ormolu paws, France, mid-19th c., 40" h., pr. (ILLUS. top of page) . **4,830**

Federal country-style "fancy" side chair, painted & decorated, the wide slightly curved crestrail over a lower rail & three short arrow slats all between the back-swept tapering stiles, shaped plank seat on ring-turned tapering legs joined by slender turned stretchers, original mustard yellow paint w/black & green foliate decoration on the back rails, branded mark under seat for S. Saiter of Marion County, Ohio, ca. 1840-50, 36" h. (ILLUS.)... **863**

Federal country-style side chair, child's, painted & decorated, a flat gently curved crestrail above a flat lower rail over the woven rush seat, ring-turned & tapering front legs w/button feet joined by a flat curved front stretcher, black ground decorated w/gold banding & gold floral stenciling on the lower rail, ca. 1830, 26" h. (ILLUS.) next page...................................... **200**

Child's Decorated Federal Side Chair - M.M.

Decorated Federal Side Chair - M.M.

Federal country-style side chair, painted & decorated pine & maple, a flat gently curved crestrail tapering at each end between tapering curved stiles flanking three arrow slats, wide plank seat over canted simple ring-turned front legs joined by a shaped stretcher, original painted & stenciled decoration w/roses & leaves on the crestrail & bands of leaves down the slats & stiles, ca. 1830, 32" h. (ILLUS.).. **200**

Federal "fancy" side chairs, painted & decorated, a rectangular crestrail fitted on stiles joined by three slender lower rails above the balloon-form woven rush seat, tapering ring- and rod-turned front legs joined by simple turned stretchers, original black on red paint simulating

rosewood, the crestrail w/gold & red shell & acanthus leaf decoration, further gilt trim, probably New York state, ca. 1820, 33" h., pr. (ILLUS. of one photo below)........ **546**

One of Two Federal "Fancy" Chairs - G

Nice Federal Revival Side Chair - M.M.

Federal Revival side chair, inlaid mahogany, rounded shield-back w/fanned & pierced center slat inlaid w/light bands, wide over-upholstered seat on square tapering front legs ending in spade feet & inlaid w/long triangular panels, refinished, early 20th c., 36" h. (ILLUS.)............. **275**

George III-Style Fancy Armchairs - N.O.

Federal Revival wingchair, mahogany, the tall upholstered back w/a curved crest above flaring rounded & tapering upholstered side wings continuing to closed upholstered arms ending in scroll-carved hand holds on tapering reeded arm supports, cushion seat above a curved reeded seatrail, round tapering reeded front legs, refinished, new upholstery, ca. 1920s, 45" h. (ILLUS. right) **350**

George III-Style armchairs, mahogany, a shell-carved crestrail on the balloon back centered by a solid scroll-carved splat & flanked by serpentine open arms terminating in a carved, curled bird head above an S-scroll arm support, the wide oblong slip seat in a molded shell-carved seatrail raised on cabriole front legs w/shell-carved knees & ending in claw-and-ball feet, England, late 19th - early 20th c., 41" h., pr. (ILLUS., above)............ **1,035**

Federal Revival Wing Chair - M.M.

George III-Style Oak Dining Chairs - N.O.

George III-Style dining chairs, oak, each w/a serpentine crestrail centered by a scroll-carved crest continuing down into the ornate pierced & scroll-carved splat, two w/serpentine molded open arms on incurved arm supports, wide over-upholstered seat, cabriole front legs w/leaf-carved knees & ending in claw-and-ball feet, England, ca. 1900, 39 1/2" h., set of four (ILLUS. bottom previous page) **1,150**

Fine Karpen Jacobean Revival Chair - M.M.

Jacobean Revival armchair, carved oak, the tall ornately carved back w/a wide pierce-carved crestrail featuring a pair of putti flanking an eagle surrounded by scrolls, the barley-twist stiles topped by knob finials, long scroll-ended padded open arms raised on barley-twist arm supports over the wide upholstered seat, narrow diamond-carved seatrail on barley-twist front legs joined by a pierce-carved stretcher matching the crestrail, knob feet, barley-twist stretchers & rear legs, original label of the Karpen Furniture Co., Chicago, ca. 1890s, 4' h. (ILLUS.) **800**

Jacobean Revival armchair, carved oak, the wide arched & pierce-carved crestrail composed of a pair of mermaids flanking a center shield above turned columnar stiles flanking the arched wide center splat centered by an upholstered panel surrounded by ornate scroll carving, shaped open arms on tall S-scroll carved arm supports above the upholstered seat, heavily carved angled front legs w/carved nude figures over scrolls joined by a wide pierce-carved front stretcher w/scrolls flanking a pair of putti flanking a basket of flowers, original dark finish, old but not original upholstery, ca. 1890s, 4' 2" h. (ILLUS. next page)............................. **700**

Upholstered Georgian Side Chair - BR

Georgian side chair, the tall squared upholstered back above a wide upholstered seat, the front cabriole legs w/acanthus-carved knees, shaped hairy ankles & scroll-carved returns, deeply carved four-toe feet w/talons, rear legs w/pad feet, needlepoint upholstery probably later 19th c., England, mid-18th c., missing several returns, foot of proper right rear leg off but present, frame loose under upholstery, extensive fading to upholstery, 37" h. (ILLUS.) **2,090**

Figural-carved Jacobean-type Chair - M.M.

Fancy Carved Late Victorian Chair - M.M.

Late Victorian armchair, oak, the wide arched & rounded crestrail carved to resemble a large shell w/scroll trim above a short vasiform splat w/carved scrolls & a pierced center opening, shaped arms on three canted slender ropetwist spindles & a matching larger arm support, wide shaped seat on canted ropetwist legs on ball feet & joined by double ropetwist stretchers, ca. 1890, 34" h. (ILLUS. left) **350**

Louis XV *fauteuil* **(open-arm armchair),** fruitwood, the squared upholstered back w/molded serpentine framing raised above the wide upholstered seat & flanked by padded molded arms w/incurved arm supports, the serpentine seatrail centered by a carved blossom, cabriole front legs w/floral-carved knees & ending in scrolled toes, France, mid-18th c., 32" h. (ILLUS.) **1,610**

French Louis XV Armchair - N.O.

Louis XV Revival Giltwood Side Chairs - M.M.

Louis XV Revival side chairs, giltwood, the caned balloon back w/a pierced scroll-carved crest & a pierced scroll-carved lower rail, wide over-upholstered seat w/a serpentine scroll-carved seatrail continuing to cabriole front legs w/carved knees & scroll feet w/pegs, France, early 20th c., 36" h., pr. (ILLUS.) **450**

Carved Louis XV Revival Chair - M.M.

Louis XV Revival wingchair, mahogany, the high tufted upholstered back w/an arched crestrail w/a pierced scroll crest flanked by serpentine flaring side wings separated from the back by narrow pierce-carved wood panels, slightly rolled upholstered arms flanking the cushion seat, serpentine scroll-carved seatrail centered by a carved shell, cabriole front legs w/carved knees & ending in scroll feet on pegs, original upholstery & finish, ca. 1920s, 4' h. (ILLUS. above) **600**

Louis XV-Style *bergeres* (closed-arm armchairs), giltwood, the tall upholstered back w/a gently arched crestrail continuing around the shaped upholstered wings that taper to the padded closed arms, wide cushion seat, molded serpentine seatrail centered by carved florals & continuing into short front cabriole legs w/floral-carved knees & ending in scrolled toes, France, late 19th c., 44" h., pr. (ILLUS. of one below left) **2,990**

Louis XV-Style Bergere Armchair - N.O.

Louis XV-Style Fauteuil Armchair - N.O.

Louis XV-Style French Provincial Dining Chairs - N.O.

Louis XV-Style *fauteuil* **(open-arm arm-chair),** giltwood, the wide caned back w/an arched crestrail centered by a pierce-carved scroll crest, scroll-carved stiles above the padded, molded open arms above the wide cushion seat, molded serpentine seatrail centered by a scroll-carved reserve & continuing to cabriole legs w/shell-carved knees & ending in scrolled toes, France, late 19th c., 43" h. (ILLUS. previous page)................... **1,265**

Louis XV-Style Provincial "ladder-back" dining chairs, fruitwood, the side chairs w/tall backs w/serpentine floral-carved crestrails above two lower slats flanked by serpentine stiles above the woven rush seats, curved & scalloped seatrails centered by floral carving, cabriole front legs w/floral-carved knees & ending in raised scroll toes, baluster-, ring- and plaque-carved front stretchers, w/two matching armchairs w/lower backs, France, late 19th c., 34" h., set of 6 (ILLUS.)................. **1,725**

Louis XVI-Style *bergere avec orielles* **(wingchair),** polychromed wood, the tall upholstered back w/an arched leaf-carved crestrail centered by a floral crest & continuing around the incurved upholstered back wings down to the low padded closed arms flanking the wide cushion seat, the seatrail carved w/leaf bands flanking a floral-carved reserve above

the turned tapering fluted legs ending in peg feet, France, first half 19th c., 46 1/4" h. (ILLUS. below)......................... **4,830**

Fine Louis XVI-Style Wingchair - N.O.

English Louis XVI-Style Tub Chair - N.O.

Louis XVI-Style tub chair, mahogany, the U-form molded bellflower band-carved crestrail above the upholstered back curving down to form the shaped out-scrolled closed arms w/incurved leaf-carved arm supports, a cushion seat above the dentil-carved seatrail over baluster- and ring-turned front legs ending in peg feet, England, ca. 1900, 35" h. (ILLUS.) **1,093**

Rare Gustav Stickley "Morris" Chair - CR

Mission-style (Arts & Crafts movement) "Morris" armchair, oak, the tall adjust-able back composed of horizontal slats between wide, flat & slightly angled arms over multiple small square spindles, cushion seat w/missing back cushion, Gustav Stickley, early 20th c. (ILLUS.) ... **37,375**

Rare L. & J.G. Stickley "Morris" Chair - CR

Mission-style (Arts & Crafts movement) "Morris" armchair, oak, the tall adjust-able back composed of horizontal slats, wide gently arched flat arms above four slats on each side over a deep apron, front arms w/corbels, slightly arched front seatrail, Model No. 406, L. & J.G. Stick-ley, early 20th c. (ILLUS.) **23,000**

Mission-style (Arts & Crafts movement) rocking chair w/arms, oak, the high back composed of horizontal slats above wide flat & slightly arched arms over four wide slats on each side, corbels under the front arms, gently arched front seat rail, leather-covered back & seat pads, Model No. 427, L. & J. G. Stickley, early 20th c. (ILLUS.) **5,750**

Classic Eames-Designed Armchair - G

Modern style Eames armchair & otto-man, laminated wood & leather, the high wide back w/a padded black leather curved upper panel above a lower panel flanked by rolled upholstered arms & wide upholstered seat, all within a laminated wood framework, raised & swiveling on a metal pedestal supported on a star-shaped metal base, produced by Herman Miller & w/original paper label, mid-20th c., worn original leather, armchair 32" h., 2 pcs. (ILLUS. of chair only) **1,265**

Moravian closed-stool chair, walnut & poplar, the high rectangular back w/vertical slats above two arms w/scrolled ends & chamfered arm supports, the lift-seat above a deep apron, mortise-and-tenon construction, front, side & back w/frame-&-panel construction, sliding panel on back, Salem, North Carolina, 1810-40, old refinishing, 19 3/4 x 22 1/4", 43 3/4" h. (ILLUS. below) **1,430**

Moroccan armchairs, inlaid & marquetry fruitwood, the stepped & blocked crestrail w/ornate mother-of-pearl & marquetry inlay above the low angular inlaid arms & a paneled & inlaid central back panel flanked by turned spindles & side panels, wide tapering ornately inlaid seat raised on deep arched & ornately inlaid base panels between the square line-incised legs ending in turned disk feet, Morocco, late 19th c., 33 1/2" h., pr. (ILLUS. bottom of next page) **920**

Moravian Closed-stool Chair - BR

Elaborate Moroccan Armchairs - N.O.

Fine Baltic Neoclassical Armchair - N.O.

Nutting "Comb-back" Armchair - G

Neoclassical armchairs, birch, the long gently curved rectangular tiger-grained crestrail raised on a squared frame enclosing a pierced & ebonized scroll-carved splat, turned rounded arms above the upholstered seat, flat seatrail raised on baluster- and ring-turned front legs ending in button feet, Baltic region, mid-19th c., 36" h., pr. (ILLUS. of one) **2,070**

Nutting-signed "comb-back" Windsor armchair, mixed woods w/golden brown finish, the slender serpentine crestrail w/curled ears raised on nine slender spindles continuing through the U-form mid-rail that forms the flat arms w/scrolled hand grips on canted, baluster-turned arm supports, wide shaped saddle seat, canted bold baluster- and ring-turned legs joined by a swelled H-stretcher, branded Wallace Nutting signature beneath seat, seat 18" h., overall 44" h. (ILLUS.) **1,955**

Chinese Dragon-armed Armchair - N.O.

Chinese Dragon-Carved Armchair - G

Oriental armchair, carved rosewood, the arched back ornately pierce-carved w/entwined dragon bodies & scrolls con-

tinuing into the arms formed by the dragon body & ending in dragon heads & raised on ornately carved arm supports, the wide seat w/a serpentine molded seatrail w/a pierced scroll carving & continuing into the heavy cabriole front legs ending in scroll feet, China, ca. 1900, 36" h. (ILLUS. top left).................... **863**

Oriental armchair, carved teakwood, the high arched crestrail pierce-carved w/a pair of facing dragons among clouds above the wide solid back panel carved w/a large coiling dragon, the open arms ending in dragon heads holding pearls on reeded incurved arm supports, the wide seat w/a serpentine molded front above a pierce-carved seatrail over the cabriole front legs w/large winged bats carved at the knees & ending in scroll feet, old reddish brown finish, China, late 19th - early 20th c., 44 1/2" h. (ILLUS. bottom left)........ **575**

Ornate Inlaid Persian Side Chair - N.O.

Persian side chair, carved & inlaid hardwood, the tall rectangular back formed by a series of interlocking spindles & balls & framed by mother-of-pearl-inlaid stiles w/urn-form finials, the upholstered seat above a similarly formed apron between square inlaid legs ending in pad feet, an inscription under the seat in an archaic Persian dialect, late 19th c., 41" h. (ILLUS.)... **805**

Country Queen Anne Side Chair - G

Queen Anne country-style side chair, painted mixed wood, the back composed of simple rails above & below the vasiform splat flanked by baluster- and block-turned stiles w/button finials, seat replaced w/old floral upholstery, sausage-turned front legs joined by a baluster-turned front stretcher, plain turned side & back stretchers, old dark surface, split in one post, America, late 18th c., 42 1/2" h. (ILLUS.).. **489**

Queen Anne Revival dining chairs, quarter-sawn oak, shaped & rounded crestrail above a solid wide vasiform splat, trapezoidal slip seat above cabriole front legs ending in paw feet, square H-stretchers, refinished, ca. 1910, nine side chairs & one armchair, 40" h., set of 10 (ILLUS. below) **2,750**

Queen Anne side chair, walnut, serpentine crestrail w/flared ears above the vasiform splat, the slip seat w/faded blue & white floral upholstery, cabriole front legs w/trifid feet & scalloped returns, the molded seat frame mortised through the rear stiles, "Hannah Jarrett Spencer" painted inside seat frame in old white, attributed to Philadelphia, 18th c., overall 38" h. (ILLUS. next page) **5,175**

Queen Anne Revival Dining Chairs - M.M.

Queen Anne Walnut Side Chair - G

Queen Anne side chair, walnut, shaped crestrail over a solid vasiform splat over an upholstered balloon-shaped seat above a shaped seatrail, cabriole front legs ending in padded disk front legs, blocked-and turned stretchers, Massachusetts or Rhode Island, 1740-60, 40 1/2" h. **9,400**

Queen Anne-Style side chairs, mahogany, scrolled ox-yoke crestrails above vasiform splats, molded stiles over the upholstered slip seat, front cabriole legs w/pad feet, turned H-stretcher base, probably England, 19th c., several replaced glue blocks, old refinishing, repairs to legs, 40" h., pr. (ILLUS. top of next page) **2,200**

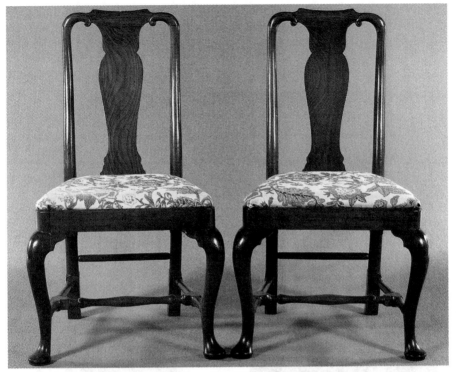

Queen Anne-Style Side Chairs - BR

Queen Anne-Style Side Chair - G

Queen Anne-Style side chairs, mahogany, the ox-yoke crestrail above a tall vasiform splat, the upholstered slip seat in a plain seatrail raised on cabriole front legs ending in pad feet, glued split at top of one leg, America, early 20th c., 41" h., pr. (ILLUS. of one).. **173**

Fancy Caned Regency Armchair - N.O.

Regency armchairs, painted & decorated, the backswept & knob-turned back stiles flanking a half-round caned panel w/a small polychrome painted tablet above two thin rails, squared open arms raised on incurved arm supports above the wide caned seat, raised on knob-turned slightly curved front legs, overall black paint w/gilt highlights, England, first quarter 19th c., 33 1/2" h., pr. (ILLUS. of one) **4,140**

Rococo-Style Side Chairs - BR

Rococo-Style side chairs, painted wood, upholstered shaped back & seat, serpentine seatrail over cabriole front legs, old grey-green paint, Italy, probably early 20th c., chips & losses to paint, several frames loose, upholstery w/stains & losses, 38" h., set of 7 (ILLUS.) **2,420**

Shaker Ladder-back Side Chair - G

Rustic Folk Art Twig Chair - BR

Rustic style folk art twig chair, rectangular back formed by crossed bent twigs, single-twig low arms slope to front legs, cross-stretcher base, chip-carved surface w/green paint, Blowing Rock, North Carolina, or East Tennessee, early 20th c., paint w/losses & chips, 47" h. (ILLUS.) **770**

Shaker "ladder-back" side chair, birch, three arched slats between turned stiles w/oval finials above the woven rush seat, slender legs & posts w/wooden tilters on back feet, double stretchers on front & sides, attributed to Enfield, New Hampshire, seat 18" h., overall 41" h. (ILLUS. top, right column) **2,070**

Fussy Aesthetic Movement Chair - N.O.

Italian Baroque Revival Side Chairs - N.O.

Victorian Aesthetic Movement side chair,
Louis XV inspiration, giltwood, the wide
ornately scroll-carved & pierced crestrail
w/a small inset marquetry panel above
an upholstered D-form back panel over
a pierced scroll-carved & spindled panel, the wide over-upholstered spring
seat above a shaped seatrail centered
by another small marquetry panel, on
scroll-carved front cabriole legs ending
in peg feet, England or America, late
19th c., 32" h. (ILLUS. bottom previous
page).. **546**

Victorian Baroque Revival side chairs,
oak, the high rectangular upholstered
back raised above the wide spring cushion upholstered seat w/a molded seatrail
centered by a scroll-carved front drop,
raised on ring- and rod-turned legs
joined by an H-stretcher w/scroll-carved

trim, Italy, mid-19th c., 38 1/2" h., set of
4 (ILLUS. top photo)............................... **1,725**

Victorian Baroque-Style side chairs, oak,
the arched crestrails carved w/designs of
fruit & flowers above upholstered back
panels above the upholstered seat,
heavily turned legs & stretchers, probably cane originally, possibly England or
Europe, ca. 1880, 34" h., set of 8 (ILLUS.
bottom photo) **800**

**Victorian Golden Oak platform rocking
chair w/arms,** oak, the wide arched crestrail carved w/leafy scrolls above a
fanned cluster of bobbin-turned spindles
above a pierced looping scroll lower rail,
ring-and-block-turned stiles w/oval finials, shaped arms on incurved arm supports over the original needlepoint seat,
platform rocker base, refinished, ca.
1895, 42" h. (ILLUS. on next page)............. **350**

Victorian Baroque-Style Side Chairs - M.M.

Pair of Gothic Revival Side Chairs - N.O.

Golden Oak Fancy Platform Rocker - M.M.

Spiral-twist Victorian Novelty Chair - M.M.

Victorian Gothic Revival side chairs, walnut, a high pierced & scroll-carved Gothic arch crestrail topped by a spire-form finial flanked by tall molded stiles w/spire finials flanking the arched upholstered back panel, short scroll-carved skirt guards on the wide rounded seat w/a line-incised seatrail raised on ring-and-rod-turned front legs, third quarter 19th c., 45" h., pr. (ILLUS. above)... **748**

Victorian novelty chairs, mahogany, two armchairs, one w/two horizontal bamboo-turned back rails forming two sections, the top section w/four spiral-twist spindles & the lower section w/six spiral-twist spindles, tall spiral-twist stiles topped w/brass ball finials, spiral twist open arms w/knob ends on spiral-twist arm supports above the wide squared seat w/a spiral-twist border, on canted spiral-twist legs joined by a spiral-twist H-stretcher; the other of similar construction but w/an angled & flat bamboo-turned rail from the top of the back stiles to shorter stiles w/brass ball finials, two small spiral-twist spindles between these rails, the front legs w/brass claw feet holding glass balls, original dark finish, ca. 1885, 38" h., pr. (ILLUS. previous page and below) **1,000**

Spiral-twist Victorian Novelty Chairs - M.M.

Hunzinger Patented Rocking Chair - M.M.

Victorian "patent" rocking chair w/arms, walnut, a tall flaring upholstered back w/top corner knob finials flanked by long angled ring-turned rails mounted w/padded ring-turned angular arms flanking the upholstered seat, ring-turned front stretcher w/two short spindles, patented by George Hunzinger Co., New York, New York, ca. 1870s, original finish, newer upholstery, 32" h. (ILLUS.) **400**

Unique Hunzinger Folding Chair - N.O.

Victorian "patent" folding armchair, walnut, the needlepoint upholstered back & seat featuring ecclesiastical designs of a communion chalice & flowers, fitted on a folding bamboo-turned frame w/large knob finials & bamboo-turned stretchers, incised stamp mark & label of George Hunzinger, New York City, ca. 1880, 37" h. (ILLUS.) **1,035**

Rosewood Renaissance Armchair - M.M.

Victorian Renaissance Revival armchair, carved rosewood, an arched crestrail carved w/a scroll-carved cartouche crest flanked by columnar stiles w/disk finials flanking the tall arched upholstered back panel, padded open arms on ring-turned arm supports over the deep spring-cushion seat, curved seatrail w/scroll-carved drop, turned inverted trumpet-form front legs on casters, old refinish, newer upholstery, ca. 1870, 44" h. (ILLUS. previous page) **1,000**

Renaissance Highchair-Stroller - M.M.

Victorian Renaissance Revival child's highchair-stroller, oak, the rounded crestrail w/applied carved scrolls above the caned back flanked by a hinged lift-up feeding tray & low shaped arms over the seat w/board replacing original caning, a curved front footrest & turned spindles above the four hinged outswept legs on metal wheels which lower to form a stroller, ca. 1880, overall 42" h., as is (ILLUS. left) **350**

Renaissance Revival Corner Chair - M.M.

Victorian Renaissance Revival corner chair, mahogany, U-form crestrail w/a raised center section carved w/scrolls, rail continues to form rounded, molded arms raised on three ring-and-knob-turned spindles alternating w/scalloped leaf-and-scroll-carved splats, rounded seat w/original leather insert, on four ring-and-knob-turned tapering legs, original finish, ca. 1880s, 32" h. (ILLUS.) **450**

Ornate European Renaissance Revival Dining Chairs - M.M.

Renaissance Revival Dining Chairs with Padded Crests - M.M.

Victorian Renaissance Revival dining chairs, fruitwood, an arched & scroll-carved crest on the crestrail molding above a large ornate scroll-cut splat centered by a carved medallion, the carved stiles decorated at the outside edge w/the head & leg of a beast, trapezoidal possibly original leather seats, seatrail w/incised carving above the turned tapering trumpet-form front legs, original finish, Europe, ca. 1875, 38" h., set of 12 (ILLUS. of part, bottom previous page) **3,600**

Victorian Renaissance Revival dining chairs, walnut, a short ring-and-block-turned crestrail above the squared back w/an upholstered crest w/a curved lower rail joined to a lower rail by a carved roundel splat, straight burl-paneled stiles w/carved detail, over-upholstered seat on a burled seatrail w/two small knob drops, block-and-ring-turned front legs on casters joined by a ring-turned front stretcher, ca. 1870s, original finish, later upholstery, 34" h., set of 4 (ILLUS. above) **1,000**

Victorian Renaissance Revival dining chairs, walnut, an arched & ornately scroll-carved crestrail centered by a shell above a pierced leaf-sprig-carved & lunette-carved splat above a lower arched rail, molded straight stiles above the over-upholstered seat, line-incised seatrail above tapering ring-turned legs w/peg feet, original finish, old vinyl upholstery, ca. 1870s, 36" h., set of 4 (ILLUS. below) **800**

Nicely Carved Renaissance Revival Dining Chairs - M.M.

Simple Renaissance Revival Dining Chairs - M.M.

Victorian Renaissance Revival dining chairs, walnut, arched & scalloped line-incised crestrail w/eared corners above a reeded splat centered by a large roundel, square stiles w/S-scroll skirt-guards flanked by upholstered seats, simple ring-turned front legs joined by double ring-and-rod-turned stretchers, probably originally had caned seats, original finish, ca. 1875, 34" h., set of 6 (ILLUS. above) **600**

form skirt guards flanking the rounded over-upholstered seat on a molded seatrail, tapering ring-and-rod-turned front legs on casters, old upholstery, refinished, ca. 1875, 36" h. (ILLUS. below left) **350**

Quality Renaissance Side Chair - M.M.

Victorian Renaissance Revival side chair, walnut, the gently arched & molded crestrail w/scroll-carved corners above a pierced back composed of large loops centered by a large palmette design, the incised stiles flanked by long S-

Child's Renaissance Revival Chair - N.O.

Victorian Renaissance Revival substyle child's armchair, gilt-incised & ebonized walnut, the arched crestrail centered by a raised platform & demi-lune crest & w/roundel-set ears above a pierced urn-form splat, the squared open arms on trumpet-turned arm supports above the wide upholstered seat, the gently curved seatrail w/a center drop & cross-incised corner blocks above the trumpet-turned front legs w/peg feet, America, ca. 1875, 26 1/2" h. (ILLUS.) **633**

Fabulous Belter "Fountain Elms" Pattern Armchair - G

Victorian Rococo armchair, carved & laminated rosewood, the high balloon back centered by an upholstered oval panel surrounded by an ornately pierce-carved frame, the arched scroll crestrail topped by a high floral-carved crest & continuing into the scroll- and leaf-carved serpentine sides above the shaped open arms w/incurved arm supports, a serpentine front seatrail centered by a carved floral cluster, demi-cabriole front legs w/floral-carved knees, "Fountain Elms" pattern by John H. Belter, New York City, ca. 1855, arm restorations & edge chips, 43" h. (ILLUS.) **10,925**

"A Rose" Pattern Rosewood Armchair - M.M.

Victorian Rococo armchair, carved & laminated rosewood, the oval upholstered back within a molded frame w/a high pierced scroll-carved crest centered by a rose blossom, open padded arms on incurved molded arm supports over the wide rounded upholstered seat w/a serpentine seatrail above demi-cabriole front legs on casters, "A Rose" patt., possibly by George Henkels, Philadelphia, refinished, ca. 1855, 44" h. (ILLUS.) **3,500**

Victorian Rococo armchair, carved & laminated rosewood, the large balloon back w/a wide arched pierce-carved frame w/an arched crest centering a carved leaf cluster flanked by ornate scrolling continuing down to frame the arched upholstered back panel, serpentine padded open arms on incurved molded arm supports above the wide upholstered seat on a scroll-and-leaf-carved serpentine seatrail continuing to demi-cabriole front legs, "Hartford" patt. by J. & J. Meeks, New York, New York, ca. 1855, original finish, new upholstery, 44" h. (ILLUS. left)........................... **4,800**

Meeks "Hartford" Pattern Armchair - M.M.

Belter "Rosalie" Pattern Armchair - M.M.

"Rosalie with Grapes" Belter Armchair - M.M.

Victorian Rococo armchair, carved & laminated rosewood, the tall balloon-form back w/a floral-carved arched crestrail continuing down to form the frame enclosing the upholstered back panel, serpentine open arms on incurved arm supports above the wide upholstered seat w/a serpentine seatrail continuing to demi-cabriole front legs on casters, "Rosalie" patt. by John H. Belter, New York, New York, ca. 1855, 40" h. (ILLUS. previous page)...... **3,000**

Victorian Rococo armchair, carved & laminated rosewood, the tall balloon-form back w/a high arched flower-carved crestrail continuing down to enclose the upholstered back panel, open serpentine arms on incurved arm supports, wide upholstered seat w/a serpentine seatrail carved w/floral scrolls flanked by demi-cabriole front legs w/flower-carved knees & raised on casters, "Rosalie with Grapes" patt., John H. Belter, New York, New York, ca. 1885, 44" h. (ILLUS. top photo) **6,000**

Rococo Armchair Attributed to Roux - M.M.

Victorian Rococo armchair, carved rosewood, the large oval back w/an ornate
pierce-carved scroll crestrail continuing
to form the oval molding enclosing the
upholstered back panel, padded serpentine open arms on incurved scroll-carved
arm supports flanking the wide upholstered seat w/a serpentine fruit-and-leaf-
carved seatrail above demi-cabriole front
legs on casters, attributed to Alexander
Roux, New York City, ca. 1860, refinished, new upholstery, 45" h. (ILLUS.
bottom of previous page) **2,500**

"Henry Ford" Pattern Meeks Chair - N.O.

Victorian Rococo armchair, pierced &
laminated rosewood, the high balloon
back w/a tufted upholstered oblong center panel enclosed by an ornately pierce-
carved frame topped by a high arched
crestrail centered by a scroll-carved crest
above a floral cluster, the serpentine
sides w/further pierced scrolls, shaped
padded open arms on incurved arm supports above the wide shaped upholstered
spring seat w/a serpentine molded seatrail centered by a carved cartouche,
demi-cabriole front legs on casters, in the
"Henry Ford" pattern by J. & J.W. Meeks,
New York City, ca. 1855, 48" h. (ILLUS.).. **6,900**

Victorian Rococo armchair, pierced & laminated rosewood, the tall corseted balloon
back w/an upholstered panel framed by
an arched crestrail w/an arched grape-
and-leaf-carved crest above pierce-
carved fruit vines continuing down the
sides & flanked by open padded arms on
incurved arm supports, wide upholstered
spring seat on a serpentine seatrail, a floral-carved reserve flanked by carved leafy
scrolls & continuing to the incurved carved
cabriole front legs ending in scroll feet on
casters, attributed to John H. Belter, New
York City, ca. 1855, 47" h. (ILLUS. top of
right column) **8,625**

Fine Carved Belter Armchair - N.O.

Victorian Rococo armchair, rosewood,
high balloon-shaped back w/leaf-and-
scroll-carved crestrail continuing down to
frame the tufted upholstered back
flanked by rolled upholstered closed
arms w/scrolled, incurved arm supports,
scroll-and-medallion-carved serpentine
seatrail on scrolled demi-cabriole front
legs on casters, ca. 1860, 45" h. **448**

One of Two Rococo Armchairs - M.M.

Nice Mahogany Rococo Armchairs - M.M.

Victorian Rococo armchairs, carved rosewood, the shaped balloon-back w/an arched crestrail carved w/fanned scrolls & continuing to form the serpentine frame around the tufted upholstered back panels, shaped padded open arms on incurved arm supports over the wide upholstered seat w/a serpentine seatrail centered by a carved cartouche, demi-cabriole front legs ending in scroll feet on casters, refinished, ca. 1860, 36" h., pr. (ILLUS. of one on previous page).......... **950**

Victorian Rococo armchairs, carved mahogany, the tall tapering balloon-form back w/a pierced scroll-carved crest on the molded back rail enclosing the tufted upholstered back panels, serpentine padded open arms on heavy scrolled arm supports above the wide upholstered seat w/a serpentine seatrail carved w/scrolls & continuing into scroll-carved demi-cabriole front legs on casters, original finish, old upholstery, ca. 1860, 46" h., pr. (ILLUS. top of page)...... **1,700**

Victorian Rococo "barrel-back" armchair, mahogany, the simple molded & scroll-carved arched crestrail above the tufted upholstered back continuing down to form the low upholstered arms flanking the upholstered spring seat, molded serpentine seatrail, molded demi-cabriole front legs, ca. 1860-70, 38" h. (ILLUS. right column).................... **2,530**

Unusual Victorian Rococo Armchair - N.O.

Victorian Rococo dining chairs, chestnut, balloon back w/molded rail enclosing a pierced splat composed of rings & scrolls above curved skirt guards flanking the seats w/original horsehair upholstery & serpentine seatrails continuing to cabriole front legs on casters, original finish, ca. 1865, one armchair & seven side chairs, 36" h., set of 8 (ILLUS. of part top of next page) **3,600**

Partial Set of Rococo Dining Chairs - M.M.

Nice Rococo Lady's Parlor Chair - M.M.

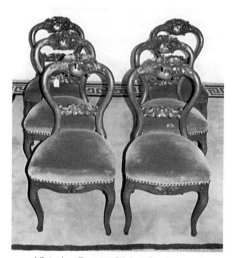

Victorian Rococo Dining Chairs - M.M.

Victorian Rococo dining chairs, walnut, the balloon back w/a pierced scroll-carved crestrail above a scroll-carved lower rail, over-upholstered seat w/serpentine leaf-carved seatrail on simple cabriole front legs, old refinish, later upholstery, ca. 1860, 32" h., set of 6 (ILLUS.) **1,500**

Victorian Rococo lady's parlor chair, walnut, tall back w/a pierced serpentine crestrail centered by carved flowers, incurved sides continuing to low arms flanking the upholstered back, wide upholstered seat w/serpentine seatrail w/carved scrolls, demi-cabriole front legs on casters, ca. 1860, refinished, new upholstery, 42" h. (ILLUS. top right column) **500**

Victorian Rococo Parlor Chairs - N.O.

Victorian Rococo parlor chairs, walnut, an armchair & side chair, each w/a wide balloon back w/an oblong tufted upholstered panel enclosed by a molded frame, the armchair w/padded open arms on incurved arm supports, both w/wide upholstered spring seats on molded serpentine seatrails continuing into demi-cabriole front legs ending in casters, ca. 1870, armchair 40" h., pr. (ILLUS.) **518**

Victorian Rococo reclining armchair, carved walnut, the tall balloon back w/a pierced scroll-carved crest w/the rail continuing to scroll-carved projections above the padded shaped arms w/eagle head-carved hand grips over incurved supports, wide seat w/serpentine seatrail w/a unique scroll-carved pullout foot rest on short turned legs, short turned front legs on main frame w/carved knees, the tall back jointed to tilt backward, original wooden casters, new leather upholstery, attributed to George Henkels of Philadelphia, ca. 1860, 46" h. (ILLUS. next page) **1,800**

Grape & Scroll-carved Side Chair - M.M.

Unique Early Rococo Recliner - M.M.

Victorian Rococo side chair, carved & laminated rosewood, the tall serpentine pierced & carved balloon back w/a floral-carved crest over bands of scrolls centered by a carved grape cluster, round needlepoint seat w/a scroll-carved apron above simple molded cabriole front legs, original finish, ca. 1855, attributed to J. & J. Meeks, New York City, 36" h (ILLUS. top rright column)............ **1,800**

Victorian Rococo side chairs, carved & laminated rosewood, a tall back w/an ornate pierced & scroll-carved framework w/a pair of cornucopia forming the crest above the tall rounded & serpentine-sided upholstered back panel, rounded upholstered seat w/an ornately carved serpentine seatrail & carved S-scroll front legs on casters, new red upholstery, attributed to John H. Belter, New York City, ca. 1855, 38" h. pr. (ILLUS. below)... **5,520**

Ornately Carved Rococo Side Chairs - N.O.

Belter "Rosalie" Pattern Side Chairs - SL

Victorian Rococo side chairs, carved rosewood, an ornate fruit-carved crest atop the tall tapering balloon back w/long carved S-scrolls at the sides above the overupholstered spring seat on a molded serpentine seat frame, demi-cabriole front legs on casters, "Rosalie" patt. by John Henry Belter, New York City, ca. 1855, pr. (ILLUS.).................................... **2,400**

Victorian Rococo side chairs, walnut, simple balloon back w/molded railing centered by a cartouche-carved crest above the original horsehair-upholstered back panel, curved skirt guards flank the rounded horsehair-upholstered seat w/a serpentine seatrail above simple cabriole front legs, refinished, ca. 1865, 34" h., set of 4 (ILLUS. below) **800**

Victorian Rococo side chairs, pierced & laminated rosewood, the tall balloon back centered by an oval upholstered panel enclosed by an ornately pierce-carved frame, the arched crestrail centered by a high arched floral-carved crest & continuing to form the pierced vine- and scroll-carved sides, the rounded upholstered spring seat on a conforming seatrail centered by a carved floral cluster, on demi-cabriole front legs on casters, the "Fountain Elms" pattern, ca. 1855, 38" h., pr. (ILLUS. of one top of next page).. **15,525**

Simple Victorian Rococo Side Chairs - M.M.

Belter "Fountain Elms" Side Chair - N.O.

turned free-standing back stiles above a scalloped lower back raise, S-scroll skirt guards flanking the wide round upholstered seat & conforming seatrail carved w/scrolls & raised on ring-turned tapering front legs on casters, ca. 1870, 40 3/4" h., pr. (ILLUS. of one below left) **920**

Fine English Papier-Maché Chair - N.O.

Victorian Rococo "tub" chair, black-lacquered papier-maché, the high arched solid back sloping down to form low rolled arms & decorated overall w/ornate gilt scrolls & inlaid mother-of-pearl accents, the upholstered seat over the serpentine matching seatrail & cabriole front legs ending in scroll feet, stamped on underside "Jennens & Bettridge," England, ca. 1850, 37" h. (ILLUS.) **2,185**

Wicker rocking chair, the wide rolled & tightly woven crestrail curving down to form a continuous band w/wide arms & seatrail, the back w/a decorative finely woven central square framed by diamond lattice weaving, tightly woven seat, scroll band under seatrail, wrapped legs on rockers, original dark green paint, ca. 1900, 36" h. (ILLUS. left with side chair on top of next page) **250**

Wicker side chair, the tall ornate back w/a long, upturned C-scroll crestrail centered by a half-round crest enclosing wicker oval loops & topped by small ball finials, the back composed of a decorative fanned woven design trimmed w/small balls & tight scrolls at the base, the caned seat over an ornate scrolled seatrail & wrapped legs w/decorative wicker trim, original varnished surface, ca. 1890, 36" h. (ILLUS. right with wicker rocker on top of next page) **300**

Victorian Rococo Slipper Chair - N.O.

Victorian Rococo slipper chairs, carved walnut, the tall back w/an oblong upholstered panel below the high arched & pierced crestrail carved w/scrolls & floral clusters & raised on baluster- and ring-

Wicker Rocker and Side Chair - G.K.

English William IV Hall Chair - N.O.

William IV hall chairs, mahogany, the tall back w/a fanned & fluted crest above large S-scrolls framing the back panel centered by a large rosette, the solid trapezoidal seat above ring-turned tapering front legs w/disk feet, England, second quarter 19th c., 35" h., pr. (ILLUS. of one) **2,990**

William & Mary Side Chairs - BR

William & Mary Side Chairs - BR

William & Mary Revival Wingchair - M.M.

William & Mary side chairs, maple, yoked & carved crestrails above vasiform splats, molded stiles over the rush seats, front skirts w/cutouts, front block & knob-turned legs, front stretcher w/bulbous turning, marked for "3" & "9" of larger set, probably America, first half 18th c., old refinishing, traces of old red paint, one leg w/repaired split, one seat w/original rail w/rose-head nails, 40 x 19 x 17", pr. (ILLUS. previous page & above) **2,530**

William & Mary Revival wingchair, mahogany & pine, the tall arched upholstered back flanked by shaped upholstered wings above the rolled upholstered arms flanking the cushion seat over a serpentine upholstered seatrail, on cabriole front legs ending in hoof feet & joined by an arched pierced scroll-carved stretcher, late 19th - early 20th c., 4' 3" h. (ILLUS. top next column).. **2,500**

Windsor "Birdcage" Side Chair - G

Windsor "birdcage" side chairs, hardwood w/old mustard paint, seven-spindle back, shield-shape seats w/incised detail around spindles & fronts, bamboo turned legs & rungs, glued split in seat of one chair, another w/wear, seats 17" h., overall 33 1/4" h., set of 4 (ILLUS. of one) **1,955**

Two early Windsor Child's Chairs - M.M.

Windsor child's "continuous-arm" rocker, painted hardwood, the slender bowed crestrail continuing down to flat arms, nine bamboo-turned back spindles & two spindles & a canted arm support under arms, wide shaped seat on heavy bamboo-turned canted legs joined by a swelled H-stretcher, inset carpet-cutter rockers, original black paint, early 19th c., 32" h. (ILLUS. above right)............................ **500**

Windsor child's "step-down" side chair, painted hardwood, the narrow stepped crestrail above six slender curved spindles flanked by curved stiles above the wide shaped seat, canted turned legs joined by box stretchers, old refinish, early 19th c., 24" h. (ILLUS. above left with rocker) **300**

Windsor "comb-back" rocker, hardwood w/old dark refinishing, curved crestrail over seven spindles continuing through the U-form mid-rail & continuing to form scrolled arms over two spindles & a canted baluster-turned arm support, "D"-shape seat w/incised edging, canted baluster- and ring-turned legs joined by a swelled H-stretcher & mortised into shaped rockers, attributed to Philadelphia, Pennsylvania, arms missing bottoms of knuckle scrolls, replaced crest, restorations, seat 14" h., overall 37" h. (ILLUS. bottom left) **863**

Windsor "Comb-back" Rocker - G

Windsor "Comb-back" Rocker - G

Windsor "comb-back" rocking chair w/arms, painted & decorated wood, the small back comb w/a rectangular crest raised on four small spindles above the flat crestrail over seven bamboo-turned spindles flanked by backswept tapering stiles, shaped arms over a turned spindle & arm supports, wide shaped plank seat raised on canted bamboo-turned legs joined by turned box stretchers & mortised into rockers, old dark green paint, restored split where comb meets crest, America, ca. 1830, 38 1/4" h. (ILLUS. previous page) **345**

George III English Windsor Chair - N.O.

Windsor "fan-back" armchair, elm & maple, the tall back w/a serpentine crestrail above an upper vasiform splat flanked by three spindles on each side over a U-form medial rail forming the flat arms & raised on another splat & spindles w/five spindles under each arm & an incurved arm support, wide shaped seat on canted rear legs & cabriole front legs ending in pad feet, joined by a turned H-stretcher, England, ca. 1800, 42" h. (ILLUS.) **1,725**

Early Windsor "Low-back" Armchair - M.M.

Windsor "low-back" armchair, painted hardwood, the U-form crestrail w/a thick center crest continuing to form flat arms w/carved hand grips above numerous simple spindles & canted baluster- and ring-turned arm supports, wide shaped saddle seat on canted baluster- and ring-

turned legs joined by a swelled H-stretcher, old repaint, early 19th c., 32" h. (ILLUS. bottom left) **500**

Windsor "Rabbit Ear" Side Chair - G

Windsor "rabbit ear" side chairs, hardwood w/reddish brown refinishing, flat slightly curved crestrail over five turned spindles between the curved & tapered styles, rounded plank seat, bamboo turned legs reinforced underneath w/shims, incised shield-shape seats, glued spindle restorations, one seat w/repaired split, seats 15 3/4" h., overall 32" h., set of 4 (ILLUS. of one).................... **518**

Nicely Decorated Windsor Rocker - G

Windsor tall-backed rocking chair w/arms, painted & decorated, the wide rectangular crestrail raised on seven slender turned spindles flanked by turned stiles, serpentine arms over two turned spindles & a canted turned arm support, wide shaped plank seat raised on bamboo-turned canted legs joined by box stretchers & mortised into rockers, original yellow paint w/gold & black line edging & fruit & scrolls in dark green & gold on the crestrail, walnut arms w/old brown finish, stamped mark under seat appears to read "E.R. Norman," New England, ca. 1830, 46 1/2" h. (ILLUS.) **1,265**

CHESTS & CHESTS OF DRAWERS

Fine Adam Revival Style Chest - N.O.

Adam Revival chest of drawers, brass-mounted & polychromed satinwood, the rectangular yellow & brown marble top w/a narrow stepped-out front section above a conforming case w/four long, graduated drawers, the front decorated overall w/continuous polychrome leafy vines & floral garlands, the third drawer centered by an oval reserve w/a black ground painted w/a shaded gold neoclassical figural scene, black banding w/further neoclassical designs framing the case, molded base raised on turned disk & peg feet, in the 18th c. style of Robert Adam, England, ca. 1900, 23 x 51", 36" h. (ILLUS.) **$4,025**

Altar chest, Oriental, pine, the long narrow plain top above a case w/a row of paneled & lotus-carved drawers above a row of four plain panels, heavy square legs w/long carved front brackets, scroll-cut long brackets down the sides of the case, China, late 19th c., 17 1/2 x 76 1/2", 33" h. (ILLUS. below) **1,035**

Chinese Pine Altar Chest - N.O.

Louis XVI-Style Bachelor's Chest - G

Bachelor's chest, Louis XVI-Style, figured veneers w/h.p. floral & gilt decoration, red, grey & white shaped marble top w/small gallery at rear holding two small drawers, body w/reeded legs & pilasters w/raised acanthus leaves & banding around door & drawer panels, holding 18 drawers including four on each side behind the doors, two in the bottom, & two at the center w/concave fronts, by "Slack Rassnick & Co, New York," 24 1/2 x 48 1/2", 4' 6" h. (ILLUS.).............. **1,150**

Spanish Baroque Vergueno - BR

Baroque vergueno, rectangular top above a dovetailed cabinet w/iron mounts, fitted w/three drawers flanking a central door opening to three drawers & above a single bottom drawer, the drawers ornately decorated w/bone-inlaid stars w/spiral columns, the door front w/architectural spiral columns w/scrolled pediment, compressed bun feet, Spain, probably 17th c., separations, repairs, inlay losses, missing one lock set, 21 x 34", 13" h. (ILLUS.) **5,720**

Blanket chest, Chippendale country-style, pine w/old blue paint & faded bittersweet trim, single-board molded top w/iron strap hinges over dovetailed case w/covered till, molded base w/shaped bracket feet, restorations, 20 1/2 x 49 1/2", 26" h. (ILLUS. below) **1,150**

Pine Blanket Chest with Old Blue Paint - G.

Chippendale Country-style Blanket Chest - BR

Blanket chest, Chippendale country-style, walnut, dovetailed construction, the rectangular molded lid w/exterior battens & original iron strap hinges opening to an interior w/lidded till, dovetailed case on a molded base w/original bracket feet w/pointed returns, interior of lid inscribed "Salem, Ohio" & interior of till lid w/"Surplus indigo, Salem (?)," w/indistinct writing on back (possibly maker's name), front & till locks missing, later brass escutcheon, stains, 18 3/4 x 50", 25" h. (ILLUS. above) **1,430**

Blanket chest, Chippendale country-style, yellow pine & poplar chest w/original painted surface decorated w/swags & tassels, on walnut, tulip poplar & yellow pine frame w/short cabriole legs w/trifid feet in front & tapered rear legs, scalloped side & front skirts, cut-nail construction, North Carolina, replaced hinges, restoration to feet, some fading & losses to paint, surface chips, scratches & scuffs, 26 1/2 x 42 x 18" (ILLUS. below) **14,300**

Country-style Chippendale Blanket Chest - BR

Early Grain-painted Blanket Chest - M.M.

Blanket chest, country-style, painted & decorated pine, rectangular hinged top w/molded edges opening to a deep well, molded base on turned double-knob bun feet, original grain-painted surface, brass keyhole escutcheon & original lock, ca. 1840, 18 x 38", 22" h. (ILLUS. above).......... **400**

Blanket chest, early American country-style, pine w/old blue paint, single board scalloped ends, the lid w/molded edge, the interior w/unusual till w/reeded lid & dovetailed drawer below, New England, end battens of lid have screws added, lock escutcheon missing, edge wear, chip, 17 x 48", 24" h. (ILLUS. below, top) **1,495**

Early American Country Blanket Chest - G

Federal Walnut Blanket Chest - BR

Fine Soap Hollow Blanket Chest - G

Blanket chest, Federal, walnut, the top w/applied molding, the interior w/lidded till & dovetailed drawer, top of front inlaid w/extensive tassel, vine, turnip & teardrop designs, sides w/shaped skirt & barberpole inlay, original French feet w/shaped skirt w/extensive fan, barberpole & tassel inlay, original glue blocks, Tennessee, first quarter 19th c., lid hinges repaired, some veneer losses, old refinishing, scattered scratches & dents, feet w/repaired tips, 17 3/4 x 38", 20 1/2" h. (ILLUS. bottom of previous page) **46,200**

Blanket chest, painted & decorated poplar, pine & chestnut, the rectangular top lifting above a well w/a lidded till, a pair of molded drawers at the bottom, molded base on simple bracket feet, original black over red painted spiral decoration, strong gold-stenciled initials "N.H." on the front w/a ghost image of the date "1904," black-painted detail on feet & moldings, floral decals on case & drawers, nailed drawers w/white porcelain pulls, Soap Hollow type, attributed to the Sala Brothers of Pennsylvania, 20 3/4 x 48", 25" h. (ILLUS. top of page) **7,475**

bly Piedmont, North Carolina, early 19th c., missing original lock, brass pulls replaced, old refinishing, some fading, 12 1/2 x 13", 16" h. (ILLUS. below) **15,400**

Federal Cherry Cellaret on Stand - BR

Early Mustard Yellow Blanket Chest - G

Blanket chest, painted poplar, the rectangular top w/a molded edge opening to a well w/a covered till, a dovetailed case w/narrow base molding & turned bun feet, old dark mustard yellow paint, mid-19th c., 18 x 38", 22" h. (ILLUS.) **460**

Cellaret (wine chest) on stand, Federal, inlaid cherry, compartmentalized dovetailed top, lid & front w/string & star or floral inlay, base w/dovetailed drawer above tapered legs w/descending bellflower inlay & extensive single & double string inlay, original brass hinges, proba-

Cherry Chippendale Chest - G

Chippendale chest of drawers, cherry, the rectangular top w/molded edges above a case of four long graduated drawers w/older replaced butterfly brasses & keyhole escutcheons, molded base on scroll-cut bracket feet, refinished, top reset & cut along back, age split in one end, restoration to drawer lips, feet & base moldings replaced, late 18th - early 19th c., 20 x 38", 36" h. (ILLUS. previous page) **1,840**

Maple & Birch Chippendale Chest - G

Chippendale chest of drawers, maple & birch, rectangular one-board top above a case of four long graduated beaded drawers w/replaced batwing brasses & escutcheons, molded base on ogee bracket feet, refinished, feet & base moldings old replacements, one baseboard missing, initialed inside "H.T.," late 18th - early 19th c., 20 1/2 x 40 3/4", 35 1/2" h. (ILLUS.) **1,093**

Fine Chippendale Chest-on-Chest - G

Chippendale chest-on-chest, curly maple, two-part dovetailed construction: the upper section w/cove molded cornice above five graduated drawers; the bottom section w/three drawers; all w/beaded trim & original brass pulls, molded waist & base, high bracket feet w/scalloped returns, a couple splits to foot facings w/section of one back facing missing, 37 1/2 x 20", 6' 5" h. (ILLUS. below left) **23,000**

Chippendale Chest-on-Chest - M.M.

Chippendale chest-on-chest, mahogany & mahogany veneer, two-part construction: the top section w/a rectangular top & flaring cornice above a border of crotch-grained mahogany veneer around a pair of drawers over three long graduated drawers; the lower section w/a mid-molding over a crotch-grain veneer band above three long graduated drawers, molded base on ogee bracket feet, old but no original brasses, refinished, ca. 1780, 20 x 38", 6' 4" h. (ILLUS.)............... **2,400**

Chippendale Walnut Chest of Drawers - BR

Chippendale Country-style Chest - M.M.

Chippendale "Chinese style" chest of drawers, walnut, four graduated dovetailed drawers w/scribed borders, original brass pulls & inlaid kite escutcheons, vertical backboards w/cut nails, bracket feet, Virginia, last quarter 18th c., old refinish-

ing, replaced feet, added drawer runners, repairs, 20 x 42", 36" h. (ILLUS. previous page) **4,400**

Chippendale country-style chest of drawers, figured maple, rectangular top w/molded edges overhanging a case w/four long graduated thumb-molded drawers w/replaced butterfly brasses & keyhole escutcheons, molded base on scroll-cut bracket feet, refinished, second half 18th c., 22 x 38", 34" h. (ILLUS. top of left column) **1,800**

Clasical butler's chest of drawers, mahogany & mahogany veneer, the rectangular top over florette-carved corner blocks flanking two long narrow round-fronted drawers projecting over a case w/a long central false drawer folding down to form a writing surface & small interior drawers above a pair of tall paneled doors, a stack of three small tall drawers down each side flanked by heavy turned side columns, flat apron on heavy acanthus leaf-carved paw feet on casters, refinished, ca. 1830s, 20 x 40", 44" h. (ILLUS. below) **1,800**

Fine Classical Butler's Chest - M.M.

Ornately Carved Classical Chest - M.M.

Classical chest of drawers, mahogany & mahogany veneer, a long narrow rectangular mirror raised & swiveling between ornately carved scrolling uprights composed of a large scrolling dolphin above a boldly scrolling cornucopia all raised on a row of three small handkerchief drawers across the rectangular top over a long round-fronted drawer projecting above three long drawers flanked by boldly carved baluster-form acanthus leaf-carved columns, flat apron raised on scroll-carved paw front feet, original finish, replaced brass hardware, ca. 1840, 22 x 44", 5' 10" h. (ILLUS.)........................ **2,400**

Dark Mahogany Classical Chest - G

Classical chest of drawers, mahogany & mahogany veneer, the rectangular top above a case w/a long top drawer w/an inset arch projecting over three long deep drawers w/original pressed glass pulls

flanked by ring-turned & leaf-carved half-columns, raised on heavy carved front paw feet, top w/old refinishing, remainder w/original dark finish, age split in top, ca. 1840, 21 1/4 x 47", 49" h. (ILLUS. below left)............ **460**

Classical Chest with Large Mirror - M.M.

Classical chest of drawers, mahogany & mahogany veneer, the superstructure w/a rectangular mirror in a wide ogee frame topped by a pointed scroll crestrail & swiveling between S-scroll uprights on short columns above a pair of handkerchief drawers on the rectangular top above double-tier apron w/a long narrow drawer in the lower tier projecting over the case w/three long graduated drawers all w/crotch-grain veneering, rounded front corners, flat base on tapering ring-turned front feet, wooden pulls, refinished, ca. 1840, 21 x 44", overall 7' 4" h. (ILLUS.) **1,000**

Classical Country-style Butler's Chest - BR

Classical country-style butler's chest of drawers, curly maple, central pull-out top drawer w/eight dovetailed graduated & cockbeaded drawers, central prospect door w/two drawers behind, six cubbyholes, three long drawers flanked by beaded pilasters, turned & reeded legs, bottom of fall-front pull-out drawer w/chalk inscription, possibly initials, faint pencil inscription on back of top graduated drawer, Tennessee, early 19th c., old refinishing, some separation to top, 46 x 43 x 23" (ILLUS. previous page) **2,310**

Grain-painted Butler's Chest - M.M.

Classical country-style butler's chest of drawers, grain-painted pine, rectangular top over a wide band divided into an arrangement of false drawers & a small door flanked by carved scrolls all folding down to expose a pullout writing surface & interior storage, the lower case w/three long drawers, scroll-carved brackets at the top corners of the front, decorated overall w/bold grain painting simulating crotch-grain rosewood, simple bracket feet, original hardware & ivory pulls on interior, ca. 1850, 16 x 38", 42" h. (ILLUS.) **1,000**

Country Classical Cherry Chest - M.M.

Classical country-style chest of drawers, cherry, a rectangular top above a long drawer slightly projecting over a case of three long graduated drawers flanked by ropetwist-turned columns, flat base on tapering knob-turned front legs, replaced glass pulls, old refinish, ca. 1840s, 20 x 42", 40" h. (ILLUS. below left) **650**

Unusual Grained Classical Chest - M.M.

Classical country-style chest of drawers, grain-painted pine, a high ornate scroll-carved crestrail centered by silhouetted lovebirds above a small chest w/a rectangular top over two long round-fronted drawers flanked by knob-turned columns & on knob feet atop the rectangular chest top over a projecting long narrow drawer above three long drawers flanked by heavy columns each w/a spiral-turned knob over a plain knob on blocks flanking the flat apron, raised on turned tapering bulbous front legs, overall original grain painting, brass bail pulls, ca. 1850, 20 x 42", 5' 4" h. (ILLUS.) **1,200**

New England Seven-drawer Chest - G

Classical country-style chest of drawers, hardwood w/old mustard paint, three set-back drawers on the rectangular top, over four dovetailed drawers w/original embossed brass pulls, turned feet, New England, evidence of later red paint, 18 x 39 1/2", 41 1/2" h. (ILLUS. previous page) **1,610**

Mahogany & Cherry Classical Chest - M.M.

Classical country-style chest of drawers, mahogany & cherry, the rectangular top over a long deep projecting drawer above three long graduated drawers flanked by ring-and-spiral-turned tapering columns, flat apron on tapering bulbous knob feet, simple wooden pulls, paneled sides, original finish, ca. 1845, 18 x 40", 4' h. (ILLUS.) **750**

Classical Country Mahogany Chest - M.M.

Classical country-style chest of drawers, mahogany & mahogany veneer, the rectangular top over an upper projecting section w/a pair of narrow drawers over a deep long drawer above a lower stack of three long graduated drawers flanked by ring-and-knob-turned columns, flat apron on ring-and-knob-turned legs, old

pressed glass pulls, original dark finish, ca. 1840s, 20 x 40", 4' h. (ILLUS. below left) **750**

Striped Maple & Mahogany Chest - M.M.

Classical country-style chest of drawers, tiger stripe maple & mahogany, a rectangular top over a deep long projecting drawer w/tiger stripe maple framed by mahogany veneer banding, the lower case w/three long graduated tiger stripe maple drawers flanked by spiraling acanthus leaf-carved columns, flat apron on leaf-carved paw front feet, replaced hardware, refinished, ca. 1840, 22 x 44", 4' h. (ILLUS.) **900**

Walnut Country Classical Chest - M.M.

Classical country-style chest of drawers, walnut, a wide peaked crestrail on the rectangular top over a projecting arrangement of two small drawers over a single long drawer all above three long graduated drawers flanked by ring-turned & leaf-carved columns, flat apron on turned tapering bulbous front feet on casters, old refinish, replaced hardware, ca. 1850, 20 x 40", 4' 4" h. (ILLUS.) **750**

Provincial Louis XIV Coffer Chest - N.O.

Coffer chest, Louis XIV Provincial, carved oak, long rectangular hinged top opening to a well, the case front heavily carved w/bands of shallow geometric designs & scrolls, heavy stile legs, back of plank construction, restorations, France, late 17th c., 22 x 67 1/2", 27 1/2" h. (ILLUS.)... **1,725**

Tall Country Pine Chest of Drawers - M.M.

Country-style chest of drawers, pine, rectangular top on a tall case w/a long deep drawer over four shorter drawers above the long bottom drawer, scalloped apron w/bracket feet, dovetailed & square nail construction, original cast-iron pulls, second half 19th c., 18 x 34", 46" h. (ILLUS.) **500**

Federal "bow-front" chest of drawers, birch, figured maple & mahogany veneer, the scroll-cut crestrail above the rectangular top w/ovolo front corners over baluster-and-ring-turned reeded columns flanking the case w/four long bow-front drawers w/crotch-grain mahogany veneer, baluster-and-ring-turned legs w/knob feet, refin-

ished, replaced hardware, ca. 1830, 22 x 42", 4' h. (ILLUS. below).................... **1,200**

Federal "Bow-front" Chest of Drawers - M.M.

Inlaid Federal Chest of Drawers - G

Inlaid Federal "Bow-front" Chest - BR

Federal "bow-front" chest of drawers, inlaid mahogany & mahogany veneer, the rectangular top w/a gently bowed front above a conforming case of four long graduated drawers each w/banded inlay panels & original oval brasses w/a running dog design, serpentine apron & tall French feet, old refinishing, early backboards possibly replacements, replaced base & feet, late 18th - early 19th c., 21 1/4 x 38 3/4", 33" h. (ILLUS. bottom right previous page) **1,380**

Federal "bow-front" chest of drawers, inlaid mahogany, the rectangular top w/a bowed front above four long graduated dovetailed & cockbeaded bow-front drawers w/string & canted corner inlay & round brass pulls, biscuit corners w/conforming reeded columns, scalloped skirt above ring-turned legs, America, late 18th - early 19th c., one leg w/repaired split, minor restorations, replaced drawer runners, top drawer bottom replacement, added support pieces on side panels, 21 1/2 x 42 1/2", 37" h. (ILLUS. top of page) **2,640**

Federal butler's chest of drawers, mahogany & cherry, the rectangular top above a row of three narrow drawers over a deep drawer w/fold-down front forming a writing surface & enclosing small compartments above three long graduated drawers, batwing brasses, molded base on incurved bracket feet, late 18th c., 20 3/4 x 48", 46" h. (ILLUS. below) **4,370**

Fine Federal Butler's Chest - N.O.

Rare Federal Chest of Drawers - BR

Federal chest of drawers, bow-front chest w/light wood corner inlay, four graduated dovetailed & cockbeaded drawers w/string & oval inlay, fancy book-matched walnut veneer drawer facings, top drawer w/compartments & ratchet for lift-up dressing mirror w/single-line inlay, inlaid pointed oval escutcheons, skirt w/light inlay & demi-lune fan apron, shaped French feet, includes box of parts, mostly interior compartment sections & supports, Tennessee, 1800-1819, repairs, veneer

chips, stains, minor separations, base missing original glue blocks, one rear glue block replaced, most of missing inlay on front present but not attached, 23 3/4 x 44", 39 1/2" h. (ILLUS. left) **33,000**

Cherry Federal Chest of Drawers - G

Federal chest of drawers, cherry, four dovetailed drawers w/beaded edges, line inlay & original oval brasses w/embossed plow designs, ring-turned legs w/raised beaded panels on ends, Kentucky, bolt missing from one brass, 21 1/2 x 42 1/2", 41 1/2" h. (ILLUS. above)......................... **3,105**

Federal Inlaid Mahogany Chest - BR

Quality Federal Mahogany Chest - M.M.

Federal chest of drawers, inlaid mahogany, rectangular top above four long graduated dovetailed & cockbeaded drawers w/original brass pulls & line inlay, drawer fronts w/book-matched figured mahogany, scalloped skirt on French feet, America, early 19th c., old refinishing, feet & skirt later replacements, 18 1/2 x 37 1/2", 36 1/2" h. (ILLUS. bottom previous page) . **1,540**

Federal chest of drawers, inlaid mahogany, the rectangular top above four long graduated drawers, the top one w/two oval inlays & leaf spring corner inlays & banding, an inlaid shield-shaped keyhole escutcheon, the three lower drawers w/leaf-sprig & banded inlay, quarter-round reeded corner columns, molded base on scroll-cut bracket feet w/some damage, original dark finish & oval brass pulls, early 19th c., 21 x 44", 36" h. (ILLUS. above) **3,500**

Federal Chest with Carved Basket - M.M.

Federal chest of drawers, mahogany & mahogany veneer, the scroll-cut crestrail decorated w/a relief-carved basket of fruit above the rectangular top w/ovolo front corners over ring-and-spiral-turned front corner columns flanking four long graduated drawers w/crotch-grain veneering, scalloped apron, baluster-and-ring-turned legs on peg feet, original brass pulls, original finish, ca. 1815-20, Boston or Salem, Massachusetts, 22 x 46", 4' h. (ILLUS. bottom, previous page) **2,500**

Mahogany Federal Chest of Drawers - M.M.

Federal chest of drawers, mahogany, rectangular top w/four ovolo corners over reeded corner columns, the case w/four long graduated drawers w/probably original oval brass pulls & keyhole escutcheons, baluster-and-ring-turned legs w/peg feet, refinished, ca. 1820s, 20 x 42", 40" h. (ILLUS.) **1,200**

Southern Federal Chest of Drawers - BR

Federal chest of drawers, walnut, rectangular top above a case w/two over three dovetailed drawers decorated w/string inlay w/canted corners & teardrop inlay at original brass pulls, triple-line inlay on edge of top & at base, base w/original skirt & French feet, vertical backboards, hand-wrought nails, American South, feet & glue blocks probable replacements, triple-line inlay possibly not original, stains, separations & scattered small repairs, 20 x 42", 37" h. (ILLUS.) **3,520**

Federal chest of drawers, walnut, rectangular top w/molded edges above a case w/four long graduated cockbeaded drawers w/simple bail pulls & brass keyhole escutcheons flanked by chamfered front corners, serpentine apron on tall French feet, Bucks County, Pennsylvania, original finish & hardware, early 19th c., 20 x 36", 40" h. (ILLUS. below) **1,800-2,000**

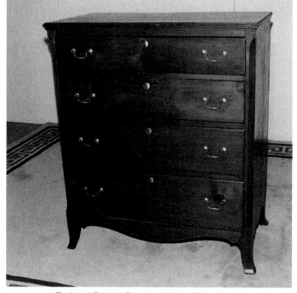

Federal Bucks County Walnut Chest - M.M.

Fine Federal Cherry Chest-on-Chest - G

Federal chest-on-chest, cherry, two-part construction: the upper section w/a rectangular top w/a coved cornice above a row of three small drawers above a stack of four long graduated drawers flanked by quarter-round reeded columns; the lower section w/a mid-molding above a case w/three long graduated drawers, original oval brasses, molded base on tall French feet, old refinish, glued splits on foot facings, late 18th - early 19th c., 22 x 40 1/2", 6' 2 1/4" h. (ILLUS.)............ **13,513**

Inlaid Cherry Chest of Drawers - BR

Federal country-style chest of drawers, cherry, double-line inlaid top over four graduated dovetailed & cockbeaded drawers w/double-string inlay, chamfered corners w/line inlay, shaped feet & skirt, chalk inscription inside at bottom of proper right side reads "Amos Downey (?)," interior bottom of top drawer w/painting of three figures including woman w/curly black hair, Kentucky, feet & skirt probably replacements, separation, splits & old paint, two backboards missing, repair to runners, replaced brass pulls, locks missing, old refinishing, 19 1/2 x 39", 39 1/2" h. (ILLUS. below left) **2,970**

Federal Country Cherry Chest - G

Federal country-style chest of drawers, cherry, rectangular top over a case w/a long deep drawer over three long graduated drawers all w/old replaced turned wood knobs, serpentine apron & simple bracket feet, old red wash, small splits in case, early 19th c., 21 1/2 x 47", 44 1/4" h. (ILLUS.) **863**

Inlaid Tennessee Cherry Chest - BR

Federal country-style chest of drawers, inlaid cherry, the top w/double-string inlay on edges w/1 1/2" overhang at back, four graduated dovetailed drawers w/string inlay, brass pulls, possibly original, & inlaid ivory kite escutcheons, French feet & shaped skirt, cherry veneers w/small band of walnut inlay, Tennessee, replaced drawer runners & support for top, backboards w/replaced nails, brass pulls lacking one post & bale, glue blocks w/added screws & reinforcement, 19 x 40", 38" h. (ILLUS.) **5,060**

Southern Federal Walnut Chest - BR

Federal "Swell-front" Chest - BR

Federal country-style chest of drawers, walnut, the rectangular top w/light-wood corner inlay, the case w/two over three dovetailed drawers w/triple dark & light string inlay, original brass pulls & inlaid kite escutcheons, shaped skirt w/French feet, yellow pine vertical backboards w/cut nails, original glue blocks for skirt & feet, American South, patches to foot, refinished, 21 1/2 x 42", 39 1/2" h. (ILLUS.) **990**

Federal "swell-front" chest of drawers, mahogany & cherry veneer, rectangular top over four graduated dovetailed & cockbeaded drawers w/brass pulls, probably original, w/inlaid diamond escutcheons, the top drawer w/compartments, original skirt w/cherry veneer, feet facings w/V joints, horizontal backboards, Kentucky, scratches, small dents, one escutcheon off but present, replaced glue blocks & rear returns, old refinishing, 22 x 39 5/8", 38 1/2" h. (ILLUS.) **15,400**

Federal Tall Chest of Drawers - BR

Federal tall chest of drawers, cherry, rectangular top above a row of three dovetailed & cockbeaded drawers, the central drawer w/interior compartments w/two interior drawers, a stack of four long graduated drawers below, oval brass pulls, frame-and-panel sides, fluted pilasters down the front sides, spiral-turned legs, horizontal backboards, America, second quarter 19th c., old refinishing, separations, traces of old white paint, drawer runners rebuilt, replaced pulls, top backboards replaced, repair & restorations, 21 x 45", 4' 6" h. (ILLUS. bottom, previous page) **2,530**

George III Mahogany Chest - N.O.

George III chest of drawers, mahogany, rectangular top above a pair of drawers over three long graduated drawers w/oval brasses, molded base on simple

bracket feet, England, ca. 1800, 21 x 40 1/2", 39 1/2" h. (ILLUS. left) **1,150**

George III Chest-on-Chest - N.O.

George III chest-on-chest, mahogany, two-part construction: the upper section w/a flaring stepped cornice above a pair of drawers over a stack of three long graduated drawers; the lower section w/a mid-molding over three long graduated drawers, molded base w/scroll-cut bracket feet, batwing brasses, England, ca. 1800, 21 x 44", 5' 8 1/2" h. (ILLUS.).......... **1,610**

Early English Jacobean Revival Chest of Drawers - N.O.

acobean **Revival chest of drawers,** black-lacquered & decorated wood, the rectangular top w/brass corner caps above a case w/a pair of drawers over two small drawers flanking a deep square drawer over a small drawer, all above a pair of bottom drawers, heavy bun feet, decorated overall w/polychrome Oriental figures & landscapes, small ring pulls, England, first quarter 19th c., 19 1/2 x 40 1/4", 33" h. (ILLUS. bottom previous page) **4,140**

French Louis Philippe Chest - N.O.

Louis Philippe chest of drawers, walnut & burl walnut, the rectangular charcoal marble top overhanging a case w/canted front corners & a paneled long frieze drawer over three long drawers, deep molded base on low block feet, wreath-form ring pulls & pierced brass keyhole

escutcheons, France, second quarter 19th c., 22 x 49 1/2", 39 1/2" h. (ILLUS. left) **3,450**

Louis XV-Style Bombé Chest - M.M.

Louis XV-Style chest of drawers, banded rosewood & oyster-shell veneer, the rectangular top w/serpentine edges above a bombé case w/three long drawers fitted w/scroll-cast ormolu mounts, the serpentine sides w/ormolu mounts, the serpentine front apron w/a long scrolling ormolu mount, flared legs w/ormolu mounts on the feet, original finish, France, second half 19th c., 16 x 28", 30" h. (ILLUS.)........ **2,500**

Louis XV-Style Console Chest - BR

Louis XV-Style chest of drawers, inlaid hardwood, rectangular serpentine-sided mottled brown & ivory marble top w/biscuit corners above a conforming case w/two hand-dovetailed drawers w/hand-planed surfaces & original locks, decorated w/elaborate floral & vine inlay, ormolu mounts w/extensive scrolled & raised openwork surfaces w/14" ormolu mounts at tops of legs, scrolled ormolu feet & apron, paper label on back of top drawer reads "Hirsch Antiquities, 32 Rue du Grinelle, Paris," France, 19th c., repairs to legs, various separations & veneer losses, missing ormolu on proper left side of top drawer, several panels loose under top, marble top broken, w/two large pieces present, repairs to marble, metal frame to reinforce marble, 25 x 63 1/2", 36" h. (ILLUS. bottom of previous page) **5,280**

Early New England Mule Chest - G

Flame-grained Country Mule Chest - G

Mule chest (box chest w/one or more drawers below a storage compartment), country-style, painted & decorated pine & poplar, the rectangular top opening to a deep well above a single long drawer w/old walnut pulls, deeply scalloped apron & short bracket feet, original reddish brown flame graining on a tan ground, top w/later sponge decoration on interior, age splits, New England, first half 19th c., 18 1/4 x 36 3/4", 31 1/2" h. (ILLUS. above).......................... **1,265**

Rare Gustav Stickley Chest - CR

Mission-style (Arts & Crafts movement) chest of drawers, oak, a low slightly peaked crestrail on the rectangular top w/through-tenon front stiles flanking a pair of small drawers over four long graduated drawers, paneled sides, original copper plate & bail pulls, signed by Gustav Stickley, early 20th c. (ILLUS.) ... **36,800**

Mule chest (box chest w/one or more drawers below a storage compartment), Chippendale country-style, painted pine, a rectangular one-board top w/molded edges & wrought-iron staple hinges opening to a deep well w/an old large brass batwing escutcheon at the top front above a long dovetailed base drawer w/replaced wood knob pulls, molded base on shaped bracket feet, rosehead nail construction, old reddish brown paint, split in one front foot, interior lid lock & drawer escutcheon missing, New England, 18th c., 19 1/2 x 42 3/4", 33 1/4" h. (ILLUS. top right column).......... **2,530**

Sponge-decorated Mule Chest - G

Mule chest (box chest w/one or more drawers below a storage compartment), country-style, painted & decorated pine, the thick rectangular top opening to a deep well fitted w/a covered till & small drawer, the lower case w/two long graduated drawers w/original turned wood knobs, decorated overall in original brown over yellow sponging on the front panels w/dark red over brown on the rest of the case, slight loss to height, pad added to one rear foot, first half 19th c., 20 x 37", 37 3/4" h. (ILLUS. bottom previous page) .. **2,415**

Tall Chinese Chest-on-Chest - N.O.

Oriental chest-on-chest, pine, three-part construction: the top section w/a rectangular top w/flaring stepped cornice above a pair of large raised-panel doors beside a small raised panel door over a small

drawer; the center & lower sections each w/two long drawers, deep molded flat base, original door brasses & simple pail drawer pulls, China, first half 20th c., 19 x 47", 5' 7" h. (ILLUS. left) **690**

Queen Anne chest-on-frame, walnut, two-part construction: the upper section w/a rectangular top w/a coved corner over a row of three small drawers above a pair of drawers & a stack of three long drawers, old replaced batwing brasses; the lower section w/a mid-molding over a deep scalloped apron on cabriole legs ending in pad feet, old refinishing, base a well done replacement, 18th c., 24 1/2 x 46 1/2", 4' 11" h. (ILLUS. below) . **2,300**

Queen Anne Chest-on-Frame - G

Inlaid Queen Anne-Style Chest - N.O.

Queen Anne-Style chest of drawers, inlaid walnut & burl walnut veneer, the rectangular top w/molded edges above a case w/a pair of drawers w/banded inlay above three long graduated drawers w/pairs of rectangular inlay bands, the bottom drawer centered by a starburst inlay, molded base on bun feet, small ring pulls, partially composed of antique elements, England, late 19th - early 20th c., 21 1/2 x 37 1/2", 34" h. (ILLUS. bottom previous page) **1,955**

Italian Rococo-Style Chest - BR

Rococo-Style chest of drawers, pine, shaped top over three dovetailed drawers w/brass pulls & mounted w/side runners, vertically bowed front, shaped skirt, curved feet, Italy, 19th or 20th c., drawers rebuilt, replaced pulls, old black paint, repairs to runners, new supports under top, 34 x 40 x 21" (ILLUS.).............................. **2,750**

Chippendale Style Spice Chest - G

Spice chest, Chippendale style, cherry & walnut, cove molded top over single raised paneled door & ten interior dovetailed drawers w/old brass pulls, molded base w/shaped bracket feet, inscription on drawer reads "Presented to Margaret

Worthington by her mother May 20th, 1836 it being the property formerly of her great grandmother Anne Strode," restorations w/replacements, wood refinished, comes w/book Thomas Worthington by Alfred Byron Sears, 11 3/4 x 19 1/4", 23 3/4" h. (ILLUS. below left) **7,475**

Cherry Sugar Chest - BR

Sugar chest, cherry, dovetailed construction, lift top w/breadboard ends, interior w/three compartments, original lock, dovetailed drawer w/original wooden pulls, turned legs, first half 19th c., top w/old separation, old refinishing, chips, light scratches, 40 x 28 x 20" (ILLUS.)...... **8,800**

American Walnut Sugar Chest - BR

Sugar chest, walnut, single-board top w/iron butt hinges above two equal interior compartments, dovetailed case & drawer, base w/finely ring-turned legs w/knob feet, America, first half 19th c., old refinishing, battens possibly later, two locks missing, chips, top slightly warped, 20 x 31", 37" h. (ILLUS) **3,520**

Short Aesthetic Movement Chest - M.M.

Victorian Aesthetic Movement chest of drawers, mahogany, the rectangular top w/flaring molded edges above two small drawers beside a large square scroll-carved door all slightly projecting over three long reverse-graduated drawers, the bottom drawer carved w/a lappet band, reeded lower side stiles, molded base, paneled sides, original dark finish, ca. 1885, 18 x 40", 44" h. (ILLUS.) **650**

Tall Aesthetic Chest with Mirror - M.M.

Victorian Aesthetic Movement chest of drawers, mahogany, the tall superstructure w/a rectangular crest panel carved w/floral vines & flanked by fan-carved & blocked corners above a narrow plain panel flanked by pierced spindled bands

above reeded stiles flanking the large beveled rectangular swiveling mirror, the rectangular white marble top above a case w/a pair of drawers over two long drawers all flanked by blocked & reeded stiles, original cast-brass pulls, refinished, ca. 1890, 20 x 40", overall 6' 8" h. (ILLUS. below left) **650**

Chest with Scandinavian Decoration - M.M.

Victorian cottage-style chest of drawers, painted & decorated oak, a large oblong beveled mirror swivels within a scroll-carved frame supported between tall S-form scroll-carved uprights on the rectangular top w/a serpentine front over a pair of serpentine drawers above two long flat drawers, gently shaped apron & bracket feet, unique folk decoration painted in the Scandinavian tradition w/a dark blue background highlighted by green, red & gold scrolls & colorful blossoms, the top w/a painted landscape w/mountains & a lake, inscribed & dated "1898" on one end, 18 x 38", overall 6' 2" h. (ILLUS.) **2,000**
Victorian cottage-style chest of drawers, painted & decorated pine, the superstructure w/a tall scroll-carved crestrail centered by a cartouche continuing to molded posts on C-scroll bases enclosing a tall arched swiveling mirror, the rectangular white marble top w/a serpentine front above a conforming case w/three long drawers flanked by ring-and-rod-turned columns on rounded base corners, painted & decorated in shades of dark brown, cream & black, each drawer front w/a grained panel decorated w/a long cluster of fruits & leaves, original finish, ca. 1875, 22 x 44", overall 7' 4" h. (ILLUS. top of next page) **800**

Unique Cottage-style Painted Chest - M.M.

Walnut Chest with Wishbone Mirror - M.M.

Victorian country-style chest of drawers, walnut, an oval mirror w/a pierced scroll-carved crest swiveling between a wishbone-form bracket on a narrow rectangular top over two narrow drawers on the rectangular top over four long drawers w/fruit-and-leaf-carved pulls, quarter-round brackets at the front corners, scalloped short apron on bracket feet, original finish, ca. 1865, 19 x 40", overall 5' 10" h. (ILLUS.) **650**

Child's Eastlake Chest of Drawers - M.M.

Victorian Eastlake substyle child's chest of drawers, birch, the tall superstructure w/a pierced serpentine crestrail above a panel w/stylized floral & roundel incised designs above a long swiveling rectangular beveled mirror all flanked by blocks & line-incised stiles above the rectangular top w/molded edges, the case w/three long graduated drawers w/line-incised leaf spring & stamped brass pulls, original wooden casters, refinished, ca. 1890, 14 x 26", 4' 8" h. (ILLUS.)............................. **600**

Tall Eastlake Cherry Chest - M.M.

Victorian Eastlake tall chest of drawers, cherry, the high crestrail w/a flat top & band of incised cross-form leaves between small roundels over line-incised bands flanked by shaped brackets on the rectangular top w/molded cornice over a tall case w/two short drawers beside a square door w/a raised panel carved w/stylized sunflowers above three long lower drawers, serpentine apron & bracket feet, paneled sides, original stamped brass pulls, paneled sides, ca. 1885, refinished, 20 x 32", 4' 10" h. (ILLUS. bottom right on previous page) **750**

Tall Eastlake Side-lock Chest - M.M.

Victorian Eastlake tall chest of drawers, walnut & burl walnut, side-lock type, the rectangular top w/molded edges & blocked corners above projecting corner blocks over tall reeded corner columns flanking the long drawers w/scroll-incised burl panels & pairs of black teardrop pulls, large corner blocks at the base flanking the flat apron, paneled sides, a single locking mechanism accessed through a side keyhole, refinished, ca. 1880, 20 x 36", 4' 10" h. (ILLUS.) **2,500**

Victorian Golden Oak style chest of drawers, quarter-sawn oak, the large serpentine-framed rectangular beveled mirror w/an arched scroll-and-bar-carved crestrail swiveling between C-scroll side brackets continuing to a serpentine scroll-carved crestrail above the rectangular top w/serpentine edges above a double-serpentine case w/a pair of drawers over two long drawers, short, slightly shaped legs on casters, original brass bail pulls, refinished, ca. 1900, 18 x 36", overall 6' 2" h. (ILLUS top of right column) **700**

Golden Oak Serpentine-front Chest - M.M.

Figured Oak Tall Chest of Drawers - M.M.

Victorian Golden Oak style tall chest of drawers, figured quarter-sawn oak, an oval horizontal beveled mirror swiveling between S-scroll uprights on the rectangular top w/a serpentine front above a pair of serpentine-front drawers over four long flat drawers, simple serpentine apron & square tapering feet, simple bail pulls, original dark finish, ca. 1895, 20 x 28", 5' 8" h. (ILLUS.)............................ **500**

Tall Flat-front Golden Oak Chest - M.M.

Victorian Golden Oak style tall chest of drawers, oak, a horizontal oblong beveled mirror in a frame w/a shell-and-scroll-carved crest swiveling between simple S-scroll uprights on the rectangular top w/molded edges, the case w/five long graduated drawers w/simple bail pulls, serpentine apron & square stile legs on casters, paneled sides, refinished, ca. 1900, 20 x 34", 5' 6" h. (ILLUS.) **550**

Tall Chest with a Serpentine Drawer - M.M.

Victorian Golden Oak style tall chest of drawers, oak, a long rectangular horizontal beveled mirror w/rounded corners in a frame w/a scroll-carved crest & swiveling between simple S-scroll uprights on the rectangular top w/a serpentine edge above one long serpentine drawer above four long flat drawers, carved keyhole escutcheons & stamped brass pulls, flat apron & square stile legs on casters, paneled sides, refinished, ca. 1900, 18 x 34", 6' h. (ILLUS. below left) **550**

Tall Bow-front Golden Oak Chest - M.M.

Victorian Golden Oak style tall chest of drawers, quarter-sawn oak, a long oval beveled mirror swiveling between simple S-scroll uprights on the rectangular bow-fronted top above a conforming case w/five long bow-fronted drawers w/simple bail pulls, serpentine apron on tapering shaped legs on casters, refinished, ca. 1900, 18 x 32", 5' 6" h. (ILLUS.) **600**

Victorian Renaissance Revival chest of drawers, rosewood, the tall superstructure w/an arched & pierced scroll-carved crest raised above an arched crestrail centered by a round medallion carved in relief w/a woman's face flanked by shaped narrow raised burl panels above carved uprights supported by carved scrolling dolphins, the tall arched mirror mounted on accordion brackets so it can be pulled forward, the rectangular white marble top w/serpentine sides & projecting front corners above a conforming case w/a single long drawer decorated w/raised oval molding flanking a carved oval medallion above a pair of large cabinet doors w/rectangular raised molding around a central oval medallion, the doors opening to reveal four long interior drawers w/figured maple fronts, the case w/chamfered front corners carved w/leafy scrolls, the wide serpentine scroll-carved apron hiding another long drawer, original dark finish, ca. 1865, 24 x 46", overall 6' 8" h. (ILLUS. next page) **4,500**

Victorian Chest with Inner Drawers - M.M.

Victorian Renaissance Revival chest of drawers base, mahogany & mahogany veneer, a rectangular white marble top w/rounded corners above a long slightly projecting top drawer w/raised oval banding & a central fruit-and-scroll-carved pull, two matching long lower drawers over a plain narrow base drawer, rounded front corners on the case, original dark finish, mirror missing from the top, ca. 1865, 20 x 44", 31" h., as is (ILLUS. below)........... **500**

Marble-top Renaissance Chest Base - M.M.

Victorian Renaissance Revival chest of drawers, walnut & burl walnut, the tall superstructure w/a tall peaked leaf-and-scroll-carved pediment over an arched crestrail w/scroll-carved rounded corners above small raised burl panels over a tall rectangular mirror flanked by burl-paneled sides w/a square candleshelf on each side above the white marble drop-well top, a small raised burl panel drawer on each side above two long drawers w/small rectangular raised burl panels, flat molded base, brass ring pulls, refinished, ca. 1870s, 20 x 40", overall 7' h. (ILLUS. below).............. **75**

Drop-well Walnut Renaissance Chest - M.M.

Tall Renaissance Revival Chest - M.M.

Victorian Renaissance Revival tall chest of drawers, walnut & burl walnut, a rectangular top w/molded edges above a case w/six long drawers w/long raised burl panels w/pointed ends, chamfered front corners, flat molded base on flat block feet, refinished, ca. 1870s, 20 x 38", 4' 6" h. (ILLUS.)............................. **900**

"Bow-front" Rococo Rosewood Chest - M.M.

Victorian Rococo "bow-front" chest of drawers, carved rosewood, a large egg-shaped mirror in a molded frame topped by an ornate pierced & scroll-carved crest & swiveling between tall slender pierced uprights carved as large serpents, the rectangular white marble top w/wide rounded front corners & a bowed front above a conforming case w/four long drawers w/leaf-carved pulls, a rounded bracket w/feet, original dark finish, ca. 1855, probably made in Philadelphia, 20 x 42", overall 7' h. (ILLUS.)..... **3,000**

Bow-fronted Rococo Mahogany Chest - M.M.

Victorian Rococo "bow-front" chest of drawers, mahogany & mahogany veneer, a tall oblong serpentine-framed mirror swiveling below a high arched & scroll-carved crestrail continuing to serpentine uprights w/scroll trim, the rectangular top w/a bowed center section above a long bowed & ogee-fronted crotch-grain veneered drawer above three long bowed drawers w/further veneering & centered by large scroll-carved pulls, bowed apron w/bracket feet, original finish, ca. 1850, 22 x 38", overall 6' 8" h. (ILLUS. below left) **1,200**

Rare Rococo Carved Rosewood Chest - N.O.

Victorian Rococo chest of drawers, carved rosewood, a tall oblong mirror within a molded serpentine frame below a tall ornately pierce-carved crest featuring allegorical figures flanked by foliage, grapes & a bird, the tall scrolled uprights continuing down to bold scrolling resting atop the rectangular white marble top w/serpentine sides above a conforming case w/three long graduated drawers centered by bold carved clusters of fruit & foliage, molded base on flattened bun feet, ca. 1855, 27 x 56 1/2", 8' 8" h. (ILLUS.) **10,350**

Fine Carved Rosewood Rococo Chest - M.M.

Victorian Rococo chest of drawers, carved rosewood, the superstructure w/a tall arched frame w/a high fruit-and-scroll-carved crest continuing to scroll-carved sides flanking large arched mirror, rectangular white marble top w/projecting front corners above a conforming case w/three long graduated drawers w/raised oval banding w/scroll-carved ends & carved keyhole escutcheons, the flat apron hiding another long drawer, the chamfered front corners carved w/scrolls above the bottom blocked corners, original dark finish, ca. 1855, 20 x 45", overall 7' 6" h. (ILLUS.)...... **2,800**

Chest with Swan-head Brackets - M.M.

Victorian Rococo chest of drawers, mahogany & mahogany veneer, a large oval beveled mirror w/a scroll-carved crest swiveling between an ornately scroll-carved wishbone bracket terminating in carved swans' heads, between two small handkerchief drawers on the rectangular top w/rounded front corners above a case w/a pair of large plain drawers w/beaded edge molding slightly projecting above three long drawers w/scroll-carved ends, beaded band above the scroll-carved apron w/bracket feet, turned wood pulls, old refinish, ca. 1860, 21 x 38", overall 6' h. (ILLUS. below left) **850**

Unique Rococo Chest with Shelves - M.M.

Victorian Rococo chest of drawers, walnut & feather-grained walnut veneer, the superstructure w/a high arched molded frame w/floral- and scroll-carved crest enclosing a large arched mirror flanked by small arched side panels below small half-round candleshelves & resting on very thin handkerchief drawers on the half-round top w/a wide flat central section, the flat center over three long paneled feather-grained drawers w/scroll-carved pulls flanked by scroll-carved pilasters, quarter-round side sections w/a curved veneer panel above two open rounded shelves w/pierced scroll-cut back brackets, deep conforming molded base, Philadelphia, ca. 1855, refinished, 18 x 44", overall 7' 2" h. (ILLUS.) **3,500**

Victorian Rococo chest of drawers, walnut & feather-grained walnut veneer, the tall oblong mirror in a molded serpentine-edged frame w/pierced shell-and-scroll-carved crest swiveling between scroll-carved uprights, the rectangular white marble top w/molded edges above a long feather-grained drawer w/central scroll-carved bands & scroll-carved corner blocks all slightly projecting above three long matching feather-grained drawers flanked by slender spiral-twist corner columns, deep flat apron w/hidden drawer, thin block front feet, made in New Orleans, ca. 1850s, old refinish, 20 x 40", overall 6' h. (ILLUS top of next page.)....... **2,800**

New Orleans-made Rococo Chest - M.M.

Rococo Serpentine-front Chest Base - M.M.

Victorian Rococo chest of drawers base, walnut, rectangular white marble top w/serpentine sides above a conforming base w/four long graduated drawers centered by shell & fan carving & flanked by angled front corners w/scroll-tipped columns, deep scroll-carved serpentine apron, possibly by Mitchell & Rammelsberg, Cincinnati, Ohio, ca. 1860, original dark finish, missing mirrored superstructure, 22 x 42", 36" h., base only (ILLUS.)..... **850**

Victorian Rococo "wig" chest of drawers, rosewood, the tall superstructure centered by a period oblong mirror in a molded frame raised between two tall narrow cupboards w/Gothic arch panels in the doors & joined at the top by a pair of scrolls w/anthemion carving, the cup-

board bases w/small drawers w/cyma-curve fronts, all resting on the rectangular top above a pair of projecting ogee-front drawers above two long drawers, serpentine scroll-carved apron & bracket feet on casters, original pulls, attributed to the New Orleans warerooms of William & James McCracken, ca. 1850, 22 x 47", overall 7' 4" h. (ILLUS. below)................... **2,070**

Unusual Victorian "Wig" Chest - N.O.

William & Mary-Style Inlaid Chest - N.O.

William & Mary-Style chest of drawers, inlaid walnut, the rectangular banded & quarter-veneered top above a case w/a pair of banded inlay drawers over three long graduated drawers w/pairs of rectangular banded inlay panels, the bottom drawer centered by a recessed sunburst inlay, molded base w/concave center raised on bun feet, partially composed of antique elements w/later veneers, England, late 19th - early 20th c., 21 x 38", 37" h. (ILLUS.) **2,185**

CRADLES

Early American Walnut Cradle - N.O.

Low cradle on rockers, walnut, dovetailed construction w/an arched & canted headboard & lower footboard flanked by scroll-carved sides w/heart-shaped rope holes, on deep arched rockers, early 19th c., 24 1/2 x 40 1/2", 22" h. (ILLUS.)............ **$460**

Victorian Eastlake Cradle - G.K.

Victorian Eastlake, walnut, the head- and footboards w/openwork panels at the top w/a flat crestrail flanked by block- and knob-turned stiles w/knob finials above a central pierce-carved wheel device & slender spokes, flat side rails above numerous simple turned spindles, on curved supports rocking on the platform base w/outswept legs on casters, original finish, ca. 1885, 20 x 38", 36" h. (ILLUS.)
.... **450-500**

Renaissance Revival Cradle - G.K.

Victorian Renaissance Revival "platform" cradle, walnut, the tall headboard w/a high scallop-cut crest over carved scrolls flanking a block-framed panel over a long rectangular panel w/a raised burl panel flanked by flat rounded finials, the low footboard w/simple arched crestrail, the sides composed of ring- and rod-turned spindles, rocking on a platform base raised on ring- and rod-turned tapering legs on casters, refinished, ca. 1875, 24 x 44", 40" h. (ILLUS.) **550-650**

CUPBOARDS

Classical Cherry Corner Cupboard - G

Corner cupboard, Classical style, cherry, two-piece construction: the upper section w/a flaring flat cornice w/blocked ends above a large 12-pane glazed cupboard door w/arched top panes opening to three shelves & flanked by half-round ring- and rod-turned colonnettes; the lower section w/a projecting mid-molding above a row of three round-fronted drawers over a pair of paneled cupboard doors flanked by half-round ring- and rod-turned colonnettes, flat base raised on knob- and ring-turned feet, old mellow refinishing, well done plugs on lower doors filling pull holes, small pieced repair on one backboard, first half 19th c., 27 x 40 3/4", 7' 1 3/4" h. (ILLUS.)............ **$4,025**

Corner cupboard, Classical style, painted poplar, two-part construction: the upper section w/a stepped molded cornice above a frieze centered by a rosette block flanked by half-round turned acorn knobs above a pair of arched eight-pane glazed cupboard doors opening to two shelves & flanked by half-round ring- and baluster-turned colonnettes w/tall acorn finials; the lower section w/a mid-molding above a row of three drawers over a pair of paneled cupboard doors, molded base on simple bracket feet, later white paint, restored splits near top, cornice partially replaced, pieced repairs to feet, possibly Ohio, ca. 1850, 25 1/2 x 55", 7' 10" h. (ILLUS. top right column) **2,300**

Painted Poplar Corner Cupboard - G

Corner cupboard, country-style 'turkey-breast' form, pine & poplar, one-piece construction, a flat top w/a pointed projecting central section above the wide stepped- and cove-molded cornice over a conforming case w/a pair of tall two-panel cupboard doors w/brass thumb latch above a double mid-molding over a pair of shorter paneled doors, flat pilasters down the front sides, molded base w/scalloped apron, old finish, original brasses, first half 19th c., 55 1/2" w. top, overall 88" h. **4,400**

Country-style Corner Cupboard - G

Corner cupboard, country-style, walnut, one-piece construction, cove molded cornice over a pair of tall paneled doors above a dovetailed drawer at the waist, two shorter paneled doors below, molded bracket base, six interior shelves, square nail construction w/flat back, old replaced brass pull & latches, cornice w/pieced restorations, part of foot facings are old replacements,   18 1/2 x 48 1/4",   6' 10 1/2" h. (ILLUS. previous page) **2,185**

Early Walnut Corner Cupboard - C.H.

Corner cupboard, country-style, walnut, two-part construction: the upper section w/a narrow flat & flaring cornice above canted corners flanking a pair of two-panel cupboard doors opening to shelves; the lower section w/a mid-molding over chamfered corners flanking a pair of paneled cupboard doors, 19th c., restoration, repairs, back replaced, 21 x 50", 7' 4" h. (ILLUS.) **1,840**

Corner cupboard, early American country-style, Southern yellow pine, one-piece construction, the top w/a stepped flaring cornice above a pair of tall 8-pane glazed cupboard doors opening to three shelves & flanked by beveled front sides, a mid-molding above a pair of paneled cupboard doors also flanked by beveled sides, flat molded base, old brown refinishing, areas of insect damage to base w/pieced repairs, top doors sized down in past, backboards renailed, first half 19th c., 23 1/4 x 45 1/2", 6' 5 1/2" h. (ILLUS. above right) **2,070**

Southern Pine Corner Cupboard - G

Federal Pine Corner Cupboard - BR

Corner cupboard, Federal country style, yellow pine, one-piece construction, the molded cornice above a pair of two-panel doors opening to shelves, a medial molding joined to vertical molding at edges, the base w/a pair of paneled doors, molded base w/original bracket feet & four interior "H" hinges, vertical backboards w/original cut nails, original iron latch, probably Georgia, early 19th c., old refinishing, losses & separations to cornice, four replaced brass butt hinges, wear to feet, 29 x 51, 7' 7" h. (ILLUS.) **6,380**

Two-piece Cherry Corner Cupboard - G

Corner cupboard, Federal country-style, cherry, two-part construction: the top section w/a deep coved cornice above a single large nine-pane glazed cupboard door w/wooden knob opening to two shelves; the lower section w/a mid-molding above a pair of drawers w/wooden knobs over a pair of paneled cupboard doors w/wooden knobs, scalloped apron & short bracket feet, old dark finish, glued split in cornice, small piece of mid-molding missing, first half 19th c., 23 1/2 x 45 3/4", 6' 6 1/2" h. (ILLUS.)........ **3,738**

Federal Country Corner Cupboard - BR

Corner cupboard, Federal country-style, hardwood, two-part construction: a cove-molded cornice above a pair of eight-pane glazed doors opening to three shelves & flanked by applied quarter-round bead molding; the base w/a pair of paneled cupboard doors flanked by half-round bobbin- and knob-turned spindles, vertical yellow pine backboards w/hand-wrought nails, original brass hinges, Buncombe County, North Carolina, 19th c., repairs to proper right bottom door, old refinishing, minor scratches, finish flaws & scattered paint drips, 24 x 52", 7' 6" h. (ILLUS. below left) **7,040**

Federal Inlaid Corner Cupboard - BR

Corner cupboard, Federal country-style, inlaid cherry, the top w/a cove-molded inlaid cornice above a pair of 6-pane glazed doors framed w/rope & tassel inlay, a medial molding above two paneled doors w/canted corner string inlay, original bracket feet, vertical backboards w/original nails, Tennessee, old refinishing, panes reglazed, hinges possibly replaced, 18 1/2 x 49", 6' 2 1/2" h. (ILLUS.) . **9,900**

Corner cupboard, Federal country-style, pine, one-piece construction, the top w/a very deep flaring & stepped cornice w/a thin dentil band above raised angled molding surrounding a large 9-pane glazed door opening to two scalloped shelves above a mid-molding above a pair of two-panel cupboard doors, molded base & shaped apron on short ogee bracket feet, old dark varnished finish, rosehead nail construction w/some re-nailing, hinges & back foot replaced, pads added to front feet, early 19th c., 27 x 50", 6' 9" h. (ILLUS top left column of next page) **4,485**

Large Early Pine Corner Cupboard - G

Virginia Pine Corner Cupboard - G

Corner cupboard, Federal country-style, yellow pine, one-piece construction, the top w/a deep stepped cornice w/dentil-carved band above a pair of tall 4-pane glazed cupboard doors opening to three shelves above a single narrow drawer over a pair of short square raised-panel doors, molded

base on scroll-cut bracket feet, rose head nails in back, old refinishing, old restorations & replacements, sized down in the past, Virginia, late 18th - early 19th c., 26 x 46", 6' 8" h. (ILLUS. below left) **1,955**

Fine Inlaid Federal Corner Cupboard - G

Corner cupboard, Federal style, inlaid cherry, two-part construction: the upper section w/a high broken-scroll pediment ending in carved rosettes & centered by a reeded platform supporting an urn-form finial, matching finials at each corner, the frieze centered by an inlaid circle above the large single arched 15-pane glazed cupboard door w/a small top reeded block, opening to three shelves; the lower section w/a mid-molding above a row of three band-inlaid drawers w/early clear pressed glass knobs over a pair of band-inlaid doors, gently curved apron above scroll-cut bracket feet, dark refinishing, restorations w/replacements to crest & top door, finials replaced, ca. 1820-30, 20 x 41 1/2", 8' 5 1/2" h. (ILLUS.) **5,175**

Corner cupboard, Georgian style, pine, two-piece construction: the top w/a deep flaring stepped cornice centered by a flaring center block above an arch-molded frieze band w/flat keystone over the arched open compartment w/three shaped shelves & barrel back flanked by molded pilasters; the lower section w/a blocked mid-molding above a pair of raised panel cupboard doors w/"H" hinges flanked by flat pilasters, blocked molded flat base, refinished, originally built-in, shelves removed from base, some molding replacements, England, late 18th c., 24 1/2 x 47 3/4", 7' 5 1/2" h. (ILLUS.top left column of next page) **1,725**

English Georgian Pine Corner Cupboard - G

Early Queen Anne Corner Cupboard - N.O.

Corner hanging cupboard, Queen Anne, lacquered & decorated, a high arched & stepped back crest w/a small quarter-

round shelf above the bowed cornice above a bow-fronted case w/a pair of tall cupboard doors, decorated w/elaborate polychrome Oriental landscapes in red & gold, molded base, England, early 18th c., 15 x 23", 43" h. (ILLUS. below left) **1,380**

Shaker-style Hanging Cupboard - G

Hanging cupboard, cherry, a flat rectangular top above the dovetailed case w/a pair of tall 4-pane glazed cupboard doors opening to three shelves, attributed to the Enfield Shaker community, 19th c., 9 x 24", 31 1/2" h. (ILLUS.) **1,380**

Painted Pine Hanging Cupboard - G

Hanging cupboard, painted pine, the rectangular top w/a deep flaring & stepped cornice above a pair of paneled cupboard doors opening to three shelves, a small brass pull, old green paint, glued split on right door, 19th c., 10 x 33 3/4", 31 1/4" h. (ILLUS.) **1,093**

Early Ohio Hanging Cupboard - G

Hanging cupboard, walnut, a narrow rectangular top fronted by a tall rectangular paneled door w/a high double-arch top flanked by arch-topped side stiles, two interior shelves, flat base, old finish, Ohio, 19th c., 9 1/2 x 14 1/2", 23" h. (ILLUS.)..... **1,265**

French Provincial Hutch Cupboard - N.O.

Hutch cupboard, Louis XV Provincial style, oak, two-part construction: the upper section w/a rectangular top w/a flaring molded cornice above a scalloped leafy scroll-carved frieze band above four open spindle-galleried shelves, the bottom shelf centered by an ecclesiastical carved door; the stepped-out lower section w/a long narrow drawer mounted w/long ornately pierced brass above a pair of paneled cupboard doors w/leafy

scroll-carved bands above the door panels, deep scalloped apron on short scrolled legs, France, first quarter 19th c., 24 x 53 1/2", 7' 6" h. (ILLUS. below left) ... **3,680**

One-piece Painted Jelly Cupboard - G

Jelly cupboard, painted pine, the rectangular top w/a molded cornice above a single tall beaded board door w/old brass ring pull opening to four shelves & flanked by wide front sides, low shaped bracket feet, old pale green paint, back half of top w/earlier grey, chips on base, rear foot replaced, 19th c., 19 1/2 x 42", 4' 5" h. (ILLUS.)............. **518**

Painted Pine Jelly Cupboard - G

Jelly cupboard, painted poplar, the rectangular top w/a narrow cornice above a single large door w/six glass panes above two lower panels, opening to four shelves, molded base on small disk feet, old red paint, interior w/later blue paint, reconstruction, 19th c., 17 x 43 1/2", 5' 5 1/4" h. (ILLUS.) **1,035**

Shaker-attributed Jelly Cupboard - G

Jelly cupboard, poplar, the rectangular top w/a low three-quarters gallery above two long narrow drawers w/small wood knobs above a pair of tall paneled cupboard doors opening to three shelves w/wooden knobs, original red wash, attributed to the Mt. Lebanon Shaker community, one back leg replaced, 20 1/4 x 49", 5' 1/4" h. (ILLUS.)... **1,953**

Tall Cherry & Walnut Cupboard - G

Jelly cupboard, walnut & cherry, the thick rectangular top above a single tall two-panel cupboard door w/wooden thumb latch & small steel lock escutcheon,

opening to four later shelves, flat apron on curved bracket feet, old finish, pegs removed from interior, one rear foot w/break, cornice replaced, 19th c., 12 1/2 x 33", 5' 7" h. (ILLUS. below left) ... **1,035**

Kitchen cupboard, Hoosier-style, oak, the central projecting cupboard section w/a rectangular top above a pair of paneled & geometrically glazed cupboard doors above a pull-down door opening to fitted kitchen accessories over a projecting white porcelain work surface above a pair of drawers over a pair of cupboard doors, flanked by tall three-panel set-back cupboard doors, original finish, ca. 1930, 28 x 84", 6' h. **1,200**

Linen press, Chippendale, walnut, two-part construction: the upper section w/a rectangular top w/a widely flaring stepped cornice above a pair of arched-panel tall cupboard doors opening to linen slides & flanked by wide reeded side panels; the lower section w/a mid-molding above a case w/three long graduated drawers w/butterfly pulls & oval keyhole escutcheons, molded base on ogee bracket feet, probably New Jersey, 1780-1800, feet replaced, 22 x 50 1/2", 6' 2" h. **3,760**

Early Southern Pine Linen Press - G

Linen press, early American country-style, painted pine, the rectangular top above a pair of tall raised-panel cupboard doors opening to three shelves above two long, deep drawers w/simple bail pulls, shaped bracket feet, cleaned down to old green paint, old replaced brasses, probably Southern, first half 19th c., 19 1/4 x 40", 5' 3/4" h. (ILLUS.)...................................... **1,438**

Fine English Georgian Linen Press - N.O.

Linen press, George III style, mahogany, two-part construction: the upper section w/a rectangular top w/a narrow molded cornice above a pair of large paneled cupboard doors opening to a shelved interior; the lower section w/a mid-molding over a pair of drawers over three long graduated drawers all w/pierced brass butterfly pulls, flat base on low shaped bracket feet, England, late 18th c., 25 x 56", 6' 8 1/2" h. (ILLUS.)................... **3,450**

Dutch Rococo Linen Press - N.O.

Linen press, Rococo style, mahogany, two-part construction: the upper section w/a deep broken-scroll dentil-carved pediment centered by a large garland-carved finial above projecting blocked front cor-

ners w/fluted Corinthian pilasters flanking a pair of tall arched & paneled cupboard doors w/carved corner rosettes opening to a shelved interior; the lower bombé-form section w/two stacks of three drawers w/pierced butterfly brasses, molded serpentine apron on squatty ball-and-claw front feet, Holland, late 18th c., 25 x 73", 8' 5 1/2" h. (ILLUS. below left) ... **6,900**

Early Eight-tin Pie Safe - BR

Pie safe, ash or chestnut, mortise-and-tenon construction, rectangular top w/a molded cornice above two frame-and-panel doors, each door w/four hand-punched tins w/circular & floral decoration, vertical tongue-and-groove backboards w/cut nails, found in Blountville, Tennessee, later red paint on front & molding, sides w/old peeling brown paint, tins w/scattered rust, 17 1/2 x 52", 73 1/2" h. (ILLUS.) **2,090**

Country Pine Punched-tin Pie Safe - M.M.

Pie safe, country-style, pine, a rectangular top w/molded edges above a pair of drawers w/fruit-and-leaf-carved pulls over a pair of tall three-panel cupboard doors fitted w/three diamond-and-circle-design punched-tin panels, three punched panels on each side, flat base raised on heavy flat stile legs, refinished, ca. 1870-80, 16 x 42", 5' h. (ILLUS. bottom right column previous page) **750**

Hardwood Country Pie Safe - S.E.

Pie safe, hardwood, rectangular top above a pair of drawers w/wooden knobs over a pair of three-panel doors fitted w/replaced punched-tin panels decorated w/circle, star & quatrefoil designs, three matching tins in each side, flat apron, square stile legs, late 19th c. (ILLUS.) **310**

Tennessee Six-tin Pie Safe - BR

Pie safe, hardwood, the rectangular top w/a shaped back panel above two tall paneled doors, each w/three punched tins w/heart & circle decoration, doors w/pegged construction, square tapering stile legs, horizontal backboards w/original cut nails, Carter County, Tennessee, old brown paint w/losses, tins w/scattered rust, 16 x 40", 59" h. (ILLUS. below left) **1,320**

Painted Double-door Pie Safe - BR

Pie safe, hardwood w/old brown paint, the rectangular top above two dovetailed drawers above two doors each w/a large four-section tin, each tin section w/diamond-shaped central medallion w/stars, punched-tin side panels, turned feet, horizontal backboards w/cut nails, Cocke County, Tennessee, scrapes, scuffs & losses to painted surface, 18 1/2 x 54 1/4", 42" h. (ILLUS.) **2,750**

Old Painted Pine Pie Safe - G

Pie safe, painted pine, single-board rectangular top w/old breadboard ends added above a pair of tall two-panel doors inset w/two pierced-tin panels decorated w/flower designs, two matching tins in each side, flat apron on angled bracket feet, old brown paint, backboards replaced, 19th c., 16 1/2 x 42", 4' 1 5/8" h. (ILLUS.) **748**

Walnut & Cherry Pie Safe - BR

Pie safe, walnut & cherry, mortise-&-tenon construction, the rectangular top above two dovetailed drawers w/cut-nail construction above two doors each fitted w/four punched-tin panels, each panel w/designs of urns & grapes & star corners, punched-tin panels in sides, turned legs, original brass hinges, vertical backboards w/cut nails, attributed to Rich fam-

ily shop, Wythe County, Virginia, 1830-80, old refinishing, drawer bottoms w/chips, traces of old blue paint, top w/stains & small separations, 17 x 50", 4' 3" h. (ILLUS. left)...................................... **6,600**

Pie Safe from Tennessee - BR

Pie safe, walnut & poplar, rectangular top above a row of three dovetailed drawers above two doors each w/two large punched-tin panels w/circular centers flanked by two candlesticks w/tulips in upper corners, chamfered horizontal backboards, turned feet, Sullivan County, Tennessee, refinished, several patches, minor surface flaws & scratches, 18 1/2 x 55 1/4", 47" h. (ILLUS. above) **9,350**

Baroque Style Side Cupboard - BR

Side cupboard, Baroque style, rectangular molded top w/dentil-carved molding above a row of three paneled drawers w/wooden knobs, a central door below w/inlaid star design flanked by two panels w/geometric light & dark wood inlay, the base w/multiple cove bed moldings & bracket feet, original rosehead nails throughout, probably Italy, 18th c., repairs to drawer bottoms, separations & losses throughout, 13 x 30", 33" h. (ILLUS. bottom, previous page) **4,620**

Child's Step-back Wall Cupboard - BR

"Jackson Press" Wall Cupboard - BR

Step-back wall cupboard, country "Jackson press" style, cherry, two-part construction: the upper section w/a cove-molded cornice above two 8-pane glazed doors opening to three shelves above two dovetailed drawers; the lower section w/a pair of dovetailed drawers above two double-panel doors, baluster-turned legs, original wooden pulls, horizontal frame-&-panel backboards, old refinishing, minor surface scratches & flaws, 21 x 43", 7' 11" h. (ILLUS.) **3,520**

Step-back wall cupboard, country-style, child's, walnut, the top w/two glass doors above four dovetailed drawers w/wooden pulls in bottom section, molded front edge, four applied turned feet, cut nails, found in Kentucky, late 19th or early 20th c., minor surface flaws, missing one glass pane, 11 x 26", 44" h. (ILLUS. top right) **1,100**

Grain-painted Wall Cupboard - BR

Step-back wall cupboard, country-style, hardwood, two-part construction: the top section w/a molded cornice above a pair of paneled cupboard doors over a row of three narrow drawers above a high open pie shelf w/a narrow open shelf at the back; the base w/a row of three dovetailed drawers over two paneled doors beside a stack of three small drawers on the left, porcelain drawer pulls & iron latches probably original, original grain-painted surface w/yellow graining, faux burlwood panels on doors & drawer fronts, probably Pennsylvania, 19th c., chips, stains & losses to painted surface, 21 3/4 x 52", 73" h. (ILLUS.) **1,210**

Tennessee Wall Cupboard - BR

Step-back wall cupboard, country-style, maple, two-part construction: a rectangular top w/a molded cornice above a pair of six-pane glazed cupboard doors open-ing to two shelves; the stepped-out lower section w/a long drawer w/carved wood pulls above two astragal-molded doors flanked by split columns, horizontal backboards w/cut nails, made by Reverend Robert Hicks, Jonesboro, Tennessee, 1880-90, old refinishing, top w/old red stain, glass panes & interior molding possibly replaced, missing lock, 19 3/4 x 48 1/2", 7' 1" h. (ILLUS. left)........ **1,320**

Step-back wall cupboard, country-style, painted wood, two-part construction: the upper section w/a long rectangular top w/a flaring cornice over a row of five tall paneled cupboard doors; the stepped-out lower section w/a pull-out cutting board above a row of three paneled cupboard doors flanked at one end by a stack of four small drawers & at the other end by a pull-out potato bin, original creamy white paint, early 20th c., 20 x 110", 7' h. (ILLUS. bottom photo)........ **800**

Step-back wall cupboard, country-style, walnut, one-piece construction, the rectangular top over a pair of two-panel doors, sides w/reverse-chamfered panels, the stepped-out lower section w/single nailed long drawer above a pair of two-panel doors, slightly tapered bracket feet, vertical backboards w/original cut nails, probably Georgia, mid-19th c., old refinishing, some rodent chew, separations, scratched, 20 x 21", 6' 1/2" h. (ILLUS. top left column next page) **1,540**

Large Step-back Wall Cupboard - M.M.

Walnut Step-back Wall Cupboard - BR

Rare Ohio Step-back Wall Cupboard - G

Step-back wall cupboard, painted poplar, two-piece construction: the upper section w/a rectangular top w/a deep flaring molded cornice above a pair of raised panel doors w/wooden knobs opening to three shelves over a high open pie shelf; the stepped-out lower section w/a pair of dovetailed drawers w/wooden knobs over a pair of raised panel cupboard doors opening to two shelves, flat apron & curved bracket feet, old red paint, painted interiors, Ohio, mid-19th c., 20 1/2 x 49", 7' 1" h. (ILLUS.).................. **10,063**

Step-back Wall Cupboard - BR

Step-back wall cupboard, country-style, yellow pine, two-part construction: the upper section w/a pitched pediment w/open front above two six-pane glazed doors opening to two shelves; the broad stepped platform base w/a long double-panel door decorated w/chip-carved flowers & vines, scalloped skirt & bracket feet, vertical backboards w/cut nails & circular saw marks, probably Piedmont, North Carolina, mid-19th c., refinished, stains, scratches, chip missing from proper left skirt, 31 x 39 1/2", 7' 1 1/2" h. (ILLUS.)....... **3,520**

French Provincial Hutch Cupboard - N.O.

Step-back wall hutch cupboard, French Provincial style, fruitwood, two-part construction: the upper section w/a rectangular top w/coved cornice above an open compartment w/a row of turned drop balls above a shelf w/a low spindled front rail above a matching lower shelf; the lower section w/a pair of drawers w/wooden knobs above a pair of paneled cupboard doors, serpentine apron & curved bracket feet, France, mid-19th c., 21 1/2 x 52 1/2", 6' 4" h. (ILLUS. previous page) **1,840**

Wall cupboard, country-style, cherry & walnut, the rectangular dark brown top w/a molded cornice over a single raised-panel door w/green vinegar grained panels, opening to five interior shelves, original red over orange vinegar graining, Ohio, chips along back of top, 11 1/2 x 34 3/4", 4' 2 1/2" h. (ILLUS. below left) **8,050**

Wall Cupboard with Pediment - BR

Italian Baroque Wall Cupboard - BR

Wall cupboard, Baroque style, walnut, a rectangular molded top above two small square drawers centered by a longer paneled drawer all w/nailed construction, over a single paneled door w/a central carved florette flanked by narrow side panels, molded base on scroll-cut bracket feet, Italy, probably 18th c., extensive worm damage, later bracket feet, separations & losses, 13 x 27 1/2", 34 1/4" h. (ILLUS.)..... **3,960**

Wall cupboard, country-style, walnut, dovetailed construction, swan's-neck pediment w/pinched center over two frame-and-panel doors, the interior w/20 small dovetailed drawers, a large dovetailed & divided drawer below, tongue-and-groove vertical backboards w/cut nails, original surface, traces of old yellow or green paint in interior dividers, probably missing two small drawers, no evidence of having had feet, missing one piece of molding beside drawer, old scratches & scuffs, missing one drawer pull, America, early 19th c., 14 x 35", 46" h. (ILLUS.) **1,045**

Country-style Wall Cupboard - BR

Vinegar Grained Wall Cupboard - G

Wall cupboard, country-style, walnut, the rectangular top over a pair of small paneled doors above two larger paneled doors, scalloped skirt w/shaped feet, chamfered panels throughout, original brass hinges, white pine vertical backboards w/cut nails, possibly Piedmont, North Carolina, early 19th c., old refinishing, top w/dents, separations & stains, probably missing molding on back of top, minor chips & scratches, 18 x 42", 4' 1/2" h. (ILLUS. previous page) **2,530**

Chinese Red Lacquered Cupboard - G

Wall cupboard, Oriental, lacquered & decorated, the rectangular top above a pair of tall flat cupboard doors w/a large fitted round brass latch, opening to an interior fitted w/two shelves & two drawers w/a bin below, a deep apron w/a carved Greek key design, short square stile legs, decorated overall in old red lacquer w/gold & black Oriental river scenes, flying bats & flowers, black-painted sides, putty restoration, feet ended out, China, 19th c., 21 x 45 1/4", 6' 1/2" h. (ILLUS. left) **920**

Nice Oak Welsh Cupboard - N.O.

Welsh cupboard, provincial-style, oak, two-part construction: the upper section w/a rectangular top w/a flaring stepped cornice above a scallop-cut frieze over two open compartments centered by a small cupboard w/a square paneled door above a lower open shelf all flanked by scallop-cut sides; the projecting lower section w/a row of two long & a short drawer w/pierced batwing pulls above a double arched & scalloped apron raised on three baluster- and ring-turned supports above an open wide bottom shelf, Britain, 19th c., 16 x 53 1/2", approximately 6' h. (ILLUS.) **1,610**

DESKS

Art Nouveau Walnut Desk & Chairs - N.O.

Art Nouveau desk & chair, walnut, the desk w/a low superstructure w/an undulating pierced crestrail over two shaped side drawers & a central shelf raised above the rectangular quarter-veneered top w/serpentine molded edges above an apron fitted w/two side drawers flanking the kneehole opening & a center drawer, rounded bottom on lower drawers continues into the cabriole legs ending in peg feet, w/a matching balloon-back side chair, Europe, late 19th c., desk 32 x 55 1/2", 42" h., the set (ILLUS.)...................................... **$2,070**

Baroque Revival style, walnut-finished hardwood, the superstructure w/a scroll-carved crest centered by a carved full-figure putto above an arcaded shelf w/three scroll-carved openings above a deep molding & carved platform behind a central slant top finely carved w/frolicking putti above a pull-out working surface projecting above deep curved brackets carved w/full-figure grotesque beasts & backed by a panel carved w/a grotesque mask, Italy, late 19th c., 31 1/2 x 47", 5' 2" h. (ILLUS. left)...................................... **3,450**

Ornately Carved Italian Desk - N.O.

Fine Biedermeier Ash Desk - N.O.

Biedermeier desk, ash, in the Gothic taste, the modified kidney-shaped top banded & w/an inlaid leather writing surface above a conforming quatrefoil inlaid frieze fitted w/a single drawer, raised on two paneled bow-front cupboards w/inlaid arches flanking a central recessed cupboard door, raised on plinth bases, Europe, early 19th c., 24 x 44", 31 1/2" h. (ILLUS.) **3,680**

Chippendale Country-style Desk - BR

Chippendale country-style slant-front desk, inlaid birch, dovetailed construction, the narrow rectangular top above a hinged slant front w/mitered corners opening to an interior w/eight drawers & six cubbyholes flanking prospect door w/single drawer, the lower case w/three graduated drawers w/oval pulls, Virginia, late 18th - early 19th c., two front feet ended out 3", front skirt & foot facings replaced, 2" of side facings replaced, brasses replaced, slant front faded, 22 x 42", 4' 1" h. (ILLUS.).......................... **2,310**

Chippendale Slant-front Desk - G

Chippendale slant-front desk, mahogany, a narrow rectangular top above a wide hinged slant front opening to an unusual interior w/a total of twenty dovetailed drawers, also pigeonholes & a hinged center door w/tombstone panel & additional hidden compartments & shelves, the lower case w/four long graduated beaded drawers w/old replaced batwing brasses, molded base on ogee bracket feet, refinished, feet expertly replaced, some other minor restorations, late 18th c., 24 x 43 1/2", 31 1/2" h. (ILLUS.) **3,450**

Rare "Oxbow-front" Boston Desk - N.O.

Chippendale "oxbow-front" slant-front desk, mahogany, a narrow rectangular top above a hinged slant lid centered by a large carved fan & opening to an interior fitted w/drawers & pigeonholes, the double-swelled "oxbow-front" case w/four long graduated drawers w/batwing brasses & keyhole escutcheons, a molded base w/central drop & short cabriole legs w/carved returns ending in claw-and-ball feet, Boston, late 18th c., 23 x 42 1/2", 44" h. (ILLUS.) **15,525**

Chippendale "Serpentine" Desk - M.M.

Chippendale slant-front "serpentine"-front desk, mahogany, a narrow rectangular top above the wide hinged slant front opening to a fitted interior above a long double-serpentine drawer flanked by pull-out supports over three long graduated double-serpentine drawers all w/butterfly brasses & keyhole escutcheons, serpentine base molding, claw-and-ball feet, old refinish, replaced brasses, late 18th c., 20 x 38", 40" h. (ILLUS.) **3,200**

Fancy Chippendale Revival Desk - M.M.

Chippendale Revival slant-front desk, quarter-sawn oak, a narrow top w/a low brass spindled gallery above the wide hinged slant front centered by a large panel carved w/large leafy scrolls enclosing an urn, the case w/a long blocked drawer centered by a carved shell above the arched scroll-carved kneehole opening flanked by two small blocked drawers, pierced brass butterfly pulls & keyhole escutcheon, molded apron on cabriole legs w/leaf-carved knees & ending in claw-and-ball feet, refinished, ca. 1890s, 18 x 30", 38" h. (ILLUS. left)......... **2,500**

Chippendale-Style library desk, steel-mounted mahogany, the rectangular top w/serpentine molded edges centering an inset gilt-tooled leather top, the front apron fitted w/pairs of small serpentine drawers w/gadrooned bottom edges flanking a single long flat central drawer w/an arched kneehole opening, the opposite side w/blind drawers, raised on cabriole legs w/acanthus-carved knees & ending in scroll feet, England, ca. 1900, 37 1/2 x 64", 30 1/2" h. (ILLUS. below, top) **1,840**

Chippendale-Style Library Desk - N.O.

Copy of Famous Chippendale Partner's Desk - N.O.

Quality Colonial Revival Desk - M.M.

Chippendale-Style partner's desk, mahogany, the shaped rectangular top w/three inset leather sections, the two large pedestals carved w/large lion mask corner pilasters & carved swag & wreath designs, opening to reveal folio compartments below shallow drawers, a central drawer above the kneehole opening, facsimile of the renowned Thomas Chippendale model from Nostell Priorary, England, late 19th - early 20th c., 39 x 72", 32 1/4" h. (ILLUS. bottom previous page) .. **6,900**

Colonial Revival partner's desk, mahogany, a wide rectangular top w/rounded corners above a case fitted on each side w/a row of three narrow ornate scroll-carved drawers over two deeper scroll-carved drawers flanking the serpentine kneehole opening, each corner carved w/a large grotesque lion head above heavy cabriole legs w/leaf-carved knees & ending in paw feet, attributed to Horner of New York City, original dark finish, ca. 1890, 28 x 56", 30" h. (ILLUS. above) **3,500**

Colonial Revival partner's desk, mahogany, the rectangular hourglass-shaped top above a conforming case w/a stack of two rounded drawers on the right side & a long drawer at the top of each end, short cabriole legs w/claw-and-ball feet, brass bail pulls, carved scrolls at the top of each corner, refinished, ca. 1900, 30 x 54", 30" h. (ILLUS. below) **1,200**

Colonial Revival Hourglass-shaped Partner's Desk - M.M.

Colonial Revival Carved Partner's Desk - M.M.

Colonial Revival partner's desk, mahogany, the wide rectangular top w/molded edges above a case fitted on each side w/a scroll-carved central drawer over the arched kneehole opening flanked on one side by a large square cupboard door carved w/ornate scrolls centering a cartouche & on the other side by two scroll-carved small drawers, large carved lion heads carved at each corner above large wing-form brackets over the cabriole legs w/leaf-carved knees & large paw feet, uncarved plain side panels, attributed to Horner of New York City, original dark finish, ca. 1880s, 30 x 60", 30" h. (ILLUS. above) **5,500**

Ornate Colonial Revival Partner's Desk - M.M.

Unusual Colonial Revival Desk - M.M.

Colonial Revival partner's desk, mahogany, the wide rectangular top w/molded edges above a case fitted on each side w/a scroll-carved central drawer over the arched kneehole opening flanked on one side by a large square cupboard door carved w/ornate scrolls centering a cartouche & on the other side by two scroll-carved small drawers, large lion heads carved at each corner above large wing-form brackets over the cabriole legs w/leaf-carved knees & large paw feet, ornately scroll-carved side panels, attributed to Horner of New York City, original dark finish, ca. 1880s, 30 x 60", 30" h. (ILLUS. bottom previous page) **7,500**

Colonial Revival slant-front bombé desk, mahogany veneer, a narrow rectangular top above the wide hinged slant front opening to a fitted interior above a pair of small square pullouts over the wide bombé case fitted w/three long drawers, serpentine apron & short curved legs w/claw-and-ball feet, original finish, ca. 1900, 20 x 42", 40" h. (ILLUS. top of page) **1,800**

Colonial Revival Bombé Desk - M.M.

Colonial Revival slant-front desk, mahogany veneer, a narrow rectangular top above a wide hinged slant front opening to a fitted interior over the bombé case w/a long drawer w/a center shell carving over the kneehole opening flanked by small drawers, butterfly brasses, simple cabriole legs w/front paw feet, original finish & hardware, ca. 1910, 16 x 32", 40" h. (ILLUS. left) **700**

Country Style Walnut Desk - BR

Country-style desk, walnut, a set-back top section w/central prospect door flanked by four drawers on the rectangular lift top opening to 20 interior compartments & a case w/two drawers above single long drawer, ring-turned tapering legs, frame-and-panel sides w/mortise joints, original turned wooden pulls, backs w/chamfered horizontal panels w/deep oxidation, cut nails, America, 19th c., 25 1/2 x 27 1/2", 39" h. (ILLUS.) **3,960**

Country-style Plantation Desk - BR

Country-style plantation desk, yellow
pine, two-part construction: the top fitted
w/a three-quarters gallery above two
paneled doors opening to an interior w/14
compartments & two drawers; the lower
section w/a slant front opening to a well,
tapered ring-turned legs, drawers w/orig-
inal leather pulls, cut nails throughout, old
refinishing, possibly a marriage, top &
bottom w/traces of old green paint, some
rebuilding, Southern U.S., 19th c.,
24 x 37", 5' 4" h. (ILLUS.)........................... **1,100**
Country-style slant-top desk, pine & pop-
lar, mortise-and-tenon construction, a narrow rectangular top over the hinged wide
slant lid opening to an interior w/eight cubbyholes, tapered square legs, hand-
wrought nails, pit-sawn lumber, possibly
original dark red/brown finish, America,

19th c., hinges replaced & reset, missing
lock, 23 x 31", 36" h. (ILLUS. below)............ **990**

Country-style Slant-top Desk - BR

Early 20th century roll-top desk, quarter-
sawn oak, a narrow rectangular top
over the S-scroll tambour roll opening
to a fitted interior, the case w/a long
center drawer w/arched apron over the
paneled kneehole opening flanked on
each side w/a pull-out writing surface
over a stack of four drawers w/long
carved pulls, paneled ends & deep
molded base, refinished, ca. 1900,
30 x 54", 45" h. **2,500**
Early 20th century writing desk, quarter-
sawn oak, the wide rectangular top
w/molded edges over a center long drawer
w/serpentine edge above the kneehole
opening w/paneled interior sides flanked
on each side by a stack of four drawers
w/simple wood pulls, a pull-out writing surface above one set of drawers, six-paneled
ends, deep molded base, refinished, ca.
1900, 30 x 60", 30" h. (ILLUS. below)......... **1,200**

Nice Paneled Oak Writing Desk - M.M.

Walnut Two-part Plantation Desk - G

Federal country-style plantation desk, walnut, two-part construction: the upper section w/a rectangular top w/a wide coved cornice above a pair of tall 6-pane glazed doors opening to two shelves above two shallow drawers w/turned wood knobs; the projecting lower section w/a pair of drawers w/turned wood knobs, raised on ring- and baluster-turned tapering legs ending in peg feet, old finish, age splits, mid-19th c., 23 1/2 x 46 1/2", overall 6' 2" h. (ILLUS.).. **1,840**

Very Fine Federal Revival Desk - M.M.

Federal Revival writing desk, inlaid mahogany, a narrow rectangular top w/a low three-quarter gallery & a concave center section above a cabinet w/three small banded inlay drawers flanking the concave central section w/vertical letter slots, the wide rectangular desk top w/bowed center section above a conforming apron w/a long line-inlaid bowed center drawer flanked by two small line-inlaid drawers flanked by inlaid paterae at each corner, on tapering square line-inlaid legs ending in spade feet, original round brasses & finish, early 20th c., 20 x 32", 40" h. (ILLUS. below left) **650**

Oak George III Slant-front Desk - N.O.

George III slant-front desk, inlaid oak, a narrow rectangular top above a hinged slant top w/banded inlay opening to a gilt-tooled leather writing surface & a variety of small drawers & pigeonholes flanking a central banded door, the case w/four long graduated & inlay-banded drawers w/pierced batwing brasses, molded base on ogee bracket feet, England, late 18th c., 22 x 48", 46" h. (ILLUS.) **1,840**

Georgian-Style slant-front desk, inlaid mahogany, a narrow rectangular top above the hinged slant front opening to two small hand-dovetailed & cockbeaded drawers flanking prospect door w/six cubbyholes, the case w/three long graduated drawers w/oval brasses, molded base on scroll-cut bracket feet, original brass hinges & pulls, full dust panels, England, probably late 19th or early 20th c., 20 1/2 x 36", 41 1/2" h. (ILLUS. top next page) **990**

Georgian-Style Slant-front Desk - BR

Walnut Roll-top Desk - G.K.

Late Victorian roll-top desk, walnut, a narrow rectangular top over the S-roll scroll opening to an interior fitted w/pigeonholes & small drawers above the writing surface, an edge molding over the kneehole opening beside a band of five small drawers w/leaf-carved pulls, paneled sides at top & bottom sides, molded base, refinished, last quarter 19th c., 30 x 48", 48" h. (ILLUS. bottom, previous page)................ **2,400**

Delicate Louis XV Revival Desk - M.M.

Louis XV Revival slant-front desk, giltwood, a narrow top shelf w/a low pierced brass gallery above the wide hinged slant front opening to an interior w/three small decorated drawers, the apron w/a single long drawer w/applied brass scroll banding, on simple tall cabriole legs, original finish, probably French, early 20th c., closed 16 x 30", 38" h. (ILLUS. open) **850**

Delicate Louis XVI-Style Desk - N.O.

Louis XVI-Style lady's writing desk, rosewood, the top w/a two-tiered open gallery w/shelves w/a delicate pierced-scroll crest & slender turned supports, the highly figured hinged slant front opening to an inset felt-work surface & small compartments, the apron w/a narrow full-width crossbanded drawer, raised on slender tapering foliate-carved & fluted legs ending in peg feet, restored original finish, New York City, ca. 1870, 18 1/2 x 30 1/2", overall 4' 5 1/4" h. (ILLUS. below left) **2,760**

Ornately Carved Chinese Desk - M.M.

Oriental desk, carved mahogany, two-part construction: the superstructure w/a high crestrail carved as a mountain & clouds above stepped compartments w/dragon-carved doors flanking central slots & further carving, the wide rectangular top w/a bead-carved edge above an apron w/two small carved drawers flanking an ornate pierce-carved panel & apron, raised on cabriole legs w/boldly carved knees & ending in scroll feet, China, late 19th c., probably refinished, 23 x 36", 4' 4" h. (ILLUS. above) ... **1,500**

Carved Chinese Desk - N.O.

Oriental writing desk, stained rosewood, the superstructure w/an ornately pierce-carved crestrail above two projecting compartments, one fitted w/three small carved drawers & the other w/a carved paneled door, backed by a delicate pierce-carved panel above a short carved panel, the projecting writing surface over a pair of elaborately carved drawers, raised on cabriole legs w/carved bats at the knees & ornately pierce-carved returns, ending in claw-and-ball feet, China, ca. 1900, 25 x 38 1/2", 46 1/2" h. (ILLUS. previous page) **1,150**

Unique Aesthetic Fall-front Desk - M.M.

Victorian Aesthetic Movement fall-front desk, walnut & burl walnut, a rectangular top w/a sawtooth crestrail & plain side rails, large round projecting ears mounted w/large brass disks w/Oriental designs, the case w/a long narrow shelf over a hinged fall-front door decorated w/lattice-incised border panels & a central burl panel & opening to a fitted interior, each side of the case mounted w/a quarter-round projecting shelf w/a pierced gallery & lattice braces, the stepped-out lower section w/a long drawer overhanging a pair of line-incised cupboard doors each centered w/a pair of small square floral-carved recessed panels, a long round-fronted veneered drawer at the very base above the flat line-incised apron, original hardware & finish, ca. 1880s, 22 x 44", 5' 6" h. (ILLUS.) **2,500**

Fine Aesthetic Cylinder-front Desk - M.M.

Victorian Aesthetic Movement cylinder-front desk, walnut & burl walnut, the high superstructure w/a narrow rectangular shelf w/a Chinese Chippendale-style pierced gallery w/corner blocks & knob finials supported on slender turned columns & backed by a high curved burl panel above another rectangular shelf above the paneled burl-veneered cylinder front opening to a fitted interior, flanked on each side w/galleried side sections over the case w/a long central burl veneer drawer w/three brass pulls over the kneehole opening w/fret brackets & a concave lower shelf, the kneehole flanked by a small veneered drawer over a tall door w/a raised veneered panel, a spindled band at the bottom of each side, short tapering square legs, refinished, ca. 1880s, 22 x 46", 5' 6" h. (ILLUS.) **2,500**

Victorian Baroque Revival partner's desk, oak, rectangular top w/a plain center & wide scroll-carved border band & gadroon-carved edges above aprons each fitted w/a pair of long scroll-carved drawers centered by a lion head, raised on full-figure carved sphinxes atop animal legs & large paw feet, a wide medial shelf w/gadrooned edges, attributed to Horner of New York City, ca. 1880s, refinished, 28 x 52", 30" h. (ILLUS. top of next page) **9,800**

Elaborate Baroque Revival Partner's Desk - M.M.

Baroque Revival Slant-front Desk - M.M.

Norwegian-American Country Desk - M.M.

Victorian Baroque Revival slant-front desk, oak, narrow rectangular top w/a gadroon-carved edge above the wide hinged slant front carved w/a pair of large leafy scrolls centering a relief-carved lion head above a pair of drawers w/scroll-carved panels over the narrow scroll-carved apron, raised on front legs carved in full-relief w/winged sphinxes above legs w/large paw feet on casters, square tapering back legs, a lower medial shelf w/a gadroon-carved border, attributed to Horner, New York City, ca. 1880s, refinished, 18 x 36", 42" h. (ILLUS.)................ **4,600**

Victorian country-style fall-front desk, butternut, a rectangular top w/ovolo front corners above a tall case w/columns down the front sides carved in the middle w/a bold ropetwist design, the case w/a long drawer w/carved fruit & leaf pulls above a wide flat fall front opening to an arrangement of five small drawers flanking a center section w/a narrow drawer above & below two pigeonholes centered by a prospect door, the lower case w/two long deep drawers w/carved pulls, low apron w/small center carved knobs, Norwegian-American influence, central Midwest, ca. 1870, 22 x 44", 5' h. (ILLUS.) **2,500**

Victorian Country Slant-front Desk - M.M.

Victorian country-style slant-front desk,
walnut, a narrow rectangular top above
two narrow drawers over the wide
hinged slant front w/two long recessed
octagonal panels opening to a fitted interior, the lower case w/three long graduated drawers w/wooden knobs, serpentine apron & square stile feet,
dovetailed construction, refinished, ca.
1875, 22 x 38", 44" h. (ILLUS.) **500**

Victorian Eastlake Captain's Desk - M.M.

Victorian Eastlake captain's desk, walnut,
the superstructure w/a crown-form crestrail
w/center sunburst & incised scrolls above a
narrow rectangular shelf raised on incurved
pierced brackets flanking a large rectangular burl panel over the hinged angled felt-
lined writing surface over a burl front panel,

raised on angular cut-out line-incised side
supports joined by two wide open shelves,
original dark finish, ca. 1880s, 22 x 30", 4'
10" h. (ILLUS. below left)................................ **800**

Country Eastlake Oak Desk - M.M.

**Victorian Eastlake country-style fall-
front desk,** oak, a high line-incised crestrail w/small carved fan devices above a
narrow shelf above the narrow rectangular top above the line-incised flat fall front
opening to a fitted interior, the lower case
fitted w/three open shelves, narrow scalloped aprons, refinished, ca. 1890,
16 x 30", 5' h. (ILLUS.)................................ **650**

Very Elaborate Eastlake Desk - M.M.

Victorian Eastlake desk, walnut & burl walnut, an ornate superstructure w/a high stepped, paneled, blocked & bobbin-trimmed crest above a narrow rectangular shelf over a pair of ring-and-urn-turned spindles flanking a cupboard w/a scroll-carved paneled door beside an open compartment w/a bobbin rail over a tiny drawer, all flanked by open shelves w/back bobbin rails & raised over a pair of burl paneled drawers centered by a recess on the wide rectangular desk top w/molded edges, the apron w/a long drawer w/a long brass escutcheon raised on turned trumpet-form legs joined by U-form end stretchers joined by a turned center stretcher w/an urn finial, original finish, ca. 1885, 28 x 40", 4' 5" h. (ILLUS. previous page) **4,800**

Victorian Eastlake fall-front desk, walnut, the superstructure w/a gallery top w/a raised rectangular center leaf-carved panel flanked by pierced sides on the rectangular shelf supported on incurved pierced brackets above the rectangular top backed by a long narrow leaf-carved panel over the wide flat fall front w/a recessed panel carved in the center w/a monogram & opening to a fitted interior, the lower cabinet w/a long drawer projecting over three long drawers flanked by carved brackets & each w/brass plate & bail pulls, deep molded base, paneled sides, original finish, ca. 1880, 20 x 30", 5' 4" h. (ILLUS. top right column) **1,800**

Nice Eastlake Fall-front Desk - M.M.

Victorian Eastlake writing desk, oak, rectangular top w/molded edges above a long center drawer w/a central panel over the paneled kneehole opening flanked on each side by a projecting drawer w/small panel & simple carved wood pulls above three additional matching drawers, molded base, paneled ends, refinished, ca. 1880s, 30 x 54", 30" h. (ILLUS. below) **1,000**

Eastlake Oak Writing Desk - M.M.

Victorian Elizabethan Revival Desk - N.O.

Victorian Elizabethan Revival lady's desk, mahogany, two-part construction: the top supporting a recessed pair of two-over-two shallow drawers w/the shelf above supported by S-scroll brackets above a low pierced back gallery; the lower section w/a felt-lined projecting writing surface over a pair of drawers supported by a trestle base w/spiral-twist supports & cross stretcher, America, mid-19th c. (ILLUS.) **805**

Simple Golden Oak Slant-front Desk - M.M.

Victorian Golden Oak slant-front desk, oak, a narrow top w/a low scroll-carved crestrail over the wide flat hinged slant front centered w/a scroll-carved band & opening to a fitted interior, a long drawer w/slightly shaped apron above the simple cabriole legs, refinished, ca. 1900, 16 x 30", 44" h. (ILLUS.) **650**

Oak Slant-front Desk with Ornate Top - M.M.

Victorian Golden Oak slant-front desk, quarter-sawn oak, the ornate superstructure w/a large serpentine-sided beveled center mirror w/a scroll-carved frame flanked by scroll-carved crests & small shaped shelves supported on baluster-turned spindles above a small narrow drawer flanked by smaller rounded square beveled mirrors, all atop the wide hinged slant front w/a small scroll-carved panel at the top & opening to a fitted interior, above a case w/a pair of glazed cupboard doors w/scroll-carved corners above a pair of round-fronted bottom drawers w/bail pulls, ogee bracket feet, original hardware, refinished, ca. 1900, 18 x 30", 5' h. (ILLUS.) **2,000**

Nicely Carved Oak Slant-front Desk - M.M.

Victorian Golden Oak slant-front desk,
quarter-sawn oak, the superstructure w/a
low scroll-carved crestrail over a narrow
shelf & incurved side brackets backed by
wainscoted boards over the narrow rectangular top above the hinged slant front
ornately carved w/a central diamond
framed by leafy scrolls over a single long
leaf-carved drawer flanked by pull-out
supports above incurved sides backed
by wainscoted boards & flanking two narrow open shelves, arched boot jack
ends, refinished, ca. 1900, 16 x 30", 4'
2" h. (ILLUS. previous page) **600**

Nice Renaissance Davenport Desk - M.M.

Unusual Renaissance Fall-front Desk - M.M.

Victorian Renaissance Revival country-
style fall-front desk, walnut & bird's-eye
maple, the superstructure composed of a
narrow top shelf w/an ornately pierce-
carved back rail & scroll-cut end brackets
supported on slender turned spindles &
back brackets flanking another pierced
rail on the rectangular top over the flat fall
front w/four recessed bird's-eye maple
panels flanked by scroll-cut brackets, the
stepped-out base w/a long drawer w/two
recessed maple panels & small ring pulls
above an arched & serpentine apron
w/two trefoil cutouts, on ring-turned tapering legs, paneled sides, original hardware, refinished, ca. 1870s, 20 x 32", 5'
8" h. (ILLUS.) **850**

Victorian Renaissance Revival Daven-
port desk, walnut & burl walnut, a low
pierced scroll-carved gallery above the
gently slanted writing surface w/leather inset opening to a well, a tiny drawer at the
side of the case, the stepped-back lower
case w/two raised burl panels flanked by
pierced scroll-cut & leaf-carved brackets,
the side fitted w/a stack of four paneled
drawers w/leaf-carved pulls, molded base
w/projecting feet, refinished, ca. 1870s,
22 x 28", 40" h. (ILLUS. top right) **1,600**

Quality Renaissance Fall-front Desk - M.M.

Victorian Renaissance Revival fall-front
desk, walnut & ebonized wood, a high
arched & scroll-carved crestrail flanked
by scroll ends & centering a pointed oblong carved cartouche above the narrow
rectangular top over the hinged flat fall
front w/a rectangular center panel w/an-
other carved cartouche, opening to a fitted interior of bird's-eye maple, the
stepped-out lower case w/a pair of drawers w/line-incised decoration & brass ring
pulls above a molding projecting above a
pair of paneled cupboard doors each
centered by a large carved shield-style
cartouche flanked by block- and scroll-
carved side brackets on the flat molded
base, overall ebonized trim molding, paneled sides, original finish, ca. 1875,
20 x 32", 4' 8" h. (ILLUS.) **2,000**

Victorian Rococo Fall-front Desk - M.M.

Victorian Rococo fall-front desk, walnut & bird's-eye maple, the high superstructure w/a central arched crest over an oval mirror flanked by ornate pierced scroll-carved rails & side brackets flanking quarter-round corner shelves over two recessed oval panels above the rectangular top w/molded edges & rounded front corners, the flat fall front opening to a bird's-eye maple interior fitted w/small drawers, letter slots & a central compartment all flanked by turned half-round side drops & carved brackets, raised on heavy molded cabriole legs joined by a serpentine medial shelf w/a low scroll-pierced crest above a conforming line-incised drawer, refinished, ca. 1860, closed 22 x 40", 6' h. (ILLUS. open, above) **400**

English William IV Mahogany Writing Desk - N.O.

William & Mary Revival Partner's Desk - M.M.

William IV writing desk, mahogany, the rectangular top w/rounded corners inset w/a gilt-tooled leather writing surface, the apron fitted w/three drawers w/wooden knobs, raised on knob-turned & reeded tapering legs ending in trumpet feet on brass casters, England, second quarter 19th c., 37 x 60", 30" h. (ILLUS. bottom right column of previous page).................. **4,600**

William & Mary Revival partner's desk, walnut, the wide rectangular top inset w/leather w/embossed edging, each side fitted w/a long center drawer w/a roundel above the kneehole opening flanked by deeper drawer w/scalloped & scroll-carved bases, raised on eight trumpet-and-ring-turned legs joined by H-stretchers, bun feet, old refinish, early 20th c., 32 x 54", 30" h. (ILLUS. top of page) **1,200**

DINING ROOM SUITES

Colonial Revival: dining table, sideboard, server, china cabinet & five side chairs & one armchair; inlaid mahogany & mahogany veneer, the Chippendale-style chairs w/an arched shell-carved crestrail over pierced carved vasiform back splat, over-upholstered seat on cabriole legs; the oval extension dining table raised on heavy C-scroll legs ending in bun feet, the two-part D-form china cabinet w/the upper section centered by a large curved door w/a large oval reserve w/inlaid floral decoration, matching details on the long sideboard & small server, Rockford Republic Furniture Co., ca. 1920s, the set **$10,450**

Baroque-Style China Cabinet from Set - G.K.

Victorian Baroque-Style: round table w/six leaves, twelve chairs, tall china cabinet, sideboard & server; oak, each piece with elaborate carving, the rounded expandable dining table w/carved apron above a heavy turned round leaf-carved center post flanked by four ornately carved winged griffins below spiral-turned support legs, each chair w/a high arched carved crest & spiral-turned stiles flanking an oval caned back panel over the caned seat on turned legs & stretchers, the china cabinet w/a high crest carved w/pierced scrolls & a center cartouche above a leaf-carved corner & scroll-carved frieze band centered by a mask carving over two tall glazed cupboard doors flanked by spiral-turned side stiles, deep molded & carved base, dark original finish, ca. 1880s, the set (ILLUS. left)
.... **25,000**

William & Mary Revival: oval table, five side chairs & one armchair; oak, each chair w/a tall back w/a yoked crest centered by a pierced scroll crest above a large pierce-carved splat enclosing an oval upholstered panel, upholstered slip seat on a carved seatrail & S-scroll front legs joined by a curved H-stretcher to the rear legs, the oval table w/a scroll-carved apron, raised on four large flat leg panels w/shell, floral & scroll carving centered by a caned oval panel & drop-down supports at each end, w/six leaves, original finish, late 19th c., table 54" l., 30" h., armchair 46" h., the set (ILLUS. below) **3,500**

William & Mary Revival Dining Suite - G.K.

DRY SINKS

Painted & Decorated Poplar Dry Sink - G

Painted & decorated poplar, the long arched splashback above a long well above a case w/a pair of large paneled cupboard doors above simple bracket feet, old dark brown graining over an amber-colored ground, evidence of earlier red, interior w/two shelves painted light green, wear, door latch missing, 19th c., 17 3/4 x 45", 36" h. (ILLUS.) **$575**

Painted pine & poplar, a narrow rectangular shelf atop the raised backboard flanked by shaped sides on the long well above a pair of drawers w/turned wood knobs over a pair of paneled cupboard doors opening to two shelves, simple bracket feet, old yellow paint over earlier colors, signed in pencil in one drawer "Thos. Underwood, Clark Co. Ohio, August 10, 1881," 18 x 42", 41" h.................. **4,025**

Early Pine Dry Sink - G.K.

Pine & tiger stripe maple, a long, deep rectangular well above a case w/a pair of drawers w/wooden knobs over a pair of paneled cupboard doors w/original butt hinges & a cast-iron latch, bracket feet, old refinish, second half 19th c., 19 x 52", 33" h. (ILLUS.) **800**

GARDEN & LAWN

English Cast-iron Garden Chairs - C.H.

Armchairs, a rounded molded & floral-designed back depicting the seasons, flanked by pierced scrolling arms over a pierced seat w/serpentine front, apron w/pierced leaf design, scroll-trimmed cabriole legs joined by leafy vine stretchers, black paint, England, early 20th c., some rust & paint loss, 37" h., set of 4 (ILLUS. of part)... **$2,415**

Bench, carved marble, the back w/shaped & scrolled pediment above frieze w/elaborate relief-carved scrolls & dragons, arm supports scrolled w/extensive leaf & pet-al carving, cable borders on seat, 19th c., stains, minor chips & discoloration, marble w/some irregularities & fissures, central pediment w/large chip, 20 x 80", 46" h. (ILLUS. below)............................. **15,400**

Bench, cast iron & wood, cast-iron ends in the form of swans, their necks serving as bench arms, seat & back formed by single boards, old white & orange paint w/repainting, 19th c., scattered rust, boards probably later replacements, 28 x 72", 38" h. (ILLUS. top of next page)............... **4,840**

Carved Marble Garden Bench - BR

Swan-form Garden Bench - BR

French Garden Bench - BR

Bench, cast iron & wood, cast-iron frame decorated w/scrolls & lion heads, canted legs ending in paw feet, curved beaded wooden slat seat & back, traces of old green paint, France, 19th c., 29 x 57", 35" h. (ILLUS. above).................................. **825**

Unusual Set of Garden Furniture - N.O.

Chair & table set: two side chairs & a matching table; a pair of folding metal side chairs w/tall rectangular patterned backs & matching square seats, the table w/a rectangular top over a narrow Greek key apron raised on slender metal cross-style folding legs, worn golden yellow paint, 19th c., chairs 31" h., the set (ILLUS. bottom previous page) **1,150**

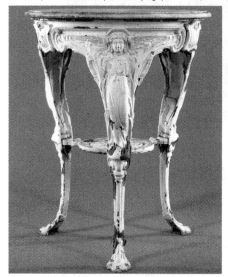

Marble-top Cast-iron Plant Stand - BR

Plant stand, cast iron & marble, round marble top on cast-iron tripod legs w/angels at tops in relief, platform stretcher below, old white paint, Europe, 19th c., scattered rust, marble w/stains & discoloration, 24" d., 30" h. (ILLUS.) **1,430**

Cast-iron Openwork Plant Stand - BR

Plant stand, cast iron, openwork round top above tripod legs w/female heads in relief, platform stretcher below, hoof feet, old green paint, England or Europe, 19th c., scattered light rust, 24" d., 28" h. (ILLUS.) **550**

Settee, a serpentine scroll-cast crestrail over a pierced back composed of small C-scrolls, the stepped arms w/tall looped scrolls flanking the seat w/a new pad, raised on scrolling cabriole legs w/scrolling leaf returns, painted green, American, 19th c., 35" l., 41" h. **1,380**

Renaissance Design Victorian Garden Settee - N.O.

Settee, Renaissance Revival style, the long pierced back centered by a wide arched fanned panel framing a large trefoil & flanked by lower square panels, the shaped tapering arms w/ pierced lacy designs, iron slat seat w/pierced scroll apron, curved saber-form legs, painted white, second half 19th c., 23 x 46 1/2", 37 1/2" h. (ILLUS. bottom, previous page) **546**

English "Strawberry Hill" Settee - N.O.

Settee, "Strawberry Hill" type, wrought-iron design w/the back composed of three overlapping Gothic arches, undulating open-end arms over the iron slat seat, on straight legs w/long angled braces, rusted white-painted surface, England, 19th c., 57 1/2" l., 41 1/2" h. (ILLUS.)................ **1,265**

Settee, the high arched & pieced back w/a flower-filled urn crest over scrolls centered by a female head above a band of large interlocking ovals, flared scroll arms above the circle-pierced seat, cabriole legs w/scroll feet, 19th c., multiple coats of old green & white paint, scattered rust, 2 1/2" piece on back broken but present, 19 x 46", 42" h. (ILLUS. below)................ **1,100**

Victorian-style Cast-iron Settee - BR

Settee, the scroll-carved serpentine crestrail above a back pierced w/rows of small arches, stepped scroll-carved arms above the scroll-pierced seat w/a shallow scroll-carved apron, scrolled cabriole legs, America or England, second half 19th c., old black paint w/scattered rust, 20 x 47", 35" h. (ILLUS. below)................ **990**

Cast-iron Openwork Settee - BR

Two Grapevine Garden Settees - N.O.

Settees, Rococo-style, the arched curved back continuing to form the arms cast overall in a pierced grapevine design, oblong pierced lattice seat w/a grapevine apron & raised on outswept grapevine legs joined by a cross-stretcher, dark green paint, early 20th c., 23 x 34", 31" h., pr. (ILLUS. above) **1,495**

Settees, the back composed of three stepped rectangular sections, the taller center section w/a sunburst & florette crest over a narrow lattice back above the ornate pierced scroll back, the lower side sections w/similar decor, simple scrolled bar arms over the pierced seat w/a flat pierced apron, on simple iron bar legs, worn old paint, American, 19th c., 45" l., pr. **978**

Stools, lacquer, barrel-shaped, a round seat above curved square supports each w/a central ring & joined at the base by flat shaped stretchers, a red & black ground decorated overall w/Oriental garden scenes & scrolling lotus designs, China, late 19th c., 12" d., 14" h., pr. (ILLUS. bottom left column) **546**

Figural Bronze & Granite Table - N.O.

Table, the demi-lune granite top supported by two bronze young mermaids w/entwined tails, Europe, 19th c., 20 x 39 1/2", 29" h. (ILLUS.) **3,450**

Chinese Decorated Lacquer Stools - N.O.

HALL RACKS & TREES

Wrought-iron & Tile Hall Rack - N.O.

Hall rack, wrought-iron & tile, a long narrow rectangular form w/iron bars above & below seven coat hooks separating a row of six colorful French faience tiles decorated w/figurines, an ornate scrolling wrought-iron crest across the top, probably France, 19th c., 5 3/4 x 39 1/2", 13" h. (ILLUS.) **$1,725**

Elaborate Cast-iron Hall Tree - BR

Hall tree, cast iron, elaborate Renaissance-style decoration of grapes, vines, full-figured putti in center, grotesque head below, female head above, seven hat/coat hooks w/lion's head above, base w/removable cast-iron shell-form basin below spiral bar flanked by two openwork sides, scattered light rust & black paint, ca. 1875, 12 x 32", 6' 6" h. (ILLUS.) **3,960**

Hall tree, late Victorian style, cherry, a high serpentine crestrail w/a large fan-carved crest & fan-carved ears above a tall rectangular beveled mirror flanked by wide serpentine sides mounted w/four double pierced iron scrolling hooks above a lower back panel w/a leaf-carved band flanked by arms composed of spindled bands joined to flat S-scroll arm supports continuing down to form the front legs, rectangular lift seat above a well, delicate beaded & scrolled apron band, old refinish, ca. 1895, 18 x 36", 7' 4" h. (ILLUS. below) **1,800**

Late Victorian Cherry Hall Tree - M.M.

Hall tree, Victorian Aesthetic Movement style, cherry, a high oval crest centered by scroll carving & enclosing small spindles above a flat molded crestrail over a circle-incised frieze band above a large rectangular beveled mirror flanked by shaped sides w/tall slender outside columns, a large scroll-embossed leather panel below the mirror & above a pierced scroll lower rail, mounted w/six brass hooks, low shaped arms flank the rectangular seat over an arched spindled apron, a bottom open shelf w/one end projecting out to support a metal drip pan below a rectangular metal bracket, original finish, ca. 1890s, 17 x 36", 7' 4" h. (ILLUS. top next page) **1,500**

Cherry & Leather Ornate Hall Tree - M.M.

Ornately Pierced Aesthetic Hall Tree - M.M.

Hall tree, Victorian Aesthetic Movement style, oak, a long arched oval crestrail enclosing ornate pierced leafy scrolls above an arched panel w/graduated rings above the flat molded rail & sides enclosing a large rectangular beveled mirror, each side mounted w/three cast-brass hooks, a pierced lattice panel below the mirror & above a narrow rectangular pad-

ded back panel, heavy C-scroll arms on the narrow rectangular seat over a long line-incised drawer w/stamped brass pulls, a projecting post & lattice panel at one side supporting a projecting rounded shelf w/a brass drip pan, square stile legs, original finish, ca. 1895, 20 x 42", 7' 6" h. (ILLUS. bottom left).......................... **2,000**

Oak Aesthetic Movement Hall Tree - M.M.

Hall tree, Victorian Aesthetic Movement style, oak, a wide flaring stepped cornice above a framework of slender square stiles & rails, a top panel w/a narrow almond-shaped panel carved w/scrolls flanking a central lion mask, a large rectangular beveled mirror over a narrow carved & pierced band above the large rectangular back panel carved w/ornate scrolls, the sides mounted w/six double scrolling iron hooks, simple shaped arms over the rectangular seat above a long narrow drawer w/stamped brass pulls, square slightly curved front legs, a pierced half-round side shelf at each side of the base for holding missing drip pans, original finish, ca. 1890s, 18 x 44", 7' 4" h. (ILLUS.) **2,400**

Hall tree, Victorian Baroque Revival style, quarter-sawn oak, a high arched & pierce-carved crest on the overhanging crestrail supported by ornate heavy carved S-scroll dragon-form brackets above the very large rectangular beveled mirror over a lower scroll-carved back panel, solid rounded arms flanking the rectangular lift seat over a deep well, mounted w/four double cast-metal hooks, flat incised apron flanked by paw feet, refinished, ca. 1900, 22 x 50", 7' 8" h. (ILLUS. top left column of next page) **3,500**

Fancy Large Baroque Style Hall Tree - M.M.

Tall Narrow Eastlake Hall Tree - M.M.

Hall tree, Victorian Eastlake style, oak, the pierced & upswept crest on a narrow flaring crestrail over a delicately pierced narrow almond-shaped panel above a small vertical rectangular mirror beside a narrow vertical pierced panel w/flat short rails flanking a figural carved crescent moon face, a large lower splat w/incurved sides & pierced narrow splat sections flanking a leaf-incised panel above a solid lower back panel flanked by narrow flat open arms on shaped supports over the rectangular seat, tapering turned front legs & a projecting rounded shelf w/metal drip pan at one side, the top mounted w/six brass hooks, refinished, ca. 1890s, 18 x 26", 7' h. (ILLUS. bottom left) **1,200**

Very Fine Eastlake Hall Tree - M.M.

Hall tree, Victorian Eastlake style, walnut & burl walnut, the high rectangular slightly projecting crest w/a flat key-pierced rail divided by four molded blocks ending in short turned bulbous spindles & two topped by angular leaf finials, two narrow burled frieze bands above the tall rectangular beveled mirror flanked by wide sides w/narrow burl panels incised w/stylized angular urn designs, the lower section w/a rectangular white marble center section over a single drawer & flanked by square frameworks for canes & umbrellas all supported on square reeded legs w/small corner ball finials, a lower paneled back above a bottom shelf joined by a flat molded base on thick wedge feet, fitted w/four projecting peg hooks on each side, refinished, ca. 1880, 14 x 48", 8' h. (ILLUS.)................................. **3,500**

Hall tree, Victorian Golden Oak style, a wide serpentine crestrail w/carved center arch over a rosette & rounded scroll-carved ears above a framework w/pierced scroll-carved brackets forming a circle centered by a diamond-shaped beveled mirror above a lower rectangular panel w/two large pierced scroll-carved corner brackets & a spindled angled center rail, simple open arms flanked by lift seat, square stile legs w/knob feet, six cast-iron hooks, refinished, ca. 1890s, 18 x 30", 7' 4" h. (ILLUS. top next page)... **1,500**

Oak Hall Tree with Pierced Panels - M.M.

Ornately Spindled Oak Hall Tree - M.M.

Hall tree, Victorian Golden Oak style, oak, a large serpentine scroll-carved crestrail on the flaring cornice above a dentil-carved band & a turned spindle rail above a large square beveled mirror flanked by side panels w/a shell carving over three tall slender spindles above another turned spindle rail over a row of five vasiform scroll-carved splats, mounted w/six cast-brass hooks, open shaped arms flanking the rectangular seat over a single long drawer w/stamped brass pulls, turned tapering front legs w/knob feet joined to square back legs w/square stretchers, a side base half-round rail for the wooden drip pan, upper support arm missing, refinished, ca. 1890s, 16 x 44", 7' 10" h. (ILLUS.) **2,400**

Scrolling Pierced Oak Hall Tree - M.M.

Hall tree, Victorian Golden Oak style, oak, the ornate upper section w/a high peaked & scroll-carved center crest & outscrolled carved ears above serpentine pierced sides enclosing a round beveled mirror & above a pierced & scroll-carved splat above a row of slender turned spindles, flat side stiles, mounted w/four ornate cast-brass double coat hooks, shaped open arms on flat S-scroll arm supports above the lift seat over a deep well, flat serpentine front legs & serpentine apron, refinished, ca. 1900, 20 x 30", 7' h. (ILLUS.) **1,500**

Oak Hall Tree with Oval Mirror - M.M.

Hall tree, Victorian Golden Oak style, oak, the wide oval top frame w/a high arched & scroll-carved crest & four cast-brass coat hooks enclosing a large oval beveled mirror above a wide shaped back panel centered by a V-form leafy scroll-carved panel above the flat serpentine arms on S-form flat arm supports flanking the lift seat over a deep apron w/scalloped base, flat S-scroll front legs, refinished, ca. 1900, 18 x 30", 7' h. (ILLUS. previous page) **1,400**

Mirrored Oak Hall Tree with Slats - M.M.

Hall tree, Victorian Golden Oak style, quarter-sawn oak, a broken-scroll crest rail w/a band of carved scrolls above double flat side stiles flanking a large diamond-form beveled mirror above a tall panel of seven flat slats, flat open arms on square arm supports flanking the wide lift seat, cabriole front legs w/scroll feet, ca. 1900, 17 x 28", 7' h. (ILLUS.) **1,250**

Hall tree, Victorian Golden Oak style, quarter-sawn oak, a wide arched crestrail w/ornate leafy scroll carving centered by an oval medallion & flanked by wide sides w/rounded scroll-carved tops all enclosing a large rectangular beveled mirror w/a gently arched top & flanked by four cast-brass double hooks, a wide lower back panel w/applied scroll carving & a serpentine bottom edge flanked by heavy serpentine arms w/scroll hand grips & leaf-carved incurved arm supports flanking the wide rectangular seat over a group of four scroll-carved drawers, scroll-carved front feet, original finish, ca. 1890s, 22 x 46", 7' 6" h. (ILLUS. top right) **4,000**

Very Large Ornate Oak Hall Tree - M.M.

Fancy Gothic Revival Hall Tree - M.M.

Hall tree, Victorian Gothic Revival style, chestnut, a high arched, scroll-carved & pierced crestrail on a molded arched rail over two arched oblong cutouts flanked by corner drops & mounted w/iron hooks above an arched center mirror flanked by ornate scroll-carved & C-form cut-out sides mounted w/further hooks over an ornately cut-out panel above a center small white marble shelf w/curved front above a conforming small drawer flanked by round wood rings above long slender serpentine support brackets on the tall base section w/scroll-cut sides & fancy shaped cutouts over a molded base w/two round side rings enclosing cast-iron drip pans, refinished, ca. 1860, 16 x 44", 7' h. (ILLUS. previous page) **1,600**

Rare Gothic Revival Hall Tree - N.O.

Hall tree, Victorian Gothic Revival style, mahogany, the tall paneled back topped by a projecting trefoil-pierced hood surmounted by crockets & over a curved panel above a central Gothic arch beveled mirror flanked by Gothic arch-carved panels above a central lift-top bench seat flanked by open arms & further Gothic arch-carved panels, fitted overall w/curved metal coat hooks & angled metal brackets to support umbrellas, probably England, late 19th c., 18 x 46", 8' 4" h. (ILLUS.)...................................... **1,380**

Hall tree, Victorian Renaissance Revival style, walnut, a small arched top cornice w/a fleur-de-lis-carved center crest over a pierce-carved arched panel above the scroll-cut wide oval framework w/narrow pierced leafy scroll-carved curved panels framing an oval mirror within a raised

molded frame, mounted w/seven coat pegs, raised above a small white marble rectangular shelf over a small drawer w/leaf-carved pulls flanked by open side rings & raised on slender ring-turned columns, the oblong base platform fitted at the sides w/round cast-iron drip pans, ca. 1870, 16 x 36", 7' h. (ILLUS. below) **1,400**

Slender Pierce-carved Hall Tree - M.M.

Slender Renaissance Hall Tree - M.M.

Hall tree, Victorian Renaissance Revival style, walnut & burl walnut, a tall central crest w/a carved shell atop an arched molding & cornice raised above canted side cornices w/scallop-cut crests over raised burl panels across the top & down the sides of the framework mounted w/six coat pegs & centering a rounded rectangular mirror, a waisted lower section w/a raised burl panel above a rectangular white marble shelf over a small burl-paneled drawer flanked by C-form supports at the sides & raised on slender ring-turned supports above the oblong platform base w/rectangular cast-iron drip pans, refinished, ca. 1875, 15 x 30", 7' 4" h. (ILLUS. previous page).................... **1,200**

High-crested Walnut Hall Tree - CP

Hall tree, Victorian Renaissance Revival style, walnut & burl walnut, an ornate high crestrail w/a fan-carved peak over a blocked center panel flanked by long pierced scrolls on a molded cornice centered by a large oval burl panel above a long rectangular burl panel above long columnar drops w/pointed drop finials flanking the framework enclosing a tall rectangular mirror above pierced scroll-cut lower brackets w/roundels above a burl panel & rounded side rings above the rectangular white marble top w/rounded corners over a small paneled drawer w/burl panels supported on turned & tapering knob-and-rod-turned supports to deep rounded base side panels holding the cast-iron drip pans, fitted w/six iron hooks, ca. 1875 (ILLUS.) **1,950**

Renaissance Hall Tree with Lady's Head - M.M.

Hall tree, Victorian Renaissance Revival style, walnut & burl walnut, the high top w/a molded, arched crestrail over a flaring molded cornice over angled side panels & blocks centered by an oval medallion w/classical relief carving of a woman's head, flaring side cornices above wide shaped sides w/narrow burl panels & mounted w/six brass hooks above a rectangular red marble top over a long narrow burl-paneled drawer above an arched & burl-paneled support, curled flat side supports & a shaped thick base platform fitted at the sides w/cast-iron drip pans, ca. 1870s, 17 x 48", 8' h. (ILLUS.) **3,500**

Hall tree, Victorian Renaissance Revival style, walnut & burl walnut, the high broken-scroll crestrail by a large projecting crest w/carved scrolls & leaves above raised burl panels & roundels over a narrow molding over the tall rectangular mirror w/rounded top flanked by narrow burl panels & slender ring-turned freestanding side columns mounted w/turned wood pegs above C-form side support loops centered by a narrow vertical burl panel over a wide rectangular white marble shelf above a narrow burl panel drawer raised on scroll-carved supports flanked by arched base brackets over round base rings enclosing the cast-metal drip pans, ca. 1870s, refinished, 20 x 50", 8' 2" h. (ILLUS. top next page)... **3,500**

Very Large Renaissance Hall Tree - M.M.

Arch-topped Renaissance Hall Tree - M.M.

Hall tree, Victorian Renaissance Revival
style, walnut & burl walnut, the wide
arched molded crestrail w/a pierced &
scroll-carved crest above narrow raised
burl panels over a deep flaring & stepped
cornice above the tall rectangular mirror
w/notched top corners, shaped scroll-
carved sides w/narrow raised burl panels
fitted w/six coat pegs, C-form side brackets above the white marble top w/con-
cave side & notched front above a long
burl-paneled drawer flanked by round
iron drip pans on the deep platform base,
refinished, ca. 1870s, 16 x 48", 8' 2" h.
(ILLUS.).. **3,600**

Victorian Rococo Walnut Hall Tree - M.M.

Hall tree, Victorian Rococo style, walnut, a
wide rounded molded frame w/grape-
carved crest w/finial & eight wooden pegs
encloses large round mirror above flat
side stiles & a scroll-carved center splat
above the white marble serpentine shelf
above a carved serpentine apron supported on cabriole front legs & the flat
back stiles, serpentine base platform
w/round drip pans at each end, second
half 19th c., 16 x 42", 7' h. (ILLUS.) **1,800**

Rococo Hall Tree with Swan Heads - M.M.

Hall tree, Victorian Rococo style, walnut, the
wide shield-form top frame composed of
flat C- and S-scrolls mounted w/coat pegs
above a small oval mirror raised on a center splat w/a cut-out heart-shaped top
curving down to figural swan's neck-
carved side rails w/pegs & continuing
down to a wide flat vasiform back behind
a tall rectangular open framework composed of slender bobbin-turned rails
above the rectangular base fitted w/a rectangular metal drip pan, original dark
finish, ca. 1860, 12 x 28", 6' 6" h. (ILLUS.) **650**

HIGHBOYS & LOWBOYS

Highboys

Cherry "Bonnet-top" Highboy - BR

Queen Anne "bonnet-top" highboy, cherry, two-part construction: the top section w/swan's-neck pediment w/three urn finials above a row of three drawers, the center one fan-carved, above four long graduated lipped & dovetailed drawers; the base w/a long narrow drawer above a row of three drawers, the center one fancarved, a scalloped skirt above cabriole legs ending in pad feet, original batwing brass pulls & keyhole escutcheons, horizontal backboards, original handwrought nails, America, 18th c., old refinishing, feet & legs repaired w/possible replacements, one finial w/repaired tip, 22 x 38 1/2", 6' 1/2" h. (ILLUS.) **$9,350**

Queen Anne "bonnet-top" highboy, walnut, two-part construction: the upper section w/a broken-scroll crest centered by an urn & flame finial w/matching corner finials above a pair of small drawers flanking a deep fan-carved drawer above a stack of three long graduated drawers; the lower section w/a mid-molding above a long drawer over a row of three drawers, the center one fan-carved, the scalloped apron fitted w/two long acorn drops, cabriole legs ending in pad feet, glued splits & pieced restoration, later finials, 18th c., 22 x 42", 7' 4 1/4" h. (ILLUS. top right column) **14,375**

Queen Anne "bonnet-top" highboy, walnut & walnut flame veneer, mortised, two-part construction: the upper section w/a broken-scroll pediment centered by an urn- and spiral-turned finial on a platform w/matching corner finials above a frieze centered by a deep shell-carved drawer over a pair of banded drawers over three

long graduated drawers; the lower section w/a mid-molding over a long narrow banded drawer above a row of three drawers over a serpentine apron centered by a carved shell, finely shaped cabriole legs ending in pad feet, America, 18th c., mellow refinishing & thin coat of old varnish, replaced brasses, lower shell an old addition, backboards of upper case are replacements, pieced restorations to case & old alterations to aprons & bonnet, 20 1/2 x 42", 7' h. (ILLUS. bottom) **17,250**

Rare American Queen Anne Highboy - G

Veneered Queen Anne Highboy - G

Queen Anne "Flat-top" Highboy - BR

Queen Anne "flat-top" highboy, maple w/fancy crotch-figure walnut drawer fronts, dovetailed, two-part construction: the rectangular top w/a cove-molded cornice above two drawers over three long, graduated dovetailed & band-inlaid drawers; the lower section w/a long narrow drawer above a row of three band-inlaid drawers, the scalloped apron above cabriole legs ending in pad feet, original brass pulls & escutcheons, original iron locks throughout, chamfered & lap-jointed vertical backboards, Boston area, 1730-60, backboards w/some added nails, several drawer runners flipped, old refinishing, 23 x 40", 5' 7" h. (ILLUS. left).................. **16,500**

Lowboys

Queen Anne Fruitwood Lowboy - N.O.

Queen Anne lowboy, fruitwood, the rectangular top w/molded edges overhanging a case w/a shallow drawer flanked by deep drawers all above the deeply arched apron, on straight cabriole legs ending in pad feet, Europe, mid-18th c., 21 x 34", 27 1/2" h. (ILLUS.) **2,530**

ICE BOXES

Fancy Oak Ice Box with Worn Finish - M.M.

Simple Early Oak Ice Box - M.M.

Early 20th century, oak, the upright case w/a rectangular top over two long rectangular three-panel doors w/original nickelplate hardware, flat molded base, paneled sides, refinished, ca. 1910, 20 x 24", 40" h. (ILLUS.) **$400**

Victorian Golden Oak style, rectangular top w/a deep flaring cornice above a long rectangular scroll-carved panel over a pair of paneled scroll-carved doors over the scalloped apron & block feet, paneled sides, original heavy brass hardware, zinc-lined w/wire shelves, old worn finish, ca. 1890s, 20 x 28", 40" h., as is (ILLUS.).. **450**

LOVE SEATS, SOFAS & SETTEES

Louis Philippe "Sleigh-form" Daybed - N.O.

Daybed, Louis Philippe style, mahogany, a sleigh-bed form w/solid outscrolled head- and foot boards joined by deep rails & flat legs w/ormolu mounts, France, second quarter 19th c., 44 1/2 x 77", 40" h. (ILLUS. left) **$920**

Daybed, Louis XVI-Style, polychromed wood & cane, the matching head- and footboards w/rolled crestrails above wide caned panels flanked by baluster-turned columns on blocks above the baluster-turned legs, joined by molded side rails, France, early 20th c., 34 x 80", 34" h. (ILLUS. below) **920**

Louis XVI-Style Caned & Polychromed Daybed - N.O.

Louis XVI-Style Polychromed Wood Daybed - N.O.

Daybed, Louis XVI-Style, polychromed wood, the matching head- and footboard w/arched crests flanked by small pineapple finials over currently velvet-uphol- stered panels, joined by molded polychrome rails, France, late 19th c., 32 x 75", 35" h. (ILLUS.) **2,530**

Rare Louis XV Beechwood Duchesse - N.O.

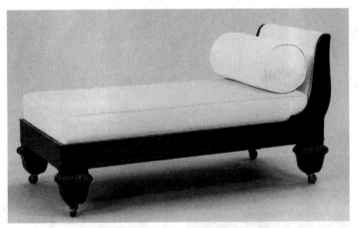

Fine American Classical Mahogany Meridienne - N.O.

Duchesse, Louis XV style, carved beech-wood, one end w/an arched upholstered back enclosed by a serpentine carved frame flanked by padded open arms & raised above the very long upholstered seat w/a molded serpentine seatrail, raised on six cabriole legs ending in peg feet, signed "H. Amand" (Henri Amand, master in 1749), France, mid-18th c., 64" l., 35" h. (ILLUS. top photo) **2,530**

Meridienne, Classical style, rosewood-banded mahogany, an upright uphol-stered end w/heavy S-scroll uprights above the long rectangular upholstered seat on the deep crotch-veneered apron w/rosewood crossbanding, raised on heavy tapering squared & carved feet on casters, America, first quarter 19th c., 23 x 48", 26" h. (ILLUS. second from top)... **2,530**

Meridienne, Victorian Rococo substyle, carved & laminated rosewood, the high arched back w/an ornate floral-carved crest atop undulating rails that taper down to form one arm & a partial back

section above the long upholstered seat w/a rounded end & serpentine molded seatrails, raised on demi-cabriole legs, the "Rosalie without Grapes" pattern by John H. Belter, New York City, ca. 1855, 36 1/2" h. (ILLUS. below)........................ **3,910**

Rare Belter Rosewood Meridienne - N.O.

Fine Neoclassical Recamier - N.O.

Recamier, Neoclassical style, mahogany, one end w/a high out-scrolled upholstered arm supported by a scroll-and-fan-carved front rail, a matching lower arm at the opposite end, joined by a tapering serpentine crestrail on the upholstered back, upholstered seat on the reeded seatrail, raised on outswept cornucopia-carved legs w/paw feet on casters, Europe, second quarter 19th c., 25 x 69", 38" h. (ILLUS. at left) **1,955**

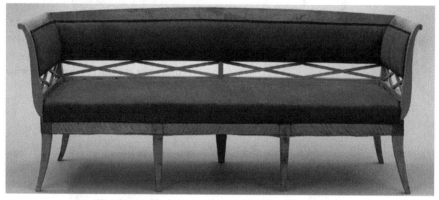

Handsome Biedermeier Blonde Fruitwood Settee - N.O.

Settee, Biedermeier style, blonde fruitwood, a long narrow crestrail flanked by even outscrolled arms all above upholstered panels over slender pierced diamond-form stretchers, the long upholstered seat on square tapering & slightly splayed legs, Europe, second quarter 19th c., 28 x 81", 34" h. (ILLUS.).............. **3,220**

Attractive English George III-Style Settee - N.O.

Settee, George III-Style, mahogany, triple-chairback style, the crestrail composed of three turned bars above three sets of rails flanking narrow horizontal diamonds over smaller vertical diamond lattice-pierced panels, the curved back stiles joined to serpentine open arms on baluster-turned arm supports flanking the long upholstered seat, three baluster- and ring-turned front legs ending in peg feet, England, late 19th c., 24 x 54", 37" h. (ILLUS.)... **690**

Fine Chippendale-Style Settee - N.O.

Settee, Chippendale-Style, mahogany, a double-chairback style w/two serpentine crestrails above scrolling foliate-pierced & carved splats, shaped open arms w/scrolled hand grips on incurved arm supports above the long upholstered seat, three front cabriole legs w/leaf-carved knees & ending in claw-and-ball feet, late 19th c., 20 x 45", 40 1/2" h. (ILLUS.) **748**

Louis XVI-Style Gilt Gesso Settee - BR

Settee, Louis XVI-Style, gilt gesso, the flat crestrail w/wreath & blossom decoration continuing down to form the padded open arms flanking the upholstered back panel, acanthus leaf & scroll arm supports, upholstered seat, France, early 20th c., upholstery badly damaged, chips & separations, 26 x 41", 57" l. (ILLUS.).............. **1,320**

Louis XVI-Style Giltwood Settee - N.O.

Settee, Louis XVI-Style, giltwood, the long oval upholstered back enclosed by a narrow carved frame topped by a small carved musical crest, shaped & padded open arms on incurved arm supports above the long upholstered seat, the flat molded two-part seatrail w/central carved panels, raised on tapering fluted front legs w/peg feet, France, early 20th c., 59 1/2" l., 37" h. (ILLUS.) **978**

Chinese Carved Softwood Settee - N.O.

Settee, Oriental, carved softwood, the long back centered by a raised carved crest w/scrolled ends enclosing a narrow carved panel above a row of three carved rectangular panels flanked by solid carved-panel arms, the deep seat above a deep apron fitted w/a row of three drawers above two small drawers flanking two larger drawers, square stile legs w/horse-hoof feet, China, 19th c., 23 x 43 1/2", 39" h. (ILLUS.) **690**

Settees, Classical style, mahogany, the serpentine back w/a leaf-carved center crest flanked by long scrolled serpentine rails

One of Two Classical Settees - N.O.

arched down to frame the long tufted upholstered back, the long serpentine upholstered seat w/a deep conforming apron w/scroll-carved corner returns, on casters, America, second quarter 19th c., 27 x 61", 38" h., pr. (ILLUS. of one) **2,300**

Settle, country-style, oak, the back composed of four paneled frames, shaped arms w/scrolled ends on turned arm supports & corner legs, long upholstered seat on a box-stretcher base w/heavy block corner legs, old mellow finish, probably England, late 17th - early 18th c., later upholstery, replaced frame under seat, other minor supports added, surface w/chips, scratches, wear & separations, made originally for rope webbing, 26 x 40", 72" l. (ILLUS. below) **2,750**

English Country-style Oak Settle - BR

Sofa in the Baroque Style - BR

Sofa, Baroque style, the long flat upholstered crestrail & back flanked by downswept upholstered arms flanking the cushion seat, cross-stretcher base w/eight serpentine & scrolled legs & stretchers, 18th c. verdure tapestry upholstery adapted to sofa using borders & figures of trees & birds, back panel w/two large birds in woodland setting, cushion w/matching borders, Dutch or German, 18th c., extensive losses, separation & repairs to tapestry, fading, pest damage, 34 x 45", 78" l. (ILLUS.)............................. **5,500**

Sofa, Biedermeier style, walnut, a narrow flat ormolu-mounted crestrail above the upholstered back flanked by outswept scroll arms within a conforming frame above the long upholstered seat on an ormolu-mounted flat seatrail, outswept flattened scroll legs, Europe, first half 19th c., 26 x 80 1/2", 35 1/2" h. (ILLUS. below) **1,725**

Early Biedermeier Walnut Sofa - N.O.

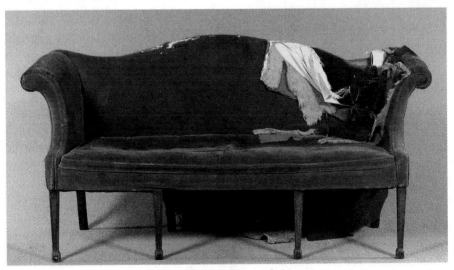

Chippendale Camel-back Sofa - BR

Chippendale-Style Upholstered Sofa - BR

American Classical Carved Mahogany Sofa - G

Sofa, Chippendale style, mahogany, the long arched camel back above out-scrolled arms above the over-upholstered seat, on square tapered front legs w/spade feet, front legs w/diamond inlay w/shield-shaped tops, England or America, probably early 19th c., upholstery badly torn, 30 x 37", 72" l. (ILLUS. bottom of previous page) **2,310**

Sofa, Chippendale-Style, the long arched & upholstered camel back flanked by out-scrolled upholstered arms above the long over-upholstered seat, raised on four square bead-trimmed front legs joined by serpentine box stretchers, England, late 19th c., the base w/several loose joints, side stretchers repaired, upholstery from several sources w/scattered losses & worn areas, 39 x 40", 8' 1" l. (ILLUS. top photo) **4,400**

Sofa, Classical, mahogany & mahogany veneer, a raised flat central crestrail flanked by scrolling leaf-carved rails above the low upholstered back flanked by rolled upholstered arms w/bolsters supported by leaf-carved scroll supports, the long upholstered seat on a narrow rounded seatrail centered by a

leaf-carved reserve & raised on carved cornucopia legs ending in paw feet, old red velvet upholstery, ca. 1830, 23 x 95", 36" h. (ILLUS. above) **1,955**

Classical Sofa with Unusual Crest - N.O.

Sofa, Classical, mahogany, the broken-scroll serpentine crestrail centered by a raised spindled crest over narrow bands above the upholstered back, the out-scrolled deep arms w/reeded rosette-tipped supports continuing down to the seatrail w/leaf-carved blocks above the carved paw feet w/wing-carved returns, refinished, ca. 1840s, later upholstery, 29 x 80", 36" h. (ILLUS.) **1,200**

Fine Quality Classical Sofa - M.M.

Sofa, Classical, mahogany, the flat bar-topped crestrail w/leaf-carved scroll ends raised above serpentine rails above the long upholstered back flanked by high in-curved padded arms w/bolsters & cornu-copia-carved arm supports, the flat se-atrail centered by a rectangular stenciled panel, raised on heavy paw front legs w/long fruit-carved returns, on casters, original polished finish, ca. 1830s, 30 x 76", 34" h. (ILLUS.) **3,600**

continuing down to form the flat seatrail, on carved paw feet w/large wing-carved returns, on casters, refinished, new upholstery, ca. 1840s, 24 x 72", 36" h. (ILLUS. left) **950**

Classical Transitional Style Sofa - M.M.

Sofa, Classical Transitional style, mahoga-ny, the triple-serpentine crestrail cen-tered by three leaf-and-fruit-carved crests above the low upholstered back, heavy outscrolled arms w/scroll-carved supports on scroll-carved blocks flanking the deep ogee seatrail, on scroll-carved front feet, original finish, ca. 1850, 28 x 80", 34" h. (ILLUS. above) **800**

Scroll-armed Classical Sofa - M.M.

Sofa, Classical, mahogany, the long flat cre-strail flanked by leaf-carved scrolls over the upholstered back flanked by high scrolled arms w/leaf-carved supports

Late Victorian Classical Revival Sofa - N.O.

Louis XV-Style Provincial Fruitwood Sofa - N.O.

Sofa, Classical Revival style, mahogany, a flat central back crestrail flanked by long S-scroll rails above the long upholstered back flanked by cylindrical arms on forked curved front arm supports flanking bolsters & a long cushion seat, the flat molded seatrail raised on carved winged-paw front legs, America, late 19th c., 27 x 78", 33" h. (ILLUS. bottom of previous page) **1,265**

Sofa, Louis XV-Style Provincial type, fruitwood, the long upholstered back w/a serpentine floral-carved crestrail continuing to form the back frame flanked by padded open arms w/incurved arm supports, the long upholstered seat w/a serpentine three-section floral-carved seatrail raised on four cabriole front legs ending in scroll feet on pegs, France, late 19th c., 25 x 74", 42" h. (ILLUS. top photo) **2,760**

Sofa, Louis XVI-Style, giltwood, a narrow beaded & rope-carved oval frame en-closing the upholstered back flanked by open padded arms on rope-carved in-curved supports above the upholstered seat, a guilloche-carved seatrail raised on four stop-fluted tapering front legs on peg feet, France, ca. 1900, 26 1/2 x 68", 39 1/2" h. (ILLUS. below) **2,530**

Fine Louis-XVI-Style Sofa - N.O.

Large Louis XVI-Style Sofa - BR

High-backed Regency-Style Fruitwood Sofa - N.O.

Sofa, Louis XVI-Style, hardwood w/carved & gilt decoration, the long rounded crestrail & arms w/ribbon, scroll & acanthus leaf decoration, padded open arms w/incurved arm supports above the over-upholstered seat on a narrow carved seatrail, on tapered & fluted front legs, France, probably early 20th c., traces of old gilt & white paint, upholstery worn & soiled, missing cushion, 32 x 38", 75" l. (ILLUS. bottom of previous page) **825**

Sofa, Regency-Style, fruitwood, the triple-arched crestrail over the high upholstered seat flanked by downswept closed arms above the long over-upholstered seat, four tall scrolled front legs joined by high serpentine front stretchers & lower serpentine H-stretchers, England, late 19th c., 75" l., 40 1/2" h. (ILLUS. top photo).................................. **3,220**

Sofa, Victorian Gothic Revival style, mahogany, the molded & carved crestrail centered by a raised panel w/Gothic style carved designs flanked by rounded stiles carved w/Gothic arches, the low upholstered back flanked by rounded upholstered arms w/wide paneled & Gothic arch-carved front supports continuing down to from the paneled block feet, the flat paneled seatrail w/carved Gothic details, New York City, ca. 1840-60, 28 x 84", 40 1/2" h................................... **4,780**

Sofa, Victorian Knole-type, upholstered, the high flat back upholstered w/three pads flanked by high flat upholstered arms all topped by large pairs of bamboo-turned corner finials, a three-cushion seat over a deep upholstered fringe-trimmed apron, England, late 19th c., 31 x 67", 35" h. (ILLUS. below)................ **2,530**

English Knole-style Upholstered Sofa - N.O.

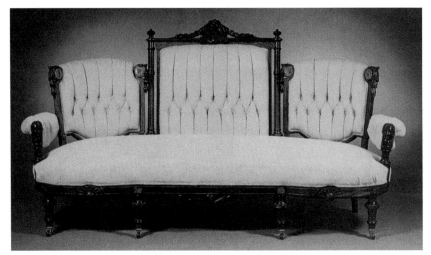

Fine Renaissance Revival Rosewood Sofa - N.O.

Sofa, Victorian Renaissance Revival style, carved rosewood, a triple-panel back, the high upholstered central panel w/pierced scroll-carved crestrail flanked by slender colonettes w/turned finials flanked by the lower upholstered side panels each w/side stiles topped by gilt-bronze inset disks w/Classical heads & trimmed w/leaf carving, the padded open arms w/arm supports carved w/figural maiden heads, long oval upholstered seat w/a conforming seatrail w/fan-carved trim & a scroll-carved center drop, on four turned & tapering front trumpet legs on casters, ca. 1870s, New York City, 31 x 82", 43" h. (ILLUS.)... **1,150**

Sofa, Victorian Rococo style, carved & laminated rosewood, a long triple-back style w/high chair-back corseted sections at each end enclosed by wide ornate pierced scroll-carved arching rails, rails continuing down & up around the lower arched central section w/a similarly carved crestrail, the side rails continuing down over the half-length closed upholstered arms w/incurved arm supports, the long serpentine-fronted seat w/a conforming seatrail carved w/scrolls & a central floral reserve, on demi-cabriole front legs on casters, attributed to John Henry Belter, New York City, ca. 1855, 31 x 88", 41" h. (ILLUS. below).............. **16,675**

Triple-back Belter-style Sofa - N.O.

Belter Victorian Rococo Sofa - BR

Sofa, Victorian Rococo style, carved & laminated rosewood, finely carved crestrail w/scrolls topped by floral-carved crests above the upholstered back, crestrail continuing down to form closed arms w/incurved arm supports, the long upholstered seat w/serpentine seatrail centered by carved florals, demi-cabriole front legs on casters, probably "Rosalie" patt., John H. Belter, New York City, ca. 1855, one rear leg repaired, 34 x 42", 5' 2" l. (ILLUS.) **3,740**

Sofa, Victorian Rococo style, carved & laminated rosewood, the high serpentine crestrail pierce-carved overall w/leafy scrolls & grape clusters & centered by a high flower- and shell-carved crest, the crestrail curving down around the high tufted upholstered back to the closed rolled arms w/incurved arm supports, a long upholstered seat w/serpentine molded seatrail centered by a scroll-carved cluster, on demi-cabriole legs on casters, the "Hawkins" pattern by J. & J.W. Meeks, New York City, ca. 1855, 40 x 65", 50" h. (ILLUS. below) .. **10,925**

Rare Meeks "Hawkins" Pattern Rosewood Sofa - N.O.

Meeks "Stanton Hall" Rococo Sofa - N.O.

Sofa, Victorian Rococo style, carved & laminated rosewood, the long serpentine crestrail pierce-carved w/ornate scrolls & centering a higher central section w/a gadrooned rail centered by a large shell- and flower-carved crest, the crestrail curving down & enclosing the tufted upholstered back above closed scrolled arms w/incurved arm supports, a long upholstered seat w/a serpentine molded seatrail centered by a carved reserve, on demi-cabriole front legs on casters, the "Stanton Hall" pattern by J.& J.W. Meeks, New York City, ca. 1855, 27 x 66", 4' 1/2" h. (ILLUS.) . **5,520**

Sofa, Victorian Rococo style, carved & laminated rosewood, the ornate pierce-carved crestrail centered by a higher peaked section w/a flower cluster flanked by beaded bands, the lower curved side rails curving down around to the closed upholstered arms w/incurved arm supports, long serpentine-front seat w/a conforming seatrail carved w/a center blossom, demi-cabriole front legs on casters, "Stanton Hall" patt. by Meeks of New York City, ca. 1855, original finish, 36 x 66", 4' h. (ILLUS. below) **5,500**

Fine "Stanton Hall" Rococo Sofa - M.M.

Meeks "Henry Ford" Pattern Sofa - FO

Sofa, Victorian Rococo style, carved & laminated rosewood, the ornate arched & pierce-carved crestrail centered by a pointed rose crest over gadrooned bands & open scrolls continuing to curved pierce-carved corners continuing down & flanking the high tufted upholstered back, closed arms w/incurved carved arm supports continuing to the serpentine finger-carved seatrail & demi-cabriole front legs on casters, "Henry Ford" patt. attributed to J. & J.W. Meeks, ca. 1855 (ILLUS.).... **13,200**

Sofa, Victorian Rococo style, carved & laminated rosewood, the very long serpentine crest topped by a very ornate high pierced & carved crestrail, the highest central arch w/an ornate flower-carved crest above a long C-scroll & fruit-and-leaf carving, continuous S- and C-scrolls across the top w/high flower-carved crests at each end & continuing down & around to the half-length upholstered arms w/incurved arm supports, the long serpentine-front seat w/conforming seatrail carved w/ornate leafy scrolls & a central flower cluster, demi-cabriole front legs on casters, attributed to John H. Belter, New York City, similar to the "Tuthill King" patt., ca. 1855, 30 x 89 1/2", 4' 1 1/2" h. (ILLUS. below) **49,450**

Fabulous Belter Rococo Sofa - N.O.

Sofa Attributed to Alexander Roux - M.M.

Sofa, Victorian Rococo style, carved & laminated rosewood, the wide serpentine crestrail centered by a high arched & pierced crest w/asymmetrical scrolls & continuing to rounded corner crests w/matching carving, closed upholstered arms w/incurved arm supports, serpentine-fronted seat w/a conforming seatrail carved w/ornate scrolls, demi-cabriole front legs on casters, attributed to Alexander Roux, New York City, ca. 1850s, original finish, later upholstery, 32 x 72", 44" h. (ILLUS.) **5,000**

Sofa, Victorian Rococo style, carved & laminated rosewood, triple-back style w/two high arched upholstered panels flanking a lower arched panel, all joined by an arched serpentine crestrail w/three carved flower basket crests over an overall pierce-carved design of grapevines continuing around to form the padded arms w/carved arm supports, the long upholstered seat w/a serpentine seatrail carved w/three floral clusters, on leaf-carved cabriole legs on casters, seven-layer lamination, America, ca. 1850, 25 x 69", 42 1/4" h. (ILLUS. below) **8,050**

Rococo Rosewood Triple-back Sofa - N.O.

Double-chairback Rococo Sofa - M.M.

Sofa, Victorian Rococo style, carved mahogany, double-chairback style, each end of the back w/a large oval upholstered medallion topped by a wide arched pierced scroll-carved crest, a low upholstered center section w/a simple serpentine crestrail, open padded arms on incurved arm supports, long serpentine-fronted seat on a simple molded conforming seatrail, demi-cabriole front legs on casters, ca. 1860, refinished, later upholstery, 28 x 64", 36" h. (ILLUS.) **2,000**

Double-chairback Rococo Sofa - M.M.

Sofa, Victorian Rococo style, mahogany, double-chair-back style w/tufted upholstery, two high balloon-shaped end sections w/high pierced & scroll-carved crestrails continuing down to the low arched center section w/another high pierced & scroll-carved crest, low upholstered half-arms on incurved arm supports, long serpentine seat w/simple conforming seatrail, on demi-cabriole front legs on casters, old refinish, older upholstery, ca. 1850s, 26 x 62", 40" h. (ILLUS.) **1,600**

Triple-back Rosewood Rococo Sofa - M.M.

Sofa, Victorian Rococo style, carved rosewood, triple-back style, a large oblong upholstered center section w/an arched rose-carved crest & scroll-carved side brackets to the flanking oval upholstered sections w/smaller rose-carved crests, padded open arms on incurved arm supports, long serpentine seat above a deep conforming seatrail carved w/leafy scrolls, on demi-cabriole front legs, original dark finish, later upholstery, ca. 1860, 26 x 66", 42" h. (ILLUS.) **2,500**

Rococo "Inverted Heart"-back Sofa - M.M.

Sofa, Victorian Rococo style, walnut, a central "inverted heart" tufted upholstered back panel w/a grape-carved crest flanked by high rounded side rails w/further grape carving, rolled upholstered closed arms w/S-scroll carved arm supports, long seat w/serpentine front above a conforming seatrail centered by a carved grape cluster, on demi-cabriole front legs, original finish, ca. 1865, 28 x 72", 40" h. (ILLUS. previous page).... **1,800**

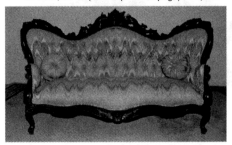

Nicely Carved Walnut Rococo Sofa - M.M.

Sofa, Victorian Rococo style, walnut, the double serpentine crestrail centered by a pierced scrolled leaf & fruit-carved crest w/similar carving on the rounded rail corners continuing down to the closed upholstered arms w/incurved arm supports, a tufted upholstered back & long serpentine seat w/a conforming seatrail carved in the center w/a blossom & leaves, on demi-cabriole front legs w/peg feet, refinished, new upholstery, ca. 1860, 28 x 70", 38" h. (ILLUS.) **2,500**

Sofa, Victorian Rococo style, walnut, the long pierce-carved crestrail centered by a pair of facing birds w/nest of eggs & flowering leafy scrolls curving down around the tufted upholstered back, open padded arms w/incurved arm supports, long upholstered seat w/a deep scalloped scroll-carved apron on semi-cabriole front legs, refinished, ca. 1850s, 31 x 71", 41" h. (ILLUS. below)................. **3,500**

Rococo Sofa with Carved Birds - M.M.

Country-style Wagon Seat - G

Wagon seat, country-style, hardwood w/old mustard paint over an earlier red, two-part back w/double arched slats, tapered round legs w/large round post at center between the two old woven splint seats w/grey paint, turned arms, wafer finials, 19th c., old gesso filler in some areas, 6 x 33 1/2", 29" h. (ILLUS.) **431**

MIRRORS

Lovely Adams-Style Gesso Mirror - M.M.

Adams-Style wall mirror, gilt gesso & paint, a large narrow oval frame topped by a high arched pierced crest composed of ornate leafy scrolls, draperies & side floral swags centered at the peak by a small oval h.p. medallion of a woman in classical dress, original finish, minor damage, late 19th - early 20th c., 30" w., 4' 10" h. (ILLUS.).. **$650**

Dutch Baroque-Style Wall Mirror - N.O.

Baroque-Style wall mirror, ebonized wood & cut glass, the wide rectangular frame composed of delicately pierce-carved corner squares & small center rails above mirrored panels & joined by a carved inner border framing the beveled mirror plate, Holland, late 19th c., 27 x 30 1/2" (ILLUS. below left) **546**

American Chippendale Wall Mirror - G

Chippendale wall mirror, mahogany & mahogany veneer, the high domed & scroll-carved crest w/incurved ears above a rectangular molding enclosing the mirror plate, an ornate scroll-carved bottom drop crest, a short ear tip replaced, minor veneer restorations, mellow refinishing, 18th c., 22 x 44 1/2" (ILLUS.)................... **2,760**

Mahogany Veneer Wall Mirror - BR

Chippendale-Style wall mirror, dark & light mahogany veneer w/string inlay border, the arched scroll-carved crestrail centered by a pierced circle w/applied bird, arched scroll-carved base drop, England, probably 19th c., old refinishing, one scroll at side bottom replaced, separations & veneer losses, 37" h. (ILLUS. previous page) **605**

Chippendale-Style Scrolled Mirror - G

Chippendale-Style wall mirror, mahogany, the high arched & boldly scroll-carved crestrail centered by an oval cut-out w/a gilt feather cluster, a rectangular molding around the mirror plate, a boldly scroll-carved bottom drop crest, America or England, late 19th c., 18 x 30 1/4" (ILLUS.) **230**

Classical Mirror-on-Stand - N.O.

Classical mirror-on-stand, mahogany & mahogany veneer, a long horizontal wide rectangular frame enclosing a mirror & tilting between tall tapering spiral-twist carved uprights w/tiny carved pineapple finials, supported on a trestle base w/reeded outswept legs ending in paw feet joined by a spiral-twist stretcher centered by a leaf-carved block, possibly from the workshop of Duncan Phyfe, New York City, ca. 1820, 35" l., 30 1/2" h. (ILLUS.) **920**

Classical overmantel mirror, carved giltwood, a long rectangular frame composed of half-round columns w/ring-turned segments alternating w/sections of delicate scrolls, corner blocks w/molded rosettes, America, second quarter 19th c., scattered minor gilt loss, 38 1/4 x 58" (ILLUS. below) **1,840**

Classical Giltwood Overmantel Mirror - N.O.

Small Classical Giltwood Mirror - N.O.

Classical wall mirror, carved giltwood, a rectangular frame w/the outer band joining large ornate scroll-carved corners enclosing an inner frame composed of half-round ring-and-baluster-turned columns & corner blocks w/rosettes, America, second quarter 19th c., 19 x 32" (ILLUS.) **748**

Classical wall mirror, molded gilt plaster, a large rectangular frame molded in each corner w/a large fleur-de-lis joined along the sides by half-round molded columns

Large Gilt Plaster Classical Mirror - M.M.

enclosing a three-part mirror, original finish, mirrors resilvered, ca. 1830s, 20 x 44" (ILLUS. above)........................... **1,800**

Classical-Style buffet mirror, gilt gesso, wide rectangular frame divided into three panels, half-column rails w/florette corner bosses, America, late 19th or early 20th c., traces of original gilding, losses & chips, replaced mirrors, 27 x 64" (ILLUS. below)... **605**

Classical-Style Buffet Mirror - BR

Giltwood and Mahogany Federal Mirrors - M.M.

Federal wall mirror, carved mahogany, the flat pediment w/rounded corners & a bowed center above a band of small spheres over a scroll-inlaid frieze band flanked by corner blocks w/metal rosettes, bold ring-and-baluster-turned & leaf-carved side columns flanking a small rectangular mirror above a tall rectangular mirror, bottom corner blocks w/metal rosettes joined by a ring-and-knob-turned half-column, the upper mirror probably replacing original reverse-painted pane, ca. 1830s, 20 x 40" (ILLUS. above right with small giltwood mirror) **450**

Federal wall mirror, giltwood, the flat flaring pediment w/blocked ends above a band of small suspended spheres above the narrow reeded frame enclosing an upper rectangular reverse-painted glass panel w/a scene of a fisherman above the rectangular mirror, small corner blocks at the bottom, ca. 1830, 18 x 32" (ILLUS. above left w/carved mahogany mirror) **350**

Federal wall mirror, mahogany veneer, the flat coved crestrail w/blocked ends above a rectangular reverse-painted glass panel brightly decorated w/a landscape scene of children playing, the sides mounted w/slender half-rounded reeded colonettes supported on lower corner blocks, original mirror plate, original paper label on the back reads "Thomas Natt & Son, Looking Glass Manufacturers, Print sellers...Philadelphia," worn silvering on mirror, slight flaking on top panel, ca. 1820, 21 x 40 1/4" (ILLUS. at right) **1,955**

Labeled American Federal Mirror - G

20th Century Federal-Style Mirror - G

Federal-Style wall mirror, gilt gesso, a
round molded frame set w/small spher-
ules & topped by ornate pierced scrolls
centered by a large spread-winged eagle, a leaf-carved base drop, America,
first half 20th c., minor gesso damage,
24 x 41" (ILLUS.)... **920**

Georgian-Style Cheval Mirror - N.O.

Georgian-Style cheval mirror, mahogany,
a tall rectangular molded frame enclosing
a mirror & swiveling between tall tapering
reeded columnar uprights w/turned tapering finials & leaf-carved base sections, above a trestle base w/reeded outswept legs on casters joined by a slender

turned stretcher, England, ca. 1900,
36 1/2" w., 5' 9" h. (ILLUS. below left)....... **2,300**

Louis XV-Style Overmantel Mirror - N.O.

Louis XV-Style overmantel mirror, giltwood, the tall arched rectangular egg-
and-dart-carved frame topped by ornate
pierced scrolls & a large shell crest, beveled mirror plate, France, late 19th c.,
36 1/2" w., 5' 1 1/2" h. (ILLUS.)................ **1,725**

Provincial Louis XVI Wall Mirror - N.O.

Louis XVI Provincial wall mirror, carved giltwood, the high arched crestrail carved w/an open oval ribbon ring over further ribbons & ornate carved flowers centered by a beaded heart reserve, the rectangular narrow frame sides carved w/flower sprigs, southern France, late 18th c., 34" w., 5' h. (ILLUS. previous page).......... **1,955**

Ornate Louis XVI-Style Tall Mirror - N.O.

Louis XVI-Style overmantel mirror, painted & parcel-gilt beechwood, the wide flat rectangular frame carved at the top center w/a large leaf & wreath swag w/ribbons below a coronet, long arrow gilt-lined side panels topped by gilt-carved floral clusters & carved at the bottom w/gilt flower-filled urns, ropetwist inner gilt molding around the mirror, France, ca. 1900, 46" w., 6' 4" h. (ILLUS.)... **3,680**

Napoleon III Mirror with Urn Finial - N.O.

Napoleon III overmantel mirror, giltwood, the tall narrow rectangular molded frame topped by an urn finial flanked by laurel leaf garlands & oak leaf sprays, France, third quarter 19th c., 46 x 78 3/4" (ILLUS. below left)... **920**

Early French Neoclassical Mirror - N.O.

Neoclassical wall mirror, rosewood-inlaid hardwood, a wide flat rectangular frame w/each corner inlaid w/delicate rosewood scrolls, later mirror plate, France, first quarter 19th c., 13 3/4 x 17" (ILLUS.) **920**

Neoclassical-Style entryway mirror, gilt & black-painted gesso, the high, widely flaring & stepped cornice w/blocked corners decorated w/a top leaf band over dentil & gadrooned bands, a blocked frieze band in black w/ornate gilt leafy scrolls in the central panel & rosette side blocks, the sides molded in full-relief w/large grotesque male caryatids on tapering bell-flower-trimmed pilasters, the wide blocked & stepped-out base w/a black band trimmed w/a molded gilt cartouche & scrolls, late 19th c., very large floor-size **1,750**

Queen Anne Wall Mirror - G

Queen Anne wall mirror, mahogany veneer, low arched & scroll-carved crestrail above the tall rectangular mirror within raised molded liner, flat bottom molding, backboards appear to be original, probably England, 18th c., old refinishing, veneer restoration, small veneer chip, 15 1/2 x 27 1/4" (ILLUS. previous page) **374**

Early Queen Anne Wall Mirror - N.O.

Queen Anne wall mirror, walnut, the scrolling cut-out crest above the arched mirror incised at the top w/a star, narrow molded frame w/wide serpentine base drop, early 18th c., 16 3/4" w., 39" h. (ILLUS.) ... **2,070**

Scroll Mirror with Urn Carving - G

Queen Anne-Style wall mirror, mahogany veneer, arched crest w/fine scrolling & incised & gilded urn & foliage decoration, molded liner & gilded gesso inner liner around the rectangular mirror, scroll-carved base apron, America or England, 19th c., refinished, minor ear restorations, staining on back, 21 1/2 x 40" (ILLUS. below left) **690**

Pair of Queen Anne-Style Mirrors - BR

Queen Anne-Style wall mirrors, in the Chinese style, top panels w/raised & painted decoration of figures in exterior landscapes, base w/gilt bellflower decoration on red ground, probably England, late 18th or early 19th c., losses to silvering, back w/additional battens for support, painted surface w/extensive losses & separations, 20 x 56", pr. (ILLUS.) **14,300**

Italian Rococo-Style Wall Mirror - N.O.

Rococo-Style wall mirrors, giltwood, the inner molded oval frame enclosed w/a wide border of serpentine pierce-carved leafy scrolls & blossoms w/a large shell-carved top crest & small shell-carved bottom drop crest, beveled oval mirror, Italy, 19th c., 35" w., 4' 11" h., pr. (ILLUS. of one previous page)... **2,530**

20th Century Italian Wall Mirror - N.O.

Fancy Engraved Venetian Mirror - N.O.

Rococo-Style wall mirrors, giltwood, the wide flat frame composed of slender leaf-carved giltwood rails enclosing long mirror panels & framing the rectangular mirror plate, Italy, early 20th c., 43 x 57", pr. (ILLUS. of one bottom left column **2,530**

Venetian wall mirror, engraved glass, the high arched & pierced crestrail decorated w/delicate engraved scrolls & blossoms, the wide arched glass frame w/further delicate engraving enclosing the conforming mirror plate, Italy, 19th c., 28 1/2 x 55 1/2" (ILLUS. bottom left column).. **1,610**

Finely Engraved Venetian Mirror - N.O.

Venetian wall mirror, giltwood, the wide cartouche-shaped frame set w/curved engraved mirror panels enclosing the shaped mirror finely engraved w/large figure of classical maiden, Italy, mid-18th c., 23 1/4 x 31 1/2" (ILLUS.)..................... **3,910**

Victorian Baroque Revival wall mirror, carved mahogany, wide rectangular frame ornately carved w/overall leafy scrolls & birds, the top crest centered by a large relief-carved cherub head w/wings, attributed to Horner of New York City, original finish, ca. 1880s, 32 x 42" (ILLUS. top photo next page)...... **2,400**

Ornate Baroque Revival Mirror - M.M.

Ornate Baroque Revival Mirror - M.M.

Victorian Baroque Revival wall mirror, gilt gesso, a wide flaring flat pediment centered by a scalloped & arched crest decorated w/ornate scrolls & flanked by pointed shell-molded corner ears, the cornice, wide sides & blocked base band molded overall w/ornate scrolling baroque designs, original surface, late 19th - early 20th c., 20" w., 36" h. (ILLUS.).......... **400**

American Beaux Arts Mirror - N.O.

Victorian Beaux Arts style mirror, carved giltwood, a wide flat frame w/a narrow outer molded band of leaves & vines, the inner frame w/a molded pebbled finish, a thin inner beaded band around the mirror, America, late 19th c., 39 3/4 x 50" (ILLUS.).. **460**

Victorian country-style cheval mirror, walnut, a tall narrow rectangular mirror frame topped w/corner brackets composed of carved pyramidal blocks centering carved fruit & leaves, enclosing a beveled mirror swiveling between tall ropetwist-turned side supports raised on arched & outswept legs w/brass claw & glass ball mounts joined by ropetwist stretcher & brackets, late 19th c., refinished, 14 x 26", 6' h. (ILLUS. top of next page)... **750**

Tall Victorian Eastlake Pier Mirror - M.M.

Victorian Eastlake style pier mirror, walnut, a high arched fan-carved crest centered by a roundel & flanked by notched corner blocks above slender half-round turned columns flanking the tall rectangular mirror above a small white marble shelf supported on a spindled apron & brackets above a large line-incised base panel, refinished, ca. 1885, 12 x 28", 9' 8" h. (ILLUS.) **1,600**

Late Victorian Cheval Mirror - N.O.

Golden Oak Mirror with Fancy Crest - M.M.

Victorian Golden Oak style hall mirror,
quarter-sawn oak, the wide rectangular
frame w/an ornate pierce-carved crest
w/facing griffins flanking an oval cartouche, the sides mounted w/four metal coat
hooks, enclosing a beveled mirror,
refinished, ca. 1900, 30 x 48" (ILLUS.
bottom previous page) **900**

Ornate Gilt Oval Mirror - BR

Renaissance Revival Pier Mirror - N.O.

Victorian Renaissance Revival pier mir-
ror, gilt-incised & ebony-trimmed walnut
burl, the narrow coved crestrail w/blocked
corners above the very tall slightly arched
mirror plate flanked by narrow sides
carved w/gilt-incised panels w/burl, the
base w/a rectangular panel centered by a
raised burl panel above a small rounded
projecting shelf & flanked by blocked corners w/further burl, America, ca. 1875,
37" w., 9' 4" h. (ILLUS.).............................. **1,265**

Victorian Renaissance Revival wall mir-
ror, gilt gesso, oval beveled mirror in ornate frame, the pediment w/the figure of
an angel & oval coat of arms flanked by
scrolls over wreath swags, sides mounted w/gilt composition full-figured images
of American Indians, one w/club, one
w/bow & arrow, extensive vine, descend-
ing bellflower & grape decoration
throughout, America, late 19th c., restoration to base, scattered repairs & regild-
ing, angel possibly missing sword,
55 x 58" (ILLUS.top right column) **4,620**

Rare American Overmantel Mirror - N.O.

Victorian Rococo style overmantel mir-
ror, carved giltwood, the large arched
frame molded w/a narrow band of small
cabochons, the crestrail further decorated w/leafy scrolls centered by a leaf
crest, delicate pierced scrolls at the bottom corners, America, second half 19th
c., 68" w., 8' 4" h. (ILLUS.) **10,925**

Victorian Rococo style overmantel mir-
ror, carved giltwood, the wide & deep
rectangular frame molded & carved overall w/scrolls & leaf bands, second half
19th c., 65" w., 7' 7" h. (ILLUS. top left
photo next page) **2,530**

Giltwood Victorian Rococo Overmantel Mirror - N.O.

Fine Victorian Overmantel Mirror - N.O.

Fancy Victorian Overmantel Mirror - N.O.

Victorian Rococo style overmantel mirror, giltwood, a long molded oval frame w/a pierce-carved crest of leafy scrolls centering a cartouche finial, large pierced & scroll-carved base brackets, burnished highlights, America, mid-19th c., 56 x 65" (ILLUS. above) **2,760**

Victorian Rococo style overmantel mirror, giltwood, the tall arched ropetwist-carved frame topped by a large pierced scroll-carved crest flanked by floral swags, the bottom corners w/large ornate carved scrolls, France, third quarter 19th c., 46" w., 6' 9" h. (ILLUS. top right column)................ **1,610**

Victorian Rococo style pier mirror, giltwood, a tall narrow molded oval frame topped by a very high openwork leafy scroll crest centering a large cartouche, ornate leafy scroll base brackets above the half-round scalloped white marble shelf raised on an ornate scroll-carved bracket centered by a full-figure cherub, mid-19th c., 15 x 34", 9' h. (ILLUS. top of next page) **11,213**

Rare Victorian Rococo Pier Mirror - N.O.

Very Tall Rococo Pier Mirror - N.O.

Victorian Rococo style pier mirror, gilt-wood, a very tall narrow rectangular mirror w/an arched top below the high arched & scroll-carved crestrail w/center scroll cartouche & incurved corners, tall narrow gadroon-molded sides above the half-round serpentine white marble bottom shelf on a conforming base of pierced leafy scrolls & scroll front feet, surface now painted w/gold paint, America, mid-19th c., 16 x 45", 10' 7" h. (ILLUS.) **1,495**

Victorian Rococo Shaving Mirror - M.M.

Victorian Rococo style shaving mirror, walnut & burl walnut, table model, a wide rectangular flat frame w/incised leaf bands mounted w/an ornate pierced scroll-carved crest centering a flower basket all enclosing a mirror swiveling between scroll-carved uprights w/scroll brackets above the serpentine platform w/projecting corners & burl veneer above a pair of narrow serpentine burl veneer drawers w/original brass knobs, original finish, mid-19th c., 12 x 20", 28" h. (ILLUS.) **1,200**

Victorian Rococo style wall mirror, gilt gesso, the wide cove-molded rectangular frame decorated at each corner w/ornate leafy scroll brackets & swags, thin inner beaded band around the two-part mirror, original finish, mid-19th c., 20 x 48" **950**

Victorian Rococo style wall mirror, walnut, a molded oval frame topped by a high arched pierced crest w/leafy scrolls, original dark finish, mid-19th c., 22 x 42" **400**

Victorian Rococo Wall Mirror - BR

Victorian Rococo style wall mirrors, gilt gesso, rectangular wide frame w/elaborate scroll decoration & shell, bead & scroll corner work, Europe, 19th c., gilding restored, several chips & losses, replaced mirrors, 47 1/4 x 57 1/2", pr. (ILLUS. of one) **3,190**

PARLOR SUITES

Unique Late Victorian Parlor Suite - G.K.

Art Nouveau: love seat & side chair; carved mahogany, each w/an ornately carved heavy framework, the back crest carved w/standing figure of an Art Nouveau maiden w/long flowing hair & wearing a diaphanous gown surrounded by swirling vines & flowers which continue down the sides of the frame, a wide upholstered seat over a heavy seatrail w/further serpentine carving & thick, short stylized cabriole front legs on casters, by the Karpen Brothers, Chicago, ca. 1890-1900, original finish, side chair 25" w., 43" h., 2 pcs. **$4,600**

Late Victorian: settee & two armchairs; walnut, unique novelty style, the settee w/a double-chair back w/each section composed of a flat upholstered crestrail over a narrow row of stick-and-ball spindles on the rail over a double-lobed upholstered panel centered by a small splat, the backrail curving around to form

the arms over another double-lobed upholstered panel, rounded overstuffed upholstered seat w/projecting blocked sections, molded conforming seatrail w/four baluster- and ring-turned front legs, matching armchairs, ca. 1890, settee 66" l., 32" h. (ILLUS. above) **1,000**

Late Victorian Rococo Revival: sofa & armchair; carved mahogany, each w/a heavy ornately carved crestrail centered by a large carved shell flanked by figural putti & flanked by further scroll carving curving down to the rolled upholstered closed arms w/bold C-scroll-carved arm supports, tufted upholstered backs & wide over-upholstered seats w/a wide serpentine seatrail carved w/a long central shell flanked by scrolls, boldly carved short cabriole front legs, original dark finish, Karpen Brothers, Chicago, ca. 1890s, ca. 1920s upholstery, sofa 70" l., 42" h., 2 pcs. (ILLUS. below) **6,500**

Karpen Rococo Revival Parlor Suite - G.K.

Louis XVI-Style Settee from Suite - N.O.

Louis XVI-Style: settee & four side chairs; painted beechwood, the settee w/a long oval upholstered back panel within a narrow molded frame flanked by padded open arms & raised above the long upholstered seat, a narrow bowed seatrail ending in blocks above turned tapering & fluted front legs, France, ca. 1900, each piece 34 1/2" h., the set (ILLUS. of settee, above) . **3,450**

Victorian Eastlake substyle: sofa & armchair; walnut, each w/an angular stepped & pierced crestrail, the sofa w/two tufted upholstered panels separated by a scroll-carved panel w/short turned spindles, padded arms on angular blocked arm supports, gently curved seatrail w/angu-

lar short center drop, ring-turned tapering front legs on casters, original finish, ca. 1880s, sofa 60" l., 2 pcs. (ILLUS. below) .. **1,000**

Victorian Renaissance Revival: sofa & armchair; upholstered walnut, each crestrail w/a pedimented crest over a round wreath enclosing a carved female face, oblong upholstered back panels flanked by block- and spindle-turned stiles above upholstered arms w/carved incurved arm supports, deep rounded cushion seat w/wide seatrail centered by carved top, tapering ring-turned front legs on casters, original dark finish, early 20th c. upholstery, ca. 1875, sofa 80" l., 45" h., 2 pcs. **2,900**

Victorian Eastlake Sofa & Armchair - G.K.

Fine Renaissance Sofa from a Set - M.M.

Victorian Renaissance Revival: sofa, two armchairs & one side chair; walnut & burl walnut, the sofa w/a triple-panel back, the vertical oval center upholstered panel within a block-carved frame topped by a high crown-form crest centered by a medallion carved in the image of a woman's head, the horizontal oval side panels in simple oval frames w/peaked scroll-carved crests, curved padded open arms w/the supports carved in the form of women's heads, long seat w/short carved drops, raised on tapering trumpet legs on casters, the chairs w/matching backs, attributed to John Jelliff, Newark, New Jersey, ca. 1870, original finish, later upholstery, sofa 72" l., the set (ILLUS. of sofa, above) **7,500**

Victorian Renaissance Revival: sofa & two side chairs; walnut & burl walnut, the sofa w/a long gently curved tufted upholstery back centered by a gently arched central crestrail w/a peaked finial over an oval medallion carved in the image of a female face over narrow burl panels & urn-form corner finials, closed upholstered half-arms w/arm supports carved as female heads, serpentine seatrail trimmed w/oval burl panels, on tapering disk-and-baluster-turned front legs on casters, the matching chairs w/similar carved crests & incurved back stiles, refinished, newer upholstery, ca. 1870s, attributed to John Jelliff, Newark, New Jersey, sofa 70" l., the set (ILLUS. below) **2,500**

Renaissance Revival Suite with Carved Heads - M.M.

Top Quality Renaissance Revival Suite - M.M.

Victorian Renaissance Revival: walnut; sofa, armchair & two side chairs, the sofa w/a long tufted upholstery back within a rectangular frame w/rounded top corners, the crestrail centered by a scroll-and ribbon-carved crest, open padded arms on incurved arm supports, long oblong upholstered seat w/a carved apron raised on turned trumpet front legs on casters, the chairs w/matching frames, refinished, new brocade upholstery, attributed to Alexander Roux, New York City, ca. 1870, sofa 70" l., the set (ILLUS.)... **6,000**

Victorian Rococo: armchair & two side chairs; carved & laminated rosewood, each back w/a central upholstered figure-8 panel enclosed w/a wide framed ornately pierced & carved w/leafy scrolls, the arched top of the sofa w/a scroll-and-floral-carved crest w/a bird, armchair w/padded open arms, wide rounded seats w/serpentine seatrails w/ornate carved scrolls, demi-cabriole front legs on casters, "Bird" patt. but bird only found on armchair crest, unknown maker, ca. 1855, refinished, armchair 46" h., the set (ILLUS. below) **18,000**

Chairs in the Rare "Bird" Pattern - M.M.

Belter "Fountain Elms" Chairs - M.M.

Victorian Rococo: armchair & two side chairs; carved & laminated rosewood, the armchair w/a high arched back w/an oval tufted upholstery panel enclosed by a wide pierced scroll-carved frame w/an arched floral-carved crestrail, serpentine wood open arms on incurved arm supports above the wide upholstered seat, serpentine seatrail w/ornate scroll carving, demi-cabriole front legs on casters, matching side chairs, "Fountain Elms" patt. by John H. Belter, New York City, ca. 1855, refinished, new upholstery, armchair 46" h., the set (ILLUS., above)................................. **28,000**

Victorian Rococo: sofa, armchair & four side chairs; carved rosewood, the sofa w/a long upholstered serpentine back w/a narrow conforming crestrail w/low carved crests, padded & closed upholstered arms w/incurved arm supports, long serpentine seatrail w/a carved trim above four demi-cabriole front legs, matching chairs w/shaped balloon backs, original finish, ca. 1860, sofa 66" l., the set (ILLUS. below, top photo) **2,300**

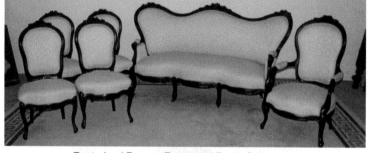

Restrained Rococo Rosewood Parlor Suite - M.M.

Restrained Rosewood Rococo Suite - M.M.

Rococo Sofa from Rare Baudouine Set - M.M.

Victorian Rococo: sofa, armchair & two side chairs; carved rosewood, the sofa w/an oval medallion w/tufted upholstery in the center below a floral-carved crest & curved crestrails continuing down to form the closed half-arms w/incurved arm supports, long serpentine seat w/a serpentine floral-carved seatrail on four demi-cabriole front legs on casters, the matching chairs w/shaped balloon backs, possibly original needlepoint upholstery, ca. 1865, original finish, sofa 72" l., the set (ILLUS. bottom of previous page) **3,000**

Victorian Rococo: sofa, armchair & two side chairs; pierce-carved rosewood, the triple-back sofa w/tall upholstered balloon-shaped end backs enclosed by wide very ornate serpentine arched frames w/pierce-carved scrolls & a top crest carved in the form of a female face, the lower arched upholstered center back section w/a similar carved crestrail &

arched crest, padded open arms w/incurved arm supports, the long upholstered seat w/a serpentine scroll-carved seatrail on demi-cabriole legs, the chairs w/balloon backs w/frames matching the end sections of the sofa, Charles Baudouine, New York City, ca. 1855, sofa 80" l., the set (ILLUS. of sofa above) **30,000**

Victorian Rococo: sofa, two armchairs & four side chairs; carved mahogany, the triple-back sofa w/two large round tufted upholstered panels flanking a lower oval tufted upholstered panel, all framed & joined by ornately pierce-carved scrolls & flowers, shaped padded open arms on scrolled arm supports above the long upholstered seat, a serpentine scroll-carved seatrail centered by a C-scroll & blossoms reserve, on S-scroll front legs ending in paw feet on casters, Eastern United States, ca. 1860, sofa 85" l., 50" h., the set (ILLUS. of sofa below) **4,140**

Ornate Victorian Rococo Sofa from Large Set - N.O.

SCREENS

Victorian Tole Bathing Screen - N.O.

Bathing screen, painted tole, a large upright convex rectangular panel w/rounded top corners raised on arched bar legs w/a center drop bar, the black ground painted in images of large stems of golden lilies & green leafy stems, England, late 19th c., 25" w., 4' 2 1/2" h. (ILLUS.) **$431**

Firescreen, Louis Philippe style, mahogany, a large rectangular tapestry panel within a molded square w/a gently arched crestrail carved w/a gadroon band & arched, pierced & scroll-carved crest, raised on outswept leaf-carved legs ending in paw feet on casters, France, mid-19th c., 25 x 42 1/2" (ILLUS. below left).... **1,035**

Louis XV-Style Brass Firescreen - N.O.

Firescreen, Louis XV-Style, gilt-brass & wire mesh, the ornate brass frame w/an arched scroll-cast crestrail topped by a loop handle, the scroll-cast upright sides joined by a scrolled bottom rail & raised on flaring arched legs, the mesh screen centered by an applied gilt-brass mount showing a young seated girl flanked by scrolls, France, late 19th c., 29 x 30 1/2" (ILLUS.) . **1,495**

Painted Louis XVI-Style Firescreen - M.M.

Firescreen, Louis XVI-Style, painted wood & gesso, the narrow upright rectangular frame w/an arched & scroll-carved crestrail centered by a cartouche above a solid panel h.p. in images of large colorful flowers in pink & white against a blue ground, on arched trestle legs, ca. 1920s, 20" w., 28" h. (ILLUS.)...................... **250**

French Louis Philippe Firescreen - N.O.

Renaissance Revival Firescreen - M.M.

Firescreen, Victorian Renaissance Revival style, walnut, the slender bobbin-and-rod-turned top rail surmounted by a large arched scroll-carved crest centered by a carved lion mask, the rail raised atop slender ring-turned columnar supports w/urn finials enclosing a square frame w/line-incised decoration & blocked corners around the machine-made tapestry panel, a lower ring- and rod-turned stretcher joining the high arched flattened outswept legs, refinished, ca. 1875, 30" w., overall 46" h. (ILLUS.).. **950**

Firescreen, Victorian Rococo style, carved rosewood, a large serpentine-sided frame carved w/a shell at the center top & bottom enclosing the original figural needlepoint panel, raised on scroll-carved supports joined by a scroll-carved stretcher & raised on four cabriole legs, original finish, mid-19th c., 12 x 24", 46" h. (ILLUS. top right column).. **750**

Firescreen, Victorian Rococo style, carved walnut, a plain flattened rectangular frame w/a high arched & scroll-carved

crest rail centered by a pair of facing figural putti flanking a central shield, a serpentine & scroll-carved rail at the bottom, supported between slender ring-, rod- and knob-turned columns w/urn finials raised on arched & scroll-carved trestle feet, Philadelphia, mid-19th c., original finish, missing textile panel, 14 x 28", 42" h. (ILLUS. bottom photo) **2,200**

Fine Victorian Rococo Firescreen - M.M.

Ornate Carved Rococo Firescreen - M.M.

Rococo Firescreen with Needlework - M.M.

Firescreen, Victorian Rococo style, pierce-carved rosewood, a narrow square molding enclosing the original needlepoint panel all framed by ornate scrolls, raised on ring-and-knob-turned supports joined by an upper scroll-carved stretcher & a simple baluster-and-knob-turned lower stretcher between the scrolled shoe feet, original finish, ca. 1850s, 24" w., overall 44" h. (ILLUS.) **1,000**

Fine Carved Japanese Screen - N.O.

Folding screen, two-fold, carved hardwood, lacquer, ivory & mother-of-pearl, the central rectangular panels w/floral-painted red lacquer border bands around black panels w/high-relief decoration in ivory & mother-of-pear of birds among flowering branches, the dark outer frame ornately carved w/Oriental motifs including birds & leaves in the crests & further designs in the rectangular bottom panels, Japan, late 19th c., overall 68" w., 6' 4" h. (ILLUS. below left) ... **4,830**

Ornate Scenic Indian Folding Screen - N.O.

Folding screen, three-fold, inlaid carved hardwood, a wide central panel flanked by narrower side panels, each w/a large central panel, the center panel depicting a scene of the Taj Mahal done in mother-of-pearl, abalone, lacquer & paint, the side panels continuing this scene, the frame of each panel w/a pierced, arched & ornately carved crestrail w/image of exotic flying bird among flowering vines, the solid bottom panels w/similar carving, India, late 19th c., overall 73" w., 6' 1 1/2" h. (ILLUS.) **748**

Painted Louis XVI-Style Screen - N.O.

Folding screen, three-fold, Louis XVI-Style, parcel-gilt & polychrome beechwood, the three arched panels painted w/a colorful continuous landscape scene w/romantic figures in 18th c. costume, France, late 19th c., 74 1/2" w., 5' 7 1/2" h. (ILLUS. previous page)............ **2,760**

Screen with Romantic Scene - N.O.

Folding screen, three-fold, Rococo-Style, the three tall arched panels painted w/a continuous colorful Italian landscape featuring figures & a large ruined Roman arch, England, early 20th c., 5' 7 1/2" h. (ILLUS.) . **1,093**

Folding screen, four-fold, decorated red lacquer, the panels decorated w/a continuous landscape scene of Chinese figures in gardens w/houses & temples in the foreground & upper background, done in gilt & polychrome paints, the reverse decorated w/colorful Oriental plants & animals, China, ca. 1900, overall 64" w., 5' 11 1/4" h. (ILLUS. below)......................... **1,150**

Ornate Chinese Lacquer Screen - N.O.

Folding screen, four-fold, hand-painted & lithographically printed wood, the front in the "Uccelli" patt. depicting a continuous scene of multi-paned windows looking out to slender trees filled w/colorful birds, faux panels at the bottom, all on a creamy white ground, the reverse painted in a monochromatic "Libreria" patt. depicting library shelves filled w/leatherbound books, trophies & knickknacks, raised on casters, designed by Piero Fornasetti, Italy, ca. 1950s, each panel 19 5/8" w., overall 6' 4 1/2" h.................... **6,463**

Ornately Painted Louis XIV-Style Screen - N.O.

Folding screen, four-fold, Louis XIV-Style, painted & gilt-trimmed continuous design of colorful exotic birds, flowering vines & fruit-filled scrolls, on an antiqued gold ground, France, ca. 1900, 88" w., 6' 6" h. (ILLUS. bottom, previous page) **2,530**

Fine English Victorian Screen - N.O.

Folding screen, four-fold, mahogany & fabric, the simple mahogany framework enclosing two yellow damask panels in each section, the reverse w/claret damask panels, England, third quarter 19th c., overall 100" w., 6' h. (ILLUS.) **1,380**

Folding screen, four-fold, painted lacquer, each panel on the front w/a black lacquer ground, a tall upper panel in each panel painted w/a standing figure of a Japanese man or woman, a small square bottom panel decorated w/image of a bird perched among pine boughs, the whole framework painted in gold w/a chain-like design, the reverse in red lacquer w/decoration of Oriental foliage, Japan, ca. 1900, overall 72" w., 5' 3" h. (ILLUS. below) **978**

Lacquer Screen with Figural Panels - N.O.

Folding screen, four-fold, Restauration style, painted paper, the four wide panels slightly arched at the top & painted w/an overall Chinoiserie design of figural vignettes enclosed by gilt scrolls, all on a black ground, France, first quarter 19th c., each panel 22 1/2" w., overall 4' 3 3/4" h. (ILLUS. below) **1,840**

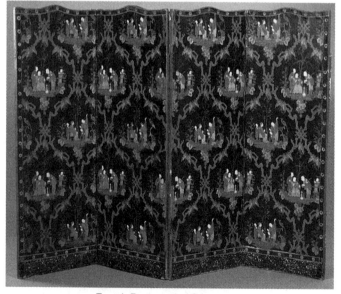

French Restauration Screen - N.O.

verse right in vermilion calligraphy, scattered minor losses in the lacquer, China, overall 144" w., 8' h. (ILLUS. below) **2,070**

Six-fold Chinese Lacquer Screen - N.O.

Folding screen, six-fold, decorated black lacquer, the front w/narrow black lacquer panels decorated w/a continuous scene of small applied mother-of-pearl Chinese figures w/a temple & trees, enclosed in narrow gilt banding, the reverse w/overall gilt foliate decoration, China, ca. 1900, overall 108" w., 8' h. (ILLUS.) **1,495**

Ornate Chinese Coromandel Screen - N.O.

Fine Tooled Leather Spanish Screen - N.O.

Folding screen, six-fold, tooled leather, each panel decorated w/richly tooled floral leather on one side & images of birds among flowering branches on the other, Spain, second quarter 19th c., overall 126" w., 6' 6" h. (ILLUS.) **1,150**

Folding screen, eight-fold, Coromandel-type, in the Ch'ien Lung taste, the primary facade decorated w/"Precious Objects" borders & "Boys at Play on a Mountain Lake" central scene, the reverse w/"Bamboo-and-Rocks" design, signed on the re-

Georgian Pole Screen with Sampler - N.O.

Pole screen, Georgian style, painted wood, a small square wood frame enclosing an alphabet sampler signed "Mary Nowne, Her work finished in the twelth (sic) year of her age. 1827," also w/fruit, butterflies, dogs & a verse, raised on a tall slender tapering & ring-turned pole above a tripod base w/a turned center drop & splayed cabriole legs ending in scroll feet, overall black paint, small holes in sampler, England, overall 4' 5 1/4" h. (ILLUS.) **748**

English Needlepoint Pole Screen - G

English Mahogany Pole Screen - N.O.

Pole screen, mahogany, the shield-shaped screen decorated w/floral découpage on a red ground, raised on a turned & foliate-carved standard above a tripod base w/cabriole legs ending in acanthus-carved feet, England, last quarter 18th c., 44" h. (ILLUS.) **518**

Pole screen, Victorian Rococo style, European walnut, rectangular scrolled frame holds needlepoint panel of spaniel lying on a pillow, small brass urn-shaped finial on top, spiral column on three scrolled cabriole legs decorated w/raised carved fruit, England, restorations to column & one leg, 4' 10" h. (ILLUS.) **1,265**

SECRETARIES

Early Biedermeier Secretary - M.M.

Biedermeier secrétaire à abattant, mahogany & mahogany veneer, the rectangular grey marble top w/rounded front corners on a deep ogee cornice above the wide rectangular fold-down writing surface opening to an interior fitted w/an arrangement of small drawers over a long narrow drawer, the lower case w/three long drawers w/bold crotch-grained veneer, original finish, Europe, ca. 1830s, 18 x 38", 5' 4" h. (ILLUS.) **$1,800**

Chippendale Mahogany Secretary - M.M.

Chippendale secretary, mahogany, two-part construction: the upper section w/a

broken-scroll pediment centered by a ball finial above a pair of arched mirrored doors w/ornate engraving opening to a large interior fitted w/numerous pigeonholes & small drawers; the lower section w/a fold-down slant top opening to an interior centered by a small square mirrored door flanked by small pigeonholes & drawers, the lower case w/a pair of drawers over two long drawers, molded back on bracket feet, old refinish, original oval brass pulls, late 18th c., Europe, possibly England, 26 x 46", 8' h. (ILLUS.) . **7,500**

Chippendale Secretary-Bookcase in Walnut - BR

Chippendale secretary-bookcase, walnut, two-part construction: the top w/molded & dovetailed cornice over two doors w/inlaid kite escutcheon, over two pull-out candle boards, built-up base molding, back w/four chamfered panels; the dovetailed base w/interior w/crotch-figure prospect door w/two dovetailed drawers behind each flanked by four dovetailed drawers, four cubbyholes above w/shaped moldings, fall board above four graduated, dovetailed & lipped drawers, hand-cut nails throughout, vertical pine backboards w/rose-head nails, America, both pieces (marriage) w/old refinishing, two cubbyhole moldings off, lock & hinges on fall board replaced, old replaced ogee bracket feet w/repairs & restorations, several backboards loose, 23 x 42", 7' 4" h. (ILLUS.) **2,420**

Chippendale Secretary-Bookcase - BR

Chippendale secretary-bookcase, walnut, two-part construction: the top w/two doors, each w/four chamfered panels, horizontal backboards; the base w/twelve stepped interior drawers below eight cubbyholes flanking prospect door, over four lipped & graduated dovetailed drawers, original dovetailed bracket feet & base w/vertical backboards & original rosehead nails, found in Georgia, replaced brass pulls & hinges, cornice missing one piece of molding, one door detached w/splintered hinge mounts, old refinishing, patches, separations & repair throughout, 24 x 39", 7' 4" h. (ILLUS.)....... **4,840**

Chippendale Revival secretary-book-case, mahogany & mahogany veneer, two-part breakfront-style: the upper section w/a tall stepped-out central section w/a pierced & scroll-carved broken-scroll pediment centered by a raised block on the flaring coved cornice above a single large glazed door w/ornate applied scrolling grillwork & opening to shelves above a narrow rectangular molded panel folding down to form the writing surface & ex-

pose the fitted interior, the lower sections each w/a scroll-pierced gallery on the coved cornice above a tall narrow glazed door w/applied scrolling grillwork & opening to shelves; the matching lower section w/a mid-molding above a pair of central doors w/serpentine scroll banding flanked by matching narrow side doors, deep molded flat base, original finish, ca. 1920s, 24 x 60", 7' 8" h. (ILLUS. below) ... **3,000**

Fine Chippendale Revival Secretary - M.M.

Classical Secretary with Scroll Feet - M.M.

Classical secretary-bookcase, mahogany & mahogany veneer, two-part construction: the upper section w/a rectangular top w/a wide flat flaring cornice above a pair of tall 6-pane glazed doors opening to shelves above two narrow drawers w/wooden knobs; the stepped-out lower section w/a fold-out writing surface above a plain long & slightly overhanging drawer above two long lower drawers w/wooden knobs flanked by long serpentine brackets w/heavy C-scroll front feet, short turned rear legs w/knob feet, refinished, ca. 1840, 21 x 40", 7' h. (ILLUS. previous page) **1,200**

Fancy Classical Secretary-Bookcase - M.M.

Simple Classical Secretary-Bookcase - M.M.

Classical secretary-bookcase, mahogany & mahogany veneer, two-part construction: the upper section w/a rectangular top w/a deep flaring ogee cornice w/rounded corners above a pair of two-pane glazed doors opening to shelves above a wide rectangular fold-down writing surface opening to an interior fitted w/numerous pigeonholes & small drawers; the stepped-out lower case w/three long graduated drawers w/original glass pulls, serpentine apron & bracket feet, original finish, ca. 1850, 20 x 42", 7' h. (ILLUS.) **2,000**

Classical secretary-bookcase, mahogany & mahogany veneer, two-part construction: the upper section w/a rectangular top w/a long serpentine & scroll-cut crestrail above the deep coved cornice over a pair of tall glazed doors w/scalloped arch tops opening to shelves; the lower section w/a thick fold-out writing surface opening to a row of small narrow drawers above a pair of paneled cupboard doors w/scalloped arch tops, scroll-cut bracket feet, original finish, ca. 1840, 22 x 44", 8' 2" h. (ILLUS. top right column) **2,500**

Ornate Colonial Revival Secretary - M.M.

Colonial Revival secretary, mahogany & mahogany veneer, two-part construction: the low top section w/a rectangular top above a pair of short rectangular glazed doors w/ornate applied scrolling grillwork & divided by a scroll-carved panel, a pair of small columns at each outside corner; the lower section w/a wide hinged slant top w/an inlaid design of a floral wreath w/plume suspended on a bow & opening to a fitted interior above a case w/three long serpentine drawers surrounded by bands of carved scrolls flanked by freestanding corner columns w/bronze capitals & bases, molded serpentine base on tall ogee feet, refinished, ca. 1900, 20 x 34", 5' 6" h. (ILLUS.) **1,800**

Rare Southern Federal Secretary - G

Federal secretary-bookcase, cherry, curly maple & mahogany veneer, two-part construction: the upper section w/a broken-scroll crest w/star-inlaid terminals & three turned urn finials above a coved cornice over a pair of tall Gothic arch-paneled cupboard doors opening to three adjustable shelves; the stepped-out lower section w/a fall-front oval-paneled drawer w/oval brasses opening to an interior fitted w/eight pigeonholes, eight small drawers w/bold curly maple facings & a center door w/variegated star inlay opening to hidden compartments, the lower case w/a pair of cupboard doors paneled to form a single large Gothic arch & flanked by small vertical panels w/a Gothic arch over a quatrefoil, short ring-turned legs w/peg feet, replaced backboard & finials, some pieced repairs, possibly from Kentucky, early 19th c., 22 3/4 x 44", overall 8' 9" h. (ILLUS.) **7,188**

Federal secretary-bookcase, cherry, two-part construction: the upper section w/a narrow upright cornice divided by three reeded blocks w/brass urn finials above a narrow molding above a pair of paneled cupboard doors w/wooden knobs opening to eleven shelves above a flat fold-down writing surface opening to two rows of small drawers above a row of pigeonholes; the projecting lower section w/three long reverse-graduated beaded drawers w/round brass pulls flanked by reeded stiles above the ring- and baluster-turned legs w/knob feet, minor restorations, wooden pulls replaced, attributed to Connecticut, late 18th - early 19th c., 20 1/2 x 42", overall 6' 6 3/4" h. (ILLUS. rop right column) **3,450**

Connecticut Federal Secretary - G

Inlaid Mahogany Secretary-Bookcase - BR

Federal secretary-bookcase, inlaid mahogany, two-part construction: shaped cornice w/three brass urn finials above two 8-pane doors w/through muntins, interior w/three drawers & seven cubbyholes; the base w/fold-out writing surface w/black string inlay above three graduated dovetailed & cockbeaded drawers, probably original brass pulls, tapered legs, pit-sawn drawer bottoms w/hand-wrought nails, old refinishing, drawer runners rebuilt, patches, repairs & separations in veneer, replaced felt writing surface, 22 x 41", 6' 4 1/4" h. (ILLUS. previous page) **3,740**

Federal Mahogany Secretary-Bookcase - BR

Federal Mahogany Secretary - G

Federal secretary-bookcase, mahogany & mahogany veneer, two-part construction: the upper section w/a rectangular top & narrow coved cornice above a pair of raised-panel doors opening to two shelves above a pair of drawers w/wooden knobs; the lower section w/a mid-molding above a fold-out writing surface above a long projecting drawer above two inset long drawers flanked by baluster- and ring-turned columns, flat apron w/blocked ends raised on ring- and baluster-turned legs w/peg feet, old finish, support pulls replaced, early 19th c., 20 x 38", 5' 1 1/4" h. (ILLUS.) **1,955**

Federal secretary-bookcase, mahogany, satinwood & mahogany veneers, two-part construction: the top w/broken-arch pediment w/turned ringed oval finials over two glazed 15-pane doors w/through muntins & central octagons, applied half-round quilted-diamond medial molding, two adjustable shelves; the base w/four dovetailed & cockbeaded drawers w/original wooden pulls & ivory inlaid shield escutcheons, the top drawer w/fall front, six interior dovetailed drawers & eight cubbyholes, reeded pilasters, turned feet, New England, first quarter 19th c., one shelf probably replaced, three broken glass panes, 23 1/2 x 44", 8' 11" h. (ILLUS.).................................... **10,450**

Federal-Style Secretary-Bookcase - BR

Federal-Style secretary-bookcase, inlaid mahogany, two-part construction: cornice w/urn finials & eagle pediment above three arched doors each side; the base w/three dovetailed & cockbeaded drawers w/brass pulls, French feet, probably Centennial, supports for fall board missing knobs, veneer chips & losses, surface worn w/scuffs & scratches, 19 x 37", 6' 3" h. (ILLUS.).......................... **1,540**

Fine Georgian Revival Secretary - M.M.

Victorian "Captain's" Secretary - M.M.

Georgian XRevival secretary-bookcase, walnut, oyster-grain walnut veneer & mahogany, one-piece construction, the rectangular top w/a high arched central coved cornice flanked by flat side cornices above a case w/a central high arched bi-fold door w/fine veneer opening to shelves & flanked by tall narrow matching doors opening to shelves, the stepped-out lower case w/a hinged fold-out writing surface above a case w/an arrangement of eight horizontal & vertical banded veneered drawers w/brass teardrop pulls, on simple cabriole legs w/pad feet, original finish, Europe, early 20th c., 16 x 28", 5' h. (ILLUS.) **850**

Late Victorian "captain's" secretary, mahogany, two-part construction: the upper section topped by a long rectangular beveled mirror within a frame w/a gently arched scroll-carved crestrail swiveling between serpentine uprights over a narrow rectangular shelf above open end compartments centered by a stack of two small drawers over a long scroll-carved oval panel; the lower section w/a wide lift-top desk opening to a well projecting over a pair of raised-panel doors, simple bracket feet on casters, original pulls, refinished, ca. 1895, 24 x 32", 6' h. (ILLUS. top right column) **1,500**

Queen Anne-Style Secretary - N.O.

Queen Anne-Style secretary-bookcase,
walnut, two-part construction: the upper
section w/a double-arch deep molded cornice above a pair of tall arched mirrored
cupboard doors; the lower section w/a
mid-molding above a hinged slant front
opening to a leather-lined writing surface,
storage well & various drawers & pigeonholes over a false drawer & another molded band above three long graduated lower
drawers, batwing brasses & keyhole escutcheons, molded base on bun feet, England, mid-18th century & later,
24 1/2 x 36", 7' h. (ILLUS. previous page) . **6,613**

Unique Aesthetic Secretary - M.M.

**Victorian Aesthetic Movement secretary-
bookcase,** walnut, unusual side-by-side
design, the top w/a three-section low
back rail w/line-incised scrolls separated
by upright narrow blocks each fronted by
a low open arched bracket on the long
rectangular top w/a wide deeply bowed
center section above a conforming case,
narrow decorative bands above the lower
case centered by the wide & tall bowed
center section w/a pair of sliding tambour
doors opening to reveal a desk w/storage
compartments above the kneehole opening, the flat side sections each w/a tall
glazed door opening to shelves above a
stepped-out scroll-incised drawer, paneled sides, ca. 1885, refinished, 24 x 54",
6' h. (ILLUS.) **2,400**

Very Fine Aesthetic Inlaid Secretary - M.M.

**Victorian Aesthetic Movement secretary-
bookcase,** walnut & inlaid burl walnut,
two-part construction: the upper section
w/a rectangular top fitted w/a tall ornate
front crestrail centered by a pointed leaf-
carved crest over a burl panel inlaid w/an
urn flanked by narrow vertical blocks
flanked by pierced side panels carved
w/stylized sunflowers below a dentil-
carved band, resting on the flaring cornice
above a pair of tall glazed doors opening
to shelves & decorated w/carved & incised
sunflowers at the top corners & flanked by
blocked & line-incised side moldings; the
slightly stepped-out lower section w/a
hinged slant-front door w/two recessed
burl panels each finely inlaid w/stylized
sunflowers & leaves & flanked by carved
side moldings, opening to a fitted interior
above a mid-molding over three long
graduated drawers w/line-incised banding
& centered by a narrow burl panel inlaid
w/pairs of stylized sunflowers & leaves,
original hinged brass pulls & keyhole escutcheons, blocked & carved side moldings, flat molded base, refinished, ca.
1885, 22 x 42", 8' h. (ILLUS.) **3,400**

Ornate Baroque Revival Secretary - M.M.

Victorian Baroque Revival secretary-bookcase, carved walnut, two-part construction: the tall upper section w/a very high arched & deeply molded cornice topped by a large crest composed of carved full-figure seated cherubs flanking a large shield, above a wide arched band at the front ornately carved w/cherubs climbing grapevines & centered at the top w/a carved lion mask all enclosing the pair of tall arched glazed doors opening to shelves; the lower section w/a raised rectangular central section w/a long rectangular fold-down writing surface carved on the front w/a panel of frolicking cherubs flanked at each corner by carved full-figure seated cherubs atop the stepped-out bottom section which features a central stack of three small drawers flanked by cupboard doors w/a round raised center molding enclosing carved cherub scenes, ornately carved end panels, all on a molded base w/large bracket feet, Europe, late 19th c., original dark finish, 22 x 50", 9' 9" h. (ILLUS. previous page) **35,000**

Country Gothic Secretary-Bookcase - M.M.

Victorian country-style secretary-bookcase, butternut, two-part construction: the upper section w/Gothic Revival influences including a narrow scalloped Gothic arch drop cornice above a pair of tall two-pane doors w/a Gothic arch grill in the top pane, flanked by applied serpentine bands down the outside edges; the lower section w/a hinged slant front w/two recessed panels each centered by carved leaves & grape clusters, opening to a fitted interior above three long graduated drawers w/carved

fruit & leaf pulls, short scalloped apron & block feet, Norwegian-American workmanship, Midwest, ca. 1870, 26 x 42", 7' h. (ILLUS.) **3,000**

Outstanding Country Secretary - M.M.

Victorian country-style secretary-bookcase, cherry & mixed woods, two-part construction: the upper section w/an arched, pierced & scroll-cut crestrail centered by an inlaid starburst & flanked by trefoil corner finials over the deep stepped & flaring cornice w/angled corner blocks above a pair of cupboard doors each w/a recessed oblong panel w/molded edges centered by an inlaid starburst & flanked by chamfered front corners w/carved drops & a raised narrow diamond all above a wide hinged slant front w/a large oblong recessed panel centered by another large inlaid starburst & opening to an interior w/numerous small inlaid drawers & pigeonholes; the slightly stepped-out lower section w/a rectangular top w/a flaring stepped cornice w/corner blocks flanking a narrow ogee-fronted drawer above another pair of doors w/octagonal recessed panels centered by inlaid starbursts, recessed panels at the sides, on a flat molded base w/a raised carved diamond at the front center & projecting block corners carved w/pyramidal blocks, original finish, Norwegian-American workmanship, Midwest, ca. 1870s, 22 x 40", 7' 6" h. (ILLUS.) **5,000**

Fine Victorian Eastlake Secretary - M.M.

Oak "Cylinder-front" Secretary - M.M.

Victorian Eastlake "cylinder-front" secretary-bookcase, walnut, the tall upper section w/a high arched crest over a leaf-carved panel flanked by block-carved panels over the coved cornice above a pair of tall glazed cupboard doors w/rounded corners flanked by quarter-round corner columns above the large cylinder front w/two recessed burled panels opening to a fitted interior, bird's-eye maple interior, a projecting mid-molding above the lower case w/a long narrow drawer slightly projecting over two long drawers flanked by small round columns, flat molded base, paneled sides, original hardware & finish, ca. 1880, 22 x 40", overall 8' 2" h. (ILLUS.) **4,500**

Victorian Golden Oak "cylinder-front" secretary-bookcase, oak, two-part construction: the upper section w/a high arched & scroll-cut crestrail w/applied carved scrolls & large corner rosettes above a pair of tall glazed cupboard doors w/a small carved scroll at the top & opening to shelves; the lower section w/a two-panel cylinder opening to a pull-out writing surface & fitted desk interior above a long curved-front drawer above two small drawers beside a small paneled cupboard door, molded flat base w/shaped bracket feet, original stamped brass hardware, refinished, ca. 1890, 22 x 42", 6' 8" h. (ILLUS. top next column) **2,500**

Fancy "Cylinder-front" Secretary - M.M.

Victorian Golden Oak "cylinder-front" secretary-bookcase, quarter-sawn oak, two-part construction: the upper section w/a high crestrail w/a band of three pierced round holes centered by an arched & pierced crest carved w/leafy scrolls & daisy-like blossoms above the narrow curved cornice w/incised lines centered by a small rectangular leaf-carved panel over a frieze band w/two applied bands of leafy scrolls, the case w/a pair of tall glazed doors opening to adjustable shelves; the lower section w/a two-panel cylinder front w/each panel boldly carved w/leafy scrolls, opening to a pull-out writing surface & fitted w/a desk interior above a long drawer slightly projecting over two shorter drawers beside a small paneled cupboard door carved in a rayed design, flat molded base, original stamped brass hardware, original dark finish, ca. 1890, 22 x 40", 7' 10" h. (ILLUS. previous page) **4,000**

Oak Secretary with Stamped Panels - M.M.

Victorian Golden Oak secretary-bookcase, oak, side-by-side-style, the rectangular top w/a high front crestrail w/pointed & rounded corner ears featuring panels of ornate stamped scrolling, a center block of three half-round knobs, the left side of the case w/a tall glazed door opening to wood shelves beside an open compartment backed by a mirror

above a drawer w/stamped brass pulls over a square fold-down writing surface decorated w/a tapering balloon panel w/stamped scrolls above another drawer w/brass pulls, the lower case w/a pair of long rectangular cupboard doors decorated w/matching tapering balloon-shaped panels w/stamped scrolls, molded base w/bracket feet, original hardware, refinished, ca. 1900, 16 x 40", 6' h. (ILLUS.) **1,200**

Oak Secretary with Leaded Doors - M.M.

Victorian Golden Oak secretary-bookcase, oak, side-by-side-style, the superstructure w/an arched crest centered by pierced scrolls above a narrow shelf raised on winged scroll supports also supporting small side shelves all backed by a long narrow beveled mirror, the case w/a tall bow-fronted glass door opening to shelves beside a pair of short doors w/leaded & stained flora-form glass panes above a flat hinged fall front decorated w/an applied oval band of molding w/a grotesque face opening to a fitted interior, a stack of three bow-fronted drawers below w/simple bail pulls, molded base on tall bracket feet, original dark finish, ca. 1895, 18 x 44", 6' 6" h. (ILLUS.) **2,800**

Rare Double Side-by-Side Secretary - M.M.

Victorian Golden Oak secretary-bookcase, quarter-sawn oak, rare double side-by-side-style, a pair of tall serpentine curved glass doors at each side of a wide central section, the center w/an arched & scroll-carved crestrail above a large arched rectangular beveled glass mirror above two small projecting open shelves raised above a narrow shelf on the long rectangular hinged fall front above a pair of deep serpentine-fronted drawers w/pierced brass pulls above a long deep bottom drawer w/top rounded brackets below each of the upper drawers, narrow serpentine apron w/scroll-carved trim, raised on tall simple cabriole legs, original hardware, refinished, ca. 1900, 20 x 68", 6' h. (ILLUS. above) **3,500**

Flat-topped Oak Double Secretary - M.M.

Victorian Golden Oak secretary-bookcase, quarter-sawn oak, rare double side-by-side-style, the flat rectangular top w/a molded cornice above a case w/tall flat glazed doors at each side, each w/a carved leafy scroll band at the top, the center section w/a pair of short flat glazed doors opening to shelves above a wide hinged fall front w/long ornate scrolled brass hinges & lockplate & decorated w/a large inverted clover-shaped panel w/clusters of fanned carved leaves, the desk above a stack of three long drawers w/stamped brass pulls, molded base over a narrow curved apron & simple bracket feet, original hardware, refinished, ca. 1900, 20 x 54", 6' h. (ILLUS.) **2,800**

Victorian Golden Oak secretary-bookcase, quarter-sawn oak, side-by-side-style, a high arched crestrail trimmed w/a band of dark-stained scrolls above a narrow open shelf over the two-section cabinet, the left side w/a dark-stained top bracket beside a long narrow rectangular shelf below a long half-round beveled mirror & above a tall flat glazed door trimmed w/dark-stained banding & opening to wooden shelves, the right side w/a pair of large dark-stained scrolls flanking a recessed oval panel w/dark-stained scrolls beside a vertical narrow quarter-round beveled mirror above a rectangular shelf above a flat hinged fall front w/a large stamped scroll-decorated & stained panel above two drawers w/pierced brass pulls above a bottom cupboard door stamped w/a long dark-stained C-scroll panel, serpentine apron & C-form bracket feet, refinished, ca. 1900, 16 x 40", 6' 3" h. (ILLUS. top left column of next page) **2,500**

Fancy Light & Dark Oak Secretary - M.M.

Oak Side-by-Side with Mirrors - M.M.

Victorian Golden Oak secretary-bookcase, quarter-sawn oak, side-by-side-

style, a high flat-topped scrolled crest board behind a long narrow shelf w/down-curved ends raised above the two-part case, the left side w/a tall curved glass door opening to wooden shelves, the right side w/a long rectangular arch-topped beveled mirror at the back & a small vertical rectangular beveled mirror at the side above an open shelf above a narrow drawer over the wide hinged fall front centered by a scroll-stamped cartouche panel, a long ogee-fronted drawer over two flat drawers below the desk, each w/pierced brass pulls, simple apron on ogee bracket feet on casters, refinished, ca. 1890s, 18 x 40", 5' 8" h. (ILLUS.).. **1,600**

Oak Secretary with Stepped Cornice - M.M.

Victorian Golden Oak secretary-bookcase, quarter-sawn oak, side-by-side-style, a two-part stepped cornice above the two-part cabinet, the left side w/a flat rolled crestrail above a narrow rectangular leafy scroll-carved panel flanked by shaped brackets on the bow-front top & tall bowed glass door opening to wooden shelves, the right side w/a stepped scroll-carved crestrail above a narrow top shelf w/scroll-cut front brackets over a tall open compartment backed by a large rectangular arch-topped beveled mirror & a small side shelf all above the wide flat fall front decorated w/a scroll-carved heart-shaped panel above a long ogee-front drawer & two long flat drawers all w/highly figured oak & pierced brass pulls, raised on ogee bracket feet on casters, refinished, ca. 1890s, 16 x 40", 6' h. (ILLUS.).. **2,000**

Secretary with Scrolls & Leaded Door - M.M.

Victorian Golden Oak secretary-bookcase, quarter-sawn oak, side-by-side-style, the high serpentine crest w/a small scroll-carved center crest & outwardly-scrolled corner ears above long C-form moldings above a wide panel w/a long flaring section of applied scrolls above the two-part case, the left side w/a tall curved & leaded glass door opening to shelves, the right side w/a large rounded beveled glass mirror over a scrolled band above a narrow shelf atop the flat rectangular fall front w/a large cartouche of carved scrolls, a serpentine long drawer below the desk w/simple bail pulls above a long flat rectangular base door, on ogee front legs w/heavy paw feet, refinished, ca. 1900, 18 x 40", 5' 10" h. (ILLUS.)............................ **2,500**

Victorian Golden Oak secretary-bookcase, quarter-sawn oak, side-by-side-style w/Classical Revival detailing, the long serpentine crestrail w/applied scrolls & a central shell above a long rectangular shelf w/an ogee apron raised on tall round columns running all the way down the sides & flanking the two-part case, a long narrow rectangular beveled mirror below the top shelf & above the case, the left side w/a tall curved glass door opening to wooden shelves, the right side w/a short rectangular leaded glass door w/a fleur-de-lis design above the wide fall front opening to a fitted interior above a stack of three long drawers w/pierced brass pulls, raised on heavy C-scroll front feet, refinished, ca. 1900, 18 x 42", 5' 8" h. (ILLUS.) **1,800**

Oak Secretary with Classical Details - M.M.

Cherry "Cylinder-front" Secretary - M.M.

Victorian Renaissance Revival "cylinder-front" secretary-bookcase, cherry & burl walnut, two-part construction: the upper section w/a gently arched & notch-cut plain crestrail on dentil-carved cornice above a pair of tall glazed doors w/angled tops trimmed w/raised triangular panels & surrounded by narrow raised panels, w/cast-iron latch opening to shelves; the lower section w/a two-panel cylinder front opening to a pull-out writing surface & fitted interior above a wide mid-molding over a pair of cupboard doors w/raised rectangular burl panels & bordered by narrow burl panels, paneled sides, flat molded base on thin square gadrooned feet, old refinish, ca. 1875, 22 x 42", 7' 8" h. (ILLUS.) **2,000**

Renaissance "Breakfront" Secretary - M.M.

Victorian Renaissance Revival secretary-bookcase, walnut & burl walnut, breakfront-style, the wide stepped-out center cabinet w/a high peaked broken-scroll pediment centered by a square burl panel w/rosette below a fan-carved crest, the sides of the pediment w/curved molding over small triangular burl panels flanked by flat arched corner ears above a flaring stepped flat cornice above a pair of tall glazed doors opening to shelves & flanked by narrow blocks & burl panels down the sides all atop a long two-panel false drawer decorated w/raised burl panels & leaf-carved pulls opening to reveal a pull-out writing surface & storage slots, a pair of large square paneled doors at the base centered by raised round medallions enclosing facing profile portraits of classical-style woman, a flat molded base; the narrow stepped-back side cabinets each w/a half-round curved crest w/burl panel above a flaring stepped cornice over a tall narrow glazed door opening to shelves & w/narrow blocks & burl panels down the outer edge, a small raised burl panel door at the bottom of each side above the molded flat base, old refinish, ca. 1870s, 24 x 90", 9' 3" h. (ILLUS. above) **9,500**

Simple Renaissance Walnut Secretary - M.M.

Victorian Renaissance Revival secretary-bookcase, walnut, two-part construction: the upper section w/a high arched serpentine crestrail centered by a cluster of carved fruit above a deep coved cornice w/rounded corners above a pair of tall glazed doors w/a small block carving at the top center & opening to adjustable shelves above a pair of long narrow drawers w/fruit-and-leaf-carved pulls; the stepped-out lower section w/a fold-out writing surface above a long drawer w/carved fruit-and-leaf-carved pulls over a pair of paneled cupboard doors, deep flat molded base, ca. 1865, refinished, 18 x 42", 8' h. (ILLUS. previous page)....... **2,300**

Unusual Rococo Walnut Secretary - N.O.

Victorian Rococo secretary, walnut & burl walnut, a large square upright shallow case w/beaded molding framing a large mirror on the drop-down front panel opening to create a writing surface w/an inset tooled leather top & fitted w/small drawers & pigeonholes, an ornate pierce-carved apron across the case bottom, raised on a trestle base w/beaded & incurved uprights above heavy angled shoe feet joined by a pair of long baluster- and ring-turned stretchers, ca. 1860, 16 x 26", 4' 2" h. (ILLUS.)....................... **1,955**

Fine Rococo "Butler's" Secretary - M.M.

Victorian Rococo "butler's" secretary-bookcase, carved mahogany, two-part construction: the upper section w/a high boldly arched & scroll-carved crestrail topped by a fully dimensional head of Shakespeare above the deep flaring & stepped cornice over a scroll-carved frieze band w/carved fruit at the corners above a pair of tall cupboard doors centered by tall oval mirrors framed w/scroll-carved corners all above a pair of long narrow drawers w/scroll-carved pulls; the stepped-out lower section w/a narrow rectangular white marble top w/serpentine front above a conforming scroll-carved long drawer pulling out to reveal a writing surface & storage all above a pair of large square cupboard doors centered by large round moldings enclosing rounded carved cartouches, scroll-carved bands at the sides, on a molded base w/flat block feet, original dark finish, ca. 1855, 24 x 55", 8' 9" h. (ILLUS.)................. **8,000**

Austrian Rococo Secretary-Bookcase - N.O.

Victorian Rococo secretary-bookcase, carved mahogany, two-part construction: the upper section w/a high arched crestrail ornately pierce-carved w/scrolls & flowers flanked by turned urn finials above the arching frieze over a pair of arched cupboard doors inset w/large mirrors framed w/scroll molding & scroll-carved corner brackets; the stepped-out lower section w/a gadrooned edge above a fall-front long drawer opening to a writing surface flanked by low spindled gallery rails & exposing four rock maple small drawers above a pair of large paneled cupboard doors w/scroll-carved molding flanked by scroll-carved corner blocks, deep molded base w/outset rounded corners & an ornate serpentine scroll-carved apron, on flat bun feet, probably Austria, mid-19th c., 20 x 43", 6' 5" h. (ILLUS. previous page).... **5,520**

Rosewood Rococo Secretary-Bookcase - M.M.

Victorian Rococo secretary-bookcase, carved rosewood, two-part construction: the upper section w/a long peaked crestrail w/carved scroll edging & a carved shell finial, the long canted corners above a conforming coved cornice above scroll-carved chamfered sides flanking a pair of tall glazed cupboard doors w/scroll-carved corners above a flat fall front opening to a series of pigeonholes & small drawers w/bird's-eye maple veneer; the lower stepped-out case w/a pair of long drawers w/raised oval molding above a row of three cupboard doors each w/rectangular panels formed by raised scroll molding, flanked by chamfered sides, flat molded base on short block feet, original dark finish, ca. 1855, 24 x 48", 9' 2" h. (ILLUS.).. **8,000**

Victorian Rococo secretary-bookcase, mahogany & mahogany veneer, two-part construction: the upper section w/a broken-scroll pediment centered by a carved fleur-de-lis & grape-carved finial & w/turned urn corner finials above a pair of tall arched glazed doors opening to shelves; the lower section w/a hinged slant front ornately carved w/scrolls & opening to a fitted interior above a case w/three long graduated drawers each decorated w/scroll-carved pulls & bands,

molded base, original dark finish w/some veneer damage on base, ca. 1860, 22 x 40", 8' 4" h. (ILLUS. below) **3,000**

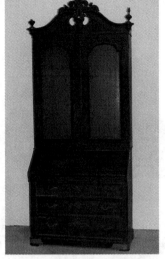

Rococo Slant-front Secretary - M.M.

Nice Rococo Rosewood Secretary - N.O.

Victorian Rococo secretary-bookcase, rosewood, two-part construction: the upper section w/a deep flaring coved cornice w/rounded corners above a wide conforming ogee frieze band over a pair of tall glazed Gothic arch designed doors carved w/leafy scrolls; the projecting lower section w/a cyma-shaped fold-out writing surface opening to a fitted interior above a pair of paneled cupboard doors w/carved scroll banding, flat apron on short bracket feet, ca. 1860, possibly made for the Southern market, 23 x 54", 7' 11 1/2" h. (ILLUS.) .. **3,680**

SHELVES

Decorated Apothecary Shelves - G

Apothecary shelves, walnut & pine, dovetailed case at top w/twelve dovetailed drawers w/old brass pulls, a shelf at base, single-board end panels w/scalloped bases & re-shaped arched top & heart cutouts, late black over red sponged decoration, 10 1/2 x 39", 37" h. (ILLUS. left) **$1,725**

Floor shelves, oak, elaborate corner posts having scalloped bracket bases & applied floral vining w/open twist columns at centers, relief carved urn finials on front, shell & grape finials on back, three shelves w/carved center aprons, old refinishing, Europe, one center apron missing, one back finial chipped, 23 1/2 x 67 1/2", 5' 10" h. (ILLUS. bottom of page) **1,725**

Wall corner shelves, hardwood w/red marble tops, approximately 2"-thick red marble top w/astragal molding, dovetailed & carved Greek key frieze, two scrolled legs w/paw feet centering on ball, probably Europe, 18th c., missing one marble top, feet w/repairs & restorations, other losses to frieze, repairs, separations, scattered worm damage, 16 x 22", 30" h., pr. (ILLUS. of one top photo next page) **1,650**

Elaborate Carved Floor Shelves - G

One of a Pair of Wall Corner Shelves - BR

Wall shelf, carved wood, a wide rectangular shelf w/rounded front corners & an arch-carved border supported atop the large carved stylized head of a man w/curly hair & a heavy mustache, the large eyes painted white, original black paint, repaired splits in shelf, 19th c., 9 x 10 7/8", 8" h. plus hangers **978**

Wall shelf, lacquered & parcel-gilt wood, folding-type, the large oblong backboard w/a fancy scroll-cut border, fitted w/a half-round shelf on a swing-out brace support, the backboard in black lacquer decorated overall in color w/various Chinese figures, England, second quarter 19th c., 5 1/2 x 9 3/4", 14 1/4" h. (ILLUS. right) **690**

Wall shelves, early American country-style, painted pine, whale-end style, a narrow rectangular top shelf above tapering rounded & scroll-cut sides flanking three narrow graduated shelves joined by a back slat, original black & red decoration & old varnishing, attributed to New England, early 19th c., minor wear, 8 1/4 x 32 7/8", 39 1/2" h. **1,840**

English Chinoiserie Wall Shelf - N.O.

Maple Whale-end Wall Shelves - G

Wall shelves, maple, whale-end style, three narrow graduated open shelves fitted between serpentine shaped sides, old brown wash, 19th c., nails of various ages & some empty nail holes, minor chips, 26" w., 25 3/4" h. (ILLUS.) **345**

Wall shelves, poplar, a three-arch crestrail above a narrow top shelf above three graduated open shelves fitted into the scalloped sides, old refinishing, square

nail construction, 19th c., 27 1/2" w., 44 3/4" h. (ILLUS.) **546**

Poplar Four-Shelf Wall Unit - G

SIDEBOARDS

Fine Calamander Art Deco Sideboard - N.O.

Art Deco sideboard, calamander, the rectangular top w/a slightly bowed front inset w/marble above a case fitted w/two wide cabinet doors opening to a fitted bar, joined by stepped side supports above a plinth base, probably France, ca. 1930s, 21 x 65 1/2", 42 3/4" h. (ILLUS.) **$6,325**

Arts & Crafts sideboard, quarter-sawn oak, the superstructure w/an arched center crest above a large beveled mirror flanked by small cupboards w/clear & blue leaded glass doors raised on sides w/heart cutouts above the long rectangular top overhanging corner corbels on the

Attractive Arts & Crafts Sideboard - M.M.

case, two long narrow drawers above a long drawer above a pair of short leaded glass doors flanked by tall narrow cupboard doors w/incised bands, a long drawer across the bottom, raised on squared tapering legs on casters, original wooden pulls, old refinish, ca. 1910, 20 x 54", 6' h. (ILLUS. above) **1,500**

Classical Country-style Sideboard - BR

Classical country-style sideboard, cherry, shaped top w/four conforming central dovetailed drawers flanked by two drawers w/chamfered fronts above two paneled doors, double split-spindle columns on front, turned feet, inlaid diamond escutcheons, back w/frame-&-panel construction w/cut nails, possibly Catawba Valley, North Carolina, missing locks, old refinishing w/surface chips, scattered old repairs, separations, losses, possibly missing splash panel, 24 x 48", 48" h. (ILLUS. bottom of previous page) **4,840**

Nice Mahogany Classical Server - M.M.

Classical server, mahogany & mahogany veneer, a high flat-topped backsplash surface-carved w/a large basket flanked by carved fans between flat corner blocks, the rectangular top above a case w/a pair of drawers w/oval brasses flanked by side panels & projecting above a pair of cupboard doors w/panels combining to form a large Gothic arch, a tapering freestanding column w/scroll-carved capital at each side, flat apron on scroll-carved heavy paw front legs, refinished, ca. 1830s, 24 x 48", 4' 4" h. (ILLUS. left) **1,200**

Classical Server with Nice Columns - M.M.

Classical server, mahogany & mahogany veneer, the high arched & scroll-cut backsplash on the rectangular top above a case w/a long veneered drawer w/round brass pulls overhanging another long drawer over a deep center drawer flanked by deep bottle drawers, spiral-turned freestanding columns at each side, on heavy baluster-turned legs, refinished, replaced pulls, ca. 1830, 22 x 46", 4' h. (ILLUS.) **650**

Classical Marble-top Server - BR

Large Classical Mahogany Sideboard - G

Classical server, mahogany w/marble top, mottled salmon & ivory marble top, conforming base w/plum pudding mahogany frieze w/brass trim above tapered circular columns & ball feet, America, 19th c., small chips & separations to Ionic capitals, old refinishing, minor chips & losses to surface, missing one piece of molding under marble at one side, missing piece of brass molding under frieze proper right side, 22 1/2 x 46 1/2", 36" h. (ILLUS. bottom of previous page) **2,860**

Classical sideboard, cherry w/mahogany veneer, the stepped flat upright crest board divided by four flat blocks above the rectangular top above a case w/a long bevel-edged drawer flanked by smaller bevel-edged drawers projecting above a pair of central paneled doors flanked by single paneled doors, all separated by a set of four heavy turned & leaf-carved col-

umns on the plinth base raised on four heavy scroll-carved paw feet, old pressed glass drawer pulls, ca. 1840, 23 x 72", 4' 5 1/2" h. (ILLUS. above) **1,725**

Classical sideboard, mahogany & mahogany veneer, a drop-well rectangular top w/an upright back composed of a pair of large finely carved cornucopias flanking the marble-topped drop well fitted w/a high central rectangular mirror w/a classical pediment & turned columns, the side sections w/a round-fronted drawer above a tall paneled door flanked by classical free-standing columns, the central section w/two long narrow drawers over a pair of paneled cupboard doors, the blocked base on leaf-carved trumpet-form front legs, early pressed glass pulls on the drawers, attributed to Anthony Quervelle, Philadelphia, ca. 1835, veneer restorations, 23 1/4 x 67", 4' 11" h. (ILLUS. below) . **3,163**

Fine Classical Sideboard Attributed to Quervelle - G

Large Carved Classical Sideboard - M.M.

Classical sideboard, mahogany & mahogany veneer, a high back rail centered by a tall plain rolled panel flanked by serpentine panels carved w/cornucopias, the drop-well top w/blocked front corners, the tall side sections w/a round-fronted drawer over a tall raised-panel cupboard door, the dropped center section w/a long round-fronted drawer above a pair of shorter raised-panel drawers, the facade divided by four tall turned & tapering freestanding columns above bulbous leafcarved & ring-turned legs w/knob feet, original finish, ca. 1830s, 24 x 72", 5' h. (ILLUS.).. **2,500**

Classical Sideboard with Gallery Top - M.M.

Classical sideboard, mahogany & mahogany veneer, a three-quarters low gallery w/shaped sides on the rectangular top w/blocked corners & gadroon-carved edges above the case w/a pair of drawers w/original ornate pierced brass butterfly pulls above a pair of large paneled cupboard doors all flanked by large spiral-turned side columns w/carved capitals & resting on shell-carved blocks above the heavy paw feet, original dark finish, ca. 1840s, 22 x 52", 4' h. (ILLUS.).. **1,600**

New York Classical Mahogany Sideboard - N.O.

Classical sideboard, mahogany & mahogany veneer, a high broken-scroll backboard centered by a large block & urn finial & w/small urn finials on each end above the rectangular top fitted w/spindled end galleries above slide-out work shelves, the main case w/a long central drawer flanked by shorter drawers above a central pair of paneled cupboard doors flanked by single paneled doors, the drawers & doors separated by reeded pilasters, raised on tapering ring- and rod-turned legs w/peg feet, New York City, ca. 1820s, 25 1/4 x 66 1/4", 5' 4" h. (ILLUS.)................................. **5,175**

Classical Boldly Veneered Sideboard - M.M.

Classical sideboard, mahogany & mahogany veneer, the rectangular top above pair of long round-fronted drawers w/round brass pulls flanked by carved corner blocks & slightly projecting over two tall turned & tapering freestanding side columns flanking an arrangement of two deep center drawers over two paneled cupboard doors flanked on each side by a stack of three tall narrow drawers all w/round brass pulls, flat apron, short front legs w/acanthus leafcarved knees over heavy paw feet on casters, refinished, ca. 1830s, 22 x 50", 4' h. (ILLUS.) **1,800**

Quality Classical Sideboard - N.O.

Classical sideboard, mahogany & mahogany veneer, the top w/a crossbanded gallery w/scrolled-end returns above a projecting section w/a pair of small drawers at each end centered by a long false drawer folding down to a writing surface, the stepped-back lower case w/a row of four paneled cupboard doors separated by four free-standing ring-turned columns on blocks above the four beehive-turned legs, round brass pulls, mid-Atlantic states, ca. 1830, 24 x 71", 4' 2" h. (ILLUS.)............................. **3,910**

Federal sideboard, cherry, rounded central section w/two conforming drawers above bay w/two doors, flanked by small drawers above cellaret drawer flanked by reeded pilasters & two swell-front drawers w/conforming doors below, dovetailed & cockbeaded drawers, six tapered & reeded legs, frame-and-panel sides, drawer faces w/fancy cherry veneer & mahogany banding, swell-front doors & drawers of stacked-block construction, old, possibly original uneven finish, brass pulls possibly original, Tennessee or Kentucky, early 19th c., some drawer surfaces replaned, possibly missing splash panel, most locks replaced, cellaret drawers missing interior dividers, several minor scratches, veneer losses & separations throughout, 25 x 44", 6' 5" h. (ILLUS. below) **15,400**

Federal sideboard in Cherry - BR

Fine Inlaid Mahogany Federal Sideboard - N.O.

Federal sideboard, inlaid mahogany, the rectangular serpentine top w/a bowed central section above a conforming case w/concave drawers over concave cupboard doors w/oval band & marquetry inlay flanking the long bowed line-inlaid drawer projecting over a pair of flat doors w/circle inlay, on four square tapering line-inlaid front legs, ca. 1800, 27 3/4 x 63", 39 1/4" h. (ILLUS.) **4,370**

Federal sideboard, mahogany & mahogany veneer, the rectangular top w/convex ends & a concave center above a case w/bow-fronted end cupboard doors flanking a concave-fronted long drawer over a pair of concave cupboard doors, front divided by four leaf-carved & reeded columns continuing down to form the reeded legs on peg feet, refinished, ca. 1820, 22 x 60", 36" h. (ILLUS. below) **1,400**

Serpentine-fronted Federal Sideboard - M.M.

Nice Federal-Style Server - M.M.

Federal-Style server, mahogany & mahogany veneer, a high gallery composed of brass rods & urn finials above the long rectangular top above a row of three drawers w/simple brass bail pulls raised on ebonized columns over a full lower shelf over a pair of drawers flanking a pair of long & low reeded cupboard doors, on tapering turned feet w/brass caps, original hardware, ca. 1920s, refinished, 20 x 64", 4' 10" h. (ILLUS. above) .. **1,000**

over an apron carved w/a band of arched leaves & supported on heavy turned front supports above two more open shelves each w/a carved apron & flanked by two heavy turned supports, short heavy cylinder & disk front legs, old dark finish, England, 19th c., reconstruction & pieced repair, 16 x 46", 4' 4" h. (ILLUS. left)......... **1,150**

English Jacobean-Style Server - G

Jacobean-Style server, carved oak, a high peaked backboard centered by a large carved rosette above the rectangular top

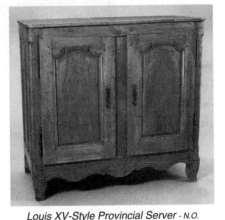

Louis XV-Style Provincial Server - N.O.

Louis XV-Style Provincial server, fruitwood, the rectangular top w/rounded corners above a conforming case w/notched front corners flanking a pair of arched paneled cupboard doors w/long brass latch mounts above the molded serpentine apron & short bracket feet, France, first half 19th c., 24 x 48 3/4", 44 3/4" h. (ILLUS.).. **3,450**

Louis XV-Style Provincial Sideboard - BR

Louis XV-Style Provincial sideboard, walnut, three-piece construction, the top w/ornate carved pediment above door w/20 beveled panes flanked by two carved side doors; the base w/two drawers above two large bay doors, cabriole legs w/carved scroll feet, panels w/detailed carving throughout, carved & paneled central backboard, France, 24 x 59", 9' h. (ILLUS.) **3,080**

Mission-style (Arts & Crafts movement) sideboard, oak, the tall superstructure w/an open crestrail joining four posts above a long rectangular shelf supported by four square posts joined by arched braces above two back panels flanking a large rectangular beveled mirror, the rectangular top overhanging a case w/four heavy stiles forming legs dividing the facade, a long recessed central drawer over a pair of double-panel recessed cupboard doors all flanked by small projecting drawers over paneled cupboard doors, arched central apron, rectangular copper bail pulls w/one bail missing, good original medium finish, unmarked Stickley Brothers, 37 x 72", overall 5' 3 1/2" h. (ILLUS. below) **4,025**

Large Stickley Brothers Oak Sideboard - CR

Renaissance Revival Sideboard - G

Renaissance Revival sideboard, walnut, three-part construction, the top w/beveled mirror glass at the back of the pie shelf & inside the top; the middle section w/relief-carved arched center crest w/glass interior shelf; the base w/grey, brown & white marble top, flat front w/bowed ends, two doors w/relief carving on raised panels w/two dovetailed drawers above, short turned wafer feet, Europe, 21 x 59 1/2", 6' 7 1/2" h. (ILLUS.)..... **1,265**

Victorian Aesthetic Movement sideboard, mahogany, the tall superstructure w/an upright cabinet on one end w/a low ball-and-stick gallery over a single beveled glass door beside a stepped-down rectangular top over an open compartment w/a full shelf & half-shelf supported by a block- and ring-turned corner post raised on slender turned columns above the rectangular top backed by a large rectangular beveled mirror, the lower case w/a long drawer over a pair of cupboard doors w/panels w/low-relief carving of dead fish & game above a long bottom drawer, the other side w/two small drawers over a similar paneled & carved door, flat molded base, original round ring brass pulls, original finish, ca. 1880, 20 x 42", 7' h. (ILLUS. below) **2,600**

Victorian Aesthetic Sideboard - G.K.

Victorian Baroque Revival sideboard, ebonized oak, two-part construction: the upper tall section w/a serpentine scroll-carved crestrail centered by an oval medallion above the egg-and-dart-carved cornice over an upper three-section frieze band carved w/acanthus leaves over lower three-section arched frieze band carved w/scrolls, each section separated by a carved lion mask, the top projecting over the tall back & supported by tall block-, baluster- and reeded knob-turned columns, the tall back divided into two horizontal sections, the upper section divided into three rectangular panels each carved w/scrolls surrounded by a ring & diamond motif, the long lower panel carved overall w/leafy scrolls; the lower section w/a rectangular top w/molded edges over a case w/a row of three plain drawers each separated by a carved lion mask above a beaded band & three paneled lower doors carved w/scrolls & the ring & diamond motif, each door separated by a large carved caryatid, a long narrow drawer across the bottom, narrow flat reeded apron w/blocked end feet, original finish, Europe, ca. 1880s, 22 x 60", 8' h. **3,200**

Victorian Baroque Revival sideboard, oak, a tall splashback w/an ornately carved crestrail w/a basket of fruit flanked by reclining dragons all above a plain recessed panel, raised block corners over carved lion masks, the long rectangular top w/blocked corners above a case w/a row of three drawers carved w/leafy scrolls & each separated by a block carved w/a stylized blossom head all above a row of three large doors w/oval carved panels, the central door w/a large scrolled cartouche framed by leafy scrolls & the matching outer doors carved w/large urns of fruit over scrolls, the central door flanked by vertical herringbone-carved blocks above the blocked apron, each outside edge w/a large barley twist-carved column, raised on bulbous squatty feet, ca. 1890, American-made, refinished, 26 x 76", 5' h. **3,500**

Huge Ornate Baroque Sideboard - M.M.

Victorian Baroque Revival sideboard, oak, the large superstructure w/a high broken-scroll pediment w/the peaked center section carved in bold relief w/a satyr face above grapevine swags continuing to the high flanking scrolls all above a long narrow rectangular shelf raised on seated griffin supports flanking a large rectangular back panel boldly carved w/grapevines centered by another large satyr mask, the rectangular top over a row of three scroll-carved drawers separated by carved satyr mask-carved blocks & projecting slightly over three large paneled doors, the central door w/full-relief carving of dead game & the matching side doors w/full-relief carving of fruit clusters, the doors separated by columns w/full-relief carving of bands of fruit, the blocked & flaring base band w/leaf & dart carving, raised on four flattened bun feet, refinished, Europe, ca. 1880, 24 x 76", 6' 8" h. (ILLUS. left) **9,500**

Unusual Eastlake Cherry Sideboard - M.M.

Victorian Eastlake style sideboard, cherry, the tall superstructure w/a long narrow rectangular shelf w/spindled gallery at the ends & front topped by turned finials raised on arched front & side brackets above two slender ring-, rod- and baluster-turned spindles resting on low spindled galleries enclosing another long shelf backed by a very large rectangular beveled mirror, a narrow paneled lower back section above the wide projecting top on the case, the case fitted w/a long narrow drawer beside a shorter narrow drawer above an asymmetrical arrangement of four drawers & two paneled scroll-carved doors, on short ring-turned front legs, original finish, ca. 1890, 20 x 52", 6' 6" h. (ILLUS.) **1,500**

Golden Oak Server with Lions - M.M.

Victorian Golden Oak server, quarter-sawn oak, a serpentine crestrail supported on seated winged lion brackets above a conforming long beveled mirror over the rectangular top, the case w/a pair of long slightly projecting drawers over a long deeper drawer above a pair of flat cupboard doors centered by a scroll-carved panel, front animal legs ending in paw feet, on wooden casters, refinished, ca. 1900, 22 x 48", 5' h. (ILLUS.)...................... **950**

Tall Carved Eastlake Sideboard - M.M.

Victorian Eastlake style sideboard, walnut & burl walnut, the very tall superstructure w/a high notched and panel-cut crestrail flanked by roundels above a molded corner of shaped blocks above a large long rectangular panel boldly carved w/sprays of fruit & leaves centered by an urn, flanked by incurved side brackets on a long narrow open shelf supported by curved brackets & baluster- and ring-turned columns, a large rectangular beveled mirror at the back above rectangular pink marble top above the case w/a pair of burl veneer drawers w/angular brass pulls over a pair of cupboard doors w/raised burl panels, reeded pilasters down the sides, flat base w/blocked feet, original finish & hardware, ca. 1885, 22 x 48", 7' 6" h. (ILLUS.) **2,800**

Victorian Golden Oak server, quartersawn oak, a flat crest rod above a long narrow oval beveled mirror flanked by curved scrolls above the long rectangular top w/rounded corners over a rounded frieze w/two long drawers above a pair of large cupboard doors w/fan-shaped leaded glass panels flanking an ornate scroll-carved center door, long round-fronted drawer across the bottom, the canted front corner headed by carved lion masks above scroll-carved tapering columns continuing to form the front legs ending in paw feet, original hardware, refinished, ca. 1895, 22 x 50", 4' 6" h. **2,400**

Golden Oak Sideboard with Mirror - G.K.

Victorian Golden Oak sideboard, a high rectangular beveled mirror w/a wide flat frame & top scroll-carved center crest enclosing a long beveled mirror, the rectangular top w/molded edges over a pair of flat cupboard doors w/arched tops flanking a long bowed central geometrically glazed cupboard door above a long drawer at the bottom w/scroll-carved trim & scalloped apron, squared outswept front legs w/paw feet, original brasses & dark finish, ca. 1910, 20 x 48", 5' h. (ILLUS.) **1,600**

Unique Oak Sideboard-Curio Cabinet - M.M.

Victorian Golden Oak sideboard, quarter-sawn oak, the superstructure w/an oblong top w/rounded ends & a bowed center section w/an arched & scroll-carved crest, the top above rounded glass display sections at each end centered by a long bow-front glass door opening to the long mirrored interior, all raised on cabriole legs w/paw feet & overhanging a long narrow rectangular beveled mirror, the top of the base w/rounded front corners above quarter-round glass doors opening to shelves & flanking the long flat central section w/a long concave-fronted drawer over a long rounded-front drawer over long deep bottom drawer w/carved scroll trim, carved cabriole front legs ending in paw feet on casters, original hardware, refinished, ca. 1890s, 24 x 56", 6' 6" h. (ILLUS.) **2,600**

Oak Sideboard with High Back - M.M.

Victorian Golden Oak sideboard, quarter-sawn oak, the tall superstructure w/a high arched & ornately scroll-carved cre-strail over a long narrow shelf w/a narrow serpentine scroll-carved apron raised on tall simple columns flanking a large oblong beveled mirror w/a small shelf at each side, the rectangular top w/a double-serpentine front over a conforming case w/a pair of drawers over a single long drawer above a pair of long rectangular cupboard doors w/applied scrolls, bottom corner scrolls above the large paw feet on casters, original brass hardware, refinished, ca. 1895, 22 x 44", 6' 8" h. (ILLUS. below left) **1,800**

Handsome Renaissance Server - M.M.

Victorian Renaissance Revival server, walnut & burl walnut, the superstructure w/a peaked pediment centered by a large fleur-de-lis finial & small raised burl panels above a flaring molding above a wide panel w/incurved sides centered by a large round raised burl panel w/a carved sunburst & shaped raised burl panels over a long narrow rectangular shelf w/rounded corners & flanked by small turned finials, the shelf supported on high pierced & scroll-cut brackets flanking a wide panel centered by a raised oval banding enclosing burl veneer, all atop the rectangular white marble top w/rounded front corners over a conforming case, the case w/a pair of drawers w/oval burl panels above a pair of cupboard doors w/large oval sunken panels w/burl veneer, deep molded flat base on casters, original finish, ca. 1875, 20 x 42", 7' 4" h. (ILLUS.) **2,600**

Elaborate Renaissance Sideboard - N.O.

Victorian Renaissance Revival side-board, carved oak, the tall superstructure w/a high arched & ornately scroll-carved crestrail centered by a large carved realistic stag head above a long half-round shelf supported on baluster-turned supports on a lower open shelf w/a closed paneled back flanked by pierced scrolls, the lower shelf supported by large projecting brackets w/fruit carving resting on the long white marble top & flanked by further pierced scrolls at the sides, the lower case w/a pair of paneled drawers w/fruit- and nut-carved pulls above a pair of arched panel doors centered by large relief-carved clusters of dead game, the beveled front corners trimmed w/carved scrolls, on a plinth base, related in style to an Alexander Roux example, ca. 1870, 23 1/2 x 59", 7' 6" h. (ILLUS.) **4,140**

Victorian Renaissance Revival side-board, chestnut, walnut & walnut veneer, the tall superstructure topped by a wide peaked scroll-carved crest w/a fan-carved finial above an arched molding above a long arched burl panel flanked by side scrolls & narrow burl panels over a long rectangular shelf w/rounded corners supported on tall blocked brackets w/turned drop finials above a long narrow rectangular mirror & scrolled side brackets, the long rectangular white marble top w/rounded front corners above a conforming case, the case w/a central stack of five small molded drawers flanked at each side w/a burled drawer w/brass ring pulls over large cupboard doors w/a rectangular raised burl panel & notch-carved dark border molding, flat molded base, original finish, 1870s, 22 x 52", 8' h. (ILLUS. top right column) **2,400**

Tall Chestnut & Walnut Sideboard - M.M.

Oak Sideboard with Carving of Game Birds - M.M.

Victorian Renaissance Revival sideboard, oak, the high superstructure topped by a tall arched crest carved w/large scrolls flanking a carved cluster of fruit above a narrow rounded shelf w/a sawtooth-cut narrow apron supported on bold scroll-carved brackets flanking a long narrow raised scroll-carved panel & scrolled side brackets above a matching longer shelf on matching brackets flanking another raised panel w/carving of a cluster of fruit all resting on the long rectangular top w/a deep flared apron w/carved scrolls at the sides & w/two long scroll-carved drawers at the front separated by three blocks w/a lion mask carved in relief, a pair of large paneled cupboard doors below each centered by relief-carved decoration of game birds, three long dividing columns down the front each carved in bold relief w/bands of fruit & leaves, blocks & scroll-carved flat base band, Europe, ca. 1875, refinished, 22 x 50", 7' 8" h. (ILLUS. previous page) **2,800**

Sideboard with Head of Robin Hood - M.M.

Victorian Renaissance Revival sideboard, walnut, burl & figured walnut, the tall superstructure topped by a high broken-scroll pediment w/an arched crest on the center section above a full-relief carved bust of Robin Hood above a wide rectangular shelf w/rounded corners supported on scroll-cut brackets above a molded narrow rectangular panel w/figured walnut & a long narrow shaped raised burl panel over another slightly

longer shelf on brackets above a larger figured walnut panel w/a large raised burl panel all flanked by scroll-cut side brackets, a half-round grey marble top w/a flattened front section above a conforming case w/a long narrow center drawer w/narrow raised burl panels flanked by curved matching swing-out trays at the sides all above three large paneled doors each centered by a large carved cartouche, deep molded base band on wafer feet, refinished, 1870s, 22 x 60", 8' 5" h. (ILLUS.) **7,500**

Walnut Sideboard with High Crest - M.M.

Victorian Renaissance Revival sideboard, walnut & burl walnut, the superstructure w/a very high arched broken-scroll pediment centered by a large pointed & carved finial above the wide smooth panel centered w/a carved cluster of fruit & two triangular raised panels, all above a long narrow shelf supported on ornate S-scroll brackets above a long narrow oval mirror over the half-round white marble top w/wide rounded corners & flat center section, on a conforming case w/a long burled drawer w/black pear-shaped drops flanked by curved side panels above a pair of flat paneled cupboard doors centered by carved fruit clusters & flanked by curved side panels w/matching carved fruit, deep molded flat base on wafer feet, refinished, ca. 1875, 20 x 48", 7' h. (ILLUS.) **2,400**

Renaissance Sideboard with Mirror - M.M.

Victorian Renaissance Revival sideboard, walnut & burl walnut, the tall superstructure w/an arched crestrail centered by a curved fanned crest & blossom-carved bands on a scroll-carved crest above narrow raised burl panels & rounded corners above brackets & tall reeded columns flanking a tall rectangular mirror w/rounded top corners, a large half-round candle shelf at each side backed by a quarter-round panel & disk-turned finials, each shelf on a large pierced C-scroll bracket ending in a vertical raised burl panel flanked by narrow burl panels all above the half-round grey marble top w/a flat central section, the conforming case w/a long narrow center drawer w/a raised burl panel & two black pear-shaped drop pulls flanked by rounded matching swing-out side trays w/pulls, the lower case w/three large cupboard doors each w/a large fine feather-grained panel, the center door w/relief carving of a group of dead game, the doors separated by large ring-turned spool over a narrow burl panel, conforming molded base, ca. 1875, 22 x 60", 8' 5" h. (ILLUS.).......................... **8,000**

Victorian Rococo server, walnut & burl walnut, the tall superstructure w/an arched crestrail decorated w/an ornate pierced & scroll-carved crest centered by carved fruit clusters above an arched panel centered by another carved fruit cluster & flanked by turned finials above a narrow serpentine shelf supported on small shaped brackets above a longer serpentine shelf supported on a large scroll-carved center bracket flanked by a pair of oblong mirrors, deeply cut scallops down the outer sides, the rectangu-

lar white marble top w/rounded corners above a conforming case w/a pair of drawers w/recessed burl oval panels centered by a scroll-carved pull flanked by black teardrop pulls, two large cupboard doors below each w/a large recessed serpentine-sided burl panel centered by large carved fruit clusters & w/carved leaf sprigs at each corner, rounded front corners & a shallow serpentine apron, refinished, ca. 1860, 20 x 44", 7' 6" h. (ILLUS. below) **2,400**

Fine Rococo Walnut Server - M.M.

Fine Rococo Mahogany Sideboard - M.M.

Outstanding Fruit-carved Rococo Sideboard - M.M.

Victorian Rococo sideboard, carved mahogany, the high superstructure w/an arched crestrail carved w/bands of fruit centering a large scroll cartouche & flanked by turned urn corner finials above an arched panel carved w/a large cluster of fruit & scrolls flanked by triangular raised panels above a long narrow shelf w/rounded corners supported by ring-and-rod-turned spindles above a long narrow rectangular back panel & another slightly longer shelf supported on bold scroll-cut brackets, pierced scroll brackets at the sides above the long rectangular white marble top w/rounded corners above a conforming case, the case w/a pair of drawers w/raised oval molding & turned wood knobs flanked by rounded corner panels above the pair of large cupboard doors w/rectangular arch-topped molding centering a boldly carved cartouche, plain curved side panels, molded flat base on casters, refinished, ca. 1855, 23 x 56", 8' h. (ILLUS. bottom of previous page)....... **8,500**

Victorian Rococo sideboard, figured walnut, the high superstructure w/an arched pediment w/a large scroll finial flanked by delicate pierced scrolls over a panel w/shaped raised panels flanking a circle of carved fruit above a long narrow shelf w/rounded corners supported w/turned & reeded spindles on another long shelf backed by a long narrow shaped mirror flanked by incurved scroll-carved sides & raised on scroll-cut brackets flanking another matching mirror & flanked at each side by asymmetrical recessed burl panels & ornate pierced C-scrolls at the outer edges, on a long half-round white marble top w/a flattened center section, the conforming case w/a pair of paneled drawers flanked by curved swing-out side storage trays above four large cupboard doors, the center two w/flat fronts w/arched panels centering oval banding enclosing a large relief-carved cluster of fruit, the curved side doors w/similar molding but centered by large scroll-carved cartouches, flat molded base, original polished finish, marked by Mitchell and Rammelsberg Co., Cincinnati, Ohio, ca. 1855, 22 x 66", 8' 6" h. (ILLUS. above)............. **10,000**

New Orleans Rococo Sideboard - N.O.

Victorian Rococo sideboard, walnut & burl walnut, the superstructure w/a low pierced & scroll-carved back crest on the long narrow top shelf supported on large ornate S-scroll front supports joined by a lower shelf & a solid back, the rectangular white marble top above a case w/a row of three ogee-front drawers above a beaded molding over three cupboard doors w/raised carved rectangular panels separated by vertical beaded moldings, a beaded base molding on the serpentine scroll-carved apron, scroll-carved bracket feet, attributed to the New Orleans warerooms of William McCracken, ca. 1850s, 22 1/4 x 54 1/2", 5' 11" h. (ILLUS. left) **2,760**

William IV sideboard, mahogany, a tall upright paneled crestboard w/rounded corners above the rectangular top w/slightly projecting ends above a conforming case w/end pedestal sections each w/a drawer over a paneled cupboard door flanking a center drawer over the open center, molded bases, England, second quarter 19th c., 23 1/2 x 78", 4' 2" h. (ILLUS. below) **1,380**

English William IV Mahogany Sideboard - N.O.

STANDS

Baker's stand, wrought iron & brass, composed of a tall rectangular back made up of narrow horizontal bars & topped by three scrolled crests, fitted w/three open half-round wire shelves w/brass band fronts & supported in the center by ornate scrolling iron brackets w/a vertical bar w/brass finial projecting at the front center, Europe, 19th c., 18 x 47 1/2", 6' 4" h. .. **$978**

Candlestand, Chippendale country-style, cherry, the top w/shaped sides & oval inlay of mixed hardwoods, on turned pedestal above three saber legs on padded snake feet, probably Massachusetts, late 18th c., 16 1/2 x 16 3/4", 25 1/2" h. (ILLUS. below left) **2,530**

Decoupage-decorated Candlestand - G

Candlestand, Chippendale country style, hardwood w/old dark surface, oval top decorated w/ornate cutouts & birds, on turned column pedestal on snake feet, decorated w/decoupage strips on the feet & up the column to resemble fluting & around the top, late 18th - early 19th c. w/later decoration, 15 x 20 3/4", 26 1/4" h. (ILLUS.) **3,220**

Early Chippendale Candlestand - M.M.

Candlestand, Chippendale, walnut, the large round dished top tilting above a ring-and-urn-turned pedestal on a tripod base w/three cabriole legs ending in raised snake feet, Pennsylvania, ca. 1790, old refinish, 16" d., 30" h. (ILLUS.)..... **800**

Cherry Candlestand with Inlaid Top - BR

Octagonal Burlwood Candlestand - BR

Candlestand, country-style, burlwood, octagonal top on four legs, the top w/inlaid frieze, the tapered legs ending in pad feet & shaped returns, probably Italian, 19th c., missing original slide-out tray for candle, 25 1/2" h. (ILLUS. previous page) **1,650**

Simple Federal Cherry Candlestand - M.M.

Candlestand, Federal country-style, cherry, round top on a heavy baluster-turned pedestal on a tripod base w/simple flattened cabriole legs on button feet, original finish, early 19th c., 18" d., 28" h. (ILLUS.) **300**

Candlestand, Federal country-style tilt-top type, birch, rectangular top w/beveled corners raised & tilting above an urn-turned pedestal on a tripod base w/spider legs, late 18th - early 19th c., traces of old red wash on base, pieced restorations to block & peg, 14 x 20", 26 1/2" h. **690**

Lobed-top Federal Candlestand - G

Candlestand, Federal country-style tilt-top type, cherry & curly maple, the oblong

four-lobed top tilting above an urn-turned pedestal on a tripod base w/spider legs, old thin red wash, late 18th - early 19th c., 17 1/2 x 21", 27 1/2" h. (ILLUS. below left) **374**

Simple Federal Candlestand - M.M.

Candlestand, Federal, mahogany, the rectangular top w/rounded corners tilting above a bold ring-and-baluster-turned pedestal on a tripod base w/outswept legs ending in knob feet, original dark finish, first quarter 19th c., 18 x 24", 28" h. (ILLUS.)... **350**

Tilt-top Federal Candlestand - BR

Candlestand, Federal, mahogany, tilt-top style, the rectangular top w/canted corners, on turned pedestal on a tripod base w/spider legs, accession number on base of pedestal, inscribed under top "From the manor house of Capt. John Overstreet's Woodland Plantation, Princess Anne County, Virginia, 1832," yellow pine plate possible replacement, repaired splits to pedestal, 18 1/8 x 21 3/4", 28 1/2" h. (ILLUS. previous page).. 1,760

Early Primitive Candlestand - G

Candlestand, primitive country-style, ash, hickory & cherry, the thin round cherry top raised on a heavy turned pedestal w/a ring-turned center raised on four simple turned canted legs, late 18th - early 19th c., rose head nails in top w/an age split, one leg damaged, 16 3/4" d., 22" h. (ILLUS.).. 575

European Provincial Candlestand - N.O.

Candlestand, primitive provincial-style, hardwood, the square top w/canted corners raised on a pedestal composed of tapering square sections centered by a large turned ball, all raised on a tripod base w/angular canted legs, peg construction, Europe, early 19th c., 12 1/4" d., 31" h. (ILLUS. below left).......... 575

Two-shelf Walnut Candlestand - BR

Candlestand, Victorian novelty type, walnut, circular top on pedestal above six-sided shelf w/petal-carved border above three heavily carved tapered square legs w/lion's head designs, iron mechanism adjusts height, England, mid-19th c., separations in top two pieces, 18 x 19", 31 to 50" h. (ILLUS.)................................... 715

Ornate Rococo Cane Stand - CP

Cane stand, Victorian Rococo style, mahogany, the arched scroll-carved crest w/pierced scroll panels above a serpentine rail raised on ring-and-rod-turned columns over the tall waisted lower back trimmed w/ornate scrolls & centered by a large heart-shaped scroll-pierced panel above the serpentine-sided platform base centering a cast-iron shell-shaped drip pan, mid-19th c. (ILLUS. previous page).... **1,320**

Federal Style Mahogany Canterbury - BR

Canterbury (music stand), Federal, mahogany, two compartments w/vertical slats, openwork hand hole, turned legs w/original brass cuffs & casters, dovetailed drawer, original surface, England or America, early 19th c., minor chips to one leg, minor surface scratches & abrasions, 13 x 18", 23" h. (ILLUS.) **1,650**

Ornate Rosewood Rococo Canterbury - N.O.

Canterbury (music stand), Victorian Rococo style, rosewood, a rectangular top frame w/knob-turned corner finials enclosing four ornately pierce-carved vertical panels centered by a lyre design & fitted at the top center w/an arched & pierced handle, bobbin-turned corner posts above an apron w/a single long drawer, bobbin-turned short feet, mid-19th c., 14 x 20", 15 1/2" h. (ILLUS.) **1,150**

Baroque Display Stand with Busts - M.M.

Display stand, Victorian Baroque Revival style, walnut & composite material, a square top w/a flaring edge over an apron w/each side decorated w/two small panels enclosing a rosette & flanking a round wreath enclosing a profile bust made from a molded composition material, the tapering rectangular sides w/molded leaf bands down each corner & two sides molded w/large busts & two sides w/floral wreaths, a lower rail over a molded base band above a molded apron & simple bracket feet, original dark finish, ca. 1870, 16" w., 36" h. (ILLUS.) **750**

Display stand, Victorian Renaissance Revival style, walnut, made for an Odd Fellows lodge, the rectangular upholstered top w/a flaring cornice above a dentil-carved band over a narrow frieze band carved in relief w/the Odd Fellows symbol above a mid-molding over sides centered by rectangular molding-trimmed panels w/grain painting, widely flaring block-incised apron on a flat platform base on later casters, original finish, ca. 1880, 18 x 26", 34" h. **500**

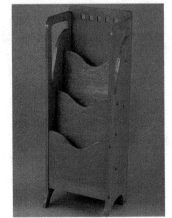

Lakeside Crafts Oak Magazine Stand - CR

Magazine stand, Arts & Crafts style, oak, the tall narrow back w/a row of small squares cutouts near the top & flanked by sides w/large curved cutouts at the top flanking three tiered magazine slots w/down-curved fronts, arched bootjack side bases, Lakeside Crafters, early 20th c., 9 3/4 x 14 1/4", 38 1/2" h. (ILLUS. previous page) **575**

Unique Ornate Inlaid Music Stand - M.M.

Music stand, Victorian Aesthetic Movement style, walnut & maple, the rectangular top w/lightly scalloped edges above a cabinet w/two paneled doors inlaid w/a stylized lyre & cross horns, paneled sides, on a lightly scalloped band above a row of four ornately pierced & carved lyres forming four tall slots above a rectangular base w/overall lattice carving, a drawer w/small ring pulls at one side, tall tapering bracket feet on casters, original finish, last quarter 19th c., 14 x 22", 40" h. (ILLUS.) **750**

Ornately Pierce-carved Music Stand - M.M.

Music stand, Victorian Baroque Revival style, mahogany, high rectangular slightly flaring side panels ornately pierce-carved w/phoenix figures & leafy scrolls centered by a grotesque mask, rotating above a tripod-base w/cabriole legs carved at the knees w/a lion mask & ending in paw feet, the legs joined by a small triangular stretcher, original finish, late 19th c., 10 x 18", 25" h. (ILLUS. below left) **1,250**

Victorian Eastlake Music Stand - M.M.

Music stand, Victorian Eastlake style, oak, the flaring rectangular sides decorated w/a border band of incised leaf bands & a roundel enclosing a central rectangular panel inlaid w/musical instruments, each side attached by slender chains to a center panel topped by an open angular handle, raised on a trestle-type base w/a narrow leafy-vine-incised apron & flat flared end legs w/incised stylized flowers & leaves joined by a medial shelf, refinished, ca. 1890, 16 x 20", 30" h. (ILLUS.) **400**

Finely Inlaid Ebonized Music Stand - M.M.

Music stand, Victorian Renaissance Revival style, inlaid ebonized wood, the rectangular top w/a low spindled gallery centered by a small arched crest, a top drawer inlaid w/a light band of stylized flower heads above inlaid side rails flanking a cabinet door ornately inlaid w/a rectangular panel w/pointed corners enclosing an ornate musical instrument trophy cluster, flat molded base, original finish, ca. 1875, 14 x 22", 44" h. (ILLUS. previous page) **1,000**

Renaissance Revival Nightstand - G.K.

Nightstand, Victorian Renaissance Revival style, walnut & burl walnut, the rectangular white marble top w/molded edges above a case w/rounded front corners flanking a single drawer w/burl panels flanking a roundel w/wooden knob, a me-

dial molding above the conforming lower case w/a paneled door centered by a raised burl panel w/a carved floral cluster & wooden knob, deep molded base on rounded thin block feet, refinished, ca. 1875, 16 x 18", 30" h. (ILLUS. left) **900-1,000**

Simple Louis XV Revival Stands - M.M.

Nightstands, Louis XV Revival style, walnut & burl walnut, the rectangular tan marble top w/serpentine sides above a bombe-shaped case w/a long drawer over a pair of cabinet doors, outset corners continuing down to form outswept legs, cast-brass mounts at the top corners & at the feet, overall banded veneering, original finish, ca. 1920s, 14 x 20", 28" h., pr. (ILLUS.) **750**

Nightstands, Louis XV Revival, walnut, demi-lune form, the half-round white marble top on a deep rounded case w/a stack of three drawers, the top drawer w/an ornate scroll-carved panel, the bottom two drawers carved w/a continuous design of a large shell, scroll-carved serpentine apron, raised on scroll-carved cabriole legs w/scroll feet, refinished, ca. 1920s, 14 x 26", 30" h., pr. (ILLUS. below) **1,600**

Fancy Louis XV Revival Nightstands - M.M.

Painted and Inlaid Louis XVI Revival Nightstands - M.M.

Nightstands, Louis XVI Revival style, inlaid mahogany, rectangular white marble top w/gently rounded ends above a conforming case w/two drawers w/patterned veneering & a delicate floral-inlaid rectangular band overlapping both drawers, the gently curved side panels w/matching inlay, a white-painted molding w/scroll-carved center drop raised on four white-painted round tapering stop-fluted legs all w/gilt trim, silvered metal teardrop drawer pulls, original finish, ca. 1920s, 16 x 20", 28" h., pr. (ILLUS. above) **650**

Neo-Grecque Metal Parlor Stand - N.O.

Parlor stand, bronze-patinated & parcel-gilt metal, a round polished black slate top above a tripod base w/three serpentine legs composed of figural Neo-Grecque-style monopoedal classical termes highlighted w/gilt trim & resting on a tripart base, France, third quarter 19th c., 42" h. (ILLUS.) **4,830**

Queen Anne-Style Nightstands - N.O.

Nightstands, Queen Anne-Style, mahogany, a square top above a single small door w/raised rectangular panel, raised on delicate tapering legs ending in pad feet, England, early 19th c., 12 1/2" sq., 31 1/2" h., pr. (ILLUS.) **2,530**

Parlor stand, Renaissance Revival style, carved oak, tapered form, dovetailed case for top portion, egg-&-leaf base molding, decorated w/carved panels w/ribbons & trophies of agriculture, England or Europe, separations & losses to carving, finish removed, 11 x 13", 4' 4" h. (ILLUS. left) **1,650**

Ornate Anglo-Indian Picture Stand - M.M.

Picture stand, easel-type, Anglo-Indian, carved mahogany, the top panel ornately pierce-carved w/bands of tiny figures & scrolls centering an ornately relief-carved three-prong panel, raised on three canted legs carved at the top w/entwined snakes ending in projecting small brackets, joined at the front by a wide pierce-carved stretcher above lower legs carved w/stylized dragons, original finish, India, ca. 1890, 28" w., 6' 6" h. (ILLUS.) ... **2,500**

Picture stand, easel-type, Victorian Golden Oak style, oak, the tall slender inwardly canted front legs w/decorative spiral-twist carving & ending in angled pointed knob finials flanking a small round beveled mirror, a plain support rail lower on the front legs above a spiral-twist stretcher, a short plain upper rail attached to the plain adjustable rear leg, original brass chain, refinished, ca. 1900, 20" w., 4' 4" h. (ILLUS. top left colum next page) **300**

Carved Oak Pedestal - BR

Turned Golden Oak Picture Stand - M.M.

Ornate Renaissance Picture Stand - M.M.

Picture stand, easel-type, Victorian Renaissance Revival style, walnut & ebonized mixed woods, the two long inwardly slanting front legs joined at the top at a high pierced scroll-carved finial centered by a small ebonized roundel inlaid w/musical in-

struments, a slender notch-cut support rail below & a large rectangular folio compartment w/the fold-out front in ebonized wood decorated w/inlaid musical instruments & gilt trim, canted scroll-carved front feet, a medial rail at the front & a plain adjustable rear leg, original decoration, ca. 1875, 24" w., 6' 4" h. (ILLUS. below left) **4,700**

Very Ornate Rococo Picture Stand - M.M.

Picture stand, easel-type, Victorian Rococo style, carved walnut, the simple inwardly slanted front legs joined by an ornate scroll-carved lower stretcher & a plain upper stretcher w/a wide support rail w/delicate scroll carving, the large top crest rounded & ornately pierce-carved overall w/leafy scrolls, the front legs ending in incurved C-scroll carved feet, a plain adjustable back leg, ca. 1860, original finish, 26" w., 5' 10" h. (ILLUS.) **1,800**

Picture stand, Victorian Renaissance Revival substyle, easel-type, gilt-incised & ebonized-accented walnut, the tall tapering front frame topped by a large carved palmette finial above an arched panel w/rosettes flanking a central gilt classical Minerva head above three slats above the lower panel w/a hinged arched folio rack decorated w/a large black scroll-trimmed cartouche, a curved & pierced front apron on scrolled front legs, a plain fold-out rear support rack, America, ca. 1875, 28 1/2" w., 6' 1/2" h. **2,530**

Plant stand, Classical country-style, painted pine, the octagonal top w/a stepped molding raised on an octagonal column w/a flaring base resting on a square platform, original overall grain-painting, ca. 1850, 10" w., 32" h. (ILLUS. top left column next page) **300**

Classical Country Plant Stand - M.M.

Fine Classical Alabaster Stand - M.M.

ramidal base w/a narrow ropetwist-carved edge band, on four carved paw feet, refinished, ca. 1900, 14" w., 34" h. (ILLUS. below) **400**

Unusual Classical Revival Stand - M.M.

Plant stand, Classical Revival style, carved alabaster, columnar form w/a square top above a ringed & reeded baluster-form pedestal on an octagonal foot, ca. 1890, 12" w., 34" h. (ILLUS.)................................... **500**

Plant stand, Classical Revival style, mahogany & mahogany veneer, a thin square top raised on a block & ring-turned short pedestal atop a square tapering tall pedestal w/brass spearhead mounts at the top, raised on a square py-

Classical Style Rosewood Plant Stand - BR

Plant stand, Classical style, rosewood, circular top above tapered & turned pedestal w/tripod scrolled feet, England, 19th c., minor surface chips & abrasions, base w/several minor separations, top band w/veneer loss, 18 1/2" d., 29 1/2" h. (ILLUS.) **990**

Ornately Turned Plant Stand - M.M.

Plant stand, late Victorian, walnut-stained maple, a wide round top above a pierced & spiral-turned heavy pedestal w/a stepped flaring ring above the wide disk foot, original finish, ca. 1900, 15" d., 36" h. (ILLUS.) **650**

Plant stand, Oriental, carved hardwood, the round dished top above a scroll-pierced apron raised on three lion head-carved cabriole legs ending in paw feet & joined by a pierced lower shelf, China, late 19th - early 20th c., 16" d., 40" h. **200-400**

Delicate Queen Anne Revival Stand - M.M.

Plant stand, Queen Anne Revival, mahogany & mahogany veneer, a small round top w/molded edge raised on a slender baluster-turned pedestal above a tripod base w/cabriole legs ending in scroll feet, original finish, ca. 1920s, 12" d., 36" h. (ILLUS. left) **300**

Plant stand, Victorian Baroque style, carved mahogany, a square top on a square tapering platform resting on the head of a figural roaring lion atop a large carved scroll pedestal tapering to a square base resting on a square platform w/square wafer feet, refinished, late 19th c., 14" w., 36" h. **850**

Tapering Baroque Plant Stand - M.M.

Plant stand, Victorian Baroque style, carved mahogany, small square top w/a gadrooned edge raised on a cluster of carved plumes above a large tapering square column carved on each side w/scroll-filled panels above a square medial rail above the square flaring lower pedestal w/panels carved w/an urn & flowering vines, square tapering base molding, late 19th c., old refinish, 14" w., 38" h. (ILLUS.) **750**

Plant stand, Victorian Baroque style, mahogany, the large round top w/incised apron raised on a finely carved full-figural standing putti swagged in drapery, on a lappet-and-scroll-carved X-form base, original finish, Europe, ca. 1890, 15" d, 32" h. (ILLUS. top photo next page)......... **2,600**

Figural Baroque Revival Plant Stand - M.M.

Decorated Golden Oak Plant Stand - M.M.

Plant stand, Victorian Golden Oak, a thick round top raised on a round pedestal w/four vertical panels of pressed leafy scrolls & beading, stepped round base on small arched feet, refinished, ca. 1900, 14" d., 34" h. (ILLUS.) **400**

Oak Eastlake Plant Stand - M.M.

Plant stand, Victorian Eastlake style, oak, a square top w/molded edges above a deep line-incised apron w/curved & reeded corner brackets raised on ring-and-rod-turned legs joined by two small square shelves, square outswept lower legs, refinished, ca. 1880s, 12" w., 36" h. (ILLUS.) **450**

Unusual Molded Renaissance Stand - M.M.

Plant stand, Victorian Renaissance Revival style, mahogany & molded plaster, the square top w/molded edges above a shallow scalloped apron pierced w/small openings holding small balls, raised on a square waisted top pedestal section resting on a molded plaster band w/two leaves on each side above a tall square tapering pedestal w/each side decorated w/a large molded plaster grotesque face, the flaring pedestal base on a shell-molded band raised on a square platform w/cut corners over flared block feet, original finish, ca. 1880, 14" w., 36" h. (ILLUS. previous page) **500**

Slender Carved Renaissance Stand - M.M.

Simple Renaissance Plant Stand - M.M.

Plant stand, Victorian Renaissance Revival style, walnut, a round white marble top above a coved apron w/two low arched & scalloped drops, raised on a baluster-and ring-turned pedestal flanked by three scalloped S-scroll legs w/outswept scroll feet, original finish, ca. 1870s, 16" d., 34" h. (ILLUS.) **350**

Plant stand, Victorian Renaissance Revival style, walnut w/ebonized trim, a round white marble top above a widely flaring carved rim band w/two stepped & incised drops raised on a ring-and-urn-turned central column flanked by two long slender curved flat brackets joining a central rosette-carved knob above a paneled knob & a tall tapering paneled & ring-turned lower pedestal resting on the tapering disk base w/a band of small ebonized blocks all raised on outswept hoof feet, original finish, ca., 1870s, 14" d., 36" h. (ILLUS. top right column) **900**

Plant Stand with Carved Putti - M.M.

Plant stand, Victorian Rococo style, carved oak, a wide thin round dished top raised on a slender round pedestal carved in full relief w/twining grapevine & two full-figure putti above a round platform issuing four outswept long scroll-carved legs each topped by a carved boar head, Europe, ca. 1870, original finish, 16" d., 26" h. (ILLUS.) **2,000**

Fine Classical Revival Plant Stands - M.M.

Plant stands, Classical Revival style, mahogany, a square top w/a tapering pointed drop finial at each corner, raised on a heavy tapering columnar pedestal w/a ring of beads above a heavy baluster-turned base section resting on a square platform w/tiny ball feet, original dark finish, late 19th c., 14" w., 40" h., pr. (ILLUS.) **2,800**

Plant Stand with Carved Dolphins - M.M.

Plant stands, Victorian Baroque style, carved mahogany, square small top w/gadrooned edges above a deep apron carved w/a band of stylized blossoms & an animal head at each corner, raised on a pedestal w/a divided ovoid reeded post atop a lower pedestal flanked by four fig-ural dolphins resting on a cross-form base w/carved paw feet, original dark finish, probably Europe, late 19th c., 14" w., 38" h., pr. (ILLUS. of one below left) **1,800**

Plant Stands with Figural Mermaids - M.M.

Plant stands, Victorian Baroque style, ebonized fruitwood, a small octagonal top w/a shallow scalloped & carved apron raised on a slender pedestal mounted w/a full-figure mermaid w/arms outstretched, the forked tail wrapping around the lower pedestal above leafy vines & a tripod base w/outswept scroll-carved legs, Europe, late 19th c., original finish, 15" w., 36" h., pr. (ILLUS.) **3,000**

Ornate Renaissance Stand - M.M.

Victorian Aesthetic Movement Portfolio Stand - BR

Plant stands, Victorian Renaissance Revival style, ebonized & inlaid walnut, a round top raised on a large bulbous ebonized urn w/large gilt-incised shells resting on a square platform w/notched corner brackets above a heavy square tapering pedestal, each side centered by a tall tapering arch-topped ebonized panel ornately inlaid w/images of a basket, bird, bow & flowering vines, on a ringed band on the square platform base w/short bracket feet, original finish, ca. 1875, one w/a round white marble top, 14" d., 36" h., pr. (ILLUS. of one without marble top bottom right column of previous page) **2,000**

Portfolio stand, Victorian Aesthetic Movement, carved cherry, frame-&-panel construction w/raised holly & berry borders, sides w/carved cranes, fall front w/recess behind for storage of prints, hinged lip forms stay of easel base, lock & key, late 19th c., leg joints reglued, minor losses & separations, several small repairs, possibly old refinishing, 19 x 33", 4' 2" h., extends to 5' 11" when back is raised (ILLUS. above)................. **1,980**

Sewing stand, Classical style, mahogany & mahogany veneer, the rectangular top w/rounded corners lifting above an interior fitted w/an outside band of small compartments centered by a lidded center well, the sides of the well forming the square tapering base of the case resting on a notch-carved band above a square short pedestal w/another carved band raised on a square panel & cross-form platform w/incurved C-scroll feet, fine figured veneering, original finish, ca. 1830s, 18 x 20", 30" h. (ILLUS. open top left column of next page) **750**

turned stretcher, original finish, ca. 1840,
14 x 20", 30" h. (ILLUS. below) **900**

Fine Classical Sewing Stand - M.M.

Finely Veneered Classical Sewing Stand - M.M.

Sewing stand, Classical style, mahogany &
mahogany veneer, the rectangular top
w/gadrooned edge lifting to a shallow
well above an apron w/an upper ogee
band w/false drawer front above a flat
lower band w/a narrow working drawer, a
pierced scroll-carved apron, raised on a
trestle-style base w/end supports composed of two pairs of molded S-scrolls
joined by a slender baluster- and-ring-

Sewing stand, Federal style, mahogany &
mahogany veneer, the rectangular top
above a deep frame w/a pull-out work surface at one end above two long drawers
w/fine crotch-grain veneering & round brass
pulls raised on spiraling acanthus leaf-
carved supports over the wide rectangular
lower shelf w/a serpentine front, raised on
small turned knob feet on original brass
casters, refinished, ca. 1820s, 16 x 20"
closed, 30" h. (ILLUS. open below) **850**

Nice Federal Veneered Sewing Stand - M.M.

Fancy Labeled Rococo Sewing Stand - M.M.

Sewing stand, Victorian Rococo style, carved walnut, the rectangular top flanked by rounded end drop leaves above a case w/two narrow drawers w/scroll-carved pulls over a thin pull-out slide w/carved pulls supporting the deep cloth bag below, trestle-style supports w/forked heavy scroll-carved uprights raised on blocked shoe feet joined by a flat scroll-carved stretcher w/a central medallion, retailer's label for George Crome Furniture Co. of Boston but produced by Mitchell & Rammelsberg, Cincinnati, Ohio, ca. 1850s, refinished, 16 x 20", 30" h. (ILLUS.) **1,400**

Aesthetic Movement Shaving Stand - M.M.

Shaving stand, Victorian Aesthetic Movement style, walnut, the superstructure w/a flat cornice over a pierced narrow band of knobs & dentil carving between the side rails flanking the square swiveling mirror above the rectangular white marble top on a case w/two narrow drawers over a narrow shaped apron & corner drops, raised on four slender square supports, the front two joined by a slender turned towel bar above a lower rectangular shelf w/a low geometrically pierced gallery, outswept front lower legs, refinished, ca. 1880s, 16 x 20", 5' 4" h. (ILLUS. below left) **1,500**

Fancy Eastlake Shaving Stand - M.M.

Shaving stand, Victorian Eastlake style, walnut & burl walnut, the tall superstructure w/an arched & bobbin-pierced crestrail flanked by corner blocks w/pointed finials above bamboo-turned uprights flanking the tall swiveling rectangular mirror above another bobbin-pierced rail, the rectangular pink marble top above a single narrow burl-veneered drawer w/a rectangular brass pull flanked by corner blocks over drop finials flanking a scalloped narrow apron, the side of the case fitted w/a small drawer, raised on turned front spindles & flat back stiles above a lower shelf w/a bobbin-turned gallery over a small rectangular door w/a recessed burl panel, arched front legs, original finish, ca. 1880s, 16 x 18", 6' h. (ILLUS.) **3,200**

Simple Golden Oak Shaving Stand - M.M.

Shaving stand, Victorian Golden Oak style, quarter-sawn oak, a rectangular beveled mirror in a narrow frame w/a scroll-carved crest swiveling between slender scrolled uprights over the rectangular top over two plain doors, raised on four slender square tapering legs joined by a lower shelf, original finish, ca. 1900, 14 x 16", 5' 6" h. (ILLUS.)............................ **750**

Fancy Golden Oak Shaving Stand - M.M.

Shaving stand, Victorian Golden Oak style, quarter-sawn oak, a shaped oval frame enclosing a beveled mirror swiveling between curved uprights over rectangular top above a deep apron w/undulating panels on the front drawer & sides, raised on spiral-turned supports above a rectangular lower shelf w/a low gallery raised on tapering spiral-turned & slightly outswept legs, refinished, ca. 1890s, 14 x 16", 5' 2" h. (ILLUS. below left) **1,600**

Fine Renaissance Shaving Stand - M.M.

Shaving stand, Victorian Renaissance Revival style, walnut & burl walnut, a rectangular mirror in a molded frame w/corner blocks & a scroll-and-shell-carved crest swiveling between scroll-tipped uprights & a pierced tapering panel over a small half-round shelf, the rectangular white marble top w/molded edges above a narrow burl veneered drawer, raised on a slender rod- and urn-turned pedestal on center post supported by four arched & scroll-trimmed legs, refinished, ca. 1870s, 14 x 16", 5' 10" h. (ILLUS.)............ **2,800**

Shaving stand, Victorian Renaissance Revival style, walnut & burl walnut, an arched rectangular mirror swiveling in a fancy framework w/a pediment centered by peaked scroll-carved crest w/roundel flanked by pointed corner finials above veneer-paneled sides, the rectangular white marble top over a single burled drawer over a scalloped narrow apron, raised on a ring-turned pedestal above a central post flanked by blocked & carved outswept legs, refinished, ca. 1870s, 16 x 18", 5' 4" h. (ILLUS. next page) **1,800**

Shaving Stand in Renaissance Style - M.M.

Rare Baudouine Shaving Stand - M.M.

Shaving stand, Victorian Rococo style, figured maple, a small oval mirror swiveling above a U-form bracket supported w/a slender turned column flanked by ornate pierced

carved scrolls, the rectangular tan marble top w/rounded front corners & bowed front above a serpentine drawer w/scroll-carved trim & turned corner drop pendants, raised on a columnar pedestal w/gadrooned base above a round post enclosed by four scroll-carved arching legs, original finish, Charles Baudouine, New York City, ca. 1850s, 16 x 18', 5' 4" h. (ILLUS. below left) **10,000**

Country-style Stand of Mixed Woods - BR

Side stand, country-style, painted mixed woods, rectangular top, tapered splayed legs w/conforming paneled door above deep front apron, probably French, late 19th c., old yellow & white paint, separations, chips, several loose parts, scattered worm damage, 19 x 20," 28" h. (ILLUS.) **770**

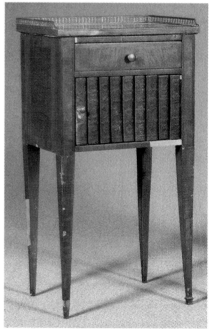

One of two Marble-top Side Stands - BR

Second of Two Side Stands - BR

Side stands, Louis XVI-Style, mahogany, rectangular tops of amber, ivory & mottled beige marble, w/three-quarters openwork brass gallery over single dovetailed drawer above door w/old leather book spines, tapered legs, France, early 20th c., extensive separations, losses to veneer, chips to leather spines, missing brass cuffs, 11 x 15", 30" h., pr. (ILLUS.)..... **880**

Simple Classical Country Washstand - M.M.

Washstand, Classical country-style, cherry, a rectangular top above a single drawer w/wooden knob, raised on tall S-scroll front supports & plain square back legs, lower platform shelf w/concave front, C-scroll front feet, ca. 1850, refinished, 14 x 18", 30" h. (ILLUS.) **275**

Veneered Classical Washstand - M.M.

Washstand, Classical style, mahogany & mahogany veneer, a high rectangular splashback w/an arched & scroll-carved crest over the long rectangular white marble top above a long ogee-fronted drawer, raised on heavy S-scroll front supports & flat back supports over a rectangular shelf, C-scroll front legs on casters, ca. 1840, refinished, 18 x 30", 38" h. (ILLUS.) **850**

Country-style Washstand - BR

Washstand, country-style, pine & poplar, dovetailed construction, three-quarters gallery w/scrolled ends on rectangular top, the case w/single drawer over paneled door, turned front feet, old, possibly original surface, ca. 1840-50, various scuffs, cracks, separations, the drawer w/loose bottom, each side w/mount, possibly for rack or towel rod, 18 x 28", 38" h. (ILLUS.).. **770**

Wide Federal Mahogany Washstand - M.M.

Washstand, Federal style, mahogany & mahogany veneer, a galleried top w/an arched crestrail & flaring stepped side rails flanking the rectangular top w/two large round cutouts & a bowed front, solid sides w/concave-cut fronts flanking a lower shelf over a pair of narrow drawers w/butterfly brasses, on short knob-and-ring-turned feet, original finish, ca. 1820s, 20 x 48", 38" h. (ILLUS.)............... **1,400**

French Directoire Washstand - N.O.

Washstand, French Directoire style, fruitwood, the rectangular top inset w/three ovoid wooden compartments above a paneled apron raised on paneled tapering legs joined by two open lower shelves, on brass caps w/casters, France, first quarter 19th c., 21 1/2" l., 30 1/2" h. (ILLUS.) **920**

Louis XVI Revival Fancy Washstand - M.M.

Washstand, Louis XVI Revival style, figured rosewood veneer, the square top inset w/white marble above the apron w/projecting round corners & a narrow paneled drawer w/wooden knob raised on four ring-turned & reeded columns above a panel-veneered shelf over a small rectangular panel-veneered door & matching sides, serpentine apron raised on short scroll-carved legs on metal casters, original finish, early 20th c., 16" sq., 30" h. (ILLUS.) **650**

English Regency Washstand - M.M.

Washstand, Regency style, mahogany, a high gallery w/a narrow shelf at the top of the back & tapering serpentine sides over the rectangular top over a deep solid apron, raised on four knob- and rod-turned tapering legs joined by a rectangular shelf w/scroll-cut front corners, on short knob-and-peg feet on original brass cap casters, original finish, England, ca. 1820, 18 x 28", 36" h. (ILLUS. on previous page)............................. **650**

Painted Country-style Washstand - M.M.

Classical Marquetry Washstand - N.O.

Washstand, Victorian Classical style, mahogany & marquetry, the rectangular top w/a tall scroll-cut backsplash & out-scrolled sides decorated w/ornate floral & scroll marquetry, the case w/a long drawer w/further decorative marquetry & pierced brass pulls above a pair of urn-inlaid cupboard doors, further marquetry on the sides, raised on carved paw front feet, England, ca. 1850, 19 x 32", 40" h. (ILLUS.)...................................... **863**

Washstand, Victorian country-style, painted & decorated pine, an ornate galleried splashback, the high serpentine back centered by a tall scroll-cut finial & flanked by stepped low sides over the rectangular top above the apron w/a small oval-fronted drawer w/porcelain knob, raised on flat serpentine front supports & turned tapering rear legs joined by a lower shelf w/a serpentine front, simple flat front feet, original mahogany-grained decorating w/yellow trim, mid-19th c., 18 x 25", 42" h. **400**

Washstand, Victorian country-style, painted pine or butternut, an arched splashback on the rectangular top over three long dovetailed drawers w/small wooden knobs, shallow scalloped apron, original worn white paint, ca. 1870, 15 x 24", 36" h. (ILLUS. top right column)................... **300**

Small Country Victorian Washstand - M.M.

Washstand, Victorian country-style, walnut, the wide serpentine splashback & serpentine front brackets joined at each side by a turned towel bar, the rectangular top over a drawer w/leaf-carved pull over a paneled cupboard door centered by a roundel, shaped bracket feet, original finish, ca. 1870, 15 x 22", 35" h. (ILLUS.) **400**

Washstand, Victorian Golden Oak style, a towel bar supported by simple S-scroll uprights above the rectangular top w/a bowed front above a long bowed drawer over a stack of two drawers beside a paneled cupboard door, serpentine side rails ending in scroll-carved feet on casters, original finish, ca. 1900, 16 x 34", 46" h. (ILLUS. top left column next page) **500**

Oak Washstand with Shaped Sides - M.M.

Washstand, Victorian Golden Oak style, oak, a large oval beveled mirror swiveling between slender S-scroll uprights w/a small towel bar to one side supported on a shorter S-scroll upright all on a serpentine backsplash over the rectangular top w/serpentine sides, the case w/a long serpentine drawer over a stack of two flat drawers beside a paneled cupboard door, serpentine apron between short shaped front feet on casters, original hardware, refinished, ca. 1900, 18 x 32", 5' h. **650**

Serpentine-fronted Oak Washstand - M.M.

Washstand, Victorian Golden Oak style, quarter-sawn oak, a long towel bar supported by tall S-scroll uprights w/scrolled ends above the rectangular top w/a serpentine front above a conforming long drawer projecting over two flat cupboard doors, serpentine apron & simple cabriole front legs on casters, original hardware, refinished, ca. 1900, 19 x 30", 4' 2" h. (ILLUS.) **450**

Washstand, Victorian Golden Oak style, quarter-sawn oak, a slender towel bar raised between tall S-scroll supports above the rectangular top w/rounded corners & a bowed front, the conforming case w/two long bowed drawers w/brass pulls above a pair of flat cupboard doors, simple cabriole front legs, refinished, ca. 1890s, 19 x 32", 4' 4" h. **500**

Washstand with Marble Splashback - M.M.

Washstand, Victorian Renaissance Revival style, walnut & burl walnut, a tall arched white marble splashback fitted w/two small shelves above the rectangular white marble top w/notched front corners, the case w/a long narrow drawer w/raised burl oblong panel & black teardrop pulls flanked by blocks at the angled corners above a pair of paneled cupboard doors each centered by a square raised burl panel & flanked by blocked angled front corners, flat molded base w/wafer feet, original finish, ca. 1870s, 17 x 30", 38" h. (ILLUS.) .. **1,350**

Fancy Renaissance Washstand - M.M.

Washstand, Victorian Renaissance Revival style, walnut & burl walnut, the fancy broken-scroll backsplash centered by an arched, pierced & scroll-carved crest over a roundel & small raised burl panels flanked by side panels w/further burl panels all flanked by short side brackets, the rectangular white marble top w/rounded front corners above a case w/a long drawer centered by an arched scroll-carved burl panel flanked by small burl panels w/pulls, carved knobs at the angled front corners above a pair of arch-paneled cupboard doors centered by carved scrolled cartouches & flanked by angled front corners carved w/tapering bead bands, deep flat base w/rounded corners, refinished, ca. 1870s, 18 x 32", 38" h. (ILLUS. on previous page)................. **1,500**

Washstand, Victorian Renaissance Revival style, walnut & burl walnut, the high peaked white marble splashback mounted w/two small shelves above the rectangular white marble top w/angled front corners over a conforming case, a long top drawer centered by a burl roundel flanked by shaped rectangular raised burl panels w/cartouche-carved pulls, two paneled cupboard doors w/arched raised burl panels above the flat molded base w/wafer feet on casters, refinished, ca. 1870s, 18 x 28", 38" h. **1,200**

Renaissance Revival Washstand - N.O.

Washstand, Victorian Renaissance Revival substyle, rosewood, the rectangular top w/projecting front corners above a conforming case w/a long paneled drawer flanked by beveled front corners w/half-round ring-turned drops above a pair of paneled cupboard doors flanked by beveled front corners w/half-round ring-turned inverted drops, molded base w/rounded front corners on disk feet on casters, ca. 1860-70, 19 x 35", 33" h. (ILLUS.) **863**

Washstand, Victorian Rococo style, figured walnut, the high arched splashback w/a fancy fruit- and scrolling leaf-carved crest & flanked by scroll-cut sides on the rectangular white marble top w/projecting corners over scroll-carved blocks flanking a long figured walnut drawer w/a raised oval band & fruit- and leaf-carved pulls over a pair of cupboard doors w/large figured walnut oval panels surrounded by carved scrolls, angled front

corners w/scroll-carved base blocks over the molded base w/rounded corners & a low scroll-carved apron, refinished, ca. 1860, 18 x 30", 42" h. (ILLUS. below)....... **1,800**

Fancy Victorian Rococo Washstand - M.M.

Mahogany Rococo Washstand - M.M.

Washstand, Victorian Rococo style, mahogany & mahogany veneer, the low serpentine white marble galleried splashback on the rectangular white marble top w/a serpentine front, a long serpentine drawer flanked by angled corners w/turned half-round drops above a pair of paneled concave doors flanked by angled corners w/half-round turned drops, serpentine scroll-cut apron & bracket feet, refinished, ca. 1850s, 18 x 32", 34" h. (ILLUS.)............................. **1,100**

Classical two-drawer stand, mahogany, two dovetailed drawers, platform-stretcher base, tapered & turned legs w/turnip feet, pencil inscription on base reads "Jan 1906 Rep. & refinished by Louis Lavoner (?) Oswego, NY," replaced brass pulls, drawer interiors painted yellow, losses & repairs to veneer, top w/repaired separations, feet w/several chips, replaced brass casters, 16 x 22", 28" h. (ILLUS. next page)............... **770**

Two-drawer Stand in Mahogany - BR

Federal country-style one-drawer stand, birch, cherry & bird's-eye maple & mahogany veneer, the nearly square top slightly overhanging the apron w/a single bird's-eye maple-veneered drawer w/original round brass pulls, on ring- and rod-turned reeded legs ending in tall tapering peg feet, ca. 1820-30, one-board birch top reset w/slight warp, 17 1/2 x 18", 25 3/4" h. **633**

Country-style One-drawer Stand - G

Federal country-style one-drawer stand, cherry, rectangular one-board top, square posts finely tapered below dovetailed drawer w/shelf above, original brass bail pull, original dark brown surface, top has been reset w/small knot hole, 16 1/4 x 22", 28 3/4" h. (ILLUS.)....... **1,150**

Federal country-style one-drawer stand, curly maple, nearly square top above an apron w/a single drawer w/wooden knob, raised on square tapering legs on tapering reeded square peg feet, old mellow refinishing, two-board top reset w/braces added, ca. 1830-40, 18 x 18 3/4", 27 3/4" h. **805**

Federal country-style one-drawer stand, painted pine & maple, the rectangular top overhanging an apron w/a single drawer w/two turned wood knobs, on turned legs ending in swelled peg feet, ca. 1840, old mustard yellow paint, pieced restoration

to drawer front, minor splits in top, 19 3/4 x 20" **546**

Federal country-style two-drawer stand, poplar, curly maple & cherry, the nearly square one-board poplar top overhanging an apron w/two curved-front drawers w/old pressed glass pulls, on square tapering legs, ca. 1850, 21 x 22", 30" h.. .... **575**

Country-style Two-drawer Stand - BR

Federal country-style two-drawer stand, walnut, square top above two hand-dovetailed drawers w/hand-planed bottoms, tapered legs, sides & back walnut veneer over pine, probably shop-made early 20th c., some elements possibly earlier, 18" sq., 31" h. (ILLUS.) **193**

Inlaid Mahogany One-drawer Stand - BR

Federal one-drawer stand, inlaid mahogany, rectangular top w/rounded corners & band of double string inlay, tapered legs w/extensive string & elliptical inlay below bird's-eye maple panels, dovetailed drawer w/three interior compartments, original oval brass pulls, original glue blocks on back skirt, American South, missing side glue blocks, which have been replaced w/small iron cleats, drawer runners flipped, top w/old separation, possibly as made, scattered old stains, 18 1/4 x 26 1/4", 28 5/8" h. (ILLUS.)........ **46,200**

STOOLS

Square Chippendale-Style Footstool - G.K.

Chippendale-Style footstool, mahogany, the rectangular upholstered top on a flat frame w/turned drop pendants in the center of each side, on cabriole legs w/leaf-carved knees & ending in claw-and-ball feet, original finish, late 19th c., 16" w., 15" h. (ILLUS.) .. **$450**

Chippendale-Style Stool - BR

Chippendale-Style stool, mahogany, muslin-covered seat, elaborately carved cabriole legs, ball-&-claw feet w/notched talons, England, probably 19th c., oval skirt w/multiple tack wounds, laminate reinforcement behind legs, old muslin covering stained, 19 x 27", 18" h. (ILLUS.)..... **1,870**

George II-Style stools, mahogany, a rectangular upholstered top & apron raised on cabriole legs w/shell-carved

knees & ending in lion paw feet, England, late 19th c., 17 1/2 x 25 1/2", 18" h., pr. (ILLUS. bottom of page) **748**

George III stool, mahogany, the rectangular over-upholstered needlepoint top raised on cabriole legs w/scroll feet, England, first quarter 19th c., 18 x 22", 19" h. (ILLUS. below)................................... **748**

English George III Upholstered Stool - N.O.

George III-Style Hoof-footed Stool - N.O.

George III-Style stool, mahogany, the rectangular upholstered seat on a shell- and scroll-carved serpentine seatrail on cabriole legs w/scroll-carved knees ending in hoof feet & joined by a curved H-stretcher, England, mid-19th c., 25 1/4 x 29 1/4", 19 1/4" h. (ILLUS. above) **1,840**

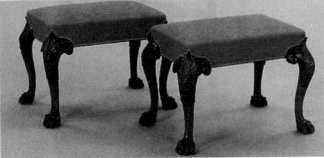

George II-Style Mahogany Stools - N.O.

Georgian-Style Stools - N.O.

Georgian-Style stools, carved mahogany, the rectangular padded & upholstered top within a gadrooned molding above the curved ornately leaf-carved serpentine apron, raised on cabriole legs ending in dolphin mask feet, England, late 19th c., 17 x 24", 21" h., pr. (ILLUS. above)......... **748**

Louis XV-Style Upholstered Stool - N.O.

Louis XV-Style stool, carved fruitwood, the rectangular needlepoint top w/serpentine sides on a conforming apron w/a carved shell at each side, raised on cabriole legs w/shell-carved knees & ending in scroll-and-peg feet, France, third quarter 19th c., 16 x 17 1/2", 16 1/4" h. (ILLUS.).............. **920**

Louis XV-Style Low Stool - BR

Louis XV-Style stool, carved rosewood, rectangular, carved frieze w/openwork shell & scroll decoration, short cabriole legs, scroll feet, upholstered seat, Europe, late 19th c., minor repairs to wood, scuffs & scratches, old worn upholstery, minor losses & chips to carving, 17 x 24 x 16" (ILLUS. below left).............. **1,210**

Louis XV-Style Giltwood Stool - N.O.

Louis XV-Style stools, giltwood, the rectangular top w/rounded corners above a serpentine apron ornately carved w/scrolls & shells, on cabriole legs w/leaf-carved knees & scroll feet joined by a shaped X-stretcher, France, 19th c., 17 1/2" h., pr. (ILLUS. of one) **1,610**

English Regency Gout Stool - N.O.

Regency gout stool, mahogany, an upholstered & rolled top over scrolled sides carved w/honeysuckle vines, on bulbous knob feet, England, early 19th c., 12 3/4 x 18", 10 1/2" h. (ILLUS.) **1,610**

Victorian Chippendale Piano Stool - N.O.

Victorian Chippendale Revival piano stool, mahogany, the rectangular needlepoint top opening to a storage space, the deep apron frame & square legs carved in the Chinese Chippendale taste w/latticework along the apron & down each leg, on block feet, legs joined by a pierced H-stretcher, probably England, late 19th c., 14 x 19 1/2", 20" h. (ILLUS.)..... **690**

English Gothic Revival Stool - N.O.

Victorian Gothic Revival stools, oak, a rectangular top above a line-incised apron raised on molded square legs w/carved quatrefoil corner brackets, England, mid-19th c., 13 1/2 x 18", 18" h., pr. (ILLUS. of one)...................................... **805**

Rose-carved Rococo Footstool - G.K.

Victorian Rococo footstool, walnut, a deep square upholstered top above a narrow dash-carved band over the serpentine apron carved w/bold rose clusters, demi-cabriole legs w/leaf-carved knees, old refinish, newer upholstery, ca. 1865, 18" w., 15" h. (ILLUS. below left) **450**

Rococo Stool Attributed to Belter - G.K.

Victorian Rococo organ stool, carved rosewood, a trilobed upholstered seat on a conforming deep apron ornately carved w/large florals, adjusting on a metal screw mechanism above an acanthus leaf-carved pedestal on a tripod base w/angled curved legs ending in S-scroll feet, original finish & upholstery, attributed to John Belter, New York, New York, ca. 1855, 14" w., 22" h. (ILLUS.) **3,500**

William IV Scroll-carved Stool - N.O.

William IV stool, mahogany & leather, rectangular w/a high S-scroll frame, sides carved w/a large rosette & leafy scroll ending in fan-carved corners, on low beveled block feet, England, first half 19th c., 20 1/2 x 35 1/2", 20" h. (ILLUS.) **748**

TABLES

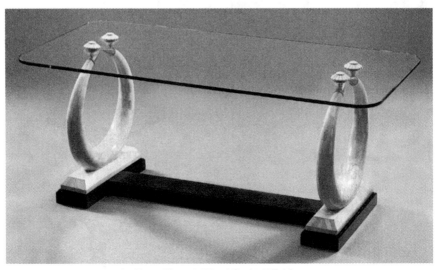

Art Deco Glass & Wood Cocktail Table - N.O.

French Art Deco Cocktail Table - N.O.

Art Deco cocktail table, blond mahogany, in the Chinese taste, the round top w/a rounded apron raised on five square legs on blocked feet & small corner blocks, w/an applied metal tag marked "Gouffé," France, ca. 1930, 35" d., 17 1/2" h. (ILLUS.)..................................... **$288**

Art Deco cocktail table, glass-topped rosewood, the rectangular glass top w/rounded corners raised on two faux ivory & brass-tipped Islamic crescents set upon the ends of H-form rosewood plinth base, France, ca. 1930, 23 x 48", 20" h. (ILLUS. top photo).. **1,093**

Baroque Revival coffee table, carved walnut, the rectangular top w/inset marble raised on large end supports carved in bold relief as spread-winged phoenixes above serpentine shoe feet, original finish, ca. 1920s, 16 x 26", 21" h. **950**

Baroque Revival Side Table - M.M.

Baroque Revival side table, walnut, a rectangular top w/rounded ends w/wide scroll-carved bands & flanked by oblong drop leaf carved to continue the scroll band & forming an oblong top when raised, on slender ring- and-rod-turned legs joined by bobbin-turned stretchers, two matching swing-out support legs, original dark finish, ca. 1920s, 20 x 30" open, 26" h. (ILLUS. open) **650**

Spanish Oak Guard Room Table - N.O.

Dutch Baroque-Style Oak Library Table - N.O.

Baroque-Style guard room table, oak, the long rectangular planked top raised on heavy serpentine end supports joined by stretchers & w/long slender scrolled iron brackets under the top, Spain, ca. 1900, 39 x 87", 29 1/2" h. (ILLUS. top photo) **2,760**

Baroque-Style library table, fumed oak, the rectangular top w/a molded edge overhanging a geometrically carved apron & raised on heavy upright rectangular panel legs carved on the outside edges w/full-figure caryatids above a shell-carved band that continues around the cross-stretcher, raised on low scroll- and shell-carved feet, Holland, ca. 1900, 42 1/2 x 82", 32" h. (ILLUS. second photo from top) **978**

Bentwood center table, the oval top supported on a central cluster of four curved & outswept continuous bentwood scrolls for the legs & trimmed w/further smaller scrolls, dark finish, Austria, possibly Thonet, late 19th c., 34 x 50 1/2", 30" h. (ILLUS. left) **5,520**

Biedermeier Cherry Center Table - N.O.

Biedermeier center table, cherry, the nearly square top overhanging an apron fitted w/one long drawer, on simple cabriole legs, good wood figure, Europe, first-half 19th c., 29 1/4 x 30 1/2", 30" h. (ILLUS.)... **1,495**

Fine Austrian Bentwood Table - N.O.

Biedermeier Blond Side Table - N.O.

Biedermeier side tables, blond wood, a round top raised on a round upper column joined by an ebonized ring to a paneled lower column w/another ebonized ring, resting on a tripartite base, Europe, first half 19th c., 20" d., 28" h., pr. (ILLUS. of one) **1,610**

Biedermeier-style Breakfast Table - G

Biedermeier-Style drop-leaf breakfast table, figured maple veneer, rectangular top w/dovetailed drawer on one side w/raised front, false front on opposite side, thick round column on platform base w/carved paw feet, Europe, 20th c., some reconstruction, 28 x 33" w. plus 9" leaves, 29 3/4" h. (ILLUS. below left) **978**

Chippendale dining table, mahogany, the rectangular top flanked by deep rectangular drop leaves, an arched apron supported on swing-out cabriole legs w/claw-and-ball feet, New York state, late 18th c., open 48 1/4 x 57", 28 3/4" h. (ILLUS. closed bottom of page)............................ **4,600**

Chippendale Tea Table - BR

Chippendale tea table, mahogany, carved Chippendale borders, "birdcage" & tilt-top mechanism, spiral-carved urn pedestal w/flower-carved band at base, three legs w/fine acanthus-carved knees w/ball-and-claw feet w/articulated talons, original iron spider & brass latch, England or America, 18th c., top w/several patches, battens probably reset, old refinishing, 33 1/8 x 34 1/8", 28 " h. (ILLUS.)............. **10,450**

Fine Chippendale Mahogany Dining Table - N.O.

Rare Chippendale Tea Table - BR

Chippendale tea table, mahogany, circular dished top w/piecrust border tilting on figured mahogany "birdcage" above the ring- & urn-turned pedestal above tripod base, pad feet, original iron spider, original spindles & plate, batten & latch appear to be original & untouched, probably original surface, Virginia family history, 18th c., stains, losses, cracks, chips & separations, 26 1/8 x 26 3/4", 27 1/4" h. (ILLUS.) **19,800**

Chippendale Revival Tea Table - M.M.

Chippendale Revival tea table, mahogany, large round top w/piecrust edge tilting above a turned pedestal on a tripod base w/three outstretched cabriole legs ending in claw-and-ball feet, original dark finish, late 19th c., 24" d., 30" h. (ILLUS.) **500**

Fine Chippendale Revival Side Table - M.M.

Chippendale Revival side table, mahogany, a rectangular top w/gadrooned ends flanked by half-round drop leaves above a deep apron w/a stack of two cockbeaded end drawers w/round brass pulls, cabriole legs w/scroll-carved knees & ending in claw-and-ball feet, original finish, 19th c., 16 x 20" closed, 30" h. (ILLUS.) ... **1,400**

Chippendale Revival Carved Table - M.M.

Chippendale Revival tea table, mahogany & mahogany veneer, the large scalloped round top w/carved shells along the border tilting above a turned pedestal on a tripod base w/three outstretched cabriole legs w/leaf-carved knees & ending in pad feet, original dark finish, ca. 1920s, 24" d., closed 4' h. (ILLUS.) **700**

Chippendale-Style Coffee Table - G

Chippendale-Style coffee table, mahogany & mahogany veneer, the rectangular mirrored tray top w/low scalloped upright sides & cut-out hand holes resting in a molded frame above square legs w/block feet & Chinese-style lattice corner brackets, old finish, early 20th c., 19 x 30", 19 1/2" h. (ILLUS.)............................... **1,208**

Chippendale-Style Tea Table - N.O.

Fine Classical Breakfast Table - M.M.

Chippendale-Style Dressing Table - BR

Chippendale-Style dressing table, mahogany & yellow pine, frieze drawer above three dovetailed drawers, central drawer w/carved fan, cabriole legs w/ball-and-claw feet, some cut nails on drawer runners, composed of parts from various pieces of furniture, probably late 19th c., small drawer is reduced, refinishing, scratches & minor separations, 19 x 27", 39" h. (ILLUS.) **1,540**

Chippendale-Style tea table, lacquered & decorated wood, the scalloped round top decorated w/gilt & gesso Oriental landscape, on a turned tapering pedestal above a tripod base w/cabriole legs w/acanthus leaf-carved knees & ending in ball-and-claw feet, England, third quarter 19th c., 19 1/2" , 28" h. (ILLUS. top right column) **805**

Classical breakfast table, mahogany & mahogany veneer, the wide rectangular top flanked by deep half-round drop leaves above a veneer-banded apron w/corner drops, raised on a heavy bulbous acanthus leaf-carved pedestal on a block platform over four outstretched leaf-carved legs w/paw feet, old refinish, ca. 1840, 24 x 48" closed, 30" h. (ILLUS.)...................................... **1,400**

Classical breakfast table, mahogany, rectangular top flanked by wide drop leaves w/rounded corners, raised on carved columns above the trestle base w/circular cross-stretcher & tapered columns, acanthus-carved saber legs, paw feet, original brass casters & iron hinges, hinges marked "JG," America, ca. 1820, 24 x 39", opens to 51", 29" h. (ILLUS. top of next page) **4,620**

Rare Classical Breakfast Table - BR

probably made in Boston, ca. 1830,
37 1/2 x 38", 30" h. (ILLUS. below) **1,955**

Late Classical Mahogany Card Table - G

Fine Classical Card Table - N.O.

Classical card table, mahogany & mahogany veneer, the rectangular fold-over top w/concave edges above a deep ogee-form apron w/a serrated edge raised on a heavy scroll-carved U-form pedestal atop a rectangular platform w/heavy outswept scroll-cut legs on casters, minor veneer chips, probably New York, ca. 1845, 18 x 34 1/2", 29" h. (ILLUS.) **345**

Classical card table, mahogany, rectangular fold-over top w/rounded corners, on a scroll-tipped apron raised on a heavy ring- and acanthus-carved center post above four arched & splayed legs w/acanthus-carved knees & ending in brass hairy-paw foot caps on casters,

Fine Round Classical Dining Table - M.M.

Classical Two-Pedestal Dining Table - M.M.

Classical dining table, mahogany & mahogany veneer, extension-type, round top w/a deep crotch-veneered apron, raised on a cluster of four columns over a cross-form base w/arch-topped flattened legs on disk feet on casters, old refinish, w/six leaves, ca. 1840, 60" d., 30" h. (ILLUS. bottom photo previous page) **4,000**

Classical dining table, mahogany & mahogany veneer, two-pedestal extension-type, each wide half-round top section w/a wide inside drop leaf, the deep apron w/a turned drop at each corner, each pedestal w/a bulbous acanthus leaf-carved post raised on four outswept leaf-carved legs ending in large paw feet on casters, original finish, replaced casters, ca. 1830s, open 54 x 100", 30" h. (ILLUS. open top photo) **4,500**

Classical dressing table, mahogany & mahogany veneer, the superstructure w/a large vertical rectangular mirror mounted in a wide frame w/half-round column sides joined by corner blocks w/brass rosettes swiveling between ornate turned & acanthus leaf-carved uprights joined at the top w/a plain pointed crestrail, the columns resting on a pair of long shallow handkerchief drawers set back on the rectangular white marble top, the case w/a long round-fronted veneered drawer over two shorter round-fronted drawers flanking an arched central panel, raised on four spiral-turned acanthus leaf-carved legs joined by a wide medial shelf w/a serpentine front, on small double-knob feet on brass casters, original hardware, refinished, ca. 1830s, 19 x 36", 6' 2" h. (ILLUS. left) **2,000**

Quality Classical Dressing Table - M.M.

Classical Inlaid Games Table - M.M.

Classical games table, inlaid mahogany, the rectangular fold-over top w/rounded corners above a conforming apron centered by an inlaid feathered maple rectangular panel, raised on a heavy pedestal w/boldly carved acanthus leaves above a round platform w/a carved border raised on four outswept legs w/leaf-carved knees & large paw feet, original finish, ca. 1830, 18 x 36" closed, 30" h. (ILLUS.) **1,200**

Philadelphia Classical Games Table - M.M.

Classical games table, mahogany & mahogany veneer, the rectangular fold-over top w/a gadrooned edge & rounded corners opening to a plain top w/a narrow half-round apron w/florette-carved front corners, raised on a pedestal composed of a cluster of columns resting on a long quadripartite platform base raised on carved paw feet, Philadelphia, ca. 1830s, original finish, 18 x 36", 30" h. (ILLUS.) **3,000**

Games Table with Unusual Base - M.M.

Classical games table, mahogany & mahogany veneer, the rectangular fold-over top w/rounded corners opening to a conforming top over a flat ogee front apron, raised on a flat flared center support atop a large flattened oval disk resting at the center of a resting platform base w/arched shoe feet, probably Boston, ca. 1840, original dark finish, 16 x 32", 30" h. (ILLUS.)........ **500**

Fork-based Classical Games Table - M.M.

Classical games table, mahogany & mahogany veneer, the rectangular fold-over top w/rounded corners above a conforming top over a deep ogee apron, raised on a widely flaring forked scroll-cut support raised on a stepped flaring platform base w/small ogee bracket feet, original finish, ca. 1845, 18 x 36", 30" h. (ILLUS. below left)........ **600**

Late Classical Games Table - M.M.

Classical games table, mahogany & mahogany veneer, the rectangular fold-over top w/rounded corners opening to a matching top over a deep crotch-grain veneered apron w/a scroll-carved border, raised on a a flattened scrolled support w/a cut-out center enclosing a scroll-carved finial, resting on a long quadripartite platform base w/outswept scroll feet, original finish, ca. 1850, 18 x 38", 30" h. (ILLUS.)...................... **750**

Games Table on Ornate Carved Base - M.M.

Classical games table, mahogany & mahogany veneer, the rectangular fold-over top w/rounded corners & a flat projecting front section opening over a conforming veneered apron, raised on a heavy cylindrical column boldly carved w/rings of acanthus leaves atop sawtooth-carved disk supported by outswept animal legs w/leaf-carved knees & large paw feet, original finish, ca. 1830s, 20 x 40", 30" h. (ILLUS.)... **2,000**

Classical games table, mahogany & mahogany veneer, the rectangular serpentine-edged fold-over top above a conforming veneered apron, raised on a flattened lyre-form pedestal above a deep rectangular coved apron & platform raised on pierced scroll-cut feet, Boston, ca. 1830, original finish, 18 x 36", 30" h. **650**

Classical parlor center table, mahogany & mahogany veneer, the rectangular top w/serpentine edges above a conforming deep scalloped apron, raised on a bulbous baluster-form octagonal pedestal resting on a domed, stepped paneled base w/notch-carved bands, raised on four flaring ogee bracket feet, refinished, ca. 1840s, 20 x 32", 30" h.) **500**

Unusual Classical Pier Table - M.M.

Classical pier table, mahogany & mahogany veneer, the rectangular white marble top above a coved apron, supported at the front by large square tapering columns w/carved acanthus leaves & gadrooning & resting on turned disk feet supported by projecting side platforms backed by matching half-columns centering a large arched mirror above a half-round acanthus leaf-carved disk which appears round in the mirror reflection, compressed carved round feet, probably Baltimore, original finish, ca. 1830s, 18 x 42", 34" h. (ILLUS.) **3,500**

Labeled Classical Pier Table - N.O.

Classical pier table, mahogany & mahogany veneer, the rectangular white marble top over a concave frieze band decorated w/stylized acanthus leaves & other foliage, supported on a pair of veneered columns w/gilt-brass capitals & bases, the edge of the lower shelf stenciled w/a classical design, a rectangular mirror in the back panel, on ebonized carved front paw feet crowned w/gilded vertical ga-

drooning, simple turned rear legs, on casters, original finish except lower shelf, stenciled label of Cook & Parkin, Philadelphia, first quarter 19th c., 20 x 47 3/4", 40 3/4" h. (ILLUS. below left) **6,900**

Fine Classical Pier Table - N.O.

Classical pier table, mahogany & mahogany veneer, the rectangular white marble top w/canted front corners above a conforming deep ogee apron, supported at the front by long heavy S-scrolls & at the back by a framed rectangular mirror all joined by a half-round lower platform on projecting C-scroll front legs, ca. 1830-40, 21 x 41", 37 1/2" h. (ILLUS.) **2,530**

Rare Classical Pier Table/Vitrine - N.O.

Classical pier table with vitrine, ormolu-mounted mahogany & mahogany veneer, the rectangular white marble top above an apron mounted in the center w/a long pierced scrolling ormolu mount w/smaller mounts at the front corners & at the sides, the front raised on tall columns w/ormolu capitals & bases that flank a pair of large glazed cabinet doors, glazed side panels, on a thick plinth base, first quarter 19th c., 17 x 39 3/4", 35 3/4" h. (ILLUS.) **2,070**

Classical Maple-inlaid Work Table - M.M.

Classical work table, mahogany & figured maple, the rectangular top w/rounded corners above a conforming deep case w/a very narrow top drawer w/a figured walnut veneer panel, brass knob pulls & a brass keyhole escutcheon above two graduated matching drawers, raised on a heavy baluster-turned & acanthus leaf-carved pedestal on outswept leaf-carved legs ending in hairy paw feet on casters, polished original finish, ca. 1830s, 16 x 22", 30" h. (ILLUS.) **1,600**

Classical work table, mahogany & mahogany veneer, a rectangular top slightly overhanging an apron w/a single drawer w/a wooden pull, raised on four ring- and knob-turned legs centered by spiral-carved sections, raised on casters, original finish, ca. 1830, 16 x 20", 30" h. (ILLUS. below left) **450**

Boston Classical Work Table - SK

Classical work table, mahogany & mahogany veneer, rectangular top flanked by half-round drop leaves flanking the case w/two drawers w/wooden knobs, raised on a square tapering pedestal w/concave sides resting on a quadripartite platform w/tapering bulbous feet on casters, Boston, Massachusetts, ca. 1830s, imperfections, 18 1/8 x 19", 29 3/4" h. (ILLUS.).. **1,380**

One-drawer Classical Work Table - M.M.

Basket-based Classical Work Table - M.M.

Classical work table, mahogany & mahogany veneer, rectangular top over a deep case w/a concave-fronted plain drawer above a flat drawer w/large rosette & ring pulls flanked by half-round ring-turned drops, raised on a bulbous pedestal carved in the form of a fruit-filled basket resting on a quadripartite platform raised on outswept fluted scroll feet on casters, refinished, ca. 1835, 16 x 20", 28" h. (ILLUS. previous page) 850

drooned edges flanked by half-round drop leaves over a case w/two round-fronted drawers w/original brass knobs flanked by leaf-carved side panels, raised on a baluster-turned leaf-carved pedestal on four outswept leaf-carved legs ending in paws on casters, refinished, late 19th c., 16 x 18", 30" h. (ILLUS. below) 750

Classical Work Table on Carved Base - M.M.

Classical Revival Work Table - M.M.

Classical work table, mahogany & mahogany veneer, rectangular top over a deep case w/two drawers w/brass ring pulls & inlaid brass keyholes, small turned drops at each corner, raised on a bulbous acanthus leaf-carved short pedestal above four outswept leaf-carved legs ending in hairy paw feet, original finish, replaced hardware, ca. 1830, 15 x 20", 28" h. (ILLUS.) 1,250

Classical Revival work table, mahogany & mahogany veneer, rectangular top w/ga-

Classical-Rococo transitional center table, rosewood, the rectangular white marble-inset top w/serpentine sides w/a gadrooned border above a serpentine apron carved at the center of each side w/leaf & blossom clusters, raised on heavy S-scroll legs w/leaf-carved knees & forming a trestle base w/an arched, shell-carved cross-stretcher, ca. 1850, 25 3/4 x 42 1/2", 29 1/4" h. (ILLUS. below) 1,265

Classical-Rococo Transitional Center Table - N.O.

Fine Classical-Style Mahogany Dining Table with Leaves - N.O.

Classical-Style Breakfast Table - N.O.

Classical-Style breakfast table, mahogany, the rectangular top flanked by deep drop leaves w/notched rounded corners, the apron w/a round-fronted drawer at each end, raised on a heavy acanthus-carved pedestal on a quadripartite platform on outswept heavy carved paw feet on casters, late 19th c., open 38 x 52 1/2", 29" h. (ILLUS. closed) **863**

Classical-Style dining table, mahogany, extension-type, the round top w/a scroll-carved border band raised on a large ring-turned split pedestal w/a bulbous reeded lower section issuing heavy acanthus-carved shaped legs ending in large paw feet, late 19th c., w/four leaves, closed 54" d., 29 1/4" h. (ILLUS. extended photo top of page) **3,220**

Classical-Style dressing table, mahogany, a large horizontal oval mirror swiveling between long outswept dolphin-carved supports above the rectangular top above a case w/a pair of round-fronted drawers flanking a leaf-carved panel over a long round-fronted drawer above a gadroon-carved apron band, the case supported by four S-scroll carved dolphin supports joining a rect-

angular serpentine-sided platform raised on outswept dolphin-carved legs, late 19th c., 20 3/4 x 27", overall 5' 6 1/2" h. (ILLUS. below) **2,300**

Fine Classical-Style Dressing Table - N.O.

Colonial Revival dining table, cherry, a long narrow rectangular top flanked by wide half-round drop heaves, raised on two baluster-, ring- and knob-turned pedestals above outswept cabriole legs w/pad feet joined by a turned medial stretcher, on casters, possibly English, late 19th - early 20th c., refinished, open 32 x 48", 30" h. (ILLUS. closed photo next page) **400**

Fine Classical Revival Mahogany Dining Table - M.M.

Oak Colonial Revival Dining Table - M.M.

Small Colonial Revival Table - M.M.

Colonial Revival Library Table - M.M.

Colonial Revival dining table, mahogany & mahogany veneer, expandable, the long rectangular top w/rounded corners above deep apron w/a thin gadroon-carved edge band, raised on six cabriole legs w/leaf-carved knees & ending in scroll feet on pads, original finish, late 19th c., w/six leaves opens to 16', closed 50" l., 30" h. (ILLUS.) **6,500**

Colonial Revival dining table, quarter-sawn oak, the rectangular top flanked by wide D-form drop leaves raised on simple trumpet-turned legs joined by box stretchers, on ball feet on casters, two swing-out support legs, refinished, early 20th c., 28 x 54" open, 30" h. (ILLUS. open right column) **450**

Colonial Revival library table, cherry, the rectangular top w/serpentine edges over-hanging a case w/a center drawer above an arched opening flanked by panels carved w/large palmette leaves, scroll-carved side aprons, on simple cabriole legs w/scroll-carved knees, refinished, late 19th c., 28 x 48", 30" h. (ILLUS.).......... **600**

Ornate Dutch Marquetry Dining Table - N.O.

Colonial Revival Sewing Table - M.M.

Colonial Revival sewing table, heavily figured cherry, the rectangular top opening to a deep divided well, the serpentine apron w/a small carved shell on each side, raised on slender cabriole legs w/leaf-carved knees & paw feet, refinished, ca. 1900, 16 x 18", 30" h. (ILLUS. open left) **450**

Country-style dining table, mahogany & marquetry, the rectangular top w/ornate floral marquetry flanked by wide rectangular drop leaves w/further marquetry in an urn & vining flower design, the apron & square legs w/further marquetry vines, on casters, Holland, third quarter 19th c., open 48 x 63", 29 1/2" h. (ILLUS. above) .. **2,760**

Country-style work table, yellow pine, two-board top w/cut nails, four turned legs w/mortise-and-tenon construction, 19th c., old refinishing, separations, two legs ended out, 30 1/2 x 123", 29 1/2" h. (ILLUS. photo below) **2,200**

Early American country-style work table, walnut, the large rectangular three-board top widely overhanging the deep apron w/two deep drawers w/wooden pulls, raised on three turned & tapering legs ending in knob-and-peg feet, old finish, early 19th c., reconstruction to base & drawers, 33 x 60", 30" h. (ILLUS. top of next page) **1,725**

Yellow Pine Country Work Table - BR

Early American Walnut Work Table - G

French Empire-Style Center Table - N.O.

Empire-Style center table, mahogany, the round top above a paneled ormolu-mounted apron raised on turned & tapering legs joined by a lower shelf w/concave sides, on short splayed feet, France, ca. 1900, 33" d., 29 1/2" h. (ILLUS.) **1,610**

Federal card table, cherry & mahogany veneer, the hinged half-round top w/projecting scroll-carved front corners above a conforming apron w/mahogany veneer, raised on ring- and knob-turned legs w/a long spiral-turned section above the ring- and baluster-turned feet, old refinish, ca. 1820, 18 x 40", 30" h. (ILLUS. right above).. **1,800**

Federal card table, inlaid mahogany, the hinged half-round top w/pointed front corners & delicate chain-inlaid edge lifting above a matching top over a conforming apron w/line-inlaid panels centering a light-colored rectangular panel enclosing an oval, a band of chain inlay along the bottom edge, raised on knob-turned & spiraled acanthus leaf-carved legs on casters, old refinish, ca. 1820s, 19 x 38", 30" h. (ILLUS. right below) **1,500**

Federal Table with Unusual Top - M.M.

Finely Inlaid Federal Card Table - M.M.

Rare Federal Mahogany Game Table - N.O.

Federal card table, mahogany & mahogany veneer, the rectangular fold-over top w/angled corners on a conforming figured mahogany veneer apron w/an applied ebony band replacing original lines of brass inlay, raised on four turned legs w/reed-carved cylindrical sections over spiral-carved egg-shaped sections, on a veneered plinth w/concave sides, supports on four rabbit-like outswept legs w/an acanthus leaf-carved knee, the paw feet on brass casters, possibly from the workshop of Duncan Phyfe, New York City, early 19th c., 18 x 36", 29 3/4" h. (ILLUS.) **10,063**

feet, some family history written inside drawer, ca. 1850, feet have been ended out, gallery is old replacement, 17 x 34 1/2", 34 3/4" h. (ILLUS. below left) **1,495**

Federal Country Dressing Table - M.M.

Federal country-style dressing table, painted mahogany, a scroll-cut crestrail above a narrow rectangular shelf over a pair of handkerchief drawers on the rectangular top over a single long drawer, ring-and-spiral-twist-turned legs on knob feet, ca. 1830, old green repaint, replaced wood pulls, refinished, 18 x 34", 40" h. (ILLUS.) **800**

Curly Maple Dressing Table - G

Federal country-style dressing table, curly maple, rectangular top w/serpentine three-quarters gallery over a single long drawer, turned tapering legs w/peg

Federal Country-style Tea Table - G

Federal country-style tilt-top tea table, cherry, two-board top w/small wooden pegs & some figure, ring-turned column, cabriole legs w/raised panels at tops & ending in tripod snake feet, decorated w/incised vining down the legs & around the top w/small fans at the corners of top, cleats w/mix of rose head & square cut nails & some later screws, attributed to Connecticut, old refinishing, 26 x 26 1/4", 27" h. (ILLUS.)... **2,128**

Federal Pembroke table, cherry, rounded leaves, tapered legs, dovetailed drawer, hand-wrought nails, probably original brass pull, pivoting drop-leaf supports,

original glue blocks, possibly Virginia, early 19th c., top reset w/some new screws, old refinishing, some insect damage, 1/2" hole, 21 x 34", opens to 43", 29" h. (ILLUS. below)........................ **1,430**

Cherry Pembroke Table - BR

Federal sofa table, mahogany & mahogany veneer, the long rectangular top above an apron w/a pair of drawers flanked by half-round drop leaves, raised on a square center pedestal carved w/a band of acanthus leaves & resting on a quadripartite platform supported by outswept acanthus leaf-carved legs ending in brass paws on casters, attributed to New York City, ca. 1820, 21 x 30 1/2" plus 11" leaves, 29" h. (ILLUS. below).... **18,400**

Rare New York Classical Sofa Table - G

Federal Three-drawer Work Table - M.M.

Federal work table, mahogany & mahogany veneer, square top flanked by hinged drop leaves w/rounded corners above a case of three shallow drawers w/round brass pulls, on ring-turned & spiral-carved legs ending in disk-and-peg feet, old finish, ca. 1820s, 16 x 30" open, 30" h. (ILLUS. half open)............................. **600**

Federal Revival Side Table - M.M.

Federal Revival side table, mahogany, the rectangular top flanked by half-round drop leaves w/leaf-carved corners above an apron w/a single paneled end drawer w/butterfly brass over line-incised brackets flanked by fluted sides, raised on turned tapering reeded supports joined by a scroll-carved cross-stretcher mounted w/a square central shelf carved w/a large rosette, on ring-turned tapering legs w/outswept brass caps, original finish, late 19th c., 18 x 20", 30" h. (ILLUS.)..... **800**

Federal Two-drawer Work Table - M.M.

Federal work table, mahogany, the square top w/ovolo corners above leaf-carved projecting corners flanking a pair of cock-beaded drawers w/original round brass pulls, raised on ring- and spiral-twist-turned legs w/a leaf-carved knob resting on peg feet w/disk angles, original brass casters, original finish, top repairs, attributed to the school of Samuel McIntyre, Salem, Massachusetts, early 19th c., 18" w., 30" h. (ILLUS.)............................. **2,000**

Nice Federal-Style Card Table - N.O.

Federal-Style card table, inlaid mahogany, the half-round serpentine fold-over top above a conforming apron inlaid at the front center by an oval enclosing an American eagle, beaded edge inlay, on square tapering legs w/bellflower inlay on the front legs, early 20th c., open 35 1/2 x 36 1/2", 29 1/2" h. (ILLUS. closed)...................................... **1,093**

Ornate George III-Style Center Table - N.O.

George III Mahogany Dining Table - N.O.

George III dining table, mahogany, the rectangular top flanked by wide rectangular top leaves, on square tapering legs, England, early 19th c., open 53 x 67", 27" h. (ILLUS. closed) **575**

George III-Style center table, polychromed & gilded wood, the rectangular top inset w/a specimen multi-colored marble top

above an apron w/a gilt Greek key band above serpentine scroll-carved edges centered by a large shell carving, the cabriole legs topped by carved gilt eagle heads above scroll-carved knees & ending in claw-and-ball feet, England, 19th c., 23 1/2 x 51 1/2", 33 1/2" h. (ILLUS. top photo) **1,840**

George III-Style dining table, mahogany, extension-type, rounded top raised on two turned pedestals on tripod bases w/cabriole legs ending in pad feet, w/original Kittinger paper label, w/one 24" w. leaf, 20th c., 48 x 92" open, 28 1/2" h. (ILLUS. open bottom photo) **1,725**

George III-Style dumbwaiter, mahogany, two graduated scalloped piecrust shelves joined by an urn-turned post & raised on a turned pedestal above a tripod base w/acanthus-carved knees ending in leaf-carved pad feet, England, ca. 1900, 23 1/2" d., 28" h. (ILLUS. photo next page) **374**

Labeled Kittinger George III-Style Dining Table - N.O.

Rare Gothic Revival Library Table - N.O.

Painted Poplar Hutch Table/Chair - G

George III-Style Dumbwaiter - N.O.

Gothic Revival library table, carved rosewood, the rectangular top inset w/variegated white marble over a wide apron w/a band of quatrefoil cutouts, raised on angled naturalistic animal legs w/scrolled hair at the top & ending in cloven hoof feet, mid-19th c., 25 1/4 x 43 1/2", 28" h. (ILLUS. top photo)............................... **16,675**

Hutch (or chair) table, poplar w/old green paint over earlier brown, two-board top w/old dark scrubbed surface, single-board tapered ends w/high arched cutouts at base, square nail & mortised construction, late 18th - early 19th c., top is warped, 31 x 40", 28 3/4" h. (ILLUS. right top)......... **1,150**

Fancy Late Victorian Side Table - M.M.

Louis XVI-Style Console Table - BR

Late Victorian side table, oak, a square top w/molded edges raised on canted legs w/ornate pierce-carved C-scrolls enclosing a slender rod all joined by a square medial shelf & ending in a brass eagle claw w/glass ball foot, original finish, ca. 1900, 20" sq., 30" h. (ILLUS. bottom of previous page) **400**

Louis XVI-Style console table, painted oak, demi-lune mottled & streaked grey marble top on conforming reeded apron w/cove-molded upper edge, supported by reeded, tapered & fluted legs, beaded cross-stretcher base, Europe, 19th c., hand-planed surfaces w/later white paint, marble w/stains, paint & tape residue, several small chips, 18 x 36", 35 1/2" h. (ILLUS. above) **2,200**

Louis XVI-Style dining table, ormolu-mounted mahogany, extension-type, the oval top w/matchbook veneers & rosewood banding above a paneled apron w/ormolu banding, raised on fluted tapering legs raised on ormolu peg feet, w/one folding leaf, France, early 20th c., open 43 x 100", 31" h. (ILLUS. open below) **2,990**

Fine Louis XVI-Style Ormolu-mounted Mahogany Dining Table - N.O.

Louis XVI-Style Gilt Table - BR

Louis XVI-Style side table, gilt hardwood, cartouche-shaped top, gilt & carved frieze, tapered stop-fluted legs, one dovetailed drawer, cross-stretcher base, France, probably early 20th c., trace of original gilding, ivory & blue paint, extensive chips & losses to painted surface, 22 x 37", 30" h. (ILLUS. above)................ **1,870**

Louis XVI-Style side table, giltwood, the oval top inset w/cream & rose marble above a ribbon-carved apron supported on six turned & fluted legs joined by two large oval caned lower shelves, on peg feet, France, mid-19th c., 19 x 31", 31" h. (ILLUS. below left)..................................... **1,495**

Louis XVI-Style Shelved Side Table - N.O.

Unusual Mission Oak Lamp Table - CR

Extremely Ornate Napoleon III Rococo Parlor Center Table - N.O.

Mission-style (Arts & Crafts movement) lamp table, oak, the square top w/rounded corners on cross-stretchers above the flat gently tapering sides w/large oblong cutouts enclosing a round lower shelf, notched base apron, good refinished condition, unmarked Limbert Furniture Co., 20" w., 29 1/2" h. (ILLUS. bottom of previous page) **4,313**

Napoleon III parlor center table, Rococo-style, gilt-brass-mounted ebonized fruitwood & marquetry, the rectangular serpentine-sided top decorated overall w/very ornate floral scrolling marquetry above the deep serpentine apron w/ormolu-banded marquetry panels centered by large ormolu mount of a putto carrying a lute, the cabriole legs mounted w/large ormolu caryatids at the knees & fitted w/brass feet, France, third quarter 19th c., 30 x 49 1/2", 30 1/2" h. (ILLUS. above) **4,370**

Neoclassical side table, inlaid mahogany, the rectangular top w/canted corners decorated w/rosewood banding above the conforming apron w/a single narrow rosewood-banded drawer, raised on square tapering legs ending in brass caps on casters & joined by a cross-

stretcher centered by a small oval shelf, Europe, mid-19th c., 13 1/2 x 19 1/2", 30" h. (ILLUS. below) **1,265**

Small Neoclassical Side Table - N.O.

Chinese Provincial Altar Table - N.O.

Finely Carved Chinese Side Table - N.O.

Oriental provincial-style altar table, hardwood, the long narrow rectangular top w/upturned scroll ends, raised on two rectangular supports w/scroll-carved brackets, China, mid-19th c., 19 1/2 x 81 1/2", 35" h. (ILLUS. bottom of previous page) **2,185**

Oriental side table, carved hardwood, the round top inset w/a porcelain Rose Medallion patt. plaque surrounded by a carved lappet band above a gadrooned band over the curved apron ornately pierce-carved w/branches of leaves & berries, raised on cylindrical legs carved w/flower swags at the top & ending in leafy scroll feet, joined by a lower round carved stretcher centered by a carved openwork diamond, China, late 19th c., 24" d., 30 1/2" h. (ILLUS. above) **2,185**

Oriental side table, carved rosewood, the round top w/beaded border centered by inset red marble, the scalloped apron pierce-carved w/leafy florals, on cabriole legs w/carved knees ending in paw feet, China, late 19th c., 21 1/2" d., 19" h. (ILLUS. left bottom photo w/Oriental rosewood side table) **250-350**

Oriental side table, carved rosewood, the rounded top w/a beaded edge inset w/red marble, the deep scalloped apron pierce-carved w/leafy florals, raised on short cabriole legs w/carved knees & paw feet, China, late 19th c., 12" d., 13 1/2" h. (ILLUS. right w/Oriental rosewood side table bottom photo) **150-300**

Queen Anne Country Tavern Table - G

Queen Anne country-style tavern table, maple w/old dark brown paint over earlier red, one-board rectangular top w/worn molded edge, dovetailed drawer w/original turned wooden pull, turned legs w/beaded stretchers & aprons, top edge has early patched knot hole, 17 1/2 x 27 3/4", 26" h. (ILLUS.) **21,850**

Two Chinese Carved Side Tables - N.O.

Queen Anne Revival Dressing Table - M.M.

Country-style Tavern Table - G

Queen Anne country-style tavern table, maple w/old red paint, pegged construction, single-board oval top, splayed & tapered legs w/pad feet, top slightly warped, age splits, pegged restorations to one leg, minor repairs to pads of two feet, 24 x 29 1/4", 27 1/2" h. (ILLUS.) **6,038**

Queen Anne Revival dressing table, mahogany & mahogany veneer, a rectangular top above a case w/a row of three small drawers over two deeper drawers flanking an arched apron, on cabriole legs w/shell-carved knees & pad feet, original teardrop brasses, original finish, ca. 1920s, 16 x 26", 30" h. (ILLUS. top right) **400**

Queen Anne tea table, mahogany, a large single-board octagonal top tilting above a turned pedestal on a tripod base w/three outswept cabriole legs ending in pad feet, possibly original finish, 32" w., 30" h. (ILLUS. right) **1,800**

Queen Anne Tea Table - M.M.

Queen Anne Work Table - BR

Queen Anne work table, walnut, one-drawer two-board top, tapered legs w/pad feet, ornate brass pull possibly original, possibly by Johannes Crouse, 18th c., rebuilt dovetailed drawer, drawer runners replaced, old refinishing, top w/stains & separations, 28 x 37 1/2 x 26" (ILLUS. bottom previous page) **3,960**

English Queen Anne-Style Table - G

Queen Anne-Style dining table, mahogany, narrow rectangular top w/rounded ends flanked by wide half-round drop leaves above an apron w/slender ring-turned blocked legs & swing-out support legs joined by simple stretchers, on small pad feet, dark finish, England, early 20th c., small pieced restorations under top near hinges, 18 1/4 x 40" plus 19 3/4" w. leaves, 29 1/2" h. (ILLUS.) **863**

Queen Anne-Style Games Table - N.O.

Queen Anne-Style games table, red-lacquered wood, the fold-over shaped top w/a polychromed & gilt scene in the chinoiserie style, opening to a baize-lined interior, the back gatelegs supporting the open top, raised on heavily turned & paneled tapering legs joined by a shaped

box stretcher & ending in bun feet, the whole w/chinoiserie gilt trim, England, third quarter 19th c., open 13 1/2 x 31 1/2", 30 1/2" h. (ILLUS. open below left) **3,680**

English Regency Sofa Table - M.M.

Regency sofa table, mahogany, the long rectangular top flanked by short half-round drop leaves, the apron w/a pair of long paneled drawers w/knobs, a trestle-form base w/a pair of slender baluster- and ring-turned supports at each end resting on cross stretchers over outswept legs w/brass paw caps on casters, a long slender baluster-turned stretcher from end to end, polished original finish, England, ca. 1820, 22 x 46", 30" h. (ILLUS.) **1,400**

Very Ornate Rococo Coffee Table - M.M.

Rococo Revival coffee table, carved walnut, the oblong tray top ornately carved w/a wide serpentine border of leafy scrolls w/loop end handles & an oval glass center inset, raised on a serpentine pierce-carved apron w/scrolls centering a large shell, leaf-carved S-scroll legs w/scroll feet joined by a scroll-carved cross stretcher centered by a scroll-carved disk, original finish, ca. 1920s, 24 x 32", 20" h. (ILLUS.) **750**

Rococo Side Table with Carved Angel - M.M.

Rococo Revival side table, carved mahogany, a black marble "turtle top" inset into a widely flaring conforming apron carved w/leaves, raised on cabriole legs, each topped by a large carved angel head w/wings & tapering down to a scroll foot, joined by a baluster-turned cross stretcher centered by a turned finial, original finish, ca. 1920s, 20" w., 20" h. (ILLUS.)...... **600**

Very Fine Rococo Revival Side Table - M.M.

Rococo Revival side table, carved mahogany, a rectangular black marble top set into a molded frame w/ovolo corners above a deep serpentine ornately pierce-carved apron w/leafy scrolls & florettes centering a large oblong lattice-inlaid panel, raised on cabriole legs, each topped by a carved full-figure putto & ending in a scroll foot, joined by an arched cross-stretcher centered by a carved flower basket finial, original finish, by Flint & Horner, New York City, ca. 1920s, 18 x 24", 30" h. (ILLUS.)................ **1,800**
Rococo Revival side table, carved mahogany, the round top over a shaped apron carved w/pairs of scrolls, raised on bulbous turned knobs atop S-scroll legs carved at

the top w/an acanthus leaf & ending in a scroll foot raised on a bun, joined by a scrolled & arched cross stretcher centered by a turned urn finial, refinished, late 19th c., 24" d., 30" h. (ILLUS. below) **450**

Rococo Revival Scroll-carved Table - M.M.

Inlaid Rococo Revival Side Table - M.M.

Rococo Revival side table, inlaid mahogany, the round top centered by a large inlaid star-shaped dark panel centered by a light circle & bordered by inlaid swags, the molded edge above the deep serpentine apron pierce-carved w/leafy scrolls, raised on four incurved slender square legs ending in paw feet & joined at the center w/a serpentine-sided shelf pierce-carved w/acanthus leaves, original finish, ca. 1920s, 22" d., 30" h. (ILLUS.) **500**

Inlaid Italian Rococo-Style Table - N.O.

Rococo-Style games table, mahogany & marquetry, the rectangular fold-over top w/large projecting rounded corners, decorated w/an elaborate inlay of putti & scrolling designs, opening to a similarly inlaid interior, the ornately inlaid apron fitted w/one drawer, on inlaid cabriole legs ending in square feet, the drawer w/paper label for Giovannia Bacci - Oggetti D'arte - Anticui E. Moderni - Via della Vigna Nuova St. - Firenze, Italy, mid-19th c., 33 1/2" l., 29" h. (ILLUS.)...................... **2,760**

Victorian Aesthetic Movement dining table, mahogany, expandable, the wide round top over a deep apron carved w/a lappet band, raised on four heavy square stop-fluted & tapering legs on casters, joined by a heavy cross-stretcher centered by four heavy solid scroll-shaped brackets w/oval carved rosettes, refinished, ca. 1890, w/six leaves, 60" d. closed, 30" h. (ILLUS. bottom photo) **2,000**

Victorian Aesthetic Movement parlor table, mahogany, the square top inset w/tiles forming a border band around a

cluster of stylized blossoms all framed by a low brass edge gallery & a narrow brass band along the outer edges, raised on four canted ring-turned & reeded tapering legs w/brass bands near the top & supports on brass claw feet w/glass balls, joined by a lower square shelf w/a brass gallery, probably England, ca. 1900, original finish, 20" w., 32" h. (ILLUS. below) **600**

Victorian Aesthetic Parlor Table - M.M.

Victorian Baroque Revival dining table, carved mahogany, extension-type, the round top w/a deep scroll-carved apron, raised on a large center post flanked by four supports carved as large seated winged griffins on the cross-form base, by Horner Furniture Co., New York City, late 19th c., refinished, w/eight leaves, 60" d., 30" h. (ILLUS. top on next page) **10,000**

Victorian Aesthetic Dining Table - M.M.

Rare Horner Baroque Dining Table - M.M.

Baroque Dining Table with Masks - M.M.

Victorian Baroque Revival dining table, oak, extension-type, the round top above a plain apron, raised on a large round reeded squatty disk above a large cylindrical base issuing four large animal legs w/paw feet on casters, original finish, w/six leaves, ca. 1895 54" d., 30" h. (ILLUS. left with leaves on the top)................ **3,000**

Baroque Table with Large Pedestal - M.M.

Victorian Baroque Revival dining table, carved mahogany, extension-type, the square top w/rounded corners above a deep apron w/carved ropetwist border, raised on six legs composed of blocks, a reeded egg-shaped knob over a large leafy scroll, all joined by angled wide scroll-carved solid panels centered by large carved grotesque faces, original finish, w/six leaves, ca. 1890s, 60" w. closed, 30" h. (ILLUS. below).................. **5,000**

Victorian Baroque Revival dining table, carved oak, extension-type, the wide square top w/a lappet-carved apron, raised on a large spiral-carved center post & four corner posts resting on the heads of carved full-figure reclining lions on the cross-form base w/carved paw feet, ca. 1890, w/six leaves, sold refinished, 60" w., 30"h. (ILLUS. with the leaves stacked on top) **4,500**

Baroque Dining Table with Lions on the Base - M.M.

Victorian Baroque Revival dining table,
oak, extension-type, the round top w/a
gadrooned edge over an apron w/a thin
knob-carved rim raised on a bulbous rosette-carved column on a heavy post issuing four outswept leafy scroll-carved
legs ending in scroll feet carved on top
w/clusters of fruit, on casters, original
finish, ca. 1890, w/four leaves, 48" d.,
30" h. (ILLUS. below) **2,000**

Smaller Fruit-carved Dining Table - M.M.

Victorian Baroque Revival library table,
carved mahogany, partner's-type, the
rectangular top w/a wide scroll-carved
border band above the deep rounded
apron carved overall w/leafy scrolls & centered on each side by a long drawer,
raised at each corner by a large full-figure
carved seated griffin on a narrow platform
connecting to a raised rectangular center
shelf w/incurved beaded edges, Horner
Furniture Co., New York City, ca. 1880s,
28 x 52", 30" h. (ILLUS. below) **5,500**

Victorian Baroque Revival library table,
carved mahogany, partner's-type, wide
rectangular top w/a wide scroll-carved
border band over a deep rounded apron
carved overall w/scrolls & fitted on each
side w/a long drawer, raised on four large
full-figure seated winged griffins at the
corners on projecting platforms extending
from a serpentine central shelf stretcher,
on four thin bun feet, attributed to the Horner Furniture Co., New York City, late 19th
c., 30 x 48", 30" h. (ILLUS. bottom photo) .. **4,500**

Fine Horner Library Desk with Carved Griffin Legs - M.M.

Horner-style Carved Mahogany Library Table - M.M.

Library Table with Paneled Ends - M.M.

Victorian Baroque Revival library table, carved oak, rectangular top w/a wide border band carved w/leafy vines & pineapple-like fruits, the edge carved w/a raised dash design, scroll-carved corner brackets, the ends supported w/legs composed of carved blocks over a bulbous turned knob over a smaller block over slender turned legs w/paw feet, the legs joined across the ends by a lattice-bar design centered by a pierced scroll-carved panel, a shaped flat stretcher shelf from end to end, sold refinished, ca. 1890, 24 x 40", 30" h. (ILLUS.) **2,000**

Baroque Table with Masks - M.M.

Victorian Baroque Revival library table, carved oak, the rectangular top covered overall w/ornate floral scrolls above a deep floral scroll-carved apron w/a relief-carved female mask at each corner above a turned drop, on a trestle-form base w/three columns at each end carved w/spiraling vines & raised on wide platforms carved at each end w/a figural sphinx, a heavy flat base stretcher centered by another carved column, fumed oak finish, late 19th c., 26 x 48", 30" h. (ILLUS.) **1,400**

Victorian Baroque Revival parlor table, carved walnut, the rectangular top fitted w/two fold-out leaves carved w/pairs of scroll-carved bands on the top side, the deep rectangular case below carved on three sides w/primitive geometric designs, one long side fitted w/a paneled door centered by a panel carved w/a

round medallion carved w/a primitive bust profile of a woman flanked by leaf-carved columns, a projecting medial band raised on four heavy square legs carved w/geometric designs & resting on a lower shelf above simple carved paw feet, original finish, ca. 1890-1900, 15 x 20" closed, 31" h. (ILLUS. below)........ **650**

Unique Folk-carved Parlor Table - M.M.

Ornately Carved Parlor Table - M.M.

Victorian Baroque Revival parlor table, carved walnut, the rectangular top w/a wide ornate scroll-carved border band & carved beveled edge overhanging a deep scroll-carved apron w/sunburst-carved corner blocks all overhanging a case w/a group of four paneled & scroll-carved drawers on each side & matching carved end panels, the projecting corners w/bold leaf-carved & ring-turned freestanding columns above blocks on bun feet, probably an exhibition piece, original finish, ca. 1870s, 22 x 40", 30" h. (ILLUS.)................ **4,500**

Victorian Baroque Revival parlor table, oak, the octagonal top above a deep line-incised octagonal apron supporting four slender legs w/bulbous scroll-carved tops over fluted sections resting on blocks above short ring-carved ankles on claw-and-ball feet, the legs joined by a squared pierce-carved medial shelf, original finish, ca. 1890s, 22" w., 30" h. **650**

Oak Baroque Drop-leaf Parlor Table - M.M.

Victorian Baroque Revival parlor table, quarter-sawn oak, a narrow rectangular top w/rounded ends flanked by wide half-round drop leaves, raised on a heavy fluted column above four outswept heavy scroll-carved feet, old refinish, ca. 1895, 36 x 46" open, 30" h. (ILLUS. closed)` **950**

Unusual Country-style Games Table - M.M.

Victorian country-style games table, oak w/maple top, the square top w/a window in the center allowing a view of a numbered scorekeeping devices, the apron w/knobs on each side used to change the

score, a small square drawer in one corner of the apron, top also w/a flush-mounted button which rings a bell when pressed, heavy ring-, rod- and baluster-turned legs, original finish, ca. 1900, 34" w., 30" h. (ILLUS. below left) **600**

Victorian Painted Country Table - M.M.

Victorian country-style work table, painted pine, the oval top widely overhanging one end, the apron centered by a small drawer w/wooden pull, on square tapering legs, original crackled light blue paint w/white on legs, ca. 1900, 18 x 28", 30" h. (ILLUS.) **175**

Victorian Eastlake style dining table, walnut, extension-type, square top w/rounded corners above a conforming block-incised apron, raised on six heavy legs w/large gadrooned & fluted bulbous knobs or ring-turned & fluted knobs over long incurved block-incised side stretchers flanking a shorter center stretcher, on bun feet on casters, original finish, ca. 1890, w/four leaves, 52" w., 30" h. (ILLUS. below) **1,800**

Six-legged Eastlake Dining Table - M.M.

Eastlake Dining Table with Bobbins - M.M.

Victorian Eastlake style dining table, walnut, extension-type, square top w/rounded corners over a simple apron

raised on six ring- and knob-turned legs, the outer pairs of legs joined by concave stretchers mounted w/high bobbin-turned bands between blocks, the flat center stretchers joining the center two legs, original porcelain casters, original finish, w/six leaves, ca. 1890, 48" w., 30" h. (ILLUS. left) **1,500**

Victorian Eastlake style dining table, walnut, extension-type, the square top w/rounded corners above a deep apron w/leaf-incised blocks supported on a heavy squared center pedestal flanked by wide flat pierce-carved panels w/a diamond motif resting on platforms joining the four corner legs, each ring- and bulbous knob-turned leg resting on a stepped block foot, original finish, w/six leaves, ca. 1880s, closed 48" w., 30" h. (ILLUS. below, top) **3,000**

Fine Eastlake Walnut Dining Table - M.M.

Fine Eastlake Oak Library Table - M.M.

Victorian Eastlake style library table, oak, partner's-type, the rectangular top w/molded edge over an apron w/a working drawer next to a false drawer on each side, each section w/a lightly carved center panel w/brass keyhole escutcheon flanked by diamond point-carved narrow panels, raised on four reeded block corner legs w/turned rings at the top & base, resting on blocked outswept legs, joined by a cross stretcher fitted w/a rectangular shelf w/a long gallery & turned corner finials, on casters, refinished, ca. 1890, 24 x 48", 30" h. (ILLUS. bottom previous page) **650**

Claw-footed Oak Dining Table - M.M.

Square Golden Oak Dining Table - M.M.

Victorian Golden Oak dining table, extension-type, the square top w/small rounded corners above an apron w/a notch-carved border, raised on five heavy columnar legs w/bulbous reeded central knobs above large bun feet on casters, the corner legs joined by a high concave panel stamped w/pairs of scrolls, a central support leg, w/four leaves, refinished, ca. 1900, 52" w., 30" h. (ILLUS. open) **2,800**

Eastlake Mahogany Parlor Table - M.M.

Victorian Eastlake style parlor table, mahogany, the rectangular top w/a narrow shell-carved band at the molded edge above the line-incised apron w/a gently arched border, raised on knob-, ring- and rod-turned legs curving out at the base, scroll-carved end stretchers joined by flat cross-stretchers centered by a small disk finial, original finish, ca. 1885, 18 x 30", 30" h. (ILLUS.).............................. **450**

Victorian Golden Oak dining table, extension-type, round top w/simple apron raised on a heavy split-post pedestal w/three incised rings flanked by four outstretched shaped legs ending in large paw feet on casters, refinished, w/four leaves, ca. 1900, 48" d., 30" h. (ILLUS. top right column) **1,250**

Simple Golden Oak Dining Table - M.M.

Victorian Golden Oak dining table, quarter-sawn oak, extension-type, round top w/plain apron raised on a heavy octagonal split pedestal resting on a cross-form base w/C-scroll feet on casters, refinished, w/four leaves, ca. 1900, 60" d., 30" h. (ILLUS.) **1,200**

Fine Column-based Golden Oak Dining Table - M.M.

Victorian Golden Oak dining table, quarter-sawn oak, extension-type, round top w/scallop-incised rim above an apron w/angled blocks above a cluster of five large reeded columns on a platform base w/scroll-carved feet, w/six leaves, refinished, ca. 1895, 60" d., 30" h. (ILLUS. above) **4,200**

Victorian Golden Oak dining table, quarter-sawn oak, extension-type, the round top w/scallop-carved edge over a plain apron & a large square split pedestal w/a fruit-carved panel on each side & spiral-carved columns at each corner, supported on a cross-form platform on tapering knob feet, w/three leaves, original finish, ca. 1890s, 60" d., 30" h. (ILLUS. below with leaves on the top) **3,500**

Fine Golden Oak Dining Table with Square Pedestal - M.M.

Golden Oak Library Table with Long Drawer - M.M.

Victorian Golden Oak library table, quarter-sawn oak, rectangular top w/molded edge above an apron w/a single very long drawer w/small brass pulls & a carved scroll at the center, each end w/a raised scroll-carved block, a narrow gadrooned edge band above the boldly ring-turned & reeded columnar supports joined by a wide flat barbell-shaped shelf-stretcher, on ring-turned short legs on lobed paw feet, refinished, ca. 1900, 26 x 42", 30" h. (ILLUS.) **650**

Shell-carved Oak Library Table - M.M.

Victorian Golden Oak library table, quarter-sawn oak, rectangular top w/wide round corners overhanging an apron w/a long drawer w/stamped brass pulls on one side, curved & shaped scroll-carved corner blocks, solid end panels carved w/a large shell within an arched band, flat slightly slanted legs ending in carved paw feet on casters, a barbell-shaped lower flat stretcher, ca. 1900, refinished, 22 x 42", 30" h. (ILLUS.) **950**

Fancy Golden Oak Side Table - M.M.

Victorian Golden Oak side table, square top w/serpentine edges above a serpentine scroll-carved apron w/a center fleur-de-lis on each side, raised on slender serpentine scroll- and bead-carved legs joined by arched scroll-carved cross stretchers supporting a small four-lobed shelf, original finish, ca. 1900, 16" w., 30" h. (ILLUS.) **350**

French Gothic Revival Game Table - N.O.

Victorian Gothic Revival game table, carved & inlaid fruitwood, the square top w/beveled corners over a deep apron w/swing-out arms containing the wells for the gaming pieces, a large arched & pierced bracket at each corner, raised on flattened slightly tapering canted legs w/panels carved w/Gothic arches above a trefoil-cut foot, lift-off top, France, ca. 1900, 29 1/2" w., 28 1/2" h. (ILLUS.) **1,150**

Victorian novelty side table, folding-type, pyrographic decoration, the round top hinged at the center over intersecting flattened & shaped legs w/Moorish-style cutouts & floral & leaf pyrographic decoration outlined in red, black & gold stain, early 20th c., wear, scratches, 24 1/4" d., 25 1/4" h. **518**

Unique Inlaid Victorian Table - M.M.

Victorian novelty side table, inlaid mixed wood, the square top ornately inlaid w/a large central checkerboard surrounded by a wide inlaid band decorated w/fan-inlaid corners & various geometric designs above the shaped apron inlaid w/rectangular panels & diamond & small stars, fitted w/a single drawer w/a black pear-shaped rope pull, large baluster-, ring- and tapering rod-turned legs composed of stacked multicolored woods, original finish, ca. 1890, 26" w., 30" h. (ILLUS. below left) **750**

Victorian Patented Folding Table - N.O.

Victorian novelty side table, walnut & cast iron, the large walnut top w/a narrow edge over a pair of tiny drawers w/wide hinged drop leaf pivoting & telescoping above the tapering columnar cast-iron pedestal on a tripod base w/flat cabriole legs ending in knob feet on casters, base w/stenciled classical decoration, marked w/a stenciled label reading "Designed and manufactured at the Washburn Machine Shop connected with the Institute of Industrial Science Worcester, Mass...Patented Nov. 19, 1872," 26 x 29", 31" h. (ILLUS.) **1,150**

Victorian Renaissance Revival dining table, oak, extension-type, square top w/rounded corners above a line-incised apron raised on a heavy paneled central column fitted w/four half-round fluted columns issuing angled heavy fluted legs w/carved roundels & supporting full-round & fluted column supports, on casters, old refinish, w/five leaves, ca. 1880, 52" w., 30" h. (ILLUS. top of next page) **2,000**

Renaissance Revival Square Oak Dining Table - M.M.

Victorian Renaissance Revival dining table, walnut & burl walnut, a square top w/wide rounded corners over a burl-banded apron, raised on a large square center post issuing four downswept carved legs ending in octagonal ends carved w/rosettes & raised on rectangular platform feet, w/four leaves, ca. 1875, 53 1/2" w., 30 1/2" h. **3,300**

Victorian Renaissance Revival dining table, walnut & burl walnut, extension-type, round top above a deep apron w/narrow burl bands separated by small roundels, raised on a heavy squared split pedestal on a cross-form platform base fitted w/large scroll-carved legs w/ebonized trim, refinished, ca. 1870s, w/four leaves, 48" d., 30" h. (ILLUS. right) **2,500**

Victorian Renaissance Revival dining table, walnut, extension-type, the round top w/molded apron raised on a heavy

split pedestal w/scroll-carved projecting legs mounted w/roundels & raised on casters, holds four 12"-wide leaves, ca. 1875, open 45 x 93", 30 1/2" h. (ILLUS. open bottom of page) **1,150**

Fine Renaissance Dining Table - M.M.

Fine Renaissance Revival Walnut Dining Table - N.O.

Exceptional Herter Bros. Renaissance Revival Library Table - N.O.

Victorian Renaissance Revival library table, marquetry-inlaid rosewood, the rectangular top w/rounded ends centered by a marquetry panel using various inlaid woods, ivory & brass & depicting a central Grecian urn draped w/ribboned garlands raised on poles grasped by winged griffins, against an ebonized ground encircled by line stringing, foliate & repeating banded marquetry around the border, the apron centered on the long sides by a turret w/gilt-incised carving flanked by a repeating marquetry band, each rounded end fitted w/a full-width drawer, the concealed interior beneath one end drawer bearing the name "Schulte" or "Schatte" in pencil, raised on trumpet-turned legs w/incised carving & marquetry banding of hexagonal panels decorated w/alternating light & dark wood triangles, the base knobs above bun feet on casters, the legs joined by flattened U-shaped stretchers connected by a flattened roundel-centered stretcher w/a turned finial, stamped mark of Herter Bros., New York City, third quarter 19th c., 33 1/4 x 52", 30" h. (ILLUS. above) **41,400**

Victorian Renaissance Revival library table, walnut & burl walnut, the rectangular top w/wide rounded ends & inset center panel above a deep conforming apron w/large corner blocks w/turned drops, a long drawer centered by a bold oblong scroll-carved burl & roundel keyhole escutcheon, raised on a trestle-style base, w/pairs of square burl posts flanking large urn-turned supports raised on angled squared legs w/scroll feet on casters, a scroll-ended slender stretcher centered by a squatty bulbous turned finial, ca. 1875, 31 x 55", 30" h.) **1,610**

Simple Renaissance Library Table - M.M.

Victorian Renaissance Revival library table, walnut, the rectangular top w/rounded ends inset w/leather, the long side fitted w/two drawers w/turned wood pulls, the rounded ends w/small raised panels, raised on four trumpet-turned & fluted legs joined by an H-stretcher w/incurved ends & centered by a small urn finial, refinished, ca. 1875, 20 x 48", 30" h. (ILLUS.) **700**

Victorian Renaissance Revival parlor table, rosewood, a round white marble top above a conforming apron carved w/four scroll cartouches & supported on four long upturned carved arms issuing from the central gadroon- and scroll-carved post raised on four scroll-carved projecting cabriole legs ending on scroll feet on casters, refinished, ca. 1875, 32" d., 30" h. (ILLUS. top next page)................... **2,500**

Rosewood Renaissance Parlor Table - M.M.

Victorian Rococo console table, rosewood, the rectangular top w/inset white marble enclosed by a narrow gadrooned band above the deep apron w/a pair of large drawers w/bead-molding enclosing panels carved w/long scroll & shell-carved bands, a bead-carved front molding over a long scroll-carved drop, raised on pair of double C-scroll endings on casters joined by a long H-stretcher composed of ornate C-scrolls, New York City, ca. 1850, original finish, 18 x 52", 30" h. (ILLUS. below) **2,500**

Victorian Rococo console table, mahogany, the half-round top w/serpentine sides & a low arched & scroll-pierced crestrail above a conforming apron w/a long drawer at the front decorated w/a scroll-carved cartouche, ornate double-scroll front legs carved w/rose clusters, flat serpentine rear legs, joined by a half-round medial shelf & a rectangular base platform w/incurved front & sides on thin bun feet, original finish, ca. 1860, 14 x 28", 34" h. (ILLUS. below) **1,800**

Ornate Rococo Console Table - M.M.

Fine Rosewood Rococo Console Table - M.M.

Victorian Rococo Dressing Table - G

Victorian Rococo dressing table, rosewood, the rectangular top w/a raised central section w/coved borders, the hinged top opening to a compartment w/mirror above two drawers, a large shell- and scroll-carved drop at the front apron, raised on four incurved serpentine legs joined by a serpentine cross-stretcher centered by a small oval shelf, attributed to John H. Belter, New York City, ca. 1855, refinished, restorations to legs & stretchers, 16 x 21", 31 1/4" h. (ILLUS. above) **863**

Fine Rosewood Rococo Games Table - M.M.

Victorian Rococo games table, rosewood, the rectangular serpentine-sided lift top opening to felt lining & a matching felt-lined top over the serpentine scalloped deep apron centered by a flute & blossom-carved mount & scroll- and flower-carved knees on the cabriole legs, one rear legs swings out for support, original finish, ca. 1850s, 20 x 40", 30" h. (ILLUS. above) **1,800**

Carved Rosewood Rococo "Turtle-top" Parlor Table - M.M.

Victorian Rococo parlor table, carved
rosewood, a white marble "turtle top"
above a conforming apron carved in the
center of each side w/a large scroll cluster, the blocked corners above heavy S-
scroll legs w/leaf-carved knees & raised
on casters, C-scroll-carved cross stretcher centered by a squatty ribbed urn finial,
original finish, ca. 1860, 26 x 48", 30" h.
(ILLUS. bottom of previous page) **2,500**
Victorian Rococo parlor table, carved
rosewood, a white marble "turtle top"
above a conforming apron carved w/large
floral & scroll clusters & a border of heavy
scrolls, raised on heavy cabriole legs
w/fruit- and scroll-carved knees & ending
in scrolled leaf feet on casters, joined by a
serpentine cross stretcher centered by a
gadrooned urn finial, original finish, ca.
1850s, 24 x 44", 30" h. (ILLUS. right) **3,600**
Victorian Rococo parlor table, carved
rosewood, a white marble "turtle top"
above a conforming apron ornately
carved w/scrolls, beaded panels & large
fruit-carved reserves, raised on bold S-
scroll legs on casters joined by a delicate
S-scroll cross stretcher centered by a
large bulbous spiral-turned urn finial, attributed to Prudent Mallard, New Orleans, Louisiana, 1850s, original finish,
28 x 50", 30" h. **6,500**
Victorian Rococo parlor table, carved
rosewood, a white marble "turtle top"
above a conforming apron ornately
pierce-carved w/scrolls centering a floral
cluster, raised on S-scroll legs w/the
knees carved w/large floral clusters, scroll
feet on casters, joined by a scroll-carved

serpentine cross stretcher centered by a
reeded carved disk finial & smaller disk
drop finial, by J. & J.W. Meeks of New
York City, original finish, ca. 1855,
25 x 48", 30" h. (ILLUS. bottom of page).. **15,000**

Fine "Turtle-top" Rosewood Table - M.M.

Victorian Rococo parlor table, carved
rosewood, a white marble "turtle top"
above a conforming apron ornately pierce-
carved w/scrolls centering a floral cluster,
raised on S-scroll legs w/large floral clusters, scroll feet on casters, joined by a scroll-carved serpentine
cross stretcher centered by a large carved
basket of flowers & smaller disk drop finial,
by J. & J.W. Meeks of New York City, old
refinish, ca. 1855, approximately 25 x 48",
30" h. (ILLUS. top of next page) **18,000**

Fine Floral- and Disk-carved Meeks Rococo Parlor Table - M.M.

Outstanding Meeks Rococo Parlor Table with a Basket of Flowers - M.M.

Signed Rococo Mahogany Table - M.M.

Simple Rococo Walnut Parlor Table - M.M.

Victorian Rococo parlor table, mahogany, a tan marble "turtle top" above a conforming apron w/each side centered by a carved floral cluster, raised on tapering S-scroll legs w/leaf-carved knees & scroll feet on casters, joined by a slender serpentine cross stretcher centered by a carved basket of flowers, signed by Doe and Hazelton, Boston, Massachusetts, original top & casters, old refinish, ca. 1860, 24 x 44", 30" h. (ILLUS.) **2,500**

Victorian Rococo parlor table, rosewood, the oblong white marble top w/notched corners above a conforming deep apron pierce-carved w/long narrow bands of scrolls over scroll-carved drops, raised on forked scroll supports joining tall C-scroll supports above a serpentine cross stretcher centered by a low carved reeded dome, on squatty disk feet, refinished, ca. 1850, 24 x 44", 30" h. (ILLUS. above right) **3,600**

Victorian Rococo parlor table, walnut, a wood "turtle top" above a conforming narrow molded apron w/large leaf-and-grape cluster drops at each side, raised on simple heavy cabriole legs w/grape-carved knees & joined by a simple arched cross stretcher centered by a small urn-turned finial, on original brass casters, ca. 1865, original finish, 20 x 34", 30" h. (ILLUS.) **500**

WARDROBES & ARMOIRES

Classical Armoire with Wreaths - N.O.

European Walnut Armoire - M.M.

Armoire, Baroque Revival, carved walnut, the rectangular top w/a low spindled gallery above the deep flaring cornice w/a scroll- and rosette-carved frieze band above a pair of tall doors, each door w/a long panel carved w/leafy scrolls & a round central medallion above a small rectangular panel over a square scroll-carved bottom panel centered by a large roundel, three slender columns across the front, each turned & fluted w/a scroll-carved capital & urn-turned base on a block, two carved drawers at the bottom w/brass pulls, flat molded base, plain matching panels down the sides, bun feet, shelved interior, Europe, original finish, late 19th c., 22 x 48", 7' 8" h. (ILLUS.)...... **$2,400**

Armoire, Classical, mahogany & mahogany veneer, demountable, rectangular top w/a widely flaring stepped cornice above a pair of tall paneled doors w/fine crotch-grain veneering & brass keyhole escutcheons opening to an interior w/shelves & hangers, flat base on bulbous tapering legs on brass caps, refinished, considerable restoration, ca. 1830, 24 x 64", 8' 4" h. **3,500**

Armoire, Classical, mahogany & mahogany veneer, rectangular top above a deep cornice w/a half-round band above a pair of tall paneled doors each centered by carved oval floral wreath, flat base on scroll-carved bracket feet on casters, the back w/an old label from an antique dealer in Virginia, ca. 1840, 21 x 57", 7' 5" h. (ILLUS. top right column).. **1,725**

Mallard-style Classical Armoire - N.O.

Armoire, Classical, mahogany & mahogany veneer, the rectangular top w/a deep flaring beaded & molded cornice over a tall cyma-molded mirrored door framed by a similar molded frame, the interior w/original central drawer, the front corners w/spiral-turned edging, a long drawer at the bottom above the deep molded flat base, attributed to Prudent Mallard, New Orleans, mid-19th c., 25 x 53", 8' 4" h. (ILLUS.) **6,613**

Empire Revival Ebonized Armoire - N.O.

Armoire, Empire Revival, ormolu-mounted ebonized wood, the rectangular top w/an arched crest centered by an ormolu wreath above a wide frieze band centered by a band of ormolu & small ribbon & wreath ormolu mounts at each corner, above a large beveled glass mirrored door flanked by slender fluted columns w/gilt trim, a long molded drawer at the bottom w/an ormolu keyhole escutcheon, the flat base band w/two ormolu swag mounts, gilt-incised bun feet, Europe, ca. 1900, 22 1/2 x 48", 7' 10" h. (ILLUS.) **2,300**

Armoire, French Provincial, painted & lacquered wood, the rectangular top w/a widely flaring stepped cornice above a pair of tall three-panel doors w/heavy molded edges & fitted w/long iron hinges, three-paneled sides, a widely flaring stepped base molding on heavy bun feet, decorated overall in cream lacquer decorated w/gilt chinoiserie scenes of figures in landscapes, France, ca. 1800, 27 1/2 x 65 1/4", 7' 7 1/4" h. (ILLUS. top right column) **12,650**

Fine French Provincial Armoire - N.O.

French Henri IV-Style Armoire - N.O.

Armoire, Henri IV-Style, oak, the rectangular top widely overhanging a dentil-carved cornice above a leafy scroll-carved frieze band above a molding & a pair of tall three-panel doors, the two larger panels carved w/scroll borders & the smaller central panel carved w/a scrolled cartouche, two-part reeded side pilasters above the carved apron band, on wide rectangular block feet, France, late 19th c., 26 1/2 x 69 1/4", 7' 10 3/4" h. (ILLUS.) **1,265**

Louis XV-Style Inlaid Armoire - N.O.

Armoire, Louis XV-Style Provincial type, fruitwood, the rectangular top w/beveled front corners on the coved cornice above a paneled frieze band centered by a star-inlaid roundel over a pair of tall three-paneled doors w/long pierced brass latches, three-panel sides, serpentine carved apron on short scrolled legs w/upturned toes, France, late 19th c., 24 1/2 x 56", 7' 1" h. (ILLUS.)................... **2,185**

Fine Neoclassical Painted Armoire - N.O.

Armoire, Neoclassical, polychrome painted wood, the rectangular top w/a molded cornice above a pair of tall doors painted overall w/elaborate scrolling heraldic patterns in shades of grey, white, maroon & gold, the side painted w/trompe l'oeil panels, on a flat plinth base, Italy, late 18th c. or later, 18 x 59", 6' 6" h. (ILLUS. below left).. **8,050**

Flat-topped Golden Oak Armoire - M.M.

Armoire, Victorian Golden Oak style, quarter-sawn oak, demountable, rectangular top w/a flat narrow flaring cornice above a scroll-carved frieze band above a pair of tall beveled glass mirrored doors w/shaped tops trimmed w/carved scrolls, half-round columns down the center & at each side, the stepped out base w/a pair of bow-fronted drawers over a long bow-fronted drawer, flat shaped sides w/block feet, open interior, mix of old & new hardware, ca. 1900, refinished, 24 x 56", 7' 8" h. (ILLUS.)................................ **3,500**

Armoire, Victorian Golden Oak style, quarter-sawn oak, demountable, rectangular top w/low arched crestrail carved w/scrolls centering wide, smooth, curved panels flanked by further scroll carving & an arched molding, above a pair of tall beveled glass mirrored doors w/arched scrolls above the rounded top, a half-round smooth column down the center & half-round columns w/reeded capitals at the sides, a mid-molding over a pair of flat-front drawers over a single long double-serpentine bottom drawer, molded flat base on ogee bracket front feet, refinished, ca. 1895, 22 x 54", 8' h. **4,000**

Armoire, Victorian Golden Oak style, quarter-sawn oak, demountable, the rectangular top w/a high arched crest board w/heavy molding & centered by a large shell-carved crest, scroll-carved rounded ears, a scroll-carved frieze band above a pair of tall beveled glass mirrored doors w/carved scrolls across the top, centered by a half-round colonette w/quarter-round colonettes down each front corner, stepped-out lower section w/a pair of bow-fronted shallow drawers over a very long bow-fronted drawer all w/brass pulls, scroll-carved front corners continuing to form short flared block feet on casters, shelved interior, original hardware, refinished, ca. 1890s, 24 x 60", 8' 4" h. **3,800**

Renaissance Revival Armoire - M.M.

Armoire, Victorian Renaissance Revival style, walnut & burl walnut, demountable, a high long arched crestrail centered by a large carved shell flanked by gadrooned moldings over carved serpentine leafy vines, all on a flaring stepped cornice above a serpentine scroll-carved burl band flanked by blocked corners over a pair of tall beveled glass mirrored doors each w/a shaped burl panel at the top & flanked by reeded pilasters, the slightly stepped-out lower case w/a pair of burl veneered drawers w/pierced brass pulls, molded base w/low serpentine apron & block feet, refinished, ca. 1875, 23 x 58", 8' 6" h. (ILLUS.) **3,500**

Armoire, Victorian Rococo style, mahogany & mahogany veneer, the rectangular top w/a deep flaring cyma- and cove-molded cornice w/angled corners above a conforming case w/a pair of narrow raised molded panels in the frieze band above a pair of tall doors, w/rectangular mirrors framed w/floral & scroll carving above a raised rectangular band of carved florals & scrolls, the beveled front sides w/a floral-carved bracket at the top & a scroll-carved bracket at the bottom, a pair of bottom drawers w/raised oblong molding enclosing leaf-carved pulls, molded base w/serpentine scroll-carved apron & angled block feet, mid-19th c., 29 x 74", 8' 4" h. (ILLUS. below) **6,613**

Ornately Carved Rococo Armoire - N.O.

Tall Narrow Rococo Armoire - M.M.

Armoire, Victorian Rococo style, mahogany, wooden peg construction, the rectangular top w/an arched scroll-carved crest centered by a rounded fleur-de-lis & shell crest above a narrow scroll-carved frieze band continuing around the sides, a single tall door w/a beveled glass mirror w/a serpentine top above a narrow scroll-carved panel, a mid-molding over a long base drawer w/brass hardware, curved serpentine apron on cabriole front legs w/paw feet, drawers & shelves inside, original finish, probably Europe, ca. 1860, 17 x 30", 7' 8" h. (ILLUS. bottom of previous page)... **2,200**

Rare Mallard Rosewood Armoire - N.O.

Armoire, Victorian Rococo style, rosewood, the rectangular top w/a wide arched crestrail w/an egg-and-dart border topped by a high arched & ornately pierce-carved crest centered by a flower-filled urn, the arched & beaded-border frieze panel over a large door w/beaded border molding framing a large rectangular mirror, the door flanked by beveled front corners w/carved half-round top & base drops, the molded base fitted w/a long paneled drawer above an egg-and-dart-carved band & flat apron on flattened bun feet, attributed to the New Orleans warerooms of Prudent Mallard, ca. 1850s, 24 1/2 x 57", 9' 5" h. (ILLUS.)............... **19,500**

Massive Walnut Rococo Armoire - M.M.

Armoire, Victorian Rococo style, walnut, demountable, rectangular top w/an arched cove-molded cornice w/rounded corners above a conforming frieze band centered w/carved oval panel flanked by narrow triangular scroll-carved panels above a pair of wide arched doors w/leaf-carved sprigs above a large arched scroll-topped door flanking a narrow fruit-and block-carved middle column & flanked by matching angled corner columns, scroll-carved serpentine apron & feet, possibly Philadelphia, ca. 1860, refinished, 22 x 62", 8' h. (ILLUS.) **4,500**

Kas (a version of the Netherlands kast or wardrobe), painted pine, rectangular top w/flared cornice above a pair of tall double raised-panel doors w/a long panel over a shorter panel, a pair of false drawer fronts at the bottom above the molded base w/scroll-cut bracket feet, original salmon red paint w/black trim, pegged construction, mid-19th c., 19 1/2 x 46", 6' 4" h.............................. **2,200**

Wardrobe, Classical style, walnut, demountable, the rectangular top w/a very deep, stepped cornice w/rounded corners above a pair of tall cupboard doors w/arched panels w/carved ribbon molding, ogee base band on ogee bracket feet, open interior, old refinish, ca. 1840s, 22 x 60", 7' 6" h. **2,800**

Wardrobe, country-style, painted & decorated pine, rectangular top w/a narrow flaring cornice above a pair of wide flat doors decorated w/a large white-painted oval reserve enclosed by a green ground decorated w/dark green, yellow & blue scrolls, tall narrow recessed panels down the sides, the green ground painted w/small yellow ovals & dark green scrolls, a long green paneled drawer across the bottom painted w/small yellow ovals & dark green scrolls, flat molded base, open interior, Europe, ca. 1840, 20 x 62", 7' h. **4,500**

Walnut Country Gothic Wardrobe - M.M.

Wardrobe, George III-Style, mahogany, the rectangular top w/narrow cornice w/dentil band & bowed front above a conforming case w/a pair of large two-panel doors opening to shelves & hanging rods, molded base on splayed bracket feet, England, early 20th c., 21 x 46", 6' 10" h. . **2,070**

Wardrobe, Gothic Revival country-style, walnut, the rectangular top w/a high serpentine crestrail w/slender projecting small scrolls above the coved cornice over a pair of tall Gothic arched feathergrained doors over a pair of deep drawers w/wooden knobs, flat apron on scroll-cut bracket feet, refinished, found in Missouri, ca. 1850, 20 x 52", 7' 2" h. (ILLUS. above) **1,800**

Wardrobe, Late Victorian, walnut, demountable, the high serpentine crestrail carved w/scrolls & centered by a large carved florette above a narrow coved cornice over a scroll-trimmed frieze band above a pair of tall beveled glass mirrored doors w/curved top edge trimmed w/carved scrolls, a mid-molding over a pair of line-incised bottom drawers w/brass pulls, flat molded base, open interior, original finish, ca. 1890, 20 x 54", 8' h. (ILLUS.)..... **2,400**

Late Victorian Walnut Wardrobe - M.M.

High-crested Victorian Wardrobe - M.M.

Wardrobe, Victorian country-style, walnut, rectangular top w/wide arched crestrail centered by a pierced fan-carved crest over scrolls & w/pointed corner ears w/pierced scrolls, a pair of wide Gothic arch paneled doors opening to a shelved interior, flat base on ring-turned feet, original finish, ca. 1850s, 18 x 52", 7' 8" h. (ILLUS.) **2,000**

Wardrobe, Victorian Eastlake country-style, walnut, the rectangular top w/a flaring stepped cornice above frieze band carved w/roundels & incised leafy bands above a pair of tall paneled doors centered by a large rosette & incised leafy scrolls & blossoms, a pair of paneled drawers w/brass pulls at the bottom, flat molded base w/cutout apron & bracket feet, refinished, ca. 1885, 18 x 48", 7' 2" h. (ILLUS. top right column) **2,400**

Wardrobe, Victorian Eastlake style, walnut & burl walnut, demountable, the rectangular top w/a wide flaring cornice above a narrow burl frieze band over a pair of tall beveled glass mirrored doors topped by narrow raised burl panels, a slender half-round colonette down the center & flanking the doors, a pair of burl veneered drawers w/stamped brass pulls at the bottom, flat molded base w/wafer feet, original hardware, refinished, ca. 1875, 20 x 52", 7' 4" h. (ILLUS.) **2,400**

Country Eastlake Walnut Wardrobe - M.M.

Victorian Eastlake Wardrobe - M.M.

Oak Wardrobe with a High Crest - G.K.

Wardrobe, Victorian Golden Oak style, a tall scalloped & scroll-carved front crest above a bead-carved flaring cornice above a scroll-carved frieze band over a pair of tall paneled cupboard doors w/carved scrolls across the top, a pair of flat drawers at the base w/original stamped brass hardware, refinished, ca. 1900, 18 x 48", 7' 10" h. (ILLUS.).... **1,800-2,000**

Victorian Golden Oak Wardrobe - G.K.

Wardrobe, Victorian Golden Oak style, demountable, the high front crest w/a scalloped, scroll-carved top centered by a large shell carving over a frieze band w/further scroll carving over a flared cornice above a frieze band trimmed in scroll carving over a pair of tall cupboard doors w/rectangular panels w/rounded corners & scroll-carved trim, a pair of drawers w/stamped brass pulls at the base above the serpentine apron & scroll-carved feet, refinished, ca. 1900, 20 x 48", 8' h. (ILLUS. below left) .. **2,500-2,800**

Crested Golden Oak Wardrobe - M.M.

Wardrobe, Victorian Golden Oak style, oak, demountable, a high scroll-cut & scroll-carved crestrail above the flaring cornice above a pair of tall doors w/recessed panels w/rounded corners, a mid-molding over the long line-incised bottom drawer, paneled sides, original brasses, original finish, ca. 1900, 20 x 48", 7' 10" h. (ILLUS.) **2,000**

Wardrobe, Victorian Renaissance Revival country-style, butternut, one-piece construction, the rectangular top w/an arched & notch-cut crestrail centered by a walnut fruit cluster above the flaring cornice over a pair of tall doors w/arched molded panels, a pair of drawers w/small wood knobs at the bottom above the notch-cut apron w/bracket feet, possibly Norwegian-American influence, Midwest, ca. 1870s, refinished, 20 x 50", 7' 4" h. (ILLUS. top of next page)............. **1,500**

Country Renaissance Wardrobe - M.M.

Wardrobe, Victorian Renaissance Revival style, walnut, demountable, the rectangular top w/a high arched crestrail w/molding flanking a large scroll- and leaf-carved center crest, rounded stepped ears at the rounded top corners above a pair of wide paneled doors w/carved scrolls across the top, open interior, flat base w/cut-down bracket feet, original finish, ca. 1875, 21 x 56", 8' h. (ILLUS. bottom left column) **1,500**

Wardrobe, Victorian Renaissance Revival style, walnut, demountable, the rectangular top w/a high arched & deeply molded crestrail above an arched panel centered by a carved ring over a pair of tall arch-paneled doors centered by a narrow tall oval panel, flat molded & flaring base, open interior, refinished, ca. 1875, 22 x 60", 7' 10" h. (ILLUS. bottom of page) **2,400**

Wardrobe, Victorian Rococo style, walnut, demountable, the rectangular top w/an arched scroll-cut & scroll-trimmed crestrail above the flaring ogee cornice above a pair of tall doors, each w/a pair of tall narrow rectangular panels w/carved scrolls at the top of each panel, a pair of drawers w/simple wood knobs below, open interior, scalloped narrow apron w/bracket feet, refinished, ca. 1860, 20 x 54", 7' 10" h. **2,500**

High-crested Walnut Wardrobe - M.M.

Massive Renaissance Wardrobe - M.M.

WHATNOTS & ETAGERES

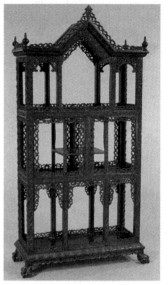

Elaborate East Asian Etagere - N.O.

Late Victorian Etagere-Curio Cabinet - M.M.

Etagere, late Victorian style, mahogany, the superstructure w/a large arched & beveled mirror flanked by slender tapering spiral-turned spindles above the half-round case over a pair of large curved glass doors centered by a narrow arched coved panel & opening to a mirrored interior, flat corner supports & single slender tapering spiral-turned center spindle on the half-round lower shelf, squared, slightly curved front legs, original dark finish, ca. 1890s, 18 x 28", 6' h. (ILLUS.) **$1,200**

Etagere, Oriental, carved rosewood, the peaked top decorated w/an ornate scroll-carved crestrail above the molded cornice w/turned corner finials & edged along the bottom w/further pierce-carved borders, supported on four slender carved supports to the top mirror-backed open shelves w/a pierce-carved gallery above five slender supports all framed by narrow pierced borders & centered by a small open shelf & backed by another mirror, all on four additional carved supports w/pierced upper borders atop the bottom shelf backed by a mirror, the flaring carved apron w/a low pierced gallery & base band, raised on carved paw feet, East Asia, early 20th c., 17 x 39", 5' 10 1/2" h. (ILLUS. top next column) **1,150**

Etagere, Victorian Rococo style, carved & laminated rosewood, the superstructure w/a high arched & ornately scroll-carved stepped crestrail centered by a rose-carved medallion crest, a large arched center mirror flanked by smaller arched mirrors each fronted by three small half-round open shelves w/pierced scroll-carved aprons, resting on the half-round serpentine-sided base w/a wide flat central section above a conforming apron centered by a long paneled scroll-carved drawer flanked by raised side panels, raised on four S-scroll legs w/fruit-carved knees, joined by a delicate scroll-carved H-stretcher, attributed to John H. Belter, New York City, ca. 1855, original finish, 20 x 50", 8' h. **16,000**

Etagere, Victorian Rococo style, carved & pierced rosewood, two-part construction: the tall upper section w/a high arched & ornately pierce-carved crest decorated w/grapevines centering a large magnolia blossom above the tall arched central mirror flanked by three half-round graduated shelves each w/ornate scroll-carved brackets; the lower section w/a long white marble top w/serpentine sides & small rounded projections above a conforming case w/serpentine scroll-carved drawer over a mirrored cupboard door flanked by concave apron panels over an open shelf above the plinth base, each side shelf supported by baluster- or columnar-turned supports & backed by a mirror, the serpentine apron w/a scroll-carved cluster in the center panel, attributed to John H. Belter, New York City, ca. 1855, 16 1/2 x 59", 8' 2" h. **52,900**

Extraordinary Carved Rosewood Signed Rococo Etagere - **N.O.**

Etagere, Victorian Rococo style, carved rosewood, the upper section w/a faceted, domed cornice surmounted by a pierced scrolling foliate-carved crest w/a center finial flanked by carved recumbent putti, projecting over a large mirror flanked by narrower mirrors fronted by four half-round open shelves supported on slender ring- and baluster-turned spindles, the half-round serpentine-fronted base w/a molded edge over a conforming deep apron w/elaborately pierce-carved decorations of leafy vines w/grape clusters & a bird, supported on four bold C-form fruit- and leaf-carved brackets joined to tapering turned spindles w/finials above the half-round serpentine lower platform backed by a mirror, a serpentine scroll-carved apron on disk feet, signed & dated by Thomas Brooks, Brooklyn, New York, 1860, 22 1/2 x 71", 9' 3" h. (ILLUS.) **105,900**

pierced floral garland-carved swags across the apron, raised on S-scroll legs w/leaf-carved knees, attributed to Meeks of New York City, ca. 1855, base only, 20 x 46", 36" h. (ILLUS. below left)............................. **4,000**

Fine Meeks Rosewood Etagere - M.M.

Etagere, Victorian Rococo style, carved rosewood, the tall superstructure w/a high arched pierced & scroll-carved crest flanked by tall baluster- and ring-turned finials & scroll-carved corners, a tall arched central mirror flanked by narrow arched mirrors fronted by small half-round open shelves supported by slender ring- and rod-turned spindles & flanked by graduated scroll-carved border brackets, the half-round white marble base w/serpentine edges above a conforming pierced & scroll-carved apron supported on a pair of large ornately turned columns above the conforming serpentine platform base w/a scroll-carved apron & centered by a rectangular mirror flanked by wide serpentine scroll-carved sides, on small knob feet, by J. & J.W. Meeks, New York City, ca. 1855, refinished, 22 x 48", 8' h. (ILLUS.) **20,000**

Late Victorian Mirrored Whatnot - G.K.

Whatnot, late Victorian, mahogany, a large round beveled mirror w/a small scroll-carved crest at the top flanked by small oblong open shelves on incurved supports above a wide oblong shelf raised on slender squared supports above a narrow vertical rectangular beveled mirror above a small open shelf on a forked bracket backed by a smaller mirror, the half-round bottom shelf w/a serpentine front, raised on simple slender cabriole front legs & straight rear legs, refinished, ca. 1910, 14 x 24", 4' 6" h. (ILLUS. above).................. **600**

Elaborate Rosewood Etagere Base - M.M.

Etagere base, Victorian Rococo style, carved & laminated rosewood, the half-round white marble top w/serpentine edges above a deep conforming case w/a pair of bowed doors ornately pierce-carved w/delicate scrolls in a rectangular scroll-bordered panel, matching pierced side panels above the

William IV Mahogany Whatnot - N.O.

Whatnot, William IV, mahogany, the rectangular top w/a low three-quarters gallery raised on slender ring-turned supports over three more open shelves w/matching turned supports, raised on trumpet-turned feet, England, second quarter 19th c., 16 1/4 x 23 1/2", 5' 10" h. (ILLUS. previous).. **1,955**

SELECT BIBLIOGRAPHY

Bivins, John, Jr. *The Furniture of Coastal North Carolina, 1700-1820.* Winston-Salem, N.C.: Museum of Early Southern Decorative Arts, 1988.

Butler, Joseph T. *Field Guide to American Antique Furniture.* New York: Facts on File Publications, 1985.

Cathers, David M. *Furniture of the American Arts & Crafts Movement.* New York: New American Library, 1981.

Comstock, Helen. *American Furniture, Seventeenth, Eighteenth, and Nineteenth Century Styles.* New York: The Viking Press, 1962.

Cooper, Wendy A. *Classical Taste in America, 1800-1840.* New York: Abbeville Press, 1993.

Dubrow, Eileen and Richard. *American Furniture of the 19th Century, 1840-1880.* Exton, PA.: Schiffer Publishing, Ltd., 1983.

Dubrow, Eileen and Richard. *Furniture Made in America, 1875-1905.* Exton, PA.: Schiffer Publishing, Ltd., 1982.

Duncan, Alastair. *Art Nouveau Furniture.* New York: Clarkson N. Potter, Inc., 1982.

Fairbanks, Jonathan L. and Elizabeth Bidwell Bates. *American Furniture, 1620 to the Present.* New York: Richard Marek Publishers, 1981.

Fales, Dean A., Jr. *American Painted Furniture, 1660-1880.* New York: Crown Publishers, 1986.

Fitzgerald, Oscar. *Three Centuries of American Furniture.* Englewood Cliffs, N. J.: Prentice-Hall, 1982.

Fredgant, Don. *American Manufactured Furniture.* Atglen, PA: Schiffer Publishing, Ltd., 1988.

Kane, Patricia E. *300 Years of American Seating Furniture.* Boston: New York Graphic Society, 1976.

Kirk, John T. *American Furniture and The British Tradition to 1830.* New York: Alfred A. Knopf, 1982.

Kovel, Ralph and Terry Kovel. *American Country Furniture, 1780-1875.* New York: Crown Publishers, 1965.

Lockwood, Luke Vincent. *Colonial Furniture in America, 2 vols.* New York: Castle Books, 1951, rpt.

Madigan, Mary Jean. *Nineteenth Century Furniture.* New York: Art & Antiques, 1982.

Marsh, Moreton. *The Easy Expert in American Antiques.* Philadelphia: J.B. Lippincott, 1978.

McNerney, Kathryn. *Pine Furniture — Our American Heritage.* Paducah, KY: Collector Books, 1989.

Montgomery, Charles F. *American Furniture, The Federal Period in the Henry Francis du Pont Winterthur Museum.* New York: The Viking Press, 1966.

Morningstar, Connie. *American Furniture Classics.* Des Moines, IA: Wallace-Homestead Book Co., 1976.

Nutting, Wallace. *Furniture Treasury, vols. I, II.* New York: Macmillan, 1928.

Nutting, Wallace. *Furniture Treasury, vol. III.* New York: Macmillan, 1933.

Sack, Albert. *The New Fine Points of Furniture.* New York: Crown Publishing, 1993.

Santore, Charles. *The Windsor Style in America.* Philadelphia: Running Press, 1981.

Santore, Charles. *The Windsor Style in America, Vol. II.* Philadelphia: Running Press, 1987.

Warner, Velma Susanne. *Golden Oak Furniture.* Atglen, PA: Schiffer Publishing, Ltd., 1992.

APPENDIX I
AUCTION SERVICES

The following is a select listing of larger regional auction houses which often feature antique furniture in their sales. There are, of course, many fine local auction services that also feature furniture from time to time.

East Coast:

Christie's
502 Park Ave.
New York, NY 10022
Phone: (212) 546-1000

Douglas Auctioneers
Route 5
South Deerfield, MA 01373
Phone: (413) 665-3530

William Doyle Galleries
175 E. 87th St.
New York, NY 10128
Phone: (212) 427-2730

Willis Henry Auctions
22 Main St.
Marshfield, MA 02059
Phone: (617) 834-7774

Dave Rago
9 So. Main St.
Lambertville, NJ 08530
Phone: (609) 397-9374

Skinner Inc.
357 Main St.
Bolton, MA 01740
Phone: (508) 779-6241

Sotheby's
1334 York Ave.
New York, NY 10021
Phone: (212) 606-7000

Withington, Inc.
R. D. 2, Box 440
Hillsboro, NH 03244
Phone: (603) 464-3232

Midwest:

DuMochelles Galleries
409 East Jefferson Ave.
Detroit, MI 48226
Phone: (313) 963-6255

Garth's Auctions
P.O. Box 369
Delaware, OH 43015
Phone: (614) 362-4771

Gene Harris Antique Auction Center
P.O. Box 476
Marshalltown, IA 50158
Phone: (515) 752-0600

Jackson's Auctioneers & Appraisers
2229 Lincoln St.
Cedar Falls, IA 50613
Phone: (319) 277-2256

Treadway Gallery
P.O. Box 8924
Cincinnati, OH 45208
Phone: (513) 321-6742

Far West:

Butterfield & Butterfield
7601 Sunset Blvd.
Los Angeles, CA 90046
Phone: (213) 850-7500

Pettigrew Auction Company
1645 So. Tejon St.
Colorado Springs, CO 80906
Phone: (719) 633-7963

South:

Neal Auction Company
4038 Magazine St.
New Orleans, LA 70115
Phone: (504) 899-5329

New Orleans Auction Galleries
801 Magazine St.
New Orleans, LA 70130
Phone: (504) 566-1849

APPENDIX II
Stylistic Guidelines: American & English Furniture

AMERICAN

Style: Pilgrim Century
Dating: 1620-1700
Major Wood(s): Oak
General Characteristics:
Case pieces: rectilinear low-relief
                carved panels
                blocky & bulbous turnings
                splint-spindle trim
Seating pieces: shallow carved panels
                spindle turnings

Style: William & Mary
Dating: 1685-1720
Major Wood(s): Maple & walnut
General Characteristics:
Case pieces: paint decoration
                chests on ball feet
                chests on frame, chests
                   with two-part construction
                trumpet-turned legs
                slant-front desks
Seating pieces: molded, carved crestrails
                banister backs
                cane, rush (leather) seats
                baluster, ball &
                   block turnings
                ball & Spanish feet

Style: Queen Anne
Dating: 1720-50
Major Wood(s): Walnut
General Characteristics:
Case pieces: mathematical proportions
                  of elements
                use of the cyma or S-curve
                broken-arch pediments
                arched panels, shell carving,
                  star inlay
                blocked fronts
                cabriole legs & pad feet
Seating pieces: molded yoke-shaped
                  crestrails
                solid vase-shaped splats
                rush or upholstered seats
                cabriole legs
                baluster, ring, ball &
                  block-turned stretchers
                pad & slipper feet

Style: Chippendale
Dating: 1750-85
Major Wood(s): Mahogany & walnut
General Characteristics:

Case pieces: relief-carved
        broken-arch pediments
        foliate, scroll, shell,
          fretwork carving
        straight, bow or
          serpentine fronts
        carved cabriole legs
        claw & ball, bracket
          or ogee feet

Seating pieces: carved, shaped crestrails
        with out-turned ears
        pierced, shaped splats
        ladder (ribbon) backs
        upholstered seats
        scrolled arms
        carved cabriole legs or
          straight (Marlboro) legs
        claw & ball feet

Style: Federal (Hepplewhite)
Dating: 1785-1800
Major Wood(s): Mahogany & light inlays
General Characteristics:

Case pieces: more delicate
        rectilinear forms
        inlay with eagle &
          classical motifs
        bow, serpentine or
          tambour fronts
        reeded quarter columns
          at sides
        flared bracket feet

Seating pieces: shield backs
        upholstered seats
        tapered square legs

Style: Federal (Sheraton)
Dating: 1800-20
Major Wood(s): Mahogany & mahogany
        veneer & maple
General Characteristics:

Case pieces: architectural pediments
        acanthus carving
        outset (cookie or ovolu)
          corners & reeded columns
        paneled sides
        tapered, turned, reeded or
          spiral turned legs
        bow or tambour fronts
        mirrors on dressing tables

Style: Federal (Sheraton) continued
Seating pieces: rectangular or square backs
           slender carved banisters
           tapered, turned or
           reeded legs

Style: Classical (American Empire)
Dating: 1815-50
Major Wood(s): Mahogany & mahogany
           veneer & rosewood
General Characteristics:
Case pieces: increasingly heavy
           proportions
           pillar & scroll construction
           lyre, eagle, Greco-Roman &
           Egyptian motifs
           marble tops
           projecting top drawer
           large ball feet, tapered fluted
           feet or hairy paw feet
           brass, ormolu decoration
Seating pieces: high-relief carving
           curved backs
           out-scrolled arms
           ring turnings
           sabre legs, curule
           (scrolled-S) legs
           brass-capped feet, casters

Style: Victorian – Early Victorian
Dating: 1840-50
Major Wood(s): Mahogany veneer, black
           walnut & rosewood
General Characteristics:
Case pieces: Pieces tend to carry over the
           Classical style with the
           beginnings of the Rococo
           substyle, especially in
           seating pieces.

Style: Victorian – Gothic Revival
Dating: 1840-90
Major Wood(s): Black walnut, mahogany
           & rosewood
General Characteristics:
Case pieces: architectural motifs
           triangular arched pediments
           arched panels
           marble tops
           paneled or molded
           drawer fronts
           cluster columns
           bracket feet, block feet or
           plinth bases

Style: Victorian – Gothic Revival continued
Seating pieces: tall backs
      pierced arabesque backs
        with trefoils or quatrefoils
      spool turning
      drop pendants

Style: Victorian – Rococo (Louis XV)
Dating: 1845-70
Major Wood(s): Black walnut, mahogany
      & rosewood
General Characteristics:

Case pieces: arched carved pediments
      high-relief carving, S- &
        C-scrolls, floral, fruit
        motifs, busts & cartouches
      mirror panels
      carved slender cabriole legs
      scroll feet
      bedroom suites (bed,
        dresser, commode)
Seating pieces: high-relief carved crestrails
      balloon-shaped backs
      urn-shaped splats
      upholstery (tufting)
      demi-cabriole legs
      laminated, pierced &
        carved construction
        (Belter & Meeks)
      parlor suites (sets of chairs,
        love seats, sofas)

Style: Victorian – Renaissance Revival
Dating: 1860-85
Major Wood(s): Black walnut, burl veneer,
      painted & grained pine
General Characteristics:

Case pieces: rectilinear arched pediments
      arched panels, burl veneer
      applied moldings
      bracket feet, block feet,
        plinth bases
      medium & high-relief
        carving, floral & fruit,
        cartouches, masks &
        animal heads
      cyma-curve brackets
      Wooton patent desks
Seating pieces: oval or rectangular
        backs with floral or
        figural cresting
      upholstery outlined
        with brass tacks
      padded armrests
      tapered turned front legs,
        flared square rear legs

Style: Victorian – Louis XVI
Dating: 1865-75
Major Wood(s): Black walnut &
ebonized maple
General Characteristics:
Case pieces: gilt decoration,
marquetry, inlay
egg & dart carving
tapered turned legs, fluted
Seating pieces: molded, slightly
arched crestrails
keystone-shaped backs
circular seats
fluted tapered legs

Style: Victorian – Eastlake
Dating: 1870-95
Major Wood(s): Black walnut, burl veneer,
cherry & oak
General Characteristics:
Case pieces: flat cornices
stile & rail construction
burl veneer panels
low-relief geometric &
floral machine-carving
incised horizontal lines
Seating pieces: rectilinear
spindles
tapered, turned legs,
trumpet-shaped legs

Style: Victorian
    Jacobean & Turkish Revival
Dating: 1870-90
Major Wood(s): Black walnut & maple
General Characteristics:
Case pieces: A revival of some heavy
17th century forms,
most commonly in dining
room pieces
Seating pieces:
Turkish Revival style features:
oversized, low forms
overstuffed upholstery
padded arms
short baluster,
vase-turned legs
ottomans, circular sofas
Jacobean Revival style features:
heavy bold carving
spool & spiral turnings

Style: Victorian – Aesthetic Movement
Dating: 1880-1900
Major Wood(s): Painted hardwoods, black
walnut, ebonized finishes
General Characteristics:
Case pieces: rectilinear forms
bamboo turnings, spaced
ball turnings
incised stylized geometric &
floral designs, sometimes
highlighted with gilt
Seating pieces: bamboo turnings
rectangular backs
patented folding chairs

Style: Art Nouveau
Dating: 1895-1918
Major Wood(s): Ebonized hardwoods,
fruitwoods
General Characteristics:
Case pieces: curvilinear shapes
floral marquetry
carved whiplash curves
Seating pieces: elongated forms
relief-carved
floral decoration
spindle backs, pierced
floral backs
cabriole legs

Style: Turn-of-the-Century
(Early 20th Century)
Dating: 1895-1910
Major Wood(s): Golden (quarter-sawn)
oak, mahogany
hardwood stained to
resemble mahogany
General Characteristics:
Case pieces: rectilinear & bulky forms
applied scroll carving or
machine-pressed designs
some Colonial & Classical
Revival detailing
Seating pieces: heavy framing or high
spindle-trimmed backs
applied carved or machine-
pressed back designs
heavy scrolled or
slender turned legs
often feature some Colonial
Revival or Classical
Revival detailing such as
claw & ball feet

Style: Mission (Arts & Crafts movement)
Dating: 1900-1915
Major Wood(s): Oak
General Characteristics:
Case pieces: rectilinear through-tenon
                     construction
                 copper decoration,
                     hand-hammered hardware
                 square legs
Seating pieces: rectangular splats
                 medial & side stretchers
                 exposed pegs
                 corbel supports

Style: Wicker
Dating: mid-19th century - 1930
Major Wood(s): Natural woven wicker or
                     synthetic fibers
General Characteristics:
Case &   Earlier examples feature tall
seating pieces: backs with ornate lacy
                      scrolling designs
                      continuing down to the
                      arms & aprons
                  tables & desks often feature
                      hardwood (often oak) tops
                  after about 1910 designs
                      were much simpler with
                      plain tightly woven backs,
                      arms & aprons
                  pieces were often given a
                      natural finish but painted
                      finishes in white or dark
                      green became popular
                      after 1900

Style: Colonial Revival
Dating: 1890-1930
Major Wood(s): Oak, walnut & walnut
                     veneer, mahogany veneer
General Characteristics:
Case pieces: forms generally following
                     designs of the 17th, 18th
                     & early 19th centuries
                 details for the styles such as
                     William & Mary, Federal,
                     Queen Anne, Chippendale
                     or early Classical were
                     used but often in a
                     simplified or stylized form
                 mass-production in the early
                     20th century flooded the
                     market with pieces which
                     often mixed & matched
                     design details & used a
                     great deal of thin
                     veneering to dress
                     up designs

Style: Colonial Revival continued
Case pieces: dining room & bedroom
              suites were especially
              popular
Seating pieces: designs again generally
              followed early period designs
              with some mixing of design
              elements.

Style: Art Deco
Dating: 1925-40
Major Wood(s): Bleached woods, exotic
                      woods, steel & chrome
General Characteristics:
Case pieces: heavy geometric forms
Seating pieces: streamlined, attenuated
              geometric forms
              overstuffed upholstery

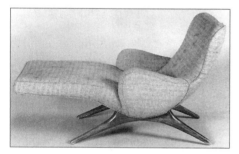

Style: Modernist or Mid-Century
Dating: 1945-70
Major Wood(s): Plywood, hardwood or
                    metal frames
General Characteristics:
Modernistic designers such as the
Eames, Vladimir Kagan, George Nelson
& Isamu Noguchi lead the way in post-
War design. Carrying on the tradition of
Modernist designers of the 1920s &
1930s, they focused on designs for the
machine age, which could be mass-
produced for the popular market. By the
late 1950s many of their pieces were
used in commercial office spaces &
schools as well as in private homes.
Case pieces: streamlined or curvilinear
              abstract designs with
              simple
              detailing
              plain round or flattened legs
              & arms commonly used
              mixed materials including
              wood, plywood, metal,
              glass & molded plastics
Seating pieces: streamlined & abstract
              curvilinear designs
              generally using newer
              materials such as plywood
              or simple hardwood
              framing

Style: Modernist or Mid-Century continued
Seating pieces: Fabric & synthetics such as
vinyl were widely used for
upholstery with finer
fabrics & real leather
featured on more
expensive pieces.
seating made of molded
plastic shells on metal
frames & legs used on
many mass-produced
designs

Style: Danish Modern
Dating: 1950-70
Major Wood(s): Teak
General Characteristics:

Case &   This variation of Modernistic
Seating pieces: post-war design originated
in Scandinavia, hence the
name.
designs were simple &
restrained with case pieces
often having simple boxy
forms with short rounded
tapering legs
seating pieces have a simple
teak framework with lines
coordinating with case
pieces
vinyl or natural fabric were
most often used for
upholstery
in the United States dining
room suites were the most
popular use for this style
although some bedroom
suites & general seating
pieces were available

ENGLISH

Style: Jacobean
Dating: Mid-17th century
Major Wood(s): Oak, walnut
General Characteristics:
Case pieces: low-relief carving,
geometrics & florals
panel, rail & stile construction
applied split balusters
Seating pieces: rectangular backs
carved & pierced crests
spiral turnings
ball feet

Style: William & Mary
Dating: 1689-1702
Major Wood(s): Walnut, burl walnut veneer
General Characteristics:
Case pieces: marquetry, veneering
                shaped aprons
                6-8 trumpet-form legs
                curved flat stretchers
Seating pieces: carved, pierced crests
                tall caned backs & seats
                trumpet-form legs
                Spanish feet

Style: Queen Anne
Dating: 1702-14
Major Wood(s): Walnut, mahogany, veneers
General Characteristics:
Case pieces: cyma curves
                broken arch pediments &
                    finials
                bracket feet
Seating pieces: carved crestrails
                high, rounded backs
                solid vase-shaped splats
                cabriole legs
                pad feet

Style: George I
Dating: 1714-27
Major Wood(s): Walnut, mahogany, veneer
                     & yewwood
General Characteristics:
Case pieces: broken arch pediments
                gilt decoration, japanning
                bracket feet
Seating pieces: curvilinear forms
                yoke-shaped crests
                shaped solid splats
                shell carving
                upholstered seats
                carved cabriole legs
                claw & ball feet, pad feet

Style: George II
Dating: 1727-60
Major Wood(s): Mahogany
General Characteristics:
Case pieces: broken arch pediments
                relief-carved foliate, scroll &
                    shell carving
                carved cabriole legs
                claw & ball feet,
                    bracket feet, ogee
                    bracket feet

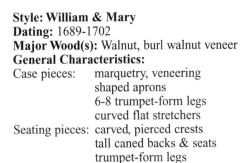

Style: George II continued
Seating pieces: carved, shaped crestrails,
     out-turned ears
     pierced shaped splats
     ladder (ribbon) backs
     upholstered seats
     scrolled arms
     carved cabriole legs or
      straight (Marlboro) legs
     claw & ball feet

Style: George III
Dating: 1760-1820
Major Wood(s): Mahogany, veneer,
     satinwood
General Characteristics:
Case pieces: rectilinear forms
     parcel gilt decoration
     inlaid ovals, circles, banding
      or marquetry
     carved columns, urns
     tambour fronts or bow fronts
     plinth bases
Seating pieces: shield backs
     upholstered seats
     tapered square legs,
      square legs

Style: Regency
Dating: 1811-20
Major Wood(s): Mahogany, mahogany
     veneer, satinwood &
     rosewood
General Characteristics:
Case pieces: Greco-Roman &
     Egyptian motifs
     inlay, ormolu mounts
     marble tops
     round columns, pilasters
     mirrored backs
     scroll feet
Seating pieces: straight backs, latticework
     caned seats
     sabre legs, tapered turned
      legs, flared turned legs
     parcel gilt, ebonizing

Style: George IV
Dating: 1820-30
Major Wood(s): Mahogany, mahogany
     veneer & rosewood
General Characteristics:
  Continuation of Regency designs

Style: William IV
Dating: 1830-37
Major Wood(s): Mahogany, mahogany
       veneer
General Characteristics:
Case pieces: rectilinear
           brass mounts, grillwork
           carved moldings
           plinth bases
Seating pieces: rectangular backs
           carved straight crestrails
           acanthus, animal carving
           carved cabriole legs
           paw feet

Style: Victorian
Dating: 1837-1901
Major Wood(s): Black walnut, mahogany,
       veneers & rosewood
General Characteristics:
Case pieces: applied floral carving
           surmounting mirrors,
             drawers, candle shelves
           marble tops
Seating pieces: high-relief carved crestrails
           floral & fruit carving
           balloon backs, oval backs
           upholstered seats, backs
           spool, spiral turnings
           cabriole legs, fluted
             tapered legs
           scrolled feet

Style: Edwardian
Dating: 1901-10
Major Wood(s): Mahogany, mahogany
       veneer & satinwood
General Characteristics:
    Neo-Classical motifs & revivals of
    earlier 18th century & early
    19th century styles.